SCOTLAND IN THE REIGN OF JAMES IV

IE FLODDEN CAMPAIGN

KING JAMES IV
OF SCOTLAND

KING JAMES IV
OF SCOTLAND

*A Brief Survey
of His Life and Times*

BY

R. L. MACKIE

OLIVER AND BOYD
EDINBURGH: TWEEDDALE COURT
LONDON: 39A WELBECK STREET, W.I

FIRST PUBLISHED 1958

PRINTED IN GREAT BRITAIN
FOR OLIVER AND BOYD LTD.
BY ROBERT CUNNINGHAM AND SONS LTD., ALVA

DEDICATION

To my Daughter

PREFACE

THE author wishes to express his gratitude to Miss A. W. Orde for the patience and accuracy with which she has filled up the gaps and verified the references in this brief account of the Life and Times of James IV of Scotland, an account which deals more fully with social than with constitutional history explored thoroughly by the late Professor Hannay. Thanks are also due to the publishers and their staff for the trouble they have taken in dealing with my manuscript.

R.L.M.

CONTENTS

ILLUSTRATIONS

SHORT LIST OF ABBREVIATIONS

for full details, see Bibliography

A.P.S.   *Acts of the Parliaments of Scotland*

Cal. Doc. Scot.   *Calendar of Documents relating to Scotland preserved in H. M. Public Record Office*

C.T.S.   *Compota Thesauriorum regum Scotorum. Accounts of the Lord High Treasurer of Scotland*

E.R.S.   *Epistolae Jacobi Quarti, Jacobi Quinti et Mariae Regum Scotorum, eorumque tutorum et regni gubernatorum, ad Imperatores, Reges, Pontifices, Principes, civitates et alios ab anno 1505 ad annum 1545*

Fac. Nat. MSS   *Facsimiles of National Manuscripts*

L. and P. Henry VIII   *Letters and Papers, Foreign and Domestic, of the Reign of Henry VIII*

L. and P. Richard III and Henry VII   *Letters and Papers illustrative of the Reigns of Richard III and Henry VII*

R.M.S.   *Registrum magni sigilli regum Scotorum, The Register of the Great Seal of Scotland*

Rot. Scot.   *Rotuli Scotiae in turri Londinensi et in domo capitulari Westmonasteriensi asservati*

R. Scac. S.   *Rotuli Scaccarium regum Scotorum, The Exchequer Rolls of Scotland*

R.S.S.   *Registrum secreti sigilli regum Scotorum, The Register of the Privy Seal of Scotland*

I

PRELUDE:

THE SCOTLAND OF JAMES III

ON 17 March 1473 was born the prince who later became King James IV of Scotland. His father, King James III, was then twenty-one; his mother, Queen Margaret, only sixteen. He had a smaller measure of Scottish blood in his veins than most of his future subjects, for his father, grandfather and greatgrandfather had all chosen foreign brides, while an Englishwoman, the Lady Jane Beaufort, had been the wife of James I. No star danced at his nativity, but a wonderful comet, visible even at noonday, blazed in the heavens from mid-January to mid-February.

Of the place of his birth no record has been preserved. It was probably Stirling Castle, his father's favourite residence. Here it is likely that he spent most of his childhood and boyhood under the eye of James Shaw of Sauchie, whom the King had made his governor while he was still an infant. The Treasurer's Accounts give us an occasional glimpse of him in the first two years of his life, wearing a little coat of blue velvet, or decked more royally in cloth of gold lined with blue silk, or sleeping in his canopied cradle with a white mutch on his head.[1]

Five months after his birth his parents made a pilgrimage to the shrine of St Ninian in the priory of Whithorn. The young prince, hereditary Duke of Rothesay, seems to have been a sickly child, for when Queen Margaret gave birth to a second son,[2] he,

---

[1] *Compota thesauriorum regum Scotorum, Accounts of the Lord High Treasurer of Scotland* (hereafter referred to as *C.T.S.*), VOL. I, ed. T. Dickson, Edinburgh 1877, pp. 39-42.

[2] Probably late in 1479 or early in 1480. See J. Herkless and R. K. Han-

too, was christened James as if to ensure that should the elder child predecease his father, the next King would still bear the name that for the last hundred years had been borne by every King of Scots. A third son, John, was born some time before 12 July 1480.[1]

Already, however, when he was barely a year old, his father had begun negotiations for his marriage to the Lady Cecilia, the youngest daughter of Edward IV.[2] In October 1474 ambassadors from England, led by Laurence Booth, Bishop of Durham, and Lord Scrope, arrived in Edinburgh, where in the Dominican Friary, on 18 October, before Lord Avandale, the Chancellor, the Earl of Argyll, Master of the Household, and James Shaw of Sauchie, the Earl of Crawford took the marriage vows on behalf of the infant Duke of Rothesay, and, clasping the hands of Lord Scrope, heard him reply for the three-year-old Princess.[3]

By the treaty of marriage, signed on 26 October, and ratified by the King on 3 November,[4] the Prince was to wed the Lady Cecilia within six months of his coming of perfect age. The dowry—20,000 marks, English money—would be paid in instalments of 2,000 marks, and the payments would be spread over a period of seventeen years.[5] In addition, the treaty seemed to guarantee an enduring peace: the truce between the two king-

nay, *The Archbishops of St Andrews*, VOL. I, Edinburgh 1907, pp. 168-9, 184.

[1] *C.T.S.*, VOL. I, p. lxv and n.

[2] *Calendar of Documents relating to Scotland preserved in H.M. Public Record Office*, ed. Joseph Bain (hereafter referred to as *Cal. Doc. Scot.*), VOL. IV, Edinburgh 1888, No. 1414.

[3] Thomas Rymer, *Foedera, conventiones, literae, et cujuscunque acta publica inter reges Angliae et alios quovis imperatores, reges, pontifices, principes vel communitates* (hereafter referred to as *Foedera*), VOL. XI, London 1710, p. 821; *Cal. Doc. Scot.*, VOL. IV, No. 1417.

[4] *Foedera*, VOL. XI, p. 824; *Cal. Doc. Scot.*, VOL. IV, No. 1418.

[5] The first three instalments of the Lady Cecilia's dowry were duly paid by Master Alexander Lye, King Edward's Almoner, at the beginning of February in each of the three succeeding years. In February 1478 he paid over only half of the accustomed sum, and did not return to Edinburgh with the arrears till the beginning of April, while in 1479 he tried to make the payment —the last recorded—in merks Scots. See *Cal. Doc. Scot.*, VOL. IV, Nos. 1425, 1437, 1446, 1448, 1450, 1452, 1456, and App. I, No. 30.

doms, made in 1465, was extended for forty-five years, till the last day of October 1519.

We get one other brief glimpse of the Prince. On 7 February 1478, when the King had reached the age of twenty-five, and had effected the customary general revocation of all grants made in his minority, he, with the consent of the Three Estates of the Realm, entrusted Queen Margaret with the Castle of Edinburgh, and, for the five years after the following Whitsuntide, with the care and direction (*regimen, gubernationem, et custodiam*) of the Duke of Rothesay, her expenses to be met every year by the King.[1]

After this, there is no mention of him in contemporary record for another ten years, though Ferrerius, writing almost a century later, declared that while all three princes showed a truly royal nature, the future King outshone the other two, and won the hearts of both gentle and simple by the beauty of his character and the brilliance of his talents.[2] It was a poverty-stricken and distracted kingdom that he seemed destined to inherit.

At the end of the third quarter of the fifteenth century Scotland was, even by medieval standards, an uncomfortable and uninviting country. Save for an occasional ambassador, an occasional merchant from France or Flanders, no stranger set foot in it. The day of the traveller in the picturesque had not dawned— would not dawn till the last wolf had been hunted down, the last cateran hanged—and the fifteenth-century poet lived too close to nature to love it much; he turned with a shudder from illimitable moorlands and lochs fading into the sunset, to the ordered beauty of a walled garden. Even the foreign merchant hesitated to make a voyage to Scotland; the risks were too great, the rewards too small. As yet no coal fire burned on the Isle of May, no warning clanged from the Bell Rock; the winter seas were thought to be

---

[1] *Registrum magni sigilli regum Scotorum, The Register of the Great Seal of Scotland* (hereafter referred to as *R.M.S.*), VOL. II (1424-1515), ed. James Balfour Paul, Edinburgh 1882, No. 1361.

[2] *Scotorum historiae . . . libri XIX Hectore Boethis Deidonato auctore continuatio per Ioannem Ferrerium* (hereafter referred to as Ferrerius, *Continuatio*), Paris 1574, p. 397.

so dangerous that no Scottish ship was allowed to leave harbour between the feast of St Simon and St Jude at the end of October, and Candlemas, at the beginning of February. Foreign traders were content to let the Scots merchants come to their Staple Port in the Low Countries—in 1479 it was Middelburg—with the wool, hides, salted salmon, and coarse woollen cloth which were the only marketable commodities that their country produced, and depart with coloured cloths, cushions, silverware, books, soap, sugar, spices, dried fruits, wines, and a hundred and one other luxuries and necessaries.

The adventurous stranger who did penetrate to Scotland would not have far to look for evidence of the poverty of the country. Walled towns, many-towered castles, great churches, were alike hard to find. Of all the Royal Burghs, only Perth and Edinburgh were protected with battlemented curtain walls; in the others the only defences, apart from the ports or gatehouses that guarded the main entrances, were the dykes at the foot of the roods or long narrow strips of garden ground that sloped upwards to the houses fronting the principal street—the "mercat gait" or "*vicus fori*" of fifteenth-century charters; in front of the new stone Tolbooth, the Mercat Cross stood on its stepped pedestal, not far from the great balance called the Tron—all three emblems of burghal dignity. In the Tolbooth met the Burgh Council, for many centuries elected every Michaelmas by an assembly of all the burgesses, now—since 1469—more quietly appointed by the retiring Council. The magistrates—the Alderman, or Provost as he was beginning to be called, the four Bailies, the Treasurer, and the Dean of Gild—were appointed by an electoral college consisting of the old and the new councils and the deacons of the various trades or crafts. After 1474 the new council was stiffened by the inclusion of four members of the old council. But though the privilege of electing the council and magistrates had been taken from the rowdy popular assemblies, the head courts of the burgh, which every burgess was expected to attend, were still held as they had been for centuries past, at Christmas, Easter and Michaelmas. The jurisdiction of the burgh magistrates over the inhabitants of the burgh was as extensive as that of the King's sheriff over his sheriffdom; there was no appeal from their decision in civil cases except to the Lords Auditors or to the Lords of the Council; in criminal matters it extended to every offence except the four "pleas of the Crown" —arson, robbery, rape, and murder.

The Tron and the Mercat Cross were symbols of other privi- leges—monopoly of the trade in wool and hides over the neigh- bouring district, sometimes over a whole sheriffdom, the right to hold a weekly market and an annual fair, and to exact toll on all goods brought into the burgh by outsiders and the right to send ships to foreign countries. But to the uninstructed eye the ordin- ary Royal Burgh, though it could claim that its first charter had been granted by David I or William the Lion, though it sent its two commissioners to Parliament and to the Convention of Royal Burghs, looked like a straggling untidy village. Most of the houses were structures of timber, covered with thatch; in the principal street, deserted except on market day, middens were piled before every door; every morning a lowing and scuffling proclaimed that the burgh herd was driving the cattle of the burgesses along the "cow gait" to the common pasture. The ordinary burgh had not yet become an exclusively trading and industrial community. The individual burgess possessed, in addi- tion to his house and rood of garden-ground, the ownership of which made him a burgess, certain rights in the broad belt of common land which surrounded the burgh. He grazed his cattle, if he had any, on the pasture, cut turf and firewood in the waste, and cultivated the ridges assigned to him by lot in the arable land. But the fact that some of the burghs had begun to feu parts of their commons, or even to sell them outright, showed that the change had begun.

Agricultural methods were as primitive in the burgh acres as in the remoter rural districts; nowhere did one find the three- field system that prevailed in the southern half of England; the twofold division into infield and outfield was universal. The infield, which received all the available manure, had been under crops for centuries without a break; the outfield was simply pasture which had been temporarily reclaimed, cropped for half a dozen years, and then allowed to revert to pasture once more. As in England, the arable land was divided into long narrow strips or rigs, separated from one another by baulks or bands of turf; as in England, it was so apportioned among the peasants who cultivated it that no man held two adjacent strips. But the peasant communities were smaller; instead of the English village one saw at wide intervals four or six wretched huts of clay or turf set in the middle of the ploughgate—the 104 Scots acres which their occupants combined to cultivate. From the sour undrained soil only scanty crops could be expected in the most favourable years; a wet summer meant famine.

The hovel of the peasant, where men and cattle sheltered under the same thatched roof, bore witness not only to his poverty but to his sense of insecurity. He held his land on a lease of five years at most; why should he trouble to build a more substantial and comfortable house when he might be turned out at the end of the time? The castle of the knight or baron told the same story; it was usually a single tower, forming one side of a narrow courtyard, which was enclosed on the other three sides by a barmekin, a wall twenty feet high. The tiny dark parish church, without aisles or transepts, unaltered since the twelfth or thirteenth century, repeated the same tale of poverty. And what was true of Scottish parish churches was true of the Scottish cathedrals. They had always been small in comparison with the corresponding buildings in England. St Andrews, the largest, was only 357 feet in length, more than 100 feet shorter than York Minster, and many a rural English parish boasted a church larger than the cathedrals of Brechin and Dunblane. But the Scottish bishops and abbots had to be content with what their twelfth- and thirteenth-century predecessors had left them. They might, as at St Andrews and Melrose, replace what fire or war had destroyed, but they embarked on no ambitious schemes of reconstruction like those which had transformed the work of the Norman architect at Gloucester and Winchester. Besides, no one built new monasteries now, because no one respected the old ones. They were not, and had never professed to be homes of learning; now they had become, in the words of the orthodox John Major, "refuges for shepherds whose only care is to find pasture for themselves, men neglectful of the duties of religion". But the proverb coined at Lindores—"The abbey bell will aye be gotten rung"—shows that the monastery was still regarded as of some spiritual value. It is easy, however, to exaggerate the poverty of the country.

The fifteenth century, when—or rather because—England had been distracted first by a series of military disasters abroad, then by civil wars at home, had been for Scotland a period of comparative prosperity. Though Homildon Hill, Crevant and Verneuil were Scottish defeats, they were not defeats on Scottish soil. Since 1385, when an English expedition had wrecked Melrose Abbey and burned Edinburgh, Dundee and Perth, no English army had crossed the borders. The damage had long since been repaired, and the size and splendour of the new parish churches of Perth and Dundee, slowly raised by the burgesses at their own expense, was only one sign of the growing wealth of the burghs. Another was the appearance, among the old timber houses, of more roomy and comfortable houses of stone. Still another was the keen rivalry manifested by Bruges and Middelburg for the Scottish Staple, for the monopoly, in other words, of the trade between Scotland and the Continent.

Outside the burghs, too, a change in the architectural fashions gave evidence of the growing prosperity of the country. Though the fifteenth-century landowner was usually content with the old tower and barmekin, or with a new castle built to the old pattern, he occasionally built something costlier and more elaborate, a castle in which the most conspicuous feature was not the tower, but a larger building, a long rectangular block, built where the curtain wall would have been, and pierced by a pend, a vaulted passage leading to the central courtyard. Below was the vaulted basement with the store rooms, buttery, and kitchen; above, the most important room was the great hall. Rarely was this palace-castle a completely new building; usually, as at Crichton Castle, the fifteenth-century masons simply pulled down a length of the barmekin, and built the new hall against the old tower. Nor was it altogether poverty that made the same landowner, grown old and solicitous for his soul's salvation, refrain from founding a monastery, as his thirteenth-century predecessor would have done; it was partly a change of fashion. He preferred to found a church larger and more ornate than the ordinary parish church, having attached to it a college or staff of some half score of secular clergy, under a Provost. The presence of such a body of chaplains was meant to ensure the regular and dignified performance of the services of the church, in a fashion impossible in the little parish church with its solitary priest. In addition, when the body of the founder was laid in the earth, prayers had to be said daily and the *De profundis* sung beside his canopied tomb. These collegiate churches were not all entirely new foundations: sometimes, like St Giles', Edinburgh, they had been parish churches; sometimes, too, they were endowed with the revenues of older churches. Still, the increase in the number of collegiate churches from two in 1400 to over a score in 1479 points to an increase in the wealth of the landowning classes.

Only to an observer capable of taking long views would this slow and irregular improvement have been perceptible; the Scotsman living in 1473 saw nothing of it; instead he was harassed by a sense of insecurity.

It is true that, so far, Fortune had seemed to smile upon King James III. He had come to the throne when he was only nine years old, but the guardianship of the sagacious Bishop Kennedy had saved his country from the worst evils of a minority. Though after Kennedy's death in 1465 he had been for a time under the control of a faction of ambitious adventurers, his marriage to the Princess Margaret of Denmark in 1469 had coincided with the sudden and dramatic fall of the Boyds. If his bride brought him only 2,000 florins out of her promised dowry of 20,000, Orkney and Shetland had been pledged for the remainder, and when three years passed without any further money payment, they were annexed to the Scottish Crown. The Treaty of 1474, as we have seen, seemed to remove all risk of hostilities between Scotland and England in the immediate future. The negotiations which preceded it, moreover, led to the discovery of some old treasons of the Lord of the Isles, who in December 1475 was declared by Parliament to have forfeited life, property, and offices.[1] A combined attack early in the following summer by an army under the King's uncle, the Earl of Atholl, and a flotilla under the Earl of Crawford, forced him to come to terms with the King.[2] Though much of his territory was restored to him, he had to surrender the Earldom of Ross, annexed in perpetuity to the Crown, and the sheriffdoms of Nairn and Inverness.[3] In 1478 the deposition of the mad and unmanageable Patrick Graham, great-grandson of a King and first Archbishop of St Andrews,[4] enabled the King to replace him by a supple prelate of lowly origin—William Schevez, astrologer and court physician,[5] whose services to the Crown had included the buying of green ginger, and the paying out of twelve shillings, "for the sewing of sarkis to the King".

But already there were signs that fortune was about to forsake one who did not know how to woo her: already John of the Isles had risen a second time in rebellion,[6] already the haggling over the payment of the Lady Cecilia's dowry showed that Edward IV had no special desire for his friendship. Edward was, in fact, laying plans for the recovery of Berwick, ceded to the Scots by Henry VI in 1461 in return for the promise of their support. And to the remoter menace of war with England was now added the more immediate threat of treason and revolt at home.

"His fatality", says a modern writer, "was that he could make himself neither loved nor feared."[7] Already Parliament had twice

---

[1] *Acts of the Parliaments of Scotland* (hereafter referred to as *A.P.S.*), VOL. II, ed. T. Thomson, London 1814, p. 108.

[2] John Lesley, *The History of Scotland from the death of King James I in the year 1436 to the year 1561*, Edinburgh 1830, p. 41; id., *De origine, moribus et rebus gestis Scotorum libri decem*, 1675 edn., p. 306 (hereafter referred to as Lesley, with page numbers Sc. and L.).

[3] *A.P.S.* VOL. II, p. 113.

[4] A. Theiner, *Vetera monumenta Hibernorum et Scotorum historiam illustrantia*, Rome 1864 (hereafter referred to as Theiner, *Vetera monumenta*) p. 479, cited in Herkless and Hannay, *Archbishops of St Andrews*, VOL. I, p. 62.

[5] Herkless and Hannay, *Archbishops of St Andrews*, VOL. I, p. 88; *C.T.S.*, VOL. I, pp. 21, 28.

[6] *A.P.S.*, VOL. II, p. 124.

[7] T. F. Henderson, *The Royal Stewarts*, Edinburgh 1914, p. 65.

taken it upon itself to censure him for dereliction of duty. In 1473, when he announced his intention of going to the Continent to mediate in person between Louis XI and Charles the Bold of Burgundy, it had pointed out to him that he would be better employed if he would "tak part of labor apone his persone and travel throw his Realme, and put sic Justice and polycy in his awne realme, that the brute [i.e. report] mycht pas in uther contreis, and that he mycht optene the name of sa Just a prince and as vertewss and as well Rewland his aune Realme."[1] In 1478 Parliament attributed the prevalence of "grit slauchter, . . . treason, refis and comoun thift . . . throuout the hale Realm" to the King's too ready granting of remissions and respites.[2] In the following year it announced hopefully, when confronted with a general breakdown of law and order, that the King meant to execute justice, and would, "in tyme to cum, with the awiss of the lordis of his counsale, attend diligently tharto".[3]

These reiterated complaints dispose of the theory advanced by some modern writers, following the lead of Buchanan, that James was a "new monarch", a Louis XI manqué, born, if not out of time, at least out of place, working deliberately and persistently to substitute government through Council—a council of experts chosen and controlled by himself—for government by Parliament —a parliament dominated by the great feudal magnates. Some support for this theory, it is true, may be found in the disappearance, sometime between 1468 and 1470, of the Sessions—judicial committees of Parliament which met twice a year, when Parliament was not sitting, to hear appeals from the ordinary courts— and the appearance, about 1466, of the Council as a new supreme civil court. But the emergence of the Council in this new capacity did not lead to the disappearance of the older court of the Lords Auditors of Causes and Complaints, which was a judicial committee of Parliament. And the two courts were not rivals; they were complementary, the Lords of Council as a rule sitting only when Parliament was not in session, and the Lords Auditors only during the session, or at most for a few days longer, with the

[1] A.P.S., VOL. II, p. 104.   [2] A.P.S., VOL. II, p. 118.
[3] A.P.S., VOL. II, p. 122.

same individuals often appearing as judges in both courts.[1] Nor can James be held responsible for the emergence in 1466 of the Council in a new role, for at that time he was a youth of fifteen, in the hands of the Boyds.

Unlike the typical "new monarch", he did not tighten up, he relaxed the administration of justice. It was James III that the anonymous author of *The Thre Prestis of Peblis* had in mind when he told the story of the King who, on two successive occasions, in return for a bribe, pardoned a courtier who had been guilty of murder, and then, when he slew a third victim, condemned him to death. The courtier was saved by Lictus the Fool, who proved that the King, by his misplaced clemency, had been responsible for the last two murders.[2] It was against James III, too, that another anonymous satirist directed his attacks:

> Bot of a thing al gude men mervalis mair:
>   Quhen grete counsale, with thine awn consent,
> Has ordanit strate justice na man to spair,
>   Within schort tym thou changis thine entent,
>   Sendand a contrar lettir incontinent,
> Chargeand that of that mater mair be nocht;
> Than al the warld murmuris that thou are bocht.[3]

James was, in truth, a "new monarch" of another stamp—an enlightened, keen-witted Renaissance prince, delighting more in the company of men as clever as himself, however lowly they might be, than in that of his illiterate and arrogant nobles. "He was ane that lowit sollitarnes", says Pitscottie, "and desyrit never to heir of weiris nor the fame thairof, but delytit mair in musik and polliecie of beging nor he did in the government of his realme; ffor he was wondrous covettous in conquissing of money rather than the heartis of his barrouns, for he delyttit mair in singing and in playing wpon instrumentis nor he did in defence

---

[1] R. K. Hannay, *The College of Justice*, Edinburgh 1933, pp. 13-14; *Acta dominorum concilii, Acts of the Lords of Council in Civil Causes*, VOL. II, edd. G. Neilson and H. Paton, Edinburgh 1918, pp. xix-xxv.

[2] *The Thre Prestis of Peblis*, ed. T. D. Robb, Edinburgh 1920, pp. 31-8.

[3] From a long poem at the end of the Marchmont manuscript of the Book of Pluscarden: printed in *The Book of Pluscarden*, ed. F. J. H. Skene, Historians of Scotland VOL. VII, Edinburgh 1877, pp. 392-400.

of the bordouris or in the ministratioun of justice."[1] The portrait drawn by Ferrerius corresponds to Pitscottie's description. James, he says, was remarkable, not for energy as a ruler, but for his intelligence and lively interest in all manner of things. He prized arts and learning, and admitted to his friendship not only scholars, but craftsmen who had shown skill above the ordinary in what were counted base and mechanic arts.[2]

But there was an ugly side to his nature. Hector Boece admitted that he was given over to licentiousness and avarice, "than which there is no disease more fatal to kings."[3] He was impatient of criticism, quick to make a foolish decision and slow to revoke it,[4] and, as events were soon to prove, superstitious out of measure.

It is little wonder that his gently-born subjects should have preferred to the unwarlike recluse, who seldom stirred from Edinburgh Castle, his two brothers, whose tastes were like their own; Alexander Duke of Albany, who "lowit nothing so weill as abill men and goode horse", and the young Earl of Mar, who "wssit mekill huntting and halking . . . archorie and wther knychtlie games".[5] Albany had remarked the King's growing unpopularity, and decided to turn it to his own advantage. But James suspected that Albany was plotting to supplant him; he was convinced, too, that his other brother had enlisted the aid of witches and warlocks to throw a spell over him and effect his destruction. In the spring of 1479 he arrested both Albany and Mar, lodged the first in Edinburgh Castle and the second in Craigmillar, and burned the supposed witches and warlocks. Albany escaped, and the story of how he slew his guards, lowered himself down the face of the Castle Rock by a rope fastened to his chamber window, hoisted his injured companion on his back, and carried him all the way to Leith, enhanced his prestige still

[1] Robert Lindesay of Pitscottie, *The History and Cronicles of Scotland*, ed. Aeneas J. G. Mackay, Edinburgh 1899-1911 (hereafter referred to as Pitscottie), VOL. I, p. 163.   [2] Ferrerius, *Continuatio*, p. 391.

[3] Hector Boece, *Murthlacensium et Aberdonensium episcoporum vitae*, ed. J. Moir, Aberdeen 1894 (hereafter referred as Boece, *Vitae*), pp. 74-5.

[4] Polydore Vergil, *Historia Anglica*, 1603 edn., VOL. II, p. 1365.

[5] Pitscottie, VOL. I, pp. 162-3.

further at the expense of the King. From Leith he escaped by sea
to his castle at Dunbar, whence he sailed for France. Dunbar
Castle was captured soon afterwards, and Albany summoned by
Parliament to stand his trial for treason,[1] but the sudden and
mysterious death of the Earl of Mar in a house in the Canongate,
slain, according to a contemporary, "becaus thai said he faworyt
the weches and warlois", dealt another blow to James's sorely
damaged reputation.[2]

The politic Louis of France received Albany hospitably, despatched an eminent Scottish theologian from the Sorbonne, John
Ireland, to the Scottish Court to plead his cause with his brother,
and in 1480 arranged his marriage[3] to Anne de la Tour, daughter
of the Count of Auvergne and Boulogne.[4]

It was not primarily solicitude for the banished Duke that had
made Louis send Ireland to the Scottish Court: he feared that his
pensioner and uncertain ally, Edward of England, might be
tempted to join forces against him along with his sister Margaret,
the widowed Duchess of Burgundy, and her son-in-law, the
future Emperor Maximilian. To insure against this he proposed
to make trouble for Edward on his northern frontier, and to this
end had instructed his ambassador to persuade the King of Scots
to break with England. James refused, but when Ireland came

---

[1] *A.P.S.*, VOL. II, pp. 125-8.

[2] An outline of the events related in the preceding paragraph is furnished
by the contemporary *Brevis cronica*, appended to one version (B.M. Royal
MS 17.DXX) of Wyntoun's *Original Chronicle* and printed in J. Pinkerton's
History of Scotland from the accession of the House of Stuart to that of Mary (hereafter
referred to as Pinkerton), London 1797, VOL. I, pp. 502-4. It is supplemented
by Lesley (pp. 43-4 Sc., 307 L.) and by Ferrerius (*Continuatio*, p. 393^v) who
state, for example, the place and manner of Mar's death. Pitscottie's highly-
coloured account (VOL. I, pp. 166-7) of the events which led to the imprisonment of the two brothers may be true, but may be a tale of superstition and
witchcraft which he thought too good to be lost; while his wonderful description (VOL. I, pp. 185-8) of the escape of Albany from Edinburgh Castle places
that event in the spring of 1483, some months after the Lauder episode.

[3] Lesley, pp. 44 Sc., 308-9 L.; Ferrerius, *Continuatio*, p. 393^v.

[4] Albany had been married before to Lady Catherine Sinclair, but had
divorced her in 1478: Sir Archibald H. Dunbar, *Scottish Kings*, Edinburgh 1899,
p. 201.

back in 1480 he succeeded in talking both the King and his nobles into making war.[1] A large army, led by the young Earl of Angus, Warden of the East Marches, crossed the Tweed, burned the Castle of Bamburgh, and after spending three days and three nights on English ground returned home unopposed— thus giving Edward the long-desired excuse for an attack on Scotland.[2]

All through the winter of 1480-1 preparations were made for a full-scale invasion to be directed by Edward in person. Ships were bought and manned and equipped for war, Lord John Howard was instructed to march to the Borders with three thousand men, and eighty butts of Malmsey were procured for the comfort of the King and his forces going to Scotland.[3] It seemed as if the elements had combined with the English against James and his unfortunate subjects, for a great tempest raged over Scotland from 1 January 1481 to 25 March.[4] James tried to avert the coming invasion by sending two envoys—a herald and a pursuivant—to the English Court, to offer redress for all breaches of the truce committed by his subjects, and also, it would appear, to warn Edward not to support Maximilian against the King of France. Edward refused to see them, nor would he allow them to return to Scotland till an English fleet had entered the Firth of Forth, plundered all the Scottish ships to be found there, and sailed away with eight of them, after burning Blackness Castle.

On the return of the envoys, "but answere owther in wourd or writ, in lichtlying of oure souerane lord", James was stung into activity; he assembled a great army and marched southwards, but before he reached the English frontier he was intercepted by an envoy from a cardinal then in England,[5] who presented him with letters from the Pope, threatening him with excommunication if he invaded the territory of another Christian prince, instead of

[1] Lesley, pp. 44 Sc., 308-9 L.; Ferrerius, *Continuatio*, p. 394.

[2] *Brevis cronica*, in Pinkerton, VOL. I, p. 503.

[3] *Cal. Doc. Scot.*, VOL. IV, No. 1466.

[4] *Brevis cronica*, in Pinkerton, VOL. I, p. 503.

[5] *A.P.S.*, VOL. II, p. 138; Lesley, pp. 45 Sc., 308-9 L.; Ferrerius, *Continuatio*, p. 394.

reserving his troops for a crusade against the Turk. Immediately James "skailit his great host", in the belief that Edward would do the same with his forces. But the "reiver Edward" had tricked him: no sooner had his army dispersed than an English fleet again appeared in the Forth, and English raiders made "grete brynyngs, hereschip, and distructioun all along the border."[1]

Though there was no large-scale invasion, raid and counter-raid continued all through the winter of 1481-2, bringing, according to the contemporary chronicler, "gret distructioun . . . of corne and catell", which "causyt bayth hungar and derth, and mony pur folk deit of hungar".[2] Even in Dundee, next to Edinburgh the wealthiest town in Scotland, the Franciscan friars were compelled to pawn their books, chalices, and ornaments, to procure food sufficient to keep body and soul together (*pro sustentatione miserabilis vite*).[3]

For the disasters that had befallen the country many people began to blame the King, and even more than the King, his counsellors; not so much his counsellors by prescriptive right, the great officers of state and busy ecclesiastics who witnessed his charters and acted as judges of appeal in civil cases, but the group of quick-witted adventurers who had become his inseparable companions, and were admitted by him, it was suspected, to the Secret Council itself. Only one of them, John Ramsay of Balmain —"a court pimp", according to Sir James Balfour—was of gentle birth. The others included William Torphichen, a fencing-master, James Hommyl, a tailor, Leonard, a shoemaker, and William Roger, an accomplished musician, who had come north in the train of an English ambassador and had been invited to stay on at the Scottish court by the music-loving King. Of the whole group, however, the most dear to the King and the most detested by his subjects was Robert Cochrane the master mason,

---

[1] According to Sir James Balfour (*Annales of Scotland*, in *Historical Works*, ed. James Haig, London 1825, VOL. I, p. 204) the Cardinal's envoy was an imposter—"a knauishe mounke" trimmed up "in the habit of the Popes Legat".   [2] *Brevis cronica*, in Pinkerton, VOL. I, p. 503.

[3] W. Moir Bryce, *The Scottish Grey Friars*, Edinburgh 1909, VOL. II, pp. 129-33.

in whom men saw, not the artist who had designed the Great Hall of Stirling Castle (mutilated today, but still beautiful), but the King's evil genius, who had persuaded him to continue the issue of "black money"—copper farthings nicknamed "Cochrane's placks"—and so brought the country to ruin. The revenues of the Earldom of Mar, bestowed on him by the infatuated King, served only to increase his arrogance.[1]

But in spite of the statement of Boece (qualified, be it noted) —*Jacobi imperium erat odiosum quod quorundam (ut ferebatur) obscurae originis, quos secretiori admoverat consilio, in publica administratione sententia utebatur*[2]—and the accusations of his nobles, there is no documentary evidence that James tried to control his Council—if by "Council" we mean the small group of great officers of state, like the Chancellor and the Master of the Household, and of permanent officials, like the Secretary, who followed him wherever he went, witnessed his charters, and gave him advice when he chose to ask for it—by excluding the great nobles and by packing it with the "skeely craftsmen" and supple adventurers who had gained his favour. The names of Cochrane, Leonard, Torphichen, and Roger, the "unworthy vile persons" who were to perish at Lauder, conspicuous in the pages of the late sixteenth-century historians, do not appear at all in the lists of witnesses in the Register of the Great Seal.[3] Nor do they figure in the sederunts of the Lords of Council,[4] which in practice was a small, sometimes a very small judicial committee of the

[1] Polydore Vergil, *Historia Anglica*, VOL. II, p. 1365; Sir David Lindesay, *The Testament of the Papyngo*, ll. 444-71, in *Works*, ed. D. Hamer, Edinburgh 1931-6, VOL. I, pp. 69-70; Lesley, pp. 48 Sc., 309 L.; Ferrerius, *Continuatio*, p. 395^v; Pitscottie, VOL. I, pp. 168-70.   [2] Boece, *Vitae*, pp. 56-7.

[3] The normal composition of the Council may be deduced from the list of witnesses to royal charters. A charter dated 8 March 1481, for example, was witnessed by: the Archbishop of St Andrews; the Bishop of Glasgow; the Bishop of Moray, Keeper of the Privy Seal; Lord Avandale, Chancellor; the Earl of Argyll, Master of the Household; the Earl of Crawford; Lord Carlyle; Master Archibald Whitelaw, Archdeacon of Lothian, Secretary; Master Alexander Inglis, Dean of Dunkeld, Clerk of Rolls and Register. *R.M.S.*, VOL. II, No. 1468.

[4] A typical sederunt of the Lords of Council in the pre-Lauder period is: the Bishops of Glasgow and Moray; the Bishop-elect of Aberdeen; the Chan-

Council, in which along with the half-dozen clerics skilled, we may assume, in civil law, there usually sat only two of the nobles, of whom the Chancellor, Avandale, was one. But we cannot say that the King excluded them; they probably excluded themselves, disinclined as they would be to endure their own ignorance of law or the tedium of the lengthy sessions. It must be admitted, however, that there are gaps in the evidence; the records of the Lords of Council between 6 November 1480 and 23 April 1483, are missing.

As for Cochrane, he can have been responsible only in part, if at all, for the debasement of the currency, which began in 1466, when Parliament sanctioned the issue of copper or "black" farthings, designed "for the eise and sustentation of the King's lieges and almous deide to be done to pure folk".[1] New pennies, too, had been issued before the time of Cochrane's ascendency, nominally of silver, really of billon-copper with only a trace of silver. To counterfeit these coins was easy and profitable; as early as 1467 Parliament had found it necessary to forbid the striking of "the black pennies"[2] under pain of death, and two years later it repeated the prohibition.[3] The acts could effect little when the Crown was the chief offender; the flood of black money of uncertain origin and diminishing value continued, and, according to the contemporary chronicler, was, along with the war, responsible for the fantastic rise in the price of food.[4] Cochrane may or may not have encouraged the King to continue a practice which in one year had brought a profit of £650 to the Exchequer[5]; what mattered was the widespread belief that he, and he alone, was responsible for it.[6]

As yet the storm did not break. There seems to have been

cellor; the Earl of Buchan; the Clerk of Rolls and Register; Master William Elphinstone; and John Ross of Montgrenane. 24 June 1480, *Acts of the Lords of council in Civil Causes*, VOL. I, London 1839, p. 51.

[1] *A.P.S.*, VOL. II, p. 86.   [2] *A.P.S.*, VOL. II, pp. 88-9.
[3] *A.P.S.*, VOL. II, p. 97.   [4] *Brevis cronica*, in Pinkerton, VOL. I, p. 503.
[5] *Rotuli Scaccarium regum Scotorum, The Exchequer Rolls of Scotland* (hereafter referred to as R. Scac. S.), VOL. IX, ed. G. Burnett, Edinburgh 1886, p. lxv.
[6] See also Sir George Macdonald, "The Mint of Crossraguel Abbey", in *Proceedings of the Society of Antiquaries of Scotland*, LIV (1919-20), pp. 20-44.

some criticism of the King's policy—or lack of it—in the Parliament which met in March 1482, criticism which James attempted to still by the declaration that "undirstanding . . . the hertfull lufe" of his lieges, he would cause justice to be evenly ministered, "with the gude and trew counsale of his prelatis, lords, and wise discrete persons".[1] Parliament then proceeded to make plans for repelling the English troops massing on the other side of the Border; among other measures of defence the fortifications of Berwick were repaired and strengthened, and a garrison of five hundred men placed in it.[2]

But the English attack did not take the precise form that the Scots had expected. Edward's next move was to open negotiations with Albany, and bring him over to England, "to serve the King his liege against his rebels in Scotland". Albany landed at Southampton on 25 April 1482 and was escorted by two esquires of the King's bodyguard to London.[3] At Fotheringay, on 10 June, he signed a treaty by which he promised to do homage to Edward "for my realm of Scotland" six months after he had gained possession of the Crown and the greater part of the Kingdom, to break the old alliance with France, to refrain from entering into any new alliance hostile to England, and to surrender Berwick a fortnight after he had reached Edinburgh.[4] By a second treaty, signed on 11 June, Edward promised to help "Alexander, King of Scotland", to gain possession of his kingdom, reserving to himself Berwick, Liddesdale, Eskdale, Ewesdale, Annandale, and Lochmaben Castle.[5] Before the end of the month an army, under the joint command of Albany and Richard, Duke of Gloucester, moved up to Alnwick.[6]

James was aware of the danger in which Berwick and the whole country stood, but when he attempted to gather an army to repel the coming invasion, he found that most of his nobles,

---

[1] *A.P.S.*, VOL. II, p. 139.   [2] *A.P.S.*, VOL. II, pp. 139-40.
[3] *Cal. Doc. Scot.*, VOL. IV, No. 1474; *Foedera*, VOL. XII, London 1711, p. 154.
[4] *Cal. Doc. Scot.*, VOL. IV, No. 1475; *Foedera*, VOL. XII, p. 156.
[5] *Cal. Doc. Scot.*, VOL. IV, No. 1476; *Foedera*, VOL. XII, p. 156.
[6] *Hall's Chronicle*, ed. Sir H. Ellis (hereafter referred to as Hall), London 1809, p. 331.

though they had called up their tenants, refused to march with him. At the head of such troops as he could muster, James, accompanied by his obnoxious favourites, advanced to the little town of Lauder, twenty-four miles south of Edinburgh, where he encamped, unaware that the disaffected nobles, the Earls of Angus, Huntly, Lennox, and Buchan, Lord Gray and Lord Lyle, were following him with an army far outnumbering his own.[1]

Marching under cover of darkness, the rebels occupied the town as day was breaking without encountering any resistance. Their leaders went to the Kirk of Lauder to discuss their next move.[2] They had already decided to present certain demands to the King: they had not yet decided how and by whom they should be presented. Lord Gray, according to the familiar story, cut the discussion short by repeating the fable of the mice, who devised the plan of fastening a bell round the neck of their enemy the cat, only to find that it had one insuperable defect. "I will bell the cat!" cried Angus, and "Bell-the-Cat" he remained to the end of his days.[3]

With one or two companions he went to the King's tent, and told him bluntly that if he wished to secure the support of his nobles in the war against England, he must withdraw the black money, and hand over his favourites to them for punishment. The King was furious—all the more so because he had already planned to withdraw the money in a fashion that would cause the minimum of inconvenience to his subjects—and dismissed

[1] According to Lesley, pp. 48 Sc., 309 L., the Earls of Argyll, Huntly, Lennox, and Buchan, Lords Gray and Lyle, and "diveris utheris"; according to Pitscottie, VOL. I, p. 173, Lord Avandale (Chancellor), the Earls of Angus, Argyll, Huntly, Orkney, and Crawford, Lords Hailes, Home, Gray, Seton, and Fleming, Sir John Drummond, and certain bishops.

[2] The Lauder episode is described briefly in the contemporary *Brevis cronica* (in Pinkerton, VOL. I, pp. 503-4) and in Boece (*Vitae*, p. 57); at greater length by Lesley (pp. 49 Sc., 309-10 L.); in more detail by Ferrerius (*Continuatio*, pp. 394^v-5^v), who furnishes the King and his adversaries with arguments; and with much picturesque circumstance by Pitscottie (VOL. I, pp. 173-6), whose account I have followed.

[3] The earliest account of the Bell-the-Cat episode is in Hume of Godscroft's *History of the Houses of Douglas and Angus* (hereafter referred to as Godscroft), which was not written till 1625.

the envoys, after refusing to grant their demands. They returned
to the church, where they repeated word for word the threats
and reproaches which the King had hurled at them. Their companions saw that there could be no going back: they must secure
the person of the King before he could attempt a counter-stroke,
and get by force what they could not achieve by persuasion.
They were anticipated by Cochrane, who appeared outside the
church at the head of a band of halberdiers attired in his livery of
black and silver. He wore a short riding-coat of black velvet,
with a heavy gold chain about his neck, and a baldrick of silk
and cloth of gold adorned with precious stones, from which hung
a hunting-horn "tipped with fine gold at every end". He
knocked loudly at the church door, and when those within asked
who knocked so rudely, answered, "It is I, the Earl of Mar."
Angus and Sir Robert Douglas, Laird of Lochleven, hurried to
the door to give him an appropriate welcome. As he entered,
Angus snatched the chain of gold from his neck, crying that "ane
raip wald sett him better", while Douglas, remarking that he
had been a "hunter of mischief owre lang", took possession of
the "fair blawing horne". "My lords, is it mowse [jest] or
earnest?" Cochrane asked. "It is good earnest," he was assured
by his captors. They spared his life for the meantime, only tying
his wrists together with a rope, despite his protests that one of
his eminence should be bound only with a silken cord; then,
snatching up their weapons, they rushed to the King's tent,
dragged out the terrified favourites, forced the King to come
with them as a spectator, and without any form of trial or any
attempt to separate the innocent from the guilty, hanged them
over the Bridge at Lauder. High "abone the lave of his complices"
dangled the body of the insolent Cochrane, "that he might be
ane exampill to all simpill personis", commented Pitscottie,
"nocht to climb so hie and proceed in so great thingis in ane
realm as he did". The Englishman William Roger, *musicus
rarissimus*, though completely innocent, perished with the rest: the
only member of the doomed company, it was commonly believed, to escape with his life, was the eighteen-year-old Ramsay
of Balmain, who clung to the King so tightly that the executioners

had to spare him, lest, in forcing him away, they should damage the royal person.[1]

The rebel lords completed the day's work by "crying down" —declaring the suppression of—the black silver. There was no longer any question of an invasion of England. With the King, now a jealously guarded captive, they withdrew to Edinburgh where, on 22 July,[2] they lodged him in the Castle under the guardianship of his uncle John Stewart, Earl of Atholl.[3] The withdrawal of the Scottish army left Berwick open to the enemy; at the end of the month Gloucester suddenly moved northward and occupied the town of Berwick. Their success was not complete: the Castle held out, but, leaving a containing force behind them, they pushed on to Edinburgh, which they entered quietly on 1 August. At the request of Albany, Gloucester refrained from sacking the town, and contented himself with "takynge only such presentes as the merchantis gentelly offered him and his capitaynes."[4] It seemed that nothing could now prevent Albany from becoming master of Scotland.

The nobles were divided: Schevez, the Chancellor Lord Avandale, and the Earl of Argyll were at variance with the King's uncles, the Earl of Atholl and the Earl of Buchan, who were determined to intrude their brother, Andrew Stewart, Dean of Moray, into the archiepiscopal see of St Andrews, and to compel Schevez to accept a poorer benefice.[5] But all were united in their distrust of Albany: the only nobles prepared to support him through thick and thin were the Earl of Angus and Lord Gray, the ringleaders in the Lauder affair. And Angus and Gray knew what the others were beginning to suspect, that the liberator of Scotland was really an English agent, pledged, if he ousted his

---

[1] At least one other escaped—James Hommyl the tailor, who is repeatedly mentioned in *C.T.S.* after 1482. There may have been others; according to the *Brevis cronica*, in Pinkerton, VOL. I, p. 503, "thai slew ane part of the Kingis hous hauld, and other part thai banyst".

[2] *Brevis cronica*, in Pinkerton, VOL. I, p. 504.

[3] Lesley, pp. 49 Sc., 310 L.   [4] Hall, p. 332.

[5] Lesley, pp. 50 Sc., 311 L. See also Herkless and Hannay, *Archbishops of St Andrews*, VOL. I, pp. 101-8.

C

brother from his throne, to do homage to England for his kingdom, and sell to him the Border passes and fortresses.

Seeing that he had no immediate chance of being accepted as
King, Albany decided to come to terms with the party that was
in the ascendant at the moment. On 2 August 1482, he closed
with the offer made to him by Schevez, Avandale, Argyll, and
the Bishop of Dunkeld,[1] to see him restored to his estates and
dignities if he would promise to remain faithful to the King.[2]
Next day he gave Gloucester a written assurance that, in spite of
any agreements that he had made or might yet make with the
Scottish lords, he would abide by the secret treaty of 10 June,[3]
whereupon Gloucester withdrew to press the siege of Berwick
Castle, which fell to him three weeks later.[4]

Albany saw that the significance of his refusal to stir a foot to
save Berwick Castle had not been hidden from his new associates,
and, fearful that their support would soon fail him, he turned in
search of other allies. He knew that the burgesses of Edinburgh
did not love Buchan and Atholl, who had forced them to promise
six thousand ducats to expedite the elevation of their brother to
the archbishopric of St Andrews.[5] But Schevez, Avandale, and
Argyll were with him when, before the end of September, he
visited Stirling Castle. Here he saw the Duke of Rothesay, now
nine years old, and talked at length with his mother about the
education proper for a young prince; then, on her advice, he rode
to Edinburgh.[6] On 29 September[7] he appeared at the gates of
Edinburgh Castle with the Provost, bailies, and burgesses, expelled Atholl, and released, or rather, made a show of releasing,
the King.[8]

[1] James Levington, d. 28 Aug. 1483.
[2] Cal. Doc. Scot., VOL. IV, No. 1479; Foedera, VOL. XII, p. 160.
[3] Hall, p. 334.   [4] Lesley, pp. 50 Sc., 310 L.
[5] Charters and other Documents relating to the City of Edinburgh 1143-1540,
ed. J. D. Marwick, Edinburgh 1871 (hereafter referred to as Edinburgh Charters),
pp. 154-6; cited in Herkless and Hannay, Archbishops of St Andrews, VOL. I,
p. 108.
[6] Lesley, pp. 50 Sc., 310 L.; Ferrerius, Continuatio, p. 396^v.
[7] Brevis cronica, in Pinkerton, VOL. I, p. 504.
[8] Lesley, pp. 50 Sc., 311 L.; Ferrerius, Continuatio, p. 396^v.

If James suspected that his release was a put-up job, he kept his suspicions to himself, and played his part convincingly in the comedy. Not only did he, within the next few days, appoint Albany his Lieutenant General in Scotland, Lord High Admiral, and Warden of the East and West Marches, and confer on him Cochrane's Earldom of Mar and Garviach[1]; he spent most of his time in his company, sharing his meals and his bed with him,[2] and showed his gratitude to the burgesses of Edinburgh by granting them, on 16 November, the Golden Charter, which made their Provost sheriff within the bounds of the city.[3]

Albany, we can guess from what happened later, was now attempting to fuse the Gray-Angus clique and the faction of the King's uncles into a single powerful party which would follow him in any course that he might pursue. He succeeded at the cost of alienating Avandale, Argyll, and Schevez, who had been compelled to exchange his archbishopric for the see of Moray. They judged it wise to retire to their castles,[4] and discreetly stayed away from the Parliament which met in Edinburgh on 2 December 1482, and prayed the King, "sen it accordis nocht to the honour of his hienes to put his noble persone daily to danger", that he should "speke to his bruther the Duke of Albany to tak apon him to be lieutenant generale of the Realme, and to defend the bordouris and Resist his ennemyis".[5]

Albany interpreted his duties after his own fashion: on 12 January 1483 he sent Angus, Gray, and Sir James Liddell to Westminster to meet King Edward's representatives,[6] and on 11 February they drafted a secret agreement. There was to be a truce for a year, but during this period Albany was to attempt daily to win the Crown for himself and "never leve that opinion for any Offre or Trety". In addition, he was to abandon finally all claim to Berwick and break the ancient league with France,

[1] R.M.S., VOL. II, No. 1541.
[2] Ferrerius, Continuatio, p. 396[v].
[3] Edinburgh Charters, pp. 157-65.
[4] Lesley, pp. 50 Sc., 311 L.; Ferrerius, Continuatio, p. 396[v].
[5] A.P.S., VOL. II, pp. 142-3.
[6] Cal. Doc. Scot., VOL. IV, No. 1486; Foedera, VOL. XII, p. 172.

while his ambassadors promised that in the event of his dying without leaving an heir, they would become subjects of King Edward, and defend their castles to the last against King James or his successors.[1]

Somehow or other the King got wind of the schemes. He dropped all show of affection. Albany, protesting that his brother had tried to poison him, withdrew to his castle of Dunbar, accompanied by Angus and Gray, and the King's three uncles.[2] The King replied by summoning Parliament. Albany saw that it had lost all its illusions about his patriotism, and on 16 March made another agreement with his brother. All he could secure from him was a promise of forgiveness and letters of security under the Privy Seal. In return, he confessed his treason, admitted that James had not attempted to poison him, and promised to repudiate his treaties with England. Further, at the King's request, he resigned his office of Lieutenant General, banished from his company his three uncles, bound himself not to come within six miles of the King's presence, and professed to "tak in hertly favouris friendship, and tenderness al the lordis and personis of our Soverain lordis counsail".[3]

For a few days, a week at most, he brooded over his thwarted schemes; then, after opening the gates of his castle to an English garrison, he fled to England.[4] There was little to be hoped for in that quarter: his ally Edward IV died on 9 April, and Richard III, insecurely seated on the throne of England, was no longer interested in the winning of thrones for other people. On 27 June the Scottish Parliament cited him to appear before it to answer the charges of conducting treasonable negotiations with the King of England, and of passing into England without the King's permission after the King had graciously pardoned him. On 8 July, at the instance of John Ross of Montgrenane, the King's Advocate, instructed by the King himself, who was present, the Three Estates, "beand deligently and Ripely avisit", found Albany guilty of all the charges. Thereupon John Dempster, the dempster

---

[1] *Cal. Doc. Scot.*, VOL. IV, No. 1487; *Foedera*, VOL. XII, p. 173.
[2] Lesley, pp. 50-1 Sc., 313 L.   [3] *A.P.S.*, VOL. II, pp. 31-3.
[4] Lesley, pp. 51 Sc., 313 L.; Ferrerius, *Continuatio*, p. 397.

or doomster of Parliament, pronounced the sentence in the accustomed fashion: "This court of parliament schewis for law, and I gif for dome, that forsamekle as it is fundin be sensiment of parliament that Alexander Duc of Albany . . . has committit and done tresoun again our souueran and his Realme in the tresonis and crimez forsaid contenit in the sumondis, for the quhilkis he has forfatit til our souueran lord his life, his landis, his gudis, officis, and all uther his possessions quhatsoeuer he had of our souueran lord within the Realme of scotland, evermair to Remain with our souueran lord, his airis and successoris as properte for his tressoun and offence. And that I give for doom." The same sentence was pronounced on his accomplice Liddell.[1]

In the summer of 1484, however, Albany appeared in Scotland with the old Earl of Douglas, banished almost thirty years earlier. At the head of five hundred horsemen they crossed the Border on 22 July, and galloped into Lochmaben, where a fair was in full swing. The Scottish Warden, however, who had come to maintain order during the fair, gave the alarm; from all sides the Border lairds and their followers rode in, and after a battle which lasted from noon to twilight, forced the raiders to flee. Albany escaped. But he had shot his bolt.[2] Richard III, who had decided to make peace with Scotland, had no further use for him. He returned to France, where, a year later, he was accidentally killed while watching a tournament.[3]

Douglas was captured and brought before the King, but, so the story goes, turned his back on him and stood silent. James, impressed by his age and dignified bearing, would order no heavier penalty than confinement in Lindores Abbey. "He that may no better be, must be a monk," was the old man's comment.[4]

It was the revelation of Albany's treason, and not any kingly virtue in James himself, that had given him the victory. For a time he walked delicately. Though he welcomed Ramsay of Balmain back to court, and on 6 September 1483 bestowed on him the lordship of Bothwell,[5] he had the good sense to call to

[1] *A.P.S.*, VOL. II pp. 151-2.
[2] Godscroft, 1644 edn., p. 205.
[3] Lesley, pp. 51 Sc., 313 L.
[4] Godscroft, p. 206.
[5] *R.M.S.*, VOL. II, No. 1565.

his aid the one statesman of genius whom Scotland possessed, William Elphinstone, who, trained in the law schools of Paris and Orleans, had returned to Scotland to become Official of Lothian. James saw to it that preferment came to one who joined learning and piety to high ability as judge and administrator; in 1481 he became Bishop of Ross,[1] and in 1483, despite some opposition in the Roman Curia, Bishop of Aberdeen.[2] Elphinstone did not hesitate to take his patron to task for his private faults, his avarice, his licentiousness, and his evident scorn of religion.[3] To his persuasions were added those of John Ireland, who, soon after the death of his patron Louis XI in August 1483, left the Sorbonne for his native Scotland,[4] to become chaplain and confessor to the King.[5] The libertine became an assiduous sermon-taster and student of theology; soon his subjects were edified by the spectacle of their sovereign kneeling in the street before some image of the Saviour or of the Virgin Mary.[6]

In all probability it was Elphinstone who inspired his policy of propping his trembling throne by establishing friendly relations with England. Though on 13 March 1484, at the instance of Bernard Stewart, Sieur d'Aubigny, and Maître Pierre Milet, ambassadors of King Charles VIII, he renewed the hundred-and-fifty-eight-year-old Treaty of Alliance with France, a treaty providing for united action against England in the event of an English attack on either of the allies,[7] he opened negotiations with England before the end of the summer.[8] On 12 September 1484, Argyll, Elphinstone, and six other Scottish ambassadors were received in the great hall of Nottingham Castle by King Richard, sitting "undyr hys clothe of ryall astate",[9] and eight

[1] Annie I. Cameron, *The Apostolic Camera and Scottish Benefices 1418-1488*, Oxford 1934, p. 77.

[2] Cameron, *op. cit.*, p. 80.   [3] Boece, *Vitae*, p. 75.

[4] Ferrerius, *Continuatio*, p. 391; John Ireland, *The Meroure of Wyssdome*, ed. C. Macpherson, Edinburgh 1926, pp. xxiii-xxiv.

[5] Ireland, *Meroure of Wyssdome*, p. 15.   [6] Boece, *Vitae*, p. 75.

[7] Register House MSS, Treaties with France, Nos. 16 (Latin), 17 (French), 18 (Ratification by Charles VIII, Paris, 9 July 1484, Latin), 19 (do. French).

[8] *Cal. Doc. Scot.*, VOL. IV, No. 1501.

[9] *Letters and Papers illustrative of the Reigns of Richard III and Henry VII*, ed.

days later articles were drawn up providing for a truce to last till
29 September 1487.[1] From this truce, however, Dunbar was excluded; it was captured by the Scots in the winter of 1485-6.[2] On
21 September too, an indenture was signed for the marriage of
the Duke of Rothesay to Anne de la Pole, niece of Richard, as
soon as it might be conveniently solemnised within the next three
years.[3]

The treaties were ratified by King James on 21 October 1484.[4]
In the Parliament which met in the following May, the Lords of
the Articles signified their approval of the truce, and nominated
commissioners to meet Richard's representatives in York and
complete the arrangements for the marriage.[5] They arrived in
England in time to be present at the Battle of Bosworth.[6]

The death of Richard III, the accession of Henry Tudor,
strengthened, if anything, the tie between the two monarchies.
If all the stories of the Scottish sixteenth-century historians are
true, Henry had good reason to be grateful to the Scots. Accord-
ing to John Major, while he lived a poverty-stricken exile in
Rouen, he took his meals in the house of one Patrick King, a
Scot, who was sorry for him and bestowed a large part of his
fortune on him.[7] The invading force with which he landed at
Milford Haven included both a French contingent, under the
command of Stewart d'Aubigny, and a Scots company, led by
John de Coningham,[8] Captain of the French King's Garde
Ecossaise, and Sir Alexander Bruce of Earlshall, a Fife laird.[9] It

James Gairdner, London 1861-3 (hereafter referred to as *L. and P. Richard III
and Henry VII*), VOL. I, pp. 63-7.

[1] *Cal. Doc. Scot.*, VOL. IV, No. 1505; *Foedera*, VOL. XII, p. 235.

[2] *R. Scac. S.*, VOL. IX, p. 433.

[3] *Cal. Doc. Scot.*, VOL. IV, No. 1504; *Foedera*, VOL. XII, p. 244.

[4] *Cal. Doc. Scot.*, VOL. IV, No. 1508; *Foedera*, VOL. XII, p. 250.

[5] *A.P.S.*, VOL. II, p. 170.

[6] See the very curious story in Pitscottie, VOL. I, pp. 196-8.

[7] John Major, *History of Greater Britain*, trans. and ed. A. Constable, Edinburgh 1892, p. 393.

[8] The editor's surmise for "John, son of Robert of Haddington". John de
Coningham was Captain of the *Garde Ecossaise* from 1478, when he succeeded
his father Robert de Coningham, until 1493. See Major, *History of Greater
Britain*, p. 393 and n.　　　　　　　　　　　　[9] Pitscottie, VOL. I, p. 191.

was this Scots company, according to Pitscottie, which formed the spear-point of Henry's attack at Bosworth.[1]

It was not gratitude alone (if indeed gratitude ever moves princes) that led Henry VII to establish friendly relations with his neighbour, it was plain commonsense. Like James, he shrank from unnecessary expenditure of money or human life; like James, he had no wish to see dangerous rebels or pretenders to his throne established just beyond the frontiers of his kingdom. On 22 September he issued safe-conducts to the Bishops of Glasgow, Aberdeen, and Dunkeld, Lord Bothwell, and two knights[2] who were present at his coronation on 30 October.[3] The recapture of Dunbar Castle in the winter of 1485-6 brought no protest from him; on 30 January 1486 he commissioned the Earl of Northumberland to open negotiations with the King of Scots,[4] and on 2 February he issued a safe-conduct to twelve Scottish ambassadors to be nominated by King James.[5] The abortive rebellion of Lovell in the north of England delayed the negotiations; it was not till 6 May that the King of Scots commissioned Elphinstone, Robert Bellenden, Abbot of Holyrood, Lord Bothwell, Lord Kennedy, Sir John Ross of Montgrenane, King's Advocate, and Archibald Whitelaw, Secretary, to conclude a truce.[6] They were received in state by Henry at Westminster on 5 June,[7] and on 3 July, after a lengthy discussion with the English commissioners they concluded a truce to last till sunset on 3 July 1489.[8] Careful arrangements were made to avoid clashes at sea or on the Borders; no traitors, fugitives from justice, or convicted criminals were to be received by either party to the truce. The problem of Berwick remained unsolved. All that was achieved was an agreement that commissioners from both king-

[1] Pitscottie, VOL. I, pp. 195-6.

[2] *Rotuli Scotiae in turri Londinensi et in domo capitulari Westmonasteriensi asservati*, London 1814-19 (hereafter referred to as *Rot. Scot.*), VOL. II, p. 469.

[3] Hon. Agnes Conway, *Henry VII's relations with Scotland and Ireland 1485-1498*, Cambridge 1932 (hereafter referred to as Conway), p. 9.

[4] *Foedera*, VOL. XII, p. 334 (dated 1488). [5] Ibid.

[6] *Cal. Doc. Scot.*, VOL. IV, No. 1520; *Foedera*, VOL. XII, p. 291.

[7] John Leland, *Collectanea*, 1774 edn., VOL. IV, p. 203, cited in Conway, p. 9.

[8] *Cal. Doc. Scot.*, VOL. IV, No. 1521; *Foedera*, VOL. XII, pp. 285-90.

doms should meet in Berwick on 8 March 1487, to delimit the ancient boundaries of town and castle, and, if these could not be discovered, to fix new ones. If the negotiations broke down, the truce would terminate on 3 July 1487. As soon as the commissioners met, however, on the assumption that the dispute would be settled amicably, ambassadors would be sent to Edinburgh to negotiate a truce of longer duration, and the marriage of James, Marquis of Ormonde, to Katharine, the second daughter of Edward IV, and so the younger sister of Henry's queen. The truce was confirmed by Henry on 26 July,[1] and by James on 24 October.[2]

Disquieting news from Ireland, where the supporters of Lambert Simnel were assembling, prevented the resumption of negotiations in March 1487. Not till August, after he had defeated the rebels at the Battle of Stoke, and found a post for the pretender in the royal kitchens, did Henry send Richard Fox, Bishop of Exeter, and Sir Richard Edgecombe to the Scottish Court,[3] where King James received them cordially, but confessed that, as his devotion to Henry was not shared by his subjects, "the Scots being so made they could not agree with the English", the ambassadors must be content with a truce for seven years only. He promised them in confidence, however, always to remain at peace with Henry, and to renew the truce every seven years. This he did, writes Polydore Vergil, because his very name was so hateful to most of his subjects, that they would disapprove utterly of anything that he might propose.[4] As it was, James's commissioners, Elphinstone and Bothwell, who obviously shared their master's fears, extended the existing truce for three months only. They agreed, however, that there should be "Communication for Marriage" not only between Ormonde and the Lady Katharine, but also between King James, left a widower by the death of Queen Margaret in the previous year, and Queen Elizabeth, the widow of Edward IV, as well as between the heir to

---

[1] *Rot. Scot.*, VOL. II, pp. 473-7, cited in Conway, p. 10.
[2] *Cal. Doc. Scot.*, VOL. IV, No. 1524; *Foedera*, VOL. XII, p. 316.
[3] *Rot. Scot.*, VOL. II, p. 480, cited in Conway, p. 10.
[4] Polydore Vergil, *Historia Anglica*, VOL. II, pp. 1459-60.

the throne and another of King Edward's daughters, "quhilk likit best to baith the said Kings". Only in this way, they declared, could an end be made to the debates and controversies over the town and castle of Berwick, of which "the said King of Scottis desiris alwais Deliverans". Negotiations about the royal marriages were to be continued at a meeting of the commissioners to be held in Edinburgh on 24 January 1488; a further meeting, to make the final arrangements for the marriage, and to settle "the seid mater of Berwik" was to be held in May, and in July the two monarchs were to meet "at sic a place as can be betwix thame agreit".[1]

The meeting never took place. James's ill-disguised advances to Henry hastened the very disaster which they were intended to avert. His negotiations with the Pope, apparently successful at first, had the same outcome. On 5 May 1484 Pope Sixtus IV, in response to his letters, and to the representations of his ambassador Robert Blacader, the new Bishop of Glasgow, issued a bull commanding the Scottish prelates and nobles to return to their obedience.[2] But even in Rome the King's affairs went awry. Clerks in the royal service, whom the King wished to see rewarded with bishoprics, found themselves, in spite of all the edicts of Parliament against the export of bullion, outbid at the Papal court by candidates better provided with ready money. Blacader, for example, had secured the see of Glasgow in spite of the King's support of the rival candidate, George Carmichael,[3] and soon afterwards Alexander Inglis, Clerk of Rolls and Register, whom both the King and the Cathedral Chapter had chosen for the see of Dunkeld, saw the prize snatched from him by George Brown, the King's Orator at the Papal court, who had ingratiated himself with Roderigo Borgia, later Pope Alexander VI.[4]

Early in the pontificate of Innocent VIII, who succeeded

[1] The terms of the agreement were set down in an indenture, witnessed by Snowdon and Carlisle Heralds on 28 Nov. 1487. *Foedera*, VOL. XII, pp. 329-30.

[2] O. Raynald, *Annales ecclesiastici*, VOL. XIX, Cologne 1693, a. 1484, No. 6.

[3] A. Myln, *Vitae Dunkeldensis ecclesiae episcoporum*, ed. T. Thomson, Edinburgh 1823 (hereafter referred to as Myln, *Vitae*), p. 27; translated in *Rentale Dunkeldense*, ed. R. K. Hannay, Edinburgh 1915, p. 302.

[4] Myln, *Vitae*, pp. 27-8; *Rentale Dunkeldense*, pp. 302-3.

Sixtus IV in August 1484, James renewed his appeals for support. They did not go unheard; early in 1486 there came to Scotland James, Bishop of Imola, legate *a latere*, bringing with him, as a special mark of the Papal favour, the Golden Rose.[1] James delighted in the conversation of the much-travelled stranger, loaded him with gifts, and took him about with him wherever he went.[2]

Imola brought not only the Golden Rose, but a more formidable spiritual weapon, a brief, written on 5 August 1485, stating that the Pope was fully aware of the recent unusually bitter disputes over the provision to Scottish benefices, and also of the insolence of certain nobles, who had not blushed to stick out their necks (*cervicem erigere non erubuerunt*) against the King, wherefore there had arisen war, sedition, slaughter, and other evils innumerable, so that not only was divine worship neglected and despised, but justice was not administered, and the whole kingdom was brought to poverty and ruin. The King, he knew, had forgiven the offenders.[3] He exhorted the King not to revoke his pardon, while admonishing clerics and laymen of every rank to live in obedience to him. Any city or burgh, university or college, which flouted the royal authority would be laid under ecclesiastical interdict. No noble was to rebel, or to associate with rebels; all treasonable confederations were to be dissolved. Fomenters of rebellion, if clerics, were to be excommunicated and deprived of their benefices; if earls, lords, knights, or chieftains of any kind (*vel quivis dominus vel primatus vel quivis alius regnicola*), their lands would be laid under an interdict, and their goods forfeited. Should an offender be absolved because his death seemed imminent, the absolution would be annulled if he recovered, and his descendants to the third generation remain incapable of holding any dignity or office that he might have enjoyed. Absolution could be granted only by the Pope himself. That no one might

---

[1] Raynald, *Annales ecclesiastici*, VOL. XIX, *a.* 1486, No. 49, cited in Herkless and Hannay, *Archbishops of St Andrews*, VOL. I, p. 124.

[2] Boece, *Vitae*, p. 76.

[3] So far, the Pope seems to quote from a letter which James and Imola had written to him.

plead ignorance, copies of the brief were to be displayed in every cathedral in the kingdom.[1]

Obedient to his instructions to restore order, Imola dealt out excommunications and interdicts with a liberal hand.[2] But the King, compassionate when compassion was out of place, shrank from applying the harsh remedies which he advised. Once when James, accompanied by Imola and Elphinstone, was on his way to the church at Restalrig, a certain nobleman, who had been found guilty of murder, broke away from the guards who were leading him to execution, flung himself at the King's feet, and weeping bitterly and holding up his fettered hands, begged the King to pardon him, since he had not meant to kill his victim. The King asked Imola for his advice. "*Fiat justitia*," he replied. Then the King turned to Elphinstone, exclaiming, "Is this the mercy of Italian priests? You used to give me very different advice. *Fiat misericordia!*" With that he ordered the prisoner's release.[3]

Imola's mission to Scotland was followed by a Scottish mission to Rome, contemplated by the King in the preceding spring, when he informed the Pope that he was sending Schevez to him as his ambassador.[4] On 9 May 1485 Parliament signified its approval of Schevez as "the maist convenient person" to lead the mission.[5] The ambassadors were instructed to secure the papal confirmation of the treaties with France and Denmark, and to attempt to right the wrong that had been done to Alexander Inglis by the intrusion of George Brown into the see of Dunkeld, which blocked the promotion of his learned protégé, John Ireland, to the Archdeaconry of St Andrews. Such disregard of the royal wishes by the Roman Curia, they were to represent, arose through the action of "certane personis, barratouris", who had obstructed the provision to benefices of persons presented by the King while the benefice was vacant, contrary to his privileges, and to the great detriment of the royal authority. They were therefore to beg the Pope to silence all such barrators, and order

---

[1] Theiner, *Vetera monumenta*, pp. 496-9.
[2] Herkless and Hannay, *Archbishops of St Andrews*, VOL. I, p. 125.
[3] Boece, *Vitae*, pp. 76-7.   [4] *A.P.S.*, VOL. II, p. 170.   [5] Ibid.

them to "cess all sic pleys in tyme to cum". What was more important, they were to beg his Holiness to take into consideration the distance of Scotland from Rome, and allow the King and his successors to delay the disposition of any prelacies or elective dignities for six months, "sa that there be na personis promovit to prelaceis nor digniteis without avise of his hienes, sen all the prelatis of his Realme has the first vote in his parliament and of his Secrete counsale".[1]

Among the privileges that the Pope was to be petitioned to grant was one destined to be fatal to the King. The Priory of Coldingham, for long a dependency, had after its disjunction become practically an appanage of the great border family of Hume. There were Humes in the cloister, Hume had succeeded Hume in the Prior's chair, and the head of the family, Alexander, Lord Hume, was hereditary bailiff of the Priory. As early as 1473, however, James had sounded Sixtus IV about the possibility of its suppression.[2] Twelve years had not taught him wisdom; though it must have been obvious that any attempt to suppress the Priory would excite the bitter opposition of the Humes, he persuaded Parliament in February 1484 to approve of its annexation to his new Chapel Royal in Stirling.[3] The ambassadors were now instructed to appeal to the Pope for "ane ereccioun of Coldingaham to our souerane lordis chapell" which would involve the alienation of its lands and revenues and the expulsion of its monks "be extinccoun of Religioun".[4]

The ambassadors, Schevez and Blacader, did not cross the Channel till late in the following year. Henry VII issued a safe-conduct to them on 7 July 1486[5]; it was not till 12 October that Schevez arrived at Dover.[6] It is possible that the death of Queen Margaret, on 14 July, delayed their departure, for, as we shall see,

---

[1] *A.P.S.*, VOL. II, p. 171.   [2] Theiner, *Vetera monumenta*, pp. 472-3.

[3] 4 Feb. 1483/4; *The Lawes and Actes of Parliament, maid be King James the First and his successours, Kingess of Scotland*, compiled by Sir John Skene, Edinburgh 1597, p. 73.

[4] *A.P.S.*, VOL. II, p. 171.

[5] *Cal. Doc. Scot.*, VOL. IV, No. 1522; Herkless and Hannay, *Archbishops of St Andrews*, VOL. I, App. IX, pp. 158-9.

[6] Herkless and Hannay, *Archbishops of St Andrews*, VOL. I, p. 127.

to the requests sanctioned by Parliament was added a petition for her canonisation.[1]

The ambassadors were in Rome in the early spring of 1487. On 27 March, to the chagrin of his fellow ambassador, the Pope raised the Archbishop of St Andrews to the rank of Primate of Scotland and *legatus natus*,[2] and a few days later he confirmed the treaty with Norway. On 20 April he issued a bull[3] in which he announced that his predecessors had delayed provision to bishoprics and to monasteries the revenues of which exceeded two hundred florins *auri de camera*[4] in order that kings and temporal lords might have an opportunity of asking for the provision of candidates whom they knew to be capable and loyal (*ad eorum regimina idoneos et eos gratos et fidos esse cognoverint*). Recognising therefore the unwavering devotion which James and his predecessors had shown to the Church, he granted to the King, at his special request, and to his successors, and their wives and children, the privilege, should they find themselves in any place lying under an interdict, of going to church as usual and hearing mass, just as if no interdict were in force. Furthermore, wishing to tread in the footsteps of his predecessors, he granted to the King and his successors the privilege that he had already promised verbally to his ambassadors, that should a cathedral or monastery of the aforementioned type fall vacant, he would delay provision to it for at least eight months, in expectation of letters and supplications from the King, and would urge those who might succeed him to do likewise.[5]

[1] Theiner, *Vetera monumenta*, pp. 499–500.

[2] Raynald, *Annales ecclesiastici*, VOL. XIX, a. 1487, No. 32.

[3] Printed in Herkless and Hannay, *Archbishops of St Andrews*, VOL. I, pp. 157–8.

[4] i.e. consistorial benefices, provision to which was made by the College of Cardinals. See Cameron, *The Apostolic Camera and Scottish Benefices*, pp. xviii–xxii.

[5] Nothing came of the supplication for the canonisation of Queen Margaret. On 2 June 1487 the Pope wrote to Schevez, Blacader, Elphinstone, and Robert Bellenden, Abbot of Holyrood, requiring them to give answers to a long list of questions about the Queen; but there the process of canonisation seems to have come to an end. Theiner, *Vetera monumenta*, pp. 499–500.

This concordat, which was to be a source of power and profit to his successor, was of little service to James; it was nullified by the fatal gift that the Pope bestowed about the same time, the bull suppressing the Priory of Coldingham, and allocating half its revenues to the Chapel Royal at Stirling.[1] And alliances and concordats were of no avail as long as James could not, or would not, devote himself entirely to the task of reducing his turbulent realm to order. Already in 1484 Parliament, acknowledging that there was still "great deuisioun, debaite, and discorde" within the kingdom, had advised the King to call the contentious great lords before his Council, and "put them in freindschip and concord" with one another.[2] In May 1485 it urged him to send out his justiciars once more on circuit, "anys on the girs and anys on the Corne"—in spring and autumn—and implored him to grant no more remissions or respites—pardons or reprieves—for reprieves were "mair agane Justice" than plain pardons.[3]

The result of the mission to Rome must have been known to the Parliament which met on 1 October 1487; one of the ambassadors, Blacader, sat among the bishops.[4] It lamented the prevalence of crimes of violence, which it attributed to "default of scharpe executioun of Justice, and over commoun granting of grace and remissiounis" to offenders, and extorted from the King a promise to grant no more pardons to criminals for the space of seven years. Even should they appear before the tender-hearted monarch in person, he was not to pardon them, but order them to be punished with the utmost rigour of the law. Further, one or two justices general, men "of will and gude mynd to execut Justice", were to be appointed to go on circuit south of the Forth, and two to the north of it.

For Parliament had the grace to recognise that there might be more than mere timidity and tenderness of heart in James's refusal to face up to his duties. It was common knowledge that the very men who called most loudly on the King to execute justice, often made the execution of justice impossible by intimi-

[1] Herkless and Hannay, *Archbishops of St Andrews*, VOL. I, pp. 132-3.
[2] *A.P.S.*, VOL. II, p. 165.
[3] *A.P.S.*, VOL. II, p. 170.   [4] *A.P.S.*, VOL. II, p. 175.

dating the judges. On this occasion, however, every member professed his readiness to take an oath that he would not stand at the bar beside anyone charged with treason, murder, theft, or robbery, even if the accused belonged to his own household. But the ancient privilege of intimidation was not completely abolished: the great lord, with his kinsman and friends, could still stand in court beside the offender, as long as he came "in sober and quiet wise" to the hearing of "honest actions".[1]

Jealousy of the increasing power of the Council might seem to have dictated the statute that all civil actions were to be brought before and decided in the ordinary courts—those of the Justiciar and Chamberlain, sheriff courts, courts of barony, and burgh courts—and should not be brought before the Lords of Council, unless they were actions affecting the Crown, or actions raised by churchmen, widows, orphans, minors ("pupillis"), and foreigners, or complaints against judges ordinary who had been parties to the dispute or had failed in their duty.[2] But this statute left the Council with a very wide jurisdiction; it attempted, moreover, to overcome the law's delays by directing that all cases already begun and left undecided should be settled by the Lords of Council, and finally, the statute was to be in force only till the next Parliament.

An attempt by the King to win the active support of the middle classes, already inclined in his favour, may be read into the series of nine statutes passed at the instance of the Commissioners of Burghs, which in general emphasised the social cleavage now becoming apparent in the larger burghs. Only "famous and worshipful men", for example, were to engage in foreign trade; merchants were to remain merchants and craftsmen craftsmen. On the other hand, these petty oligarchies were to be defended against the encroachments of the neighbouring great lord. The Act of 1469, which made the burgh councils practically self-elective, was to be enforced, so that the provost and bailies might be "the best and worthiest indwellars of the toun", not chosen by "parcialite nor mastership, quhilk is undoing of the borowis".[3]

[1] *A.P.S.*, VOL. II, pp. 176-7.   [2] *A.P.S.*, VOL. II, pp. 177-8.
[3] *A.P.S.*, VOL. II, p. 178. By the Act of 1469, the new Council was to be

JAMES III AND HIS SON, LATER JAMES IV

Hugo van der Goes   *National Gallery of Scotland*

Finally, recognising that one of the obstacles to the proper administration of justice was the universal ignorance of what laws were really in force, Parliament appointed a committee of twelve, drawn in equal numbers from each of the three estates, to submit to the next Parliament or General Council a digest of the existing laws, to be authorised and put in one volume, after which all other copies would be destroyed.[1] Two days later, on 15 October, Parliament was continued—or prorogued—to 11 January 1488, when the treaties with England, the fate of Berwick, and the matter of Coldingham would fall to be discussed.[2]

But Parliament dispersed in no conciliatory mood. In the absence of the Humes, it had been persuaded by the King to hold guilty of treason, punishable with loss of life, lands and goods, anyone who made, or even acquiesced in, any attempt to obstruct the union of the Priory of Coldingham to the Chapel Royal, or appealed to the Roman Curia against the union, or made use of bulls or other decrees purchased in Rome to quash the erection.[3]

The King had used the spiritual arm; the Humes resolved to resort to the temporal one. Every day they gained allies, the most formidable of whom was their ambitious neighbour, Patrick, Lord Hailes, the head of the house of Hepburn.[4] Diverse motives brought them together; some were honest patriots, doubtful of the pro-English policy of the King and of those members of his Council who had most influence over him, and confirmed in their suspicions that he meant to sell out his country to England when they learned that his uncle, the Earl of Buchan, had gone on a secret mission to the English court.[5] Others, who saw in the King's ineptitude the main source of the evils that afflicted the country, wished no harm to befall him, but would have been glad to see the Crown put into commission for a time. Others, like Bell-the-Cat, were convinced that James had not forgiven the crime of Lauder, and that they would not be safe as long as

elected by the old Council; both bodies would then proceed to elect the alderman or provost, bailies, dean of gild, and other burgh officials.

[1] *Lawes and Actes of Parliament*, comp. Skene, pp. 72 ʳ⁻ᵛ.
[2] *A.P.S.*, VOL. II, p. 180.   [3] *A.P.S.*, VOL. II, p. 182.
[4] Pitscottie, VOL. I, p. 200.   [5] Conway, pp. 16-17 and 17 n.

D

he remained alive. But the King could still count on the support of the great northern lords, Crawford, Huntly, Glamis, Errol, and the like, and of the bulk of the middle and lower classes, for he was "weill lowit witht all the commons and burrowis".[1]

The members of his Council who were accused of misleading the King were not "kinless loons" like the favourites who perished at Lauder, but men of learning, like the wise and upright Elphinstone, or of rank and substance, like his uncle, the Earl of Buchan, and his advocate, Sir John Ross of Montgrenane.[2] Best hated of them all was one of the few survivors of Lauder, Ramsay of Balmain, now Lord Bothwell. He, according to Ferrerius, sensing the growing discontent, persuaded James to allow no one to bear arms in the royal palaces except himself. But his enlisting of a large bodyguard of mercenaries, and his attempts to enforce the ban by threats and imprisonment, only brought nearer the danger which, he knew, threatened both himself and his master.[3]

Parliament reassembled in Edinburgh on 11 January 1488, but did not begin its deliberations till 29 January. The King was obviously looking about for supporters; his first action, after creating his second son Duke of Ross, was to raise four simple lairds to the dignity of Lords of Parliament.[4] He succeeded in gaining the approval of Parliament for the despatch of ambassadors to England to negotiate the three royal marriages, on condition, however, that they should secure the cession, or at least the destruction, of Berwick, else they were "in no wise to conclude upon the said marriage"[5]. The Act of 1487 limiting the

---

[1] Pitscottie, VOL. I, p. 203.

[2] In Aug. 1488 summonses for treason, i.e. for giving aid and counsel to the late King, were issued against Buchan, Bothwell, Ross of Montgrenane, Lord Forbes, Sir Alexander Dunbar, and various lesser gentry like Fotheringham of Powrie and Murray of Cockpule. C.T.S., VOL. I, pp. lxxvi, 92-3.

[3] Ferrerius, Continuatio, p. 398ᵛ.

[4] John Drummond of Cargill, who became Lord Drummond; Robert Crichton of Sanquhar, who became Lord Sanquhar; John Hay of Yester, who became Lord Hay of Yester; and Sir William Ruthven, who became Lord Ruthven. At the same time he knighted Robert Cunningham of Polmaise, and the eldest sons of Lords Kennedy and Carlyle. A.P.S., VOL. II, p. 181.

[5] A.P.S., VOL. II, pp. 181-2.

jurisdiction of the Lords of Council was annulled, on the ground that it left without any remedy the suitor to whom the ordinary courts could not or would not listen. Aggrieved persons were therefore once more at liberty to bring any civil case before the Council.[1] Confronted with the increase in cases of murder and other crimes of violence, the King gave "sharp command" to wardens, justiciars, and sheriffs to seek out and arrest malefactors, and inflict on them such punishment "that throw the terroure and exempill therof sic like trespass may be forborn in tyme tocum".[2] At the same time, he cancelled the justice aires previously arranged and chose new justiciars, in whose loyalty he confided, to ride out on circuit in the early summer—Bothwell, Glamis, Drummond, and Lyle[3] south of the Forth, and the Earls of Crawford and Huntly north of it.[4]

These measures for the restoration of order were never put into operation. The Humes had already taken steps, by the threat of rebellion at home, by bribery and intrigue at the Roman Curia, to overturn the annexation of Coldingham. The King therefore persuaded his Parliament, from which Humes and Hepburns were alike absent, to summon to appear before it in May any laymen who had infringed the statute forbidding opposition to the annexation, and to direct their ordinaries to deal with clerical offenders in the ecclesiastical courts. Furthermore, on 29 January he prorogued Parliament to 5 May, or, rather, conferred the full powers of Parliament upon a committee of fifty, and charged it to proceed against the "personis secularis" who had broken the statute made against the annexation of Coldingham.[5]

He had signed his own death warrant. The herald sent to summon the Humes and their confederates returned bruised and battered, and without his papers, which had been snatched and torn up, "at the quilk the King tuik great displesour and knew weill that thair was nothing bot rebellieioun".[6] Worse news arrived a few days later: the Prince was no longer in Stirling

---

[1] *A.P.S.*, VOL. II, p. 183.   [2] Ibid.

[3] To be precise, two of the four only. *A.P.S.*, VOL. II, p. 182.

[4] Ibid.   [5] *A.P.S.*, VOL. II, p. 184.   [6] Pitscottie, VOL. I, p. 201.

Castle. On 2 February[1] Shaw of Sauchie, seduced by "wheedling words and golden promises"—*blandulis verbis et aureis quoque promissis*[2]—handed him over to a party of the disaffected lords who carried him off to Linlithgow.

This they did, they proclaimed, to save him from his father, who had grown suspicious of him, and was coming with a great army to seize him and put him in prison.[3] The King retaliated by announcing that, on the advice of his Council, he had, for "certane Ressonable and gret Cause", dissolved the present Parliament, and ordered a new "general" Parliament to meet in Edinburgh on 12 May.[4] At the same time he appointed Elphinstone Chancellor in room of the Earl of Argyll, whose loyalty had become suspect.[5] Argyll, however, and Angus, remained with him for a few days longer, probably to lull his suspicions, but at the beginning of March they both disappeared from the Court.[6]

The disaffected nobles, it appears, were now massing their forces under the banner of the still unwilling Prince, and declaring to the world that they were going to war, but to remove a wicked king from the throne.

Faced with this threat, James hesitated to appeal to force, not through fear, according to Polydore Vergil, but through humanity. He was loath to draw the sword against his own subjects, especially if among them was "the one whom he loved most dearly in the whole world, next to himself." He decided, therefore, after rallying the loyal northern lords to his standard, to open negotiations with the rebels. At the same time, he would send appeals to the Pope, and to the Kings of England and France, for moral support, at least, against his contumacious subjects. His appeals were answered, but to the remonstrances of Henry VII and Charles VIII the nobles replied that they would be satisfied with nothing short of the abdication of the King, and the papal

---

[1] *A.P.S.*, VOL. II, p. 223.   [2] Ferrerius, *Continuatio*, p. 399[v].
[3] Pitscottie, VOL. I, pp. 203-4.   [4] *A.P.S.*, VOL. II, p. 184.
[5] *R.M.S.*, VOL. II, No. 1707.
[6] Argyll witnessed a royal charter on 27 Feb. (*R.M.S.*, VOL. II, No. 1709), Angus another of 7 March (*R.M.S.*, VOL. II, No. 1717).

envoy, Adriano Castelli, when he arrived at the English court, was told by Henry that he had come too late, and should go no further.[1]

The King remained in Edinburgh Castle, which was blockaded by the rebel forces, till the end of March or the beginning of April, when, hotly pursued, he rode down to Leith, and, leaving his baggage behind, embarked on a ship bound for Flanders, commanded by the loyal Sir Andrew Wood of Largo.[2]

He landed, not in Flanders, as the rebels thought he would, but in Fife; then riding northward to Aberdeen, he ordered the sheriffs of the counties through which he passed to summon all men between sixteen and sixty to follow him, on a day that he should appoint, "to dantoun this new rebellieoun".[3] According to Hume of Godscroft, on his journey north he went to Lindores Abbey to appeal to his old enemy, the Earl of Douglas, who answered wearily, "Sir, you have kept me and your black coffer in Stirling too long, neither of us can do you any good".[4]

The King reached Aberdeen on or a little before 16 April, when he confirmed to his uncle, the Bishop of Moray, for his faithful and devoted service, a charter granted to an earlier bishop in the preceding reign. It was witnessed by Elphinstone, by the Bishop of Orkney, and by his "well-beloved cousins," the Earl Marischal, the Earls of Crawford, Huntly, Errol, and Buchan, and Lords Glamis, Forbes, Innermeath, and Ruthven—the loyal nobles who, a few days later, followed his banner southwards across the Forth.[5]

Late in April or early in May the royal army came in contact with the rebel forces near Blackness. The King decided to avoid a battle if possible. Negotiations for a peaceful settlement were begun between Elphinstone, the Earl Marischal, the Earls of Huntly and Errol, Lord Glamis, and Alexander Lindsay, on the King's side, and the Earls of Angus and Argyll, Lord Hailes, and

---

[1] Polydore Vergil, *Historia Anglica*, VOL. II, pp. 1470-2. Adriano Castelli stayed on in England, to become Bishop of Hereford and the patron of Polydore Vergil.　　　　[2] Pitscottie, VOL. I, p. 202.　　　　[3] Ibid.

[4] Godscroft, p. 206.

[5] *Registrum episcopatus Moraviensis*, ed. C. Innes, Edinburgh 1837, p. 234.

Lord Lyle, on the side of the rebels. Bell-the-Cat and his associates drove a hard bargain: while they agreed that the King's authority should be "exalted, conservit, and borne up", they insisted that there should be "prelates, Erlis, lordis, and baronis, and uther persons of wisdome" about him every day "to the gud giding of his realme and lieges".[1] In addition, he must give "honourable sustentatioun" to the Prince, and permit "wise lords and honourabill persons of discrecioun" to be with him every day "for good governance of him and securite of his person".[2]

The King gave his consent to the agreement, but a few days later, persuaded, it was later alleged, by Buchan, Bothwell, Ross of Montgrenane, and other members of his Council,[3] he decided to repudiate what promised to be an act of abdication, and lead out his army against the rebel lords, whereupon Huntly, Errol, Marischal, and Glamis, shocked, perhaps, at his breach of faith, suspicious, more probably, of his efforts to secure English intervention, left him, and went home with their followers.[4] James arrayed his depleted forces near Blackness Castle. After a brief skirmish, in which the Earl of Crawford showed great valour in defending the King's person,[5] a second agreement was negotiated. This time, however, the rebel lords insisted that Buchan, Ruthven, Fotheringham of Powrie, and Murray of Tullibardine, should be delivered to them as hostages.[6]

The King withdrew to Edinburgh, where on 18 May he created Crawford Duke of Montrose.[7] He made a grant of land about the same time to Turnbull of Greenwood, who had borne the royal banner on the field of battle.[8] Other grants he made to others who had been with him at Blackness and had risked their lives in his defence, on condition, however, that they served him faithfully, and remained in his company all through the present discords.[9]

For James, with the obstinacy of the weak, was contemplating

[1] *A.P.S.*, VOL. II, p. 210.   [2] Ibid.
[3] *A.P.S.*, VOL. II, p. 201.   [4] *A.P.S.*, VOL. II, pp. 210-1.
[5] *R.M.S.*, VOL. II, No. 1725.   [6] *A.P.S.*, VOL. II, p. 201.
[7] *R.M.S.*, VOL. II, No. 1725.   [8] *R.M.S.*, VOL. II, No. 1724.
[9] *R.M.S.*, VOL. II, Nos. 1727, 1728, 1730.

a renewal of the struggle. At the beginning of June he decided to march on Stirling, where he would be in touch with his supporters from the north of the Forth. Mindful of another battle fought in June near Stirling, he ordered an old sword to be brought from the strong room in Edinburgh Castle, and buckled it to his side. It was the sword which Bruce had borne at Bannockburn.[1]

The town of Stirling was occupied without much difficulty by the King and his supporters, though they found the Castle barred against them.[2] Hearing that the rebels were advancing against him in strength, and without waiting for the reinforcements that were coming from the north,[3] the King on 11 June led out his forces to meet them. The two armies confronted each other on or near the old battlefield of Bannockburn.[4] Conspicuous in the vanguard of the rebel army were the Humes and Hepburns; behind them rode the Prince, surrounded by a bodyguard of the rebel lords; above his head floated the red and gold banner of the Scottish kings.[5] His conscience was uneasy: torn between young ambition and filial piety, he had given orders, it was said, that no one was to lay violent hands upon his father in the coming battle.[6]

The trumpets sounded, the arrows flew "as thick as hail in autumn"[7]; spears clashed and splintered. But while the King's men fought half-heartedly under a leader who sat irresolute on his great grey charger, their opponents pressed forward confident of victory, secure in the knowledge that the King "was newer hardie nor yeit constant in battell".[8] The loyal nobles, fearful of

---

[1] C.T.S., VOL. I, pp. lxxi, lxxiii.

[2] Pitscottie, VOL. I, p. 205.   [3] Ferrerius, Continuatio, p. 400.

[4] Called in contemporary record (A.P.S., VOL. II, p. 211) "the Field of Stirling"; by Pitscottie, "the Field of Bannockburn"; by Lesley located "at Bannockburn"; and by Ferrerius "ad Bannockburn vicum." Drummond of Hawthornden, History of the Lives of the fife James's, kings of Scotland, in Works, 1711 edn., p. 59, is the first to mention "the small Brook named Sawchy Burn" which later gave its name to the battle.

[5] Pitscottie, VOL. I, p. 207.

[6] Lesley, pp. 57 Sc., 316 L.; Ferrerius, Continuatio, p. 400^v.

[7] "Non secus ac per autumnum grande de caelo ruens," Ferrerius, Continuatio, p. 400^v.   [8] Pitscottie, VOL. I, p. 207.

the effect that his example might have, urged him to remove himself to a place of safety, while they fought his battle for him. James took their advice and galloped wildly through the village of Bannockburn, hoping to make for Stirling and the Forth, where Sir Andrew Wood's ship lay. He was thrown from his horse, and dragged, badly bruised, into the mill of Bannockburn by the miller and his wife.[1]

When the noise of battle had died away, he begged his rescuers to fetch a priest. They asked who he was. "I was your King this day at morn," he replied, whereupon the miller's wife ran out, crying, "A priest for the King!" "Here am I, ane priest, where is the King?" answered a passer-by. He was admitted, and, kneeling by the King, asked him if he would recover from his injuries with proper care. The King said that he believed he would, but insisted that the stranger should shrive him and give him the sacrament. "That shall I do hastily," cried the "priest", and pulling out a sword, drove it four or five times through the heart of the King.[2] So, in the Mill of Bannockburn, under the steel of an unknown assassin,[3] the King found the death that he had avoided on the field of battle.

[1] Pitscottie, VOL. I, pp. 207-8.   [2] Pitscottie, VOL. I, pp. 208-9.
[3] The assassin's identity was never discovered. Pitscottie, whose great-uncle, Lord David Lindsay of the Byres, had given the King his "great grey courser", says (VOL. I, p. 290) that by some he was believed to be a servant of Lord Gray. According to Lesley and Ferrerius, a report was current that the murder was premeditated, and though many of the rebels wished to spare the King, some had resolved on his death. They therefore observed the letter of the Prince's command by waiting till the battle was over before they attempted to lay hands on his father; they then set off in pursuit of their victim, and traced him to his hiding-place, according to the version of the story given by Ferrerius, by noticing his great grey courser wandering riderless about the mill (Lesley and Ferrerius, ut supra).

II

APPRENTICESHIP

1488-1493

THE victory in the Field of Stirling—to give the Battle of Sauchieburn its earliest name—brought no comfort to the nominal leader of the rebels. For a few days he buoyed himself up with the fancy that his father might have escaped to one of Sir Andrew Wood's ships,[1] but the discovery of the King's body in the Mill of Bannockburn shattered that hope.

The murdered King was buried in Cambuskenneth Abbey, not far from the grave of his Queen,[2] and a fortnight after the battle the unwilling victor was crowned at Scone.[3]

To outward appearance the new King was a high-spirited boy of fifteen, fond of hunting and hawking, of listening to stories and watching dancers and tumblers, delighting in the new-found liberty which allowed him to put his hand in the Treasurer's purse whenever he pleased. He showed no inclination for more serious pursuits.[4] Though his father's chaplain, John Ireland, presented him with a "Mirror of Wisdom" in five books, written expressly for his instruction,[5] he spent little time over it.[6] Altogether he seemed destined to be a puppet king, whom the rebel lords could manipulate as they pleased.

[1] Pitscottie, VOL. I, pp. 213-16.

[2] Cambuskenneth Abbey, James told Pope Leo X in 1513, was reverenced by him above all other places in his kingdom, because his father and mother were buried there. *Letters*, ed. R. L. Mackie, Edinburgh 1953, No. 542.

[3] Shortly before 26 June. *C.T.S.*, VOL. I, pp. lxxiii-lxxiv.

[4] *C.T.S.*, VOL. I, *passim*.   [5] In 1490. Ireland, *Meroure of Wyssdome*, p. xxx.

[6] *Meroure of Wyssdome*, pp. 5-16. The most that Ireland seemed to hope for was that James would consent to listen to a chapter of it on a holy day or every day during Lent (p. 15).

But the very completeness of their triumph forced a statesman-like moderation upon the victors. The murder of the King had, it is true, left their opponents without a leader or a cause to fight for, but it also alarmed neighbouring princes and created distrust and resentment at home. To still "the hevy murmor and voce of the people"[1] they must produce some evidence that they had been moved, not by animosity to the dead King, but by zeal for good government. Almost at once the machinery of administration was restarted; on 7 July the King presided at a meeting of the Lords of the Exchequer[2]; on 12 July the Lords of Council resumed their sessions,[3] and before the end of August the King was in Lanark, presiding over the Justice Aire by day and watching the gambols of dancers and guisers at night.[4] In September we see him, with his hawks and falconers, being ferried across the Forth to Dunfermline.[5] From Dunfermline he went to Dundee, to preside over the Justice Aire, buy horses for his falconers,[6] and make Lord Hailes Great Admiral of Scotland.[7]

This was only one of many offices that fell to the Hepburns and their allies. Lord Hailes had also become Master of the Household and Keeper of Edinburgh Castle[8]; his uncle, the Prior of St Andrews, was made Keeper of Falkland Castle,[9] and another kinsman became Sheriff of Fife.[10] Alexander, Lord Hume, was made Lord Chamberlain[11] and Lord Lyle Justiciar, while the Earl of Argyll was reinstated in the office of Chancellor.[12] But Angus, who had run with the hare too long to please the hounds, was sent empty away, and the Justiciar was dissatisfied with a division of the plunder which left him with the dish as his share of the treat.

Really there was little plunder to share. The examination of the treasure chests recovered from the baggage of the defeated army and of the black boxes in the vaults of Edinburgh Castle,

---

[1] *A.P.S.*, VOL. II, p. 230.
[2] *C.T.S.*, VOL. I, p. lxxiv; *R. Scac. S.*, VOL. X, p. I.
[3] *Acts of the Lords of Council in Civil Causes*, VOL. I, p. 121.
[4] *C.T.S.*, VOL. I, pp. lxxix, 93.   [5] *C.T.S.*, VOL. I, p. 93.
[6] *C.T.S.*, VOL. I, p. 94.   [7] *R.M.S.*, VOL. II, No. 1774.
[8] *R.M.S.*, VOL. II, No. 1742.   [9] *R.M.S.*, VOL. II, No. 1732.
[10] *R.M.S.*, VOL. II, No. 1733.   [11] *R.M.S.*, VOL. II, No. 1781.
[12] *A.P.S.*, VOL. II, p. 199.

showed that either much of the King's hoard had been stolen, or
that rumour had greatly exaggerated its amount.[1] The estates of
the late King's supporters could have been confiscated, it is true,
had not the policy of reconciliation which had been forced upon
the victors forbidden any scheme of wholesale spoliation. Altogether only ten[2] of the late King's supporters were summoned,
between 5 and 16 August, to stand their trial for treason, and the
charges against all but four of them—Buchan, Bothwell, Ross of
Montgrenane, and Murray of Cockpule[3]—were tacitly deserted
before Parliament assembled. Elphinstone, who had stood by the
late King to the end, was deprived of the Chancellorship, which
reverted to the Earl of Argyll, but the young King's supporters
knew his value, and did not leave him long unemployed: he
appeared in Parliament at the beginning of October, when he
was chosen to be one of the Lords Auditors of Causes and Complaints, and at the end of the month we find him sitting once more
on the bench with the Lords of Council.

On Monday, 6 October 1488, the first Parliament of the new
reign met in Edinburgh. A larger assembly than usual crowded
the Tolbooth: thirty-four bishops, abbots and clerics of lower
degree; ten earls and twenty-five lords; and commissioners from
sixteen burghs. As was the custom, the King did not appear in
person on the first day of the session, but commissioned certain
nobles—on this occasion Argyll, Hailes, Lyle and Hume—to act
on his behalf. The business of the Commissioners was to "fence"
the Parliament—to declare that it had been duly summoned by
the King and that all must obey and none molest it. Next the list
of suitors, those entitled or obliged to attend, was read by the
Clerk, and the names of absentees noted.[4]

[1] C.T.S., VOL. I, pp. lxxi-lxxii, 79-87; A.P.S., VOL. II, p. 230.

[2] The Earl of Buchan, Lords Bothwell and Forbes, Sir John Ross of
Montgrenane, Sir Alexander Dunbar, the Lairds of Amisfield, Cockpule,
Fotheringham, Innermeath, and Innes.

[3] According to Pitscottie (VOL. I, p. 219) there was a fifth, David, second
Lord Lindsay of the Byres (the chronicler's great-uncle); but there is no
mention of him in the list of summonses on pp. 92-3 of C.T.S., VOL. I, nor in
the proceedings of the Parliament of October 1488.

[4] A.P.S., VOL. II, pp. 199-200.

On the second day of the session, when the King attended in person, the Lords Auditors of Causes and Complaints and the Lords of the Articles were elected. To the first of these committees, composed of three clerics, of whom Elphinstone was one, two nobles, and three burgesses, Parliament delegated its powers as a civil court. To the second, on which sat nine clerics, fourteen nobles, and five burgesses, it entrusted the drafting of new legislation. In addition, it appointed an assize of six nobles, specially constituted for the occasion as commissioners of Parliament and royal justiciars, to sit in judgment on Buchan and his confederates on the following day.[1] In the meantime, the members who had not been elected to any committee were free to follow their own business or pleasure.

None of the accused appeared to stand trial on the day appointed. On 9 October the Earl of Buchan appeared alone, pled guilty to the charges of engaging in treasonable negotiations with England and encouraging the late King to break his first agreement with his nobles, threw himself on the King's mercy, and received an unconditional pardon.[2] Bothwell and Ross of Montgrenane, who were "owre the Border and awa", were found guilty of treason and sentenced to lose life, land, and goods. The case against the Laird of Cockpule was continued for another three months.[3]

---

[1] *A.P.S.*, VOL. II, p. 200.   [2] *A.P.S.*, VOL. II, p. 201.

[3] *A.P.S.*, VOL. II, pp. 201-5. One would like to accept Pitscottie's story (VOL. I, pp. 219-26) that his great-uncle David, second Lord Lindsay of the Byres, a stout warrior "of small ingyne and rude langage", along with other supporters of the late King, appeared in answer to the summons, but could get no advocate to speak for him, since all the men of law were afraid to offend the young King, who sat with the Chancellor and the other justiciars. Nothing daunted, he denounced his judges to the King as "fallis lurdanis and tratouris", who, if he did not deal with them speedily, would murder him as they had murdered his father. Argyll, thinking that his accuser "hatt thame ower neir", explained to the King that Lindsay was "bot ane mane of the auld world", then, turning to him, advised him to throw himself on the King's mercy. At this his brother Patrick Lindsay—Pitscottie's grandfather—trod on his foot to warn him not to accept the Chancellor's advice. "Bot the strampe of Mr Patrick's was so sade wpoun his brother's footte, quho had ane sair toe, for the paine was werie dolorous wnto him", that Lord David roared, "War thow

On 17 October all the members reassembled for the final meeting of the Parliament, when the acts drafted by the Lords of the Articles were submitted for approval or disapproval.[1] The defeated had been punished; the successful must now receive their rewards. To another Hume, the Laird of Fastcastle, went the lands of Montgrenane[2]; Lord Hailes was granted the estates of the proscribed Lord Bothwell, including his castles of Bothwell and Crichton, and in addition was created Earl of Bothwell, "that

out of the King's presentis I sould tak the on the mouth." Patrick, afraid of the consequences of his brother's "warm words", asked leave to act as his advocate, adding, "thocht hie and I hes not bene at ane thir money yeiris, yit my hairt may nocht suffer me to sie my natiue house, that I ame of, to perische and the memorie thairof abolischit." When permission was granted, he reminded the Chancellor that the King was bound by his coronation oath not to sit in judgment in a dispute, like the present one, in which he himself was one of the parties. His objection was sustained, and the King advised "to ryse and gang ben to the invart Tollbouth, quhilk was werie unplessand to him for the tyme, beand ane young prince sittand wpon the sait royall." When the King had "gone ben", Patrick pointed out a flaw in the indictment—his brother had been summoned to appear at the end of forty days, and now forty-one days had elapsed. The summons was quashed, Parliament duly fenced, and the other lords who had been summoned to thole their assize, released after giving surety that they would return when required. Unfortunately Lord David, in the King's hearing, congratulated his brother on his unwonted eloquence—"I wald not have trowit that ye had sic wordis; be Sanct Marie, ye sall have the Mains of Kirkforther for it", whereupon the King told Patrick that he "sould gar him sit quhair he sould nocht sie his feit thair for ane yeir" and lodged him for a twelvemonth in prison in the Isle of Bute.

Pitscottie is certainly retelling an often-repeated tale of a grandfather which must have some foundation in fact. Certain details—the "toe-stramping" episode, the young King's unwilling withdrawal to the inner Tolbooth, the other accused crowding into the "bose window", are clearly not invented. But old men's memories may play them tricks; the very full account of the treason trials in October 1488 does not mention Lord Lindsay of the Byres or any other of the late King's supporters except Buchan, Bothwell, Ross of Montgrenane, and Murray of Cockpule: Pitscottie, on the other hand, asserts that the Parliament before which his grandfather and great-uncle appeared met on 10 May 1489, though no session of Parliament between January and June 1489 is recorded.

[1] *A.P.S.*, vol. II, p. 206.
[2] *R.M.S.*, vol. II, No. 1785 (14 Oct. 1488).

others, imitating his virtue, might strive to gain similar honours".[1]
But Parliament showed no disposition to treat the vanquished
harshly: though royal officials who had appeared on the losing
side were to be suspended from office for three years, and merchants and other men of substance who had supported James III
were refused compensation for goods taken from them before
the Battle of Sauchieburn,[2] the goods of "pure unlandit folks"
taken before the battle, and all goods whatever taken after the
battle were to be restored to their owners,[3] while the heirs of
those who had fallen on either side were to be allowed to succeed
to their estates without impediment.[4] In addition, it was declared
that the King, "movit of piete", remitted to "all the burges,
merchandis and unlandit men forsaid the rancor of his hert".[5]

But the victors were conscious that they themselves were on
trial. To justify themselves in the eyes of neighbouring rulers
they persuaded Parliament to declare that the agreement which
they had made with the late King had been broken "by the
puerst counsale of divers persons beand with him", who had
made him bring in Englishmen "to the perpetuale subieccione of
the realm", and that the present King and his supporters were
therefore innocent of any part in his death.[6] Copies of this vindi-
cation were to be sent to the Pope, and to the Kings of France,
Spain, and Denmark.[7] Ambassadors also were to be sent to the
continent "to see and consider an honourable princess" who
would be a suitable bride for the King, and to renew the old
alliance with France. The cost of the mission was to be defrayed
by a "matrimonial" tax of £5,000, one fifth to be found by the
burgesses, and two fifths by each of the other two estates.[8]

As an emergency measure for "the stanching of thift, reff, and
utheris Innormitez", the whole country was divided into districts,
each of which was committed to the charge of some powerful
noble, who swore in presence of King and Parliament, with his
hand upon the Gospels, that he would search out all malefactors

[1] *A.P.S.*, VOL. II, p. 206. [2] *A.P.S.*, VOL. II, p. 207.
[3] Ibid. [4] *A.P.S.*, VOL. II, p. 208.
[5] *A.P.S.*, VOL. II, p. 207. [6] *A.P.S.*, VOL. II, pp. 210-1.
[7] Lesley, pp. 60 Sc., 318 L. [8] *A.P.S.*, VOL. II, p. 207.

within its bounds and "justify" them himself, or else send them to the King to be punished. This arrangement was to last till the King came of age.[1] Royal burghs were no longer to be allowed to repledge their burgesses from the justice aire.[2] The King himself was to attend all justice aires, accompanied by the Justiciar.[3]

Finally, after it had elected a committee of sixty-four to whom it entrusted its powers, Parliament was adjourned to 14 January 1489.[4] The Lords Auditors, however, sat for another nine days.

Meantime the King's apprenticeship continued. We find him sitting with the Lords of Council,[5] riding to the Justice Aires at Selkirk and Peebles[6] (with his Justiciar and falconers), losing a hawk in Tweeddale and rewarding the finder with eighteen shillings,[7] distributing five shillings to the "seke folk at Crawmond Brig",[8] borrowing thirty pounds from Prior Hepburn in St Andrews,[9] then riding through Perth to celebrate Christmas in Linlithgow.[10] On Christmas morning he offered twenty-eight shillings in the chapel; on Christmas night he lost twenty-eight pounds at dice and cards.[11] On 2 January 1489 he rode to Stirling; on 13 January we find him kneeling before the altar of St Kentigern, in St Giles' Church in Edinburgh.[12]

His devotions were ominous for Schevez, who since 1487 had been not only Archbishop of St Andrews, but Primate of Scotland and *legatus natus*. But Robert Blacader, who visited Rome along with Schevez in that year, succeeded in getting from Innocent VIII a verbal promise that his diocese would be free from the jurisdiction of St Andrews as long as he lived.[13] Schevez was furious; he upbraided Blacader violently on the way home. The Pope's formal confirmation of the exemption a year later[14] enraged

---

[1] *A.P.S.*, VOL. II, p. 208.   [2] Ibid.
[3] Ibid.   [4] *A.P.S.*, VOL. II, p. 211.
[5] e.g. on 26 Oct. and 25 Nov., in cases in which he himself was a party. *Acts of the Lords of Council in Civil Causes*, VOL. I, p. 99.
[6] *C.T.S.*, VOL. I, pp. 98, 104.   [7] *C.T.S.*, VOL. I, p. 98.   [8] Ibid.
[9] *C.T.S.*, VOL. I, p. 99.   [10] *C.T.S.*, VOL. I, pp. 99-100.
[11] *C.T.S.*, VOL. I, p. 100.   [12] *C.T.S.*, VOL. I, p. 102.
[13] Theiner, *Vetera monumenta*, p. 502. For the whole Schevez-Blacader contest see Herkless and Hannay, *Archbishops of St Andrews*, VOL. I, pp. 129-45.
[14] Theiner, *Vetera monumenta*, p. 502.

him still more and failed to satisfy Blacader, who now determined that the exemption should be perpetual, and that his cathedral should be raised to the dignity of a metropolitan church.

On 26 January 1489 Parliament decreed that the see of Glasgow should be erected into an archbishopric like the Archbishopric of York, with such dignities, immunities and privileges as should be agreed upon by the bishop and an advisory committee of prelates and nobles.[1] The Chancellor communicated this decision to the Pope. Nothing happened. The King, who was an honorary canon of Glasgow Cathedral, wrote again and again, and in the autumn of 1490 sent his clerk, Andrew Forman, to Rome. Still Innocent remained silent. James became impatient.

On 1 December he wrote to the Pope reminding him that he had already written many letters requesting that Glasgow, "which surpasses the other cathedral churches of my realm by its structures, its learned men, its foundations, its ornaments", should be raised to the rank of a metropolitan church, and that its bishop should be made primate and *legatus natus*, and expressing astonishment that the Holy Father had not listened to the prayers of so obedient a son.[2] The letter had no effect—probably the agents of Schevez had been busy in Rome. A second letter followed in January 1491, a third in February, and a fourth in April.[3] Not till 9 January 1492 did the Pope issue a bull separating the dioceses of Glasgow, Dunblane, Dunkeld, Galloway and Lismore from the province of St Andrews, and making Glasgow a metropolitan church, with the archiepiscopal dignity, and with jurisdiction over the other four dioceses. The new archbishop, however, was not to be styled primate and *legatus natus*, nor was the pallium to be sent to him.[4] The strife continued between the two Archbishops, each backed by his faction of nobles hungry for crumbs from the archiepiscopal table, each sending money overseas that

[1] *A.P.S.*, vol. II, p. 212.

[2] *Calendar of State Papers and Manuscripts relating to English Affairs existing in the archives and collections of Venice and in other Libraries of Northern Italy*, ed. Rawdon Brown (hereafter referred to as *Cal. of State Papers, Venice*), vol. I, London 1864, No. 596.

[3] *Cal. of State Papers, Venice*, vol. I, Nos. 604, 607, 611.

[4] *Cal. of State Papers, Venice*, vol. I, No. 615.

JAMES IV

Jacques le Boucq   *Bibliothèque Municipale, Arras*

Photo: Giraudon

was badly needed at home, till in June 1493 Parliament advised
the King, in view of "the unestimable dampnage" that they had
done to the realm, to send them letters exhorting them to leave
their "contentiounis, litis, and pleyis" in the court of Rome, and
threatening that, if they refused, he would order their tenants to
pay no more rent. It was made plain to them, furthermore, that
the King would "gar Justice be ministerit to thame" in their own
country by the competent ecclesiastical judge.[1]

Meantime Scotland had narrowly escaped another civil war.
When the King returned to Edinburgh at the end of March 1489,
after presiding at the justice aires in the south-west,[2] he found that
the Justiciar himself had formed a treasonable league with the
Earl of Lennox and his son, Lord Matthew Stewart, to whom
Dumbarton Castle had been entrusted.[3] James knew that trouble
was threatening, that a few months earlier Lord Forbes had ridden
through Aberdeen and the neighbouring towns, displaying the
torn and bloodstained shirt of the murdered King at the point of
a long spear, and calling on all who saw it to avenge his death.[4]
He did not know that on 8 January the Master of Huntly had
written from Edinburgh to solicit King Henry's support for the
friends and kinsfolk of the late King, of whom the Earl of Buchan
was one, who had banded themselves together to punish his
murderers.[5] To add to the King's perplexities, a Danish pirate,
Lutkyn Mere, had begun to plunder Scottish merchantmen, and
not even Sir Andrew Wood had been able to stop him.[6]

In April Lennox and Lyle were summoned to surrender.[7]
They refused and preparations for war were begun. Nothing had
been accomplished, however, when the Parliament before which
the rebels had been summoned to appear met on 26 June. In

---

[1] *A.P.S.*, VOL. II, pp. 232-3. See also Lesley, pp. 62 Sc., 319 L.

[2] *C.T.S.*, VOL. I, pp. 105-6.   [3] *R.M.S.*, VOL. II, No. 1794.

[4] Buchanan, *Rerum Scoticarum historia*, BK. XIII, in *Opera omnia*, ed. T.
Ruddiman, Edinburgh 1715, VOL. I, p. 241.

[5] B.M. MS Caligula B.III, 19, dated 8 Jan., no year given, printed in
Pinkerton, VOL. II, App. I, p. 437, dated as "perhaps 1491". Conway, p. 26,
following W. Busch, *England under the Tudors*, trans. A. M. Todd, London
1895, p. 344, dates it 1489.

[6] *A.P.S.*, VOL. II, p. 214.   [7] *C.T.S.*, VOL. I, p. 107.

E

their absence they were found guilty of treason, and sentenced to lose life, land, and goods. A price of a thousand marks was put upon their heads. It was arranged that on 19 July the King would march against Lennox's castle of Crookston and Lyle's castle of Duchal with the feudal levies from the south of the Forth, and that when the King reached Glasgow the Earl of Argyll, with the western levies, would move to Dumbarton.[1] Parliament also chose the King's Council for him. All prelates, it decreed, and all great lords, like Crawford and Huntly, were entitled to take part in its deliberations whenever they came to court, but in addition it chose four clerics, including Blacader and Elphinstone, and eight barons to be "contenualy of consale to his hienes" along with the permanent officials. Only if the King or the Chancellor gave them permission, could any of them stay away even for a short time; at least six of them must always be on duty "to deliver apon all debatable matters" and advise and direct the King. This arrangement was to remain in force till the next Parliament.[2]

Parliament also decided that ambassadors should be sent to Denmark to renew the alliance with that country and to complain about the depredations of Lutkyn Mere.[3] A few days after Parliament rose, however, Lutkyn's ship was captured in the Forth. Thirty-six of the pirates were "justifiit", but the King spared the lives of nine who volunteered to go with him to Duchal, and ordered them to be fitted out with clothes.[4]

On 18 July he left Linlithgow with his siege train, in which was Mons Meg. He reached Glasgow that night, leaving the guns miles behind. Fresh teams of oxen had to be provided; gangs of workmen with picks and shovels had to be despatched to make a track for the unwieldy pieces; even then a week elapsed before they were in position before the walls of Duchal.[5] The castle surrendered before the end of the month; at the beginning of August the oxen were dragging the guns back to Linlithgow.[6]

At Dumbarton Argyll met with less success. He occupied the

[1] *A.P.S.*, VOL. II, pp. 214-5.   [2] *A.P.S.*, VOL. II, p. 215.
[3] *A.P.S.*, VOL. II, p. 214.   [4] *C.T.S.*, VOL. I, p. 118.
[5] *C.T.S.*, VOL. I, p. 117.   [6] Ibid.

town but was driven out when the rebels set fire to it, and was compelled to withdraw to Dunglass Castle, about three miles further up the Clyde.[1] At the beginning of October the news that Lennox and the Master of Huntly were meditating a dash into the north-east brought the King to Dunblane. On the 11th, hearing that the rebels were somewhere about the head waters of the Forth, he rode westward with Lord Drummond, after sending an urgent message to Stirling for light artillery.[2] The culverins were not needed; a spy brought in the news that the enemy was at Gartalunane, near Aberfoyle. That night, after darkness had fallen, Drummond led the royal forces against the sleeping camp. The rebels were routed, but their leaders succeeded in making their way back to Dumbarton.[3] The King followed them, and appeared before the castle on 18 October,[4] but it was not till the second week of December,[5] after "the gun callit Duchal" had been brought up,[6] that he received their submission.

Evidently the surrender was not unconditional. When Parliament met at the beginning of February 1490 Lennox protested that the sentence of forfeiture passed in the previous June was invalid, as the precise hour at which he had to appear to stand his trial was not mentioned in the summons, and his protest was accepted. On 5 February, in presence of the King, who was wearing his crown and sceptre, the decree annulling the sentence and restoring the rebel lords to their estates was read by the Dempster.[7] Parliament was still working for internal peace: ten days later it urged the King and his Council to take steps to make "all persones and parties be at frendschip and concord" and to "put scharp Justice" on any who refused, so that they might be "in hartly amyte, frendschip and quiet".[8]

As in 1488, Parliament chose the members of the Secret Council. It was to include, in addition to the officers of state—

---

[1] C.T.S., VOL. I, p. xciv; A.P.S., VOL. XII, Edinburgh 1875, p. 34.

[2] C.T.S., VOL. I, p. 122.

[3] Buchanan, Rerum Scoticarum historia, BK. XIII, in Opera omnia, VOL. I, p. 241.

[4] C.T.S., VOL. I, p. 142. [5] C.T.S., VOL. I, pp. xcvi, 126.

[6] C.T.S., VOL. I, p. 123. [7] A.P.S., VOL. II, pp. 217-8.

[8] A.P.S., VOL. II, p. 218.

Chancellor, Master of the Household, Chamberlain, Chamberlain of the Chamber,[1] Privy Seal, Secretary, Treasurer, and Clerk of Rolls and Register—two bishops, one abbot or prior, and six barons. Its composition seemed a guarantee that there would be no renewal of civil war. Bishop Elphinstone and the Duke of Montrose, whose title, conferred by James III, had been automatically forfeited at the beginning of the new reign, and restored in the previous autumn,[2] sat with their late adversaries, Hume of Fastcastle and his kinsman, the Prior of Coldingham. More surprising was the presence of Ross of Montgrenane, condemned to death in 1488 and recently pardoned at the instance of the King of England and the Pope,[3] and of Lyle and Lennox, who found themselves in company with Lord Drummond, who had scattered their forces at Gartalunane.[4]

To the Secret Council Parliament committed the authority to decide the terms on which alliances with France, Spain, and Denmark were to be made.[5] More important still, it tried to conserve the resources of the monarchy by subjecting the monarch to the control of the Council. For James, profuse and generous to the end of his days, was only seventeen, easily duped into signing away valuable crown lands on the authority of valueless documents, or even into giving away his plate and jewels. He was now persuaded "to promitt and grant in parliament" that he would submit to be guided completely by the Secret Council, and to make no grants of lands or goods, safe-conducts, respites, or remissions, without its consent. As a safeguard, every document signed by him was to be countersigned by the Chancellor, and by all the other members of the Council who might be present. In addition, the King promised to be "ruled and gov-

[1] "Chaumerlane of chaumer", *A.P.S.*, vol. II, p. 220.

[2] *R.M.S.*, vol. II, No. 1895 (19 Sept. 1489).

[3] *Cal. of State Papers, Venice*, vol. I, No. 549.

[4] *A.P.S.*, vol. II, p. 220. In addition to the eight named, Blacader, Alexander Inglis, Archdeacon of St Andrews, the Duke of Montrose, Lords Glamis, Oliphant, and Borthwick, Walter Ogilvy of the Boyne, and the Justice Clerk, Master Richard Lawson, were elected. Lennox, like the Earl Marischal and the Earls of Errol and Huntly, was to attend when he was at court or when the King sent for him.   [5] *A.P.S.*, vol. II, p. 219.

erned" by the Council "in the dispositioun and gevin of his tressour, silver veschale, Cheinyeis, Jowellis, and uther abilyiements perteining to his maist noble person".[1]

At first sight this edict seems to mark the final triumph of Parliament in a constitutional struggle that had begun eight years earlier, and which now culminated in the complete subjection of the monarch to a Council chosen in Parliament and responsible to it. But there is no evidence that the 1490 Parliament meant "this maner of doing" to be more than a temporary expedient. It declared that "the said council now chosen in this present Parliament" was to function only "quhill the time of the nixt Parliament", and similarly secured from the King a promise to submit to its guidance "quhill the next Parliament, as said is".[2] In any case, neither in the proceedings of the 1491 Parliament nor in those of any subsequent Parliament of the reign is there any mention of the election of members of the Secret Council, or of any injunction to the monarch to submit to its guidance.

It was the kinsmen of Lord Drummond who next disturbed the "amity, peace, and quiet" of the country, and brought on themselves the "sharp justice" recommended by Parliament. A clash between the Drummonds, led by the second son of Lord Drummond, and the Murrays ended in the burning alive of six score Murrays in the church of Monzievaird. His father's services could not save George Drummond; he was sentenced to death at Edinburgh in the presence of the King, and executed at Stirling along with several of his followers.[3]

The chief concern of the Parliament which met in Edinburgh from 28 April to 18 May 1491,[4] was still "the stanching of cummers, slauchters, reffes, thifftis, extorsions and oppressiones". It re-enacted, with slight modifications, a series of statutes sixty-five years old, designed to secure the speedy arrest and punishment of those guilty of killing or maiming. When a sheriff, steward, baron bailie, or head officer in a regality learned that anyone "happenes to be slane or demembrit", he was to raise the country at once, pursue the offender till he was arrested, and instead of

[1] *A.P.S.*, VOL. II, pp. 220-1. [2] *A.P.S.*, VOL. II, p. 220.
[3] *C.T.S.*, VOL. I, pp. cii-ciii, 170. [4] *A.P.S.*, VOL. II, p. 223.

ordering him to appear for trial at the end of the customary forty days, either deliver him at once to the King or Justiciar, or "kepe him in sikker surete" till the King's pleasure was known. If the offender fled into a neighbouring sheriffdom, the sheriff of that district was required to continue the pursuit as soon as the first sheriff had notified him "and Swa furth fra schireffe to schireffe, quhill he be owrtakin or put out of the Realme". A sheriff who failed in this duty would be deprived of his office altogether unless it happened to be hereditary, in which case he would be suspended for three years.[1] Copying the Parliament of 1440, it ordained that justice aires should be held twice a year, in spring and autumn, and begged the King to "move his maist noble person" to preside when it was expedient.[2] It empowered the Chancellor or Justiciar to impose as heavy a monetary penalty as he pleased for manslaughter and premeditated assault, and professed to guarantee that any complainant would be "harmeles and scaithles in his persone or gudis".[3]

One cause of disorder was removed by a statute which forbade the immediate eviction of the old tenants when an estate changed hands, and required the new proprietor to let them remain till the following Whitsuntide.[4] The pushful burgess was warned that if he entered into a "band of manrent" either with his fellow burgesses or with a neighbouring noble, he was taking part in a treasonable league, and that his goods would be forfeit and his life at the King's mercy.[5]

Other problems confronted this Parliament: trouble was brewing in the Western Isles,[6] encounters between Scottish and English ships were frequent, and the attitude of the King of England was ambiguous. Perhaps it was fear of an English invasion that made Parliament prohibit "futeball, golfe, or uther sic unprofitable sportes", and enjoin the practice of archery instead, ordering weapon-schawings to be held four times a year in every sheriffdom and regality. Gentlemen having land worth

---

[1] *A.P.S.*, VOL. II, p. 225.   [2] Ibid.   [3] Ibid.   [4] Ibid.
[5] *A.P.S.*, VOL. II, p. 227.
[6] *A.P.S.*, VOL. II, p. 228; Donald Gregory, *History of the Western Highlands and Isles of Scotland*, 2nd edn., London and Glasgow 1881, pp. 55-7.

ten pounds a year or more were to come equipped with helmet, gorget or pisane, armour for the legs, sword, spear, and dagger; yeomen and burgesses were to come either mounted and fully equipped as men-at-arms, or else on foot, with sword, buckler, knife, spear, and an axe or a bow and a sheaf of arrows.[1]

At the same time provision was made for the renewal of old friendships. Lack of money had probably prevented the despatch of the various diplomatic missions sanctioned by Parliament in October 1488 and again in February 1490. A substantial portion of the matrimonial tax imposed by the first Parliament of the reign was still unpaid eighteen months later, and defaulting sheriffs, provosts and bailies had been warned to pay up "to a short day", or else enter their persons in ward at Blackness Castle; while certain prelates, lords, and burgh councils, who had been excused payment by the youthful King, were informed that their letters of discharge were invalid.[2] In spite of these admonitions, messengers had again to be sent out "with letters for the taxt" in January 1491.[3]

Evidently the response was satisfactory, for Parliament now sanctioned the payment of £5,000 to the Earl of Bothwell, Bishop Blacader, Richard Murehede, Dean of Glasgow, and a lord, whom the King had ordered to go to France, Spain, or any other country to find a bride for him. In addition, the ambassadors were to renew the old treaties of alliance with France, and attempt to secure for Scotsmen "sic fredoume within the Realme of france" as was enjoyed by Frenchmen in Scotland.[4] At the same time Parliament gave instructions that Sir James Ogilvie of Airlie, with a herald and a clerk, should proceed to Denmark to renew the treaty with that country.[5]

The final arrangements for the embassies, along with "the mater of the Ilis and utheris parteis brokin", were referred to a committee of thirty-six, which was to exercise the full power of Parliament till its reassembly on 2 August.[6]

The Franco-Scottish alliance, which the learned in both coun-

[1] A.P.S., VOL. II, p. 226.
[2] A.P.S., VOL. II, p. 217.
[3] C.T.S., VOL. I, p. 175.
[4] A.P.S., VOL. II, p. 224.
[5] Ibid.
[6] A.P.S., VOL. II, p. 228.

tries firmly believed to date from the time of Charlemagne,[1] and which some now trace to the abortive treaty concluded by John Balliol and Philippe le Bel in 1295,[2] had its real origin in the treaty made by King Robert the Bruce and King Charles IV of France in 1326.[3] By this treaty each of the contracting parties bound himself to attack England if war should break out between England and his ally, and to make no peace or truce with England in which his ally was not included. The treaty was renewed in 1359, and in 1371 it was expanded, and the obligations of the two allies were defined more precisely.[4] It contained nine articles:

(1) In view of the injuries which the King of England had inflicted on them, they were to give each other aid and counsel against the King of England both in peace and war. (2) If war broke out between one of the allies and the King of England, the other was obliged to make war with all his might, provided that any truce which he had made with that monarch had been broken, or had expired. Each of the contracting parties bound himself (3) to prevent his subjects' helping the King of England and his allies; (4) to refuse shelter to anyone who had rebelled against his ally; (5) to refuse to enter into a truce with the King of England if his ally were not included, unless his ally declared that he did not want to be included; and, similarly, (6) to refuse to make peace with the King of England unless his ally were included. (7) If either King died without issue, the other was not to interfere in the dispute for the crown, but to await the decision of the prelates and other magnates of the realm. (8) The treaty was to be confirmed by the Pope, and neither of the contracting parties was to try to be absolved from it. (9) If the Pope absolved either party, that party was to act as if the absolution had not been granted.

The Treaty of 28 October 1371 was confirmed by Robert III

[1] e.g. Boece, *Scotorum historiae prima gentis origine . . . libri XIX*, 1574 edn., p. 185^v.

[2] *Foedera*, VOL. II, p. 695. For a brief history of the Franco-Scottish alliance between 1295 and 1513, see J. D. Mackie, "The Auld Alliance and the Battle of Flodden", in *Transactions of the Franco-Scottish Society*, VIII (1919-35), pp. 37-56.   [3] Register House MSS, Treaties with France, No. 1.

[4] Register House MSS, Treaties with France, No. 2.

in 1390[1] and by the Duke of Albany in 1407.[2] It was again confirmed by James II and Charles VII of France in 1448,[3] when an attempt was made to clarify the ambiguous fifth clause. If one of the princes concluded a truce with England, he was to notify his ally within nine months; he was to protest if the King of England refused to admit his ally to the truce, and to take measures against him if he persisted in his refusal. Even if one of the allies remained out of the truce which the other entered, they were to remain good and loyal friends. With this modification, and with the addition of a clause confirming all previous treaties between the two countries, it was confirmed by James III and Charles VIII in 1484.[4]

On 14 June the King obtained from Henry VII a safe-conduct for a year for Bishops Blacader and Elphinstone, the Earls of Bothwell and Morton, Lord Glamis, Lord Oliphant, the Prior of St Johns, and Master Richard Murehede, who were going as his ambassadors to France and Spain.[5] Before the end of July Bothwell left for France in the ship *Katharine*.[6] With him went two envoys from the French court, Champagne King-of-Arms and Lord Monypenny or the Sieur de Concressault, a French nobleman of Scottish descent,[7] and also, it would appear, William Dunbar, who, if a rival poet is to be trusted, was violently sick before the ship reached the Bass.[8] Bothwell returned to Edinburgh on 29 November, bringing with him a treaty signed by Charles VIII at

[1] Register House MSS, Treaties with France, No. 3.
[2] Register House MSS, Treaties with France, Nos. 4 and 5.
[3] Register House MSS, Treaties with France, No. 13.
[4] Register House MSS, Treaties with France, Nos. 16-19.
[5] *Cal. Doc. Scot.*, VOL. IV, No. 1574.
[6] *C.T.S.*, VOL. I, p. 179.   [7] *C.T.S.*, VOL. I, pp. 179-80.
[8] Walter Kennedy. See "The Flyting of Dunbar and Kennedy", ll. 449-72, in William Dunbar, *Poems*, ed. W. M. Mackenzie, Edinburgh 1932. J. W. Baxter's denial (in *William Dunbar, a biographical Study*, Edinburgh 1952, p. 43) of the possibility of Dunbar's sailing in the *Katryn* in 1491, on the ground that "if the *Flyting* is dated correctly at 1500, and traces of Dunbar's discomfort remained on the ship 'this twenty year', 1491 would be too late for the poet's misadventure", is unconvincing. "This twenty year" is an obvious exaggeration, meant to amuse, like "Thou spewit . . . faster than all the maryneris coud pomp" a few lines further down.

Beaujeu, which, except for the omission of the tenth clause, was identical with the treaty of 1484.[1] On 20 February 1492 Parliament thanked the ambassadors for what they had accomplished but, as they had returned without a bride for the King, ordered another mission to be sent to bring the matter to completion, and sanctioned the raising of another matrimonial tax of £1,000.[2] Though James ratified the Treaty on 4 March 1492,[3] the quest for a French princess was abandoned.

No ambassador appears to have gone to Spain, but at the end of May Sir James Ogilvie sailed for Denmark. A treaty of peace and alliance, defensive and offensive, between Scotland and Denmark was concluded on 21 June,[4] and two years later, on 5 May 1494, it was confirmed by King James.[5]

With England relations were much less happy. Officially the two sovereigns were on terms of friendship: on 23 October 1488 Henry had ratified a treaty, concluded at Coldstream a few days earlier, for a truce to last till 5 October 1491,[6] and towards the end of 1489 he had exchanged gifts with King James.[7] But Henry had every reason to mistrust the dominant faction at the Scottish court, which had found in the pro-English policy of the murdered King a pretext for rebellion; he had expected the victory at Sauchieburn to be followed by an attack on Berwick, and on 19 July 1488 had ordered special precautions to be taken for its defence.[8] Followers of the late King of Scots who had committed themselves too deeply to his cause found sanctuary at the English

[1] Register House MSS, Treaties with France, No. 20.

[2] A.P.S., vol. II, p. 230.

[3] J. B. A. T. Teulet, Inventaire chronologique des documents relatifs à l'histoire d'Ecosse conservés aux archives du royaume à Paris, Edinburgh 1839, p. 53, cited in Francisque Michel, Les Ecossais en France, les Français en Ecosse, London 1862, vol. I, p. 300.

[4] 46th Report of the Deputy Keeper of Public Records, London 1886, App. II, p. 52.

[5] Ibid.

[6] Cal. Doc. Scot., vol. IV, No. 1545.

[7] C.T.S., vol. I, p. 126; Teller's Rolls, Public Record Office E. 405, 78, Mich. Term 5 Henry VII, Pierson mem. 3, cited in Conway, p. 32.

[8] Cal. Doc. Scot., vol. IV, No. 1542.

court, and one of them, Ramsay of Balmain, whom Henry still styled Lord Bothwell, was granted a pension of a hundred marks a year.[1]

In addition Henry overlooked, if he did not actively encourage, breaches of the truce at sea. According to Pitscottie, in the summer of 1489 five heavily-armed English ships repeatedly attacked and plundered Scottish merchantmen in the Firth of Forth, till Sir Andrew Wood of Largo with his two ships, the *Yellow Carvel* and the *Flower*, attacked them off Dunbar, forced them to surrender after a long and obstinate struggle, and escorted them in triumph to Leith.[2] Pitscottie cannot always be trusted, but it is certain that before 29 September the English King had paid a substantial sum to Henry Wyatt, his Clerk of the Crown Jewels, who with Ramsay of Balmain and two other exiled Scots, was taking a cargo of corn, beer, wax, brass, lead and cloth to the rebels at Dumbarton.[3] We do not know whether Wyatt and his companions succeeded in running the blockade; we do know, however, that in February 1490 a ship which King James had recently bought was so closely pursued by an English ship that she "tynt her cabillis and odir grayth", and had to take refuge under the guns of Dumbarton Castle,[4] and that in May he complained to the Pope that his subjects had been harrassed by his old enemies in England.[5] And while we may disregard Pitscottie's story that Stephen Bull was promised a pension of £1,000 a year by King Henry if he would bring back Sir Andrew Wood dead or alive,[6] it is not easy to dismiss as wholly fictitious his circumstantial account of the battle between the English and the Scottish sea-captain.[7]

According to Pitscottie, Stephen Bull, with three heavily-armed ships, sailed into the Firth of Forth in the summer of 1490 and lay off the Isle of May, in the hope of intercepting Sir Andrew Wood, whom he knew to be on his way back from Flanders.

[1] *Cal. Doc. Scot.*, VOL. IV, No. 1549.   [2] Pitscottie, VOL. I, pp. 226-7.
[3] Teller's Rolls *ut supra*.   [4] *C.T.S.*, VOL. I, p. 129.
[5] *Cal. of State Papers, Venice*, VOL. I, No. 568.
[6] Pitscottie, VOL. I, pp. 227-8.
[7] Pitscottie, VOL. I, pp. 228-30.

Early on the morning of 10 August one of the Englishmen sighted two ships sailing up by St Abb's Head. Bull straightway made some Scottish fishermen whom he had captured climb to the fighting tops, with orders to tell him if the ships were the *Yellow Carvel* and the *Flower*, "bot the Scottismen had no will to schew the weriete, bot feinyeit and said they knew them not". A promise of their freedom, however, induced them to tell the truth. "Then the captane was blyht and gart peirse the wyne, and drank about to all his skipperis and captans that was wnder him, prayand them to tak goode curage, ffor the enemeis was at hand."

Meantime Sir Andrew had seen the three great ships, bristling with guns, bearing down upon him, and prepared for battle. "Sett your sellffis in order everie man to his awin rowme," he cried, "lat the gounaris chairge thair artaillye and the croce bowis and mak thame ready, with thair lyme pottis and tua handit suordis in your for-rowmes". "And thairto," continues Pitscottie, "he caussit to fill the wyne and ewerie man drank to wther. Be this the sone begane to ryse and schynnit bright wpoun the saillis." The English opened fire with their heavier guns, but Wood, knowing that he would be outmatched in a game of long bowls, got to windward and closed with them. All through "ane lang sommer day" the farmers and fisherfolk on the coast of Fife watched the fighting, "quhilk was werie terrabill to sie". The coming of darkness interrupted the battle, but when "the day begane to break fair . . . thair trumptis blew on everie syde", and the fight was resumed with such blind fury that neither captains nor sailors noticed that the ships were drifting on to the sandbanks at the mouth of the Tay. The three English vessels ran aground, surrendered, and were towed into Dundee. King James, however, "as one that fought not for plunder, but for honour", gave money to the captives, and sent ships and men back to the English King.

Pitscottie's narrative finds scanty corroboration in contemporary records. If Stephen Bull's ships were as roughly handled as the story would suggest, the six pounds which he received from King Henry in Michaelmas Term 1490 for his expenses at sea would seem to be an inadequate recompense.[1] But a Scottish naval victory of some kind there certainly was: a charter of James IV dated 18 May 1491 mentions English prisoners captured by Andrew Wood, and employed by him in building houses and a fortalice "to resist and expel those pirates and raiders who have often attacked from the sea our kingdom and subjects".[2] There were English reprisals too, about which Pitscottie maintains a patriotic silence.

Henry took other measures to embarrass his young rival. On 16 April 1491, he lent £266.13.4 to the Earl of Buchan, King James's great-uncle, and Sir Thomas Tod, his Master of the Mint, on condition that they delivered into his hands either the King and his younger brother, James, Duke of Ross, or the King alone. Tod and Ramsay of Balmain guaranteed the repayment of the money before Michaelmas if the conditions were not fulfilled.[3] How far Buchan was sincere in his insincerity, whether he even knew that Tod and Ramsay were using his name to get four hundred marks from the parsimonious Henry, are questions that cannot now be answered. James seems to have remained ignorant of the whole mysterious affair.

Disappointed in Buchan, Henry turned to Angus, whose great fortress of Hermitage in Liddesdale commanded the western approach to Scotland. This time James suspected something, and on 29 July 1491 ordered Angus to enter into ward in his own castle of Tantallon.[4] Angus obeyed, but, it would appear, began to strengthen the castle and make plans for a rebellion. But the contumacious noble had now to reckon with the royal siege train; guns were shipped from Blackness Castle or hauled by road from Edinburgh. On 13 October workmen were digging trenches about the rebel stronghold,[5] and a few days later it surrendered.

Henry's subjects shared his suspicions of the Scots. On 17

[1] Register of Writs of Great and Privy Seals, P.R.O. E. 403, 2558, fol. 25, cited in Conway, p. 31.

[2] R.M.S., VOL. II, No. 2040; A.P.S., VOL. II, p. 227.

[3] Cal. Doc. Scot., VOL. IV, No. 1571; Foedera, VOL. XII, p. 440.

[4] C.T.S., VOL. I, p. 180.   [5] C.T.S., VOL. I, p. 181.

October his Parliament protested that as any agreement concluded on the part of the King of Scots was always broken by his subjects, open war with them was better than feigned peace, and it decreed the banishment of all Scots in England who were not made denizens within forty days.[1] Five days later Henry granted a safe-conduct to the ambassadors whom James proposed to send to England to discuss a renewal of the truce, but on 16 November, while the official representatives of the two Kings were debating at Coldstream, Sir William Tyler, Lieutenant of Berwick, and Sir John Cheyney concluded some unofficial negotiations with Angus. The Earl and his son, George, Master of Angus, pledged themselves to do all that was possible to make the King of Scots keep the peace, and, if war broke out, to use their utmost endeavour against those who had hindered an agreement with England. If they were to be hard pressed by their enemies in Scotland, and their lands and revenues endangered, they would deliver Hermitage Castle to King Henry, on condition that they obtained lands in England of at least the same value. They would enter into no agreement with and accept no pardon from the King of Scots without Henry's consent. The agreement was to be ratified by King Henry before 13 January.[2]

On 21 December the official representatives of the two sovereigns concluded a truce for five years.[3] Some rumour of the unofficial negotiations seems to have reached the ear of the Scottish King: he summoned his Council, and, after a lengthy discussion[4] had taken place, compelled Angus to surrender Liddesdale and Hermitage.[5] But the King and his counsellors knew better than turn him into an implacable foe: he received the lordship and castle of Kilmarnock in exchange,[6] and in the following year was granted Bothwell Castle and made Chancellor in place

---

[1] *Statutes of the Realm*, VOL. II, London 1816, p. 553, cited in Conway, p. 38.

[2] *L. and P. Richard III and Henry VII*, VOL. I, pp. 385-7; *Cal. Doc. Scot.*, VOL. IV, No. 1578 and App. I, No. 32.

[3] *Foedera*, VOL. XII, p. 465; *Rot. Scot.*, VOL. II, pp. 503-5, cited in Conway, p. 39.

[4] *R.M.S.*, VOL. II, No. 2072.   [5] *R.M.S.*, VOL. II, No. 2074.

[6] *R.M.S.*, VOL. II, Nos. 2072-3.

of Argyll, now near his death.[1] On 6 March 1492 James transferred Hermitage to the Earl of Bothwell,[2] and twelve days later he ratified the truce with England, not for five years, as had been agreed at Coldstream, but for eight months only.[3]

It was a gesture that might have had dangerous consequences, but though Henry might want to weaken and harrass the Scottish government, he had no intention of subverting it altogether. Now that he had a French campaign on his hands, now that he knew that a youth who claimed to be the son of Edward IV was at the French court, there were few things that he desired less than war with Scotland. James too began to see that with Inverness sacked and ruined and the island chiefs preparing for fresh conquests, war with England was a luxury in which he dare not indulge. On 17 October 1492 he commissioned Elphinstone and five other ambassadors to treat with Henry's representatives for the redress of injuries and an extension of the truce.[4] The ambassadors of the two sovereigns met at Coldstream and on 3 November agreed to extend the truce till 30 April 1494.[5]

King Henry's mind was not yet at ease. Though in accordance with the Treaty of Etaples, signed also on 3 November, Charles VIII had expelled Perkin Warbeck from his realm, the pretender had been welcomed as a nephew by Edward IV's sister Margaret, Duchess of Burgundy, whose court had long been a place of refuge for Yorkist plotters. On 28 May 1493 Henry commissioned the Bishop of St Asaph, Sir William Tyler, and two other ambassadors to negotiate a "real peace" with the King of Scots, if possible for the duration of the life of both princes, and to suggest that James should marry his distant kinswoman, the Lady—Henry styled her the Princess—Katharine, daughter of the Countess of Wiltshire.[6] James, however, would marry only

---

[1] *R.M.S.*, VOL. II, No. 2172; Sir W. Fraser, *The Douglas Book,* Edinburgh 1885, VOL. III, p. 134.
[2] *R.M.S.*, VOL. II, No. 2092.
[3] *Cal. Doc. Scot.*, VOL. IV, No. 1580; *Foedera*, VOL. XII, p. 473.
[4] *Cal. Doc. Scot.*, VOL. IV, No. 1585; *Foedera*, VOL. XII, p. 489.
[5] *Cal. Doc. Scot.*, VOL. IV, No. 1586; *Foedera*, VOL. XII, p. 494.
[6] *Cal. Doc. Scot.*, VOL. IV, No. 1588; *Foedera*, VOL. XII, p. 529.

a real princess; and instead of a real peace the English ambassadors, though they promised to pay reparations to the extent of a thousand marks, had to be content with another truce, to last till 30 April 1501. The treaty, concluded at Edinburgh on 24 June 1493, was confirmed by Henry on 18 July[1] and by James on 25 July.[2]

How far the King at this period was responsible for shaping the foreign policy of his country it is difficult to say, but signs are not lacking that he had begun to think and act for himself, and that the prestige of the Crown was again increasing. Whether the arrangement had been meant to be permanent or not, after 1490 Parliament ceased to nominate the members of the Secret Council. And if the King now chose the Council, he also chose when to follow and when to disregard its advice. "He decides nothing without his Council," wrote a Spanish observer a year or two later, "but in great matters he acts according to his own judgment."[3]

Many of his subjects still lamented his father, and complained that nothing had been done to avenge his death. To still "the hevy murmor and voce of the peple", the Parliament which met on 6 February 1492 had offered a reward of a hundred marks' worth of land to any one who should reveal, "suthfastly nawin of veray verite", the names of those who had put violent hands on the unfortunate King, that they might be brought to trial and punished "after their demerits".[4] But the King's evident remorse for his part in his father's death moved to admiration those who had once censured him. Acting on the advice of his confessor, he wore a heavy iron chain about his waist. He vowed never to accept absolution from this penance, even should the Pope offer it, but to wear the chain till the day of his death, because, he declared, "my presence [on the battlefield],

[1] *Cal. Doc. Scot.*, VOL. IV, Nos. 1590-1; *Foedera*, VOL. XII, p. 545.

[2] *Cal. Doc. Scot.*, VOL. IV, No. 1592; *Foedera*, VOL. XII, p. 545.

[3] De Ayala, in *Calendar of Letters, Despatches and State Papers relating to the negotiations between England and Spain* (hereafter referred to as *Cal. of State Papers, Spain*), VOL. I, ed. G. A. Bergenroth, London 1862, No. 210.

[4] *A.P.S.*, VOL. II, p. 230.

even though unwilling was the occasion of my father's death".[1]

But his impecuniosity kept pace with his popularity. Convinced that at the time of his death James III possessed "gret tressor and substance of gold and silver, cunyeit and uncunyeit, and utheris prisious Jowells", of which only a small portion had been recovered, Parliament ordered the sheriffs to make secret enquiries, and instructed the Justice Clerk to investigate carefully any case involving stolen treasure that might be brought to his notice. It was all in vain; the King had to resort to other methods of augmenting his financial resources.[2]

The Parliament which met in the summer of 1493 witnessed a further consolidation of the royal authority. On 25 June, the last day of the session, the Estates assembled to signify their approval or disapproval of the acts submitted to them by the Lords of the Articles, and to hear the King, who had now reached his twenty-first year, revoke all grants of crown property, including customs, burgh mails, and advowsons, that had been made during his minority. All lands that had been Crown property in the time of James II were to be restored; all heritable jurisdictions granted by his father or himself were to be annulled. The Earl of Bothwell, however, and Ross of Montgrenane, were not to be affected by this revocation.[3] A series of statutes relating to the Church did something to make the King's financial position more stable. The days were long past when a King of Scots could make a bishop by granting the cathedral chapter permission to elect the candidate whom he himself had chosen. It had been a profitable system for the King: it enabled him not only to secure salaries and places in Parliament for his clerks and counsellors, but also to divert the temporalities—the revenues from land and jurisdictions belonging to the bishopric—into the royal treasury by delaying his *congé d'élire* for six months or more. Before the middle of the fifteenth century the Pope had made

[1] Father Hay's Chronicle of the Observantine Province of Scotland, in W. Moir Bryce, *The Scottish Grey Friars*, VOL. II, pp. 177, 188. According to Pitscottie (VOL. I, pp. 217-8), the penance was self-imposed, and the King increased the weight of the chain by a certain number of ounces every year.

[2] *A.P.S.*, VOL. II, p. 230.   [3] *A.P.S.*, VOL. II, pp. 236-7.

F

good his claim to present, not only to bishoprics, but to monasteries of an annual value of over two hundred florins according to "Bagimond's Roll"—the register made in 1275 by the Papal Envoy Boiamund de Vicei and still preserved in Rome. The most that the King could now do if a benefice fell vacant was to petition the Pope to accept his nominee. But if the King acted promptly, he deprived himself of the much-needed temporalities; if he delayed he might find that some pushful ecclesiastic had forestalled him. There was the risk, too, that after the King's petition had reached the Pope, some outsider might bid higher than the royal nominee. For in Rome nothing was given for nothing; many a bishopric was purchased with borrowed money.[1]

As we have seen, Innocent VIII and James III had arrived at a concordat: by the bull of 1487 the Pope agreed to delay presentation for eight months to all benefices worth over two hundred florins. But the bull did not expressly bind Innocent's successors; and it was silent about benefices of less than two hundred florins a year. So money continued to flow from Scotland to Rome, and so the King often found that benefices of which he considered himself to be the patron had been awarded by the Pope to claimants of whom he knew nothing. At that moment the Archbishop of St Andrews was squandering the revenues of his see that he might obtain a decision against the new-made Archbishop of Glasgow in the papal courts.[2] In addition, cases which should have been tried in the Scottish courts were often taken to Rome.

Parliament therefore, while declaring that the privileges of Holy Church were to be observed,[3] announced that the bull of 1487 was still binding, and that anyone who sued for a benefice at the court of Rome within the forbidden period of eight months without having first secured the King's permission would be banished, declared a rebel, and never suffered to "bruke honor, benefice, nor dignitie within the realme".[4] Any merchant who lent money to such an unauthorised suitor for preferment would lose life, land, and goods. No suits for benefices which had not been

[1] See Cameron, *The Apostolic Camera and Scottish Benefices*, pp. xli-lix.
[2] *A.P.S.*, VOL. II, p. 232.   [3] Ibid.   [4] Ibid.

in the patronage of the Pope in the time of James I were to be taken to the papal court. The next ambassador who went to Rome was to order all who had taken cases there to abandon them and return to Scotland, where the King would "gar justice to be ministerit to thame" by the proper judge. As for the Archbishops, if they did not "leif thair contentiounis, litis, and pleyis . . . in the court of Rome", the King would forbid his subjects to pay rent or make loans to them.[1]

The ultimate effects of this legislation were to be disastrous for the Scottish Church. More startling in its immediate effects however, was the declaration that the whole of the vast possessions of John, Lord of the Isles, were forfeit to the Crown.

[1] *A.P.S.*, VOL. II, p. 233.

III

THE ISLES AND ENGLAND

THE modern Scottish man of letters, like the modern tourist, professes to find the real Scotland only in the glens and islands of the West; he even declares that if English comes awkwardly to his lips and pen, it is because his mind still keeps to the pattern of his ancestral Gaelic. It was different in the late fifteenth century: no traveller from foreign parts ventured beyond the Highland line; to the Spaniard Pedro de Ayala the Gaelic-speaking inhabitants of Scotland were simply "the savages who live in some parts of Scotland and in the islands"; and the poet Dunbar heard in their lilting speech only the "roup [croak] of raven and rook". The Lothian-born John Major, the philosopher who long adorned the schools of Paris, admired their music, "a most pleasing melody" drawn from the clareschaw, a harp with brazen strings, but he did not mention the elaborate and intricate patterns of their poetry, and the equally elaborate arrangements of formalised flowers and leaves and interlacing stems which they carved on standing crosses and recumbent grave-slabs. The island craftsman owed nothing to the example of the contemporary French or Lowland Scottish stone-carver; his work recalls rather, for all its difference in detail, the Celtic cross-slabs of the tenth and eleventh centuries.

In Major's eyes the Highlander or Islesman differed from the Lowlander only for the worse. "Just as among the Scots we find two distinct tongues," he wrote, "so we likewise find two different ways of life and conduct. For some are born in the forests and mountains of the north, and these we call men of the Highland, but the others men of the Lowland. By foreigners the former are called Wild Scots, the latter householding Scots. . . . One-half of Scotland speaks Irish, and all these as well as the

Islanders we reckon to belong to the Wild Scots. In dress, in the manner of their outward life, and in good morals, for example, these come behind the householding Scots—yet they are not less, but rather much more, prompt to fight. . . . One part of the Wild Scots have a wealth of cattle, sheep, and horses, and these . . . yield more willing obedience to the courts of law and the king. The other part of these people delight in the chase and a life of indolence . . . taking no pains to earn their own livelihood, they live upon others, and follow their own worthless and savage chief in all evil courses. . . . They are full of mutual dissensions, and war rather than peace is their normal condition." Their dress, as well as their speech, set them apart from the Lowland Scot. "From the mid-leg to the foot," wrote Major, "they go uncovered; their dress is, for an over-garment, a loose plaid, and a shirt saffron-dyed." While the Lowland laird went out to battle in armour of plate, the Highland chief protected himself with the old-fashioned coat of mail, made of iron rings; his followers were arrayed, not in helmet and quilted jack, but in an ample linen garment "sewed together in patchwork, well daubed with wax or with pitch, and with an over-coat of deerskin".[1]

So in one small country there were two languages and two cultures—one is tempted to say, two races. But the division did not indicate a difference of race—the Lowlander was as much a Celt as the Highlander, and as little: it was rather, as Major himself hinted, a manifestation of the immemorial strife between the dweller in the hills and the dweller in the plains, between the herdsman and the tiller of the soil. Nor was the difference between the Lowland and the Highland temperament so very great: De Ayala discovered in the Lowland Scot precisely those faults which Major denounced in the Highlander—indolence, vanity and envy. The records of baron and justiciary court alike show that the civilised Lowlander was as quick to strike, as slow to forget an offence, and as ready on a slender pretext to help himself to his neighbour's goods as the savage Highlander or Islesman.

But while the Lowland thief or homicide might be hanged at

[1] John Major, *History of Greater Britain*, pp. 48-9.

the justice aire, the Wild Scot had nothing to fear from sheriff or justiciar. The Western Isles were supposed to lie within the sheriffdom of Inverness, but it was not to the King's sheriff, it was to his own chieftain that the aggrieved Hebridean looked for justice. If he failed to obtain satisfaction he appealed, not to the Council, but to the Lord of the Isles, the head of the great Clan Donald, who held his high court of judicature in his island stronghold on Loch Finlagan in Islay. Here, according to a tradition current in the Western Isles two centuries later, lay a stone seven feet square, with a deep-cut hollow in its upper surface. Into this hollow each new chief of the Clan Donald placed his feet at his investiture, while he swore to his attendant vassals that he would continue them in the possession of their lands and mete exact justice to all his subjects. His father's sword was then put in his hand, the Bishop of the Isles, who was accompanied by seven priests, anointed him, and a bard recited the names and deeds of his ancestors.[1] All the island chiefs were his vassals, not only those who bore his name and claimed to be his kinsmen, but the chiefs of the MacLeans in Mull, the MacLeods in Skye, the MacNeils in Barra, of the Camerons, the MacIntoshes, and the MacKinnons. In effect, the Isles formed an independent kingdom, the rulers of which had repeatedly leagued themselves with the enemies of the King of Scots. The first Lord of the Isles had supported Edward Balliol, then, by marrying a daughter of Robert the Steward, afterwards King Robert II, had "grown, from pardoned rebel, to be considered kinsman to the throne". It was Donald, the second Lord, who in 1411 led his "Wild Scots" to within a few miles of Aberdeen in an attempt to vindicate his claim to the Earldom of Ross, an attempt which, in spite of his defeat at Harlaw, proved successful. Alexander, the third Lord of the Isles and Earl of Ross, sacked Inverness in 1429 and was warded in Tantallon for two years. He remained quiet while James I was alive, but in the reign of James II he entered into a treasonable band with the Earls of Crawford and Douglas. John, fourth and last Lord, remained true to the traditions of his house: in 1451 he

[1] Martin Martin, Gent., *A Description of the Western Islands of Scotland*, ed. Donald J. Macleod, Stirling 1934, p. 288.

rose in rebellion and seized the royal castles of Urquhart, Inverness and Ruthven; four years later he sheltered the defeated Earl of Douglas after the Battle of Arkinholme and, gathering a fleet, ravaged the islands in the Firth of Clyde. In the following year he sued for peace. The King pardoned him, and, probably to keep him away from his island strongholds, made him a Warden of the Marches. He accompanied the King to the fatal siege of Roxburgh, but in 1462, in return for a pension of £200 a year in time of war, and 100 marks in time of peace, he undertook to become the sworn vassal of Edward IV and to assist him in his military enterprises. In the event of Scotland's being conquered, he was to get one third of the land north of the Forth and lose his pension.[1] Not till 1475, when the negotiations for a treaty between England and Scotland were in progress, did his treason come to light. The result we know: his life and lands were declared forfeit, but on 1 July 1476 James III, at the prayer of the Queen and Parliament, granted him his life, and restored his lands. John, however, prudently surrendered to the King Knapdale and Kintyre, the office of Sheriff of Inverness and Nairn, and the Earldom of Ross.[2]

But it was difficult to break the spirit of the Clan Donald, "the noblest race of all created"—so sang an island bard—"a race kindly, mighty, valorous; a race the hottest in time of battle . . . a race without arrogance, without injustice, who seized naught save spoil of war". Some of the island chiefs could not forgive John for what they believed to be a pusillanimous and unnecessary surrender, and supported his illegitimate son, the savage-tempered and hard-drinking Angus, when he rose in rebellion a few years later. "The king of festive goblets" defeated his father's fleet at Bloody Bay in the Sound of Mull, but nothing came of his victory: he was killed soon afterwards by an Irish harper. He left a son, Donald Owre, who had been kidnapped in infancy by the Earl of Atholl, who handed him over to the Earl of Argyll.[3] He grew up apparently careless of his high descent and forgetful of his own people.

[1] *Foedera*, VOL. XI, p. 484.   [2] *A.P.S.*, VOL. II, p. 113.
[3] Gregory, *History of the Western Highlands and Isles of Scotland*, pp. 52–4.

The next troubler of the peace was Alexander of Lochalsh, the nephew of the Lord of the Isles, who as his nearest kinsman seemed destined to be his successor. In 1491 he invaded Ross, destroyed the castle and town of Inverness, and reduced the inhabitants to penury. The invaders were driven out by the MacKenzies, who, however, burned and looted with the same abandon.[1]

The lesson was plain. If the Lord of the Isles could not or would not restrain his vassals, he must be removed, and his lands brought under the direct control of the Crown. In May 1493 Parliament passed the sentence of forfeiture,[2] and in August the King sailed for the Western Isles. The mere sight of a royal fleet in these remote waters, where no Scottish monarch had come since the days of Bruce, seemed to overawe the island chiefs, who came to Dunstaffnage Castle to make their submission to the King.[3] Nowhere did he meet with armed resistance, and before the end of the month he was able to set out with an easy mind on his annual pilgrimage to the shrine of St Ninian in Whithorn.

It would appear that in the following year the aged Lord of the Isles had already surrendered.[4] James maintained him as a member of the royal household, gave him a pension of 200 marks, presented him with sombre but costly raiment at Yule,[5] and at the end of two years allowed him to enter the monastery of Paisley. He died there about four years later, and was buried, as he had wished, before the high altar of the abbey church, in the tomb of his royal kinsman, the unfortunate Robert III.[6]

To those chiefs who had submitted James granted fresh charters of the lands which they had held hitherto of the Lord of the Isles; two of the most formidable, Alexander of Lochalsh and John of Islay, he knighted.

But the Isles were not yet tamed. Twice in 1494 James had

[1] Gregory, *History of the Western Highlands and Isles of Scotland*, pp. 56, 57.
[2] The only Parliament at which the sentence could have been pronounced met on 31 May, and was adjourned till 26 June. *A.P.S.*, VOL. II, pp. 231, 232.
[3] *R.M.S.*, VOL. II, Nos. 2200, 2201, 2216.
[4] *Acts of the Lords Auditors of Causes and Complaints*, London 1839, p. 177.
[5] *C.T.S.*, VOL. I, pp. cxviii, 233, 235, 266, 308.
[6] Gregory, *History of the Western Highlands and Isles of Scotland*, p. 58.

to return. Of his first expedition, which took place in May, nothing is known.[1] Two months later he summoned his lords from the east, west, and south of Scotland to meet him at Tarbert, where an old royal castle guarded the isthmus between Kintyre and Knapdale.[2] After repairing and provisioning the castle, he sailed to the south of Kintyre, where he captured the Castle of Dunaverty.[3] After placing a garrison in it he sailed for home, satisfied that he had established two useful bases for operations in future campaigns. His satisfaction was short-lived; before he had left the Isles—some say while he was still in sight of Dunaverty— John of Islay, whom he had knighted a few months earlier, stormed the castle, and hanged the governor over the walls. Sir John's treachery profited him little: along with four of his sons he was captured by MacIan of Ardnamurchan, taken to Edinburgh to stand his trial, and hanged before the year was out.[4]

All through the winter of 1494-5 the shipwrights were busy at Dumbarton, repairing the ship *Christopher* and building boats, including a great row-barge for the King.[5] In May the King, accompanied by Sir Andrew Wood in the *Flower*, sailed up the Firth of Lorn to Mingary Castle on the Sound of Mull.[6] The expedition was successful; Maclean of Duart, MacDonald of Sleat, MacNeil of Barra and the Captain of Clan Cameron judged it expedient to make their submission to the King. Later in the year they were confirmed by him in the possession of their lands, held hitherto of the Lord of the Isles.[7]

James returned to Glasgow before the end of June, persuaded that he had done enough to keep the island chieftains quiet while he matched himself with a more formidable opponent. He took the precaution, however, of warding in Edinburgh Castle two potential troublers of the peace, Kenneth MacKenzie and Farquhar MacIntosh, both kinsmen of the Lord of the Isles.[8]

---

[1] C.T.S., VOL. I, p. cxv; R. Scac. S., VOL. XI, p. 181.
[2] C.T.S., VOL. I, p. 237.   [3] C.T.S., VOL. I, p. 244.
[4] Gregory, *History of the Western Highlands and Isles of Scotland*, pp. 89, 90.
[5] C.T.S., VOL. I, pp. 245-54.   [6] C.T.S., VOL. I, p. cxx.
[7] R.M.S., VOL. II, Nos. 2264, 2281, 2287.
[8] Gregory, *History of the Western Highlands and Isles of Scotland*, p. 91.

James lingered in Glasgow till the middle of July, waiting for the Irish chieftain Hugh O'Donnell of Tyrconnel, who came to swear fealty to him, and, it would appear, to concert measures with him against the King of England.[1]

Even when allowance is made for his "young adventurousness" and his belief in his own powers—"he esteems himself as much as though he were lord of the world," said De Ayala[2]—his readiness to provoke a war with England is at first sight inexplicable. He could not have forgotten that the truce which he had ratified in July 1493 still had six years to run, or that he had accepted, as full compensation for the injuries done by the English on land and sea, the thousand marks and fifty pounds offered by King Henry.[3] Apparently he had a livelier memory of Henry's underhand dealings with Angus, nor could he forget that the banner of England still floated over Berwick. And he had been converted to the belief that the rightful King of England was not Henry Tudor, but the youth whom Margaret, Dowager Duchess of Burgundy and sister of Edward IV, had declared to be her nephew, Richard, Duke of York. As early as 2 March 1492 James had received letters from Perkin Warbeck—to give the Pretender his real name.[4] In the meantime Warbeck had gone from Ireland to France, where he had been welcomed by Charles VIII, then at war with England, who gave him a bodyguard of a hundred men, commanded by the Scots Lord Monypenny. Expelled from France in November 1492, when the Treaty of Etaples ended the war, he went to the court of Margaret of Burgundy, who secured for him the support of her step-son Maximilian, soon to be Emperor, and of the Archduke Philip, his son. With Maximilian's help he assembled "a multitude of desperate characters, gathered promiscuously from neighbouring states and from English sanctuaries, called from their labour in the fields and their daily task by the hope of plunder", and at the beginning of July 1495 he set sail for England.[5]

[1] C.T.S., VOL. I, pp. 227, 242.   [2] Cal. of State Papers, Spain, VOL. I, No. 210.

[3] Cal. Doc. Scot., VOL. IV, No. 1597; Foedera, VOL. XII, p. 548.

[4] C.T.S., VOL. I, p. 199.

[5] Polydore Vergil, Historia Anglica, VOL. II, p. 1508.

At least five months earlier Henry had begun to suspect that he must number James among his enemies. On 22 March he commissioned the Earl of Surrey, Vice-Warden of the West and Middle Marches, to array all men between Trent and Tweed capable of bearing arms, that they might resist the threatened invasion by the Scots and other enemies, and empowered the Bishop of Durham to call up the men of Northumberland, Tynedale, Redesdale and his own bishopric.[1]

Warbeck landed at Deal on 3 July, but his motley host was driven back to its ships by the Kentish peasants. He next sailed to Ireland and attempted to capture Waterford, but was forced to raise the siege on 3 August. James's intentions had already been made plain by Elphinstone and the other Scottish Ambassadors who, early in July, had arrived at the court of Maximilian. They asked the Emperor to enter into an alliance with Scotland against England, and to marry his daughter to the King. They assured Maximilian that the Scots would favour the Duke of York, and that they hoped to get Berwick as the price of their support.[2]

It was November before Perkin and the remnants of his army appeared in Scotland. James prepared to welcome him as a veritable prince; the royal plate was brought in haste from Edinburgh to glitter on the board in Stirling Castle, where, on 20 November, he received the adventurer.[3] Shortly afterwards he summoned a meeting of the Great Council to which it was now his custom to refer every matter of importance. But the decisions of the Council always coincided with the King's own wishes; though some of the members declared that Perkin's statements "were but dreames and fantasies", most of them welcomed the prospect of a war with England. It was a safe investment, they argued: if the attempt succeeded Perkin would give them whatever they chose to ask; if it failed, Henry would pay them handsomely to prevent its repetition.[4]

James showed the sincerity of his belief in Perkin's pretensions

[1] *Cal. Doc. Scot.*, VOL. IV, No. 1608.
[2] *Cal. of State Papers, Venice*, VOL. I, Nos. 645, 647; Boece, *Vitae*, pp. 80-1.
[3] *C.T.S.*, VOL. I, pp. 256n., 263, 267.
[4] Polydore Vergil, *Historia Anglica*, VOL. II, pp. 1512-3; Hall, p. 474.

by marrying him, within two months of his arrival, to his kinswoman, the Lady Katharine Gordon.[1] He arranged a tournament to crown the marriage festivities, decked Perkin for the
occasion in armour covered with purple damask, took part in the
tournament himself, and was wounded in the hand.[2] Not content
with paying the expenses of his followers, reckoned to number
1,400, he bestowed on Perkin a pension of £1,344 a year.[3] But
he hesitated to invade England; though in May 1496 he sent
letters as far as Caithness and the Isles ordering the lieges to
assemble at Lauder,[4] he let the summer pass without striking a
blow for his protégé.

His mind was occupied with other schemes of conquest. At
the end of April, as the Treasurer's Accounts seem to indicate,[5] he
had begun his impetuous wooing of Margaret Drummond, the
eldest daughter of John, Lord Drummond:

> Joy wes within and joy without
> Under that unlenkest waw,
> Quhair Tay ran down with stremis stout
> Full strecht under Stobshaw.

Nor, if the "Mild, meek, mansuete Margaret" of the anonymous
poet was indeed Margaret Drummond, can he be blamed.

> To creatur that wes in cair,
>   Or cauld of crewelty,
> A blicht blenk of her vesage bair
>   Of baill his bute micht be . . .
> The blosummes that wer blycht and brycht
>   By hir wer blacht and blew
> Scho gladit all the foull of flicht
>   That in the forrest flew;
> Scho mycht haif comfort king or knycht
>   That ever in cuntre I knew. . . .[6]

---

[1] Polydore Vergil, *Historia Anglica*, VOL. II, pp. 1513-4; Hall, p. 474;
C.T.S., VOL. I, p. cxxvii.

[2] *C.T.S.*, VOL. I, pp. 257, 262-4.   [3] *C.T.S.*, VOL. I, pp. 335, 340, 342.

[4] *C.T.S.*, VOL. I, p. 269.   [5] *C.T.S.*, VOL. I, p. 273.

[6] Anonymous poem "Tayis Bank" in *Early Popular Poetry of Scotland and
the Northern Border*, ed. D. Laing, rearranged and revised W. C. Hazlitt,
London 1895, VOL. I, pp. 170-4.

At the beginning of June he installed her in Stirling Castle, whence, later in the year, she went to Linlithgow Palace.[1] But she was not his first mistress, nor was she to be his last. Three years earlier Mariot Boyd, the daughter of the Laird of Bonshaw, had borne him a son, Alexander Stewart, the future Archbishop of St Andrews.[2]

A more formidable obstacle to war was Spain. The Scottish ambassadors at the court of Maximilian had failed to obtain a bride for their master. But James had already sent Archbishop Blacader to the court of Ferdinand and Isabella to ask for the hand of a Spanish princess. Blacader had arrived in Spain towards the end of August 1495, and had obtained a sympathetic hearing from the King and Queen.[3] The invasion of Italy by the French in the previous year had made them join the Pope, the Emperor, and the rulers of Venice and Milan in a Holy League directed against France. England, faithful to the Treaty of Etaples, remained outside the League. Only with the support of England, they believed, would success in the coming struggle with France be assured; to obtain it they were ready to consent to the marriage of their youngest daughter, Katharine of Aragon, and Arthur, the elder son of King Henry. But England could not lend effective support if she were distracted by the threat of a Scottish invasion. The Scottish ambassador and the King of Scots must therefore be amused by promises of the hand of an imaginary Spanish princess, that amity between England and Scotland might be established. Accordingly in September the Spanish sovereigns tried to persuade the Pope to make Blacader a Cardinal,[4] and when Blacader left for Scotland at the end of the year they sent two ambassadors, Don Martin de Torre and Garcia de Herera, along with him. Their instructions were to procure a peace, or at least a lasting truce, between England and Scotland, that England might be free to launch an attack on France.[5]

---

[1] C.T.S., VOL. I, pp. 277, 304.

[2] C.T.S., VOL. I, p. 378; J. Dowden, The Bishops of Scotland, ed. J. Maitland Thomson, Glasgow 1912, p. 37.

[3] Cal. of State Papers, Spain, VOL. I, No. 103.

[4] op. cit., No. 104.   [5] op. cit., No. 107.

The Spaniards arrived at Stirling on 23 December 1495, and were received somewhat coldly by the King.[1] He had read their instructions, which had arrived before them, and had concluded that their visit had been suggested by King Henry.[2] He was interested, however, in the possibility of his marriage to an Infanta. In the spring of 1496 he sent Blacader back to Spain, along with Garcia de Herera, and promised that he would attempt nothing against England before his ambassador's return. Blacader was instructed to insist on the marriage, and to promise that if it took place James would make a perpetual peace with Henry and abandon the Duke of York.[3]

So the Parliament which met at Edinburgh on 13 July 1496 discussed, not preparations for war, but the cost of living, the scarcity of money, the suits at the court of Rome which both increased that scarcity and nullified the right of presentation to important benefices that was claimed by the King, and the lack of well-trained judges. "Sua that thai that are shereffis or Jugeis Ordinaris under the kingis hienes may have knawledge to do Justice"—so ran the preamble to the first Scottish Education Act—all barons and substantial freeholders were instructed to send their eldest sons to the grammar school when they reached the age of eight or nine, there to remain till "thai be competentlie foundit and have perfite latyne, and thereftir to remane thre yeris at the sculis of art and Jure, sua that thai may have knawledge and understanding of the lawis. Throw the quhilkis Justice may reigne universalie throw all the realme". Parliament could not stop the sending of petitions for benefices to the papal Curia, but it attempted to regulate the traffic. No suits were to go to Rome without a licence from the King; no suitor was to do anything contrary to the terms of his licence. Offenders against the statute were to be outlawed and their benefices declared vacant. The scarcity of money was to be remedied by the appointment of "ane famous and wise man" to be Master of the Mint, and by the enforcement of the existing statutes prohibiting the export and requiring the import of bullion. The cost of living was to

[1] R. Scac. S., VOL. X, p. 580.
[2] Cal. of State Papers, Spain, VOL. I, No. 132.   [3] op. cit., No. 137.

be reduced by the fixing of a fair price for "breid, aill, and all uther necessar thingis".[1]

Before the end of the month, however, Blacader returned from Spain, accompanied by a new ambassador, the flamboyant Don Pedro de Ayala. He reported that from Ferdinand he had got only tactful and evasive speeches.[2] James saw that he had been tricked, and decided to invade England as soon as the harvest had been gathered in. The unexpected proposal by King Henry that James should marry his daughter Margaret, then a child of seven, failed to arrest the preparations for war.[3] On 2 September the King, in the presence of his Council, announced to Perkin the price of his support—the town and castle of Berwick and 100,000 marks, payable within five years. Perkin, however, beat him down to Berwick and 50,000 marks, payable in two years.[4]

On 14 September, when the King and the Pretender knelt side by side before the high altar in Holyrood,[5] the rehearsal of the Flodden campaign began. While the guns, escorted by a long train of labourers equipped with spades, picks and mattocks, rumbled through Haddington and over the Lammermuirs to the rendezvous at Ellem,[6] heralds were despatched into England to announce that no harm would be done to those who came at once into the allegiance of the Duke of York.[7]

The Scottish artillery reached Ellem on 19 September[8]; on the following day, it would seem, James and Perkin crossed the

[1] A.P.S., VOL. II, pp. 237, 238.

[2] C.T.S., VOL. I, pp. cxxxv, cxxxvi; Cal. of State Papers, Spain, VOL. I, Nos. 137, 150.

[3] Cal. Doc. Scot., VOL. IV, No. 1622. It is possible that James did not receive it. Although on 5 May 1496 a commission to treat of the espousals of the King of Scots and the Princess Margaret was issued to the Bishops of Carlisle and Durham and the Earl of Surrey, there is nothing to show that any of them visited Scotland that summer.

[4] Letter of John Ramsay, formerly Lord Bothwell, to Henry VII, Pinkerton, VOL. II, p. 438.

[5] C.T.S., VOL. I, p. 296.   [6] C.T.S., VOL. I, pp. 296-9.

[7] Polydore Vergil, Historia Anglica, VOL. II, p. 1514; Hall, p. 475.

[8] C.T.S., VOL. I, p. 299.

Tweed near Coldstream. With them went De Ayala, who had already been attracted by the impetuous, adventurous prince.[1] Instead of flocking to the standard of their deliverer, the country-folk fled with their sheep and cattle to the castles and towers that guarded the valley of the Till. If James had been moved partly by chivalrous regard for a disinherited prince, his followers were moved wholly by love of plunder. At Tilmouth, at Twizel, at Duddo, it was the same story—the tower was assailed and captured, its occupants were slain and their sheep and cattle driven off, and only a heap of blackened stones left to show where it had been.[2]

Two days of this inglorious warfare were enough for Perkin. "O iron-hearted!" he exclaimed, "not to be moved by the sufferings of my own people!" then, turning to the King, he implored him to do no more harm to his subjects and his country. "You seem to worry yourself over what does not concern you," retorted the King, "for you have called . . . the English your subjects, yet not one of them has offered to help in a war waged on your behalf."[3] Perkin returned to Scotland on 21 September[4]; De Ayala remained, to see James display at the siege of Heton Castle those military virtues and failings which were to be his undoing at Flodden. "He is courageous, even more than a king should be," wrote the ambassador a year later. "I have seen him often undertake most dangerous things in the last wars. . . . He is not a good captain, because he begins to fight before he has given his orders. He said to me that his subjects serve him with their persons and goods, in just and unjust quarrels, exactly as he likes, and that therefore he does not think it right to begin any warlike undertaking without being himself the first in danger."[5]

[1] *Cal. of State Papers, Spain*, VOL. I, No. 210. Four of his servants were slain in the wars, and three wounded.

[2] Polydore Vergil, *Historia Anglica*, VOL. II, pp. 1514-5; Hall, p. 475; John Hodgson, *History of Northumberland*, PT. III, VOL. II, Newcastle upon Tyne 1828, pp. 178, 191 (Report by Sir Robert Bowes and Sir Ralph Elleker on the condition of Border strongholds, B.M. Cotton MS, Caligula B. VIII).

[3] Polydore Virgil, *Historia Anglica*, VOL. II, p. 1515: Hall, p. 475.

[4] *C.T.S.*, VOL. I, p. 299.

[5] *Cal. of State Papers, Spain*, VOL. I, No. 210.

JAMES IV

Daniel Mytens (after an earlier portrait)   *Keir*

By permission of Lt.-Col. W. J. Stirling of Keir

On 25 September a mine was driven under the wall of the castle,[1] but about midnight the King, who had probably been warned that the English army was advancing from Newcastle, with "his hool power retourned and stale awey into Scotland".[2]

James was still convinced that the war should go on, but he was no longer prepared to wage it on behalf of Perkin. In the middle of October he shipped Perkin's followers out of the country at a cost of £200.[3] Perkin himself he treated with increasing coolness, though he paid his pension regularly.[4] Perkin lingered in Scotland till the following summer, when James chartered and provisioned a Breton ship—the *Cuckoo*—for him.[5] At the beginning of July 1497 he sailed from Ayr,[6] to encounter defeat before the walls of Exeter, imprisonment in the Tower, and—two years later—death on the gallows at Tyburn.

The Raid of Ellem had broken down the patience of King Henry. In October 1496 he issued a proclamation declaring that through the "wilful headiness" of the King of Scots war between the two countries was now "open and at large", and urging his subjects "to doo from hensfurth by land and by see all thanoyaunce possible to the Scottes".[7] He also summoned a meeting of the Great Council, and persuaded it to authorise the raising of a loan of £40,000, and to grant him—or rather, to guarantee that Parliament would grant him—the sum of £120,000.[8] In January 1497 Parliament obediently granted him two fifteenths and tenths, and a subsidy of equal amount.

Though in the winter and spring James, usually accompanied by his master-gunner Hans, was flitting from one Border castle

---

[1] *C.T.S.*, VOL. I, p. 300.

[2] *Cal. Doc. Scot.*, VOL. IV, App. I, No. 35.   [3] *C.T.S.*, VOL. I, p. 303.

[4] Hall, p. 483. A payment was made on 27 June 1497, a few days before Warbeck left Scotland. *C.T.S.*, VOL. I, p. 342.

[5] *R. Scac. S.*, VOL. X, p. 43; *L. and P. Richard III and Henry VII*, VOL. I, pp. 185-7.   [6] *C.T.S.*, VOL. I, pp. 343, 344.

[7] *Cal. Doc. Scot.*, VOL. IV, No. 1637, printed in full App. I, No. 35. Assigned by Bain to Oct. 1498, but it obviously belongs to the previous year.

[8] C. L. Kingsford, *Chronicles of London*, Oxford 1905, p. 211; *Cambridge Modern History*, edd. A. W. Ward, G. W. Prothero *et al.*, VOL. I, Cambridge 1902, p. 469.

G

to another, though workmen were toiling feverishly to enlarge and strengthen the castle of Dunbar, though in February a small Scottish force, using Home Castle as a base, made a successful raid into England,[1] it seemed that nothing could save the Scots from the vengeance of King Henry. A powerful army, which he had put under the command of Lord Daubeny, was waiting for him to give the word to move northwards.[2]

The word was never given. In May 1497 the men of Cornwall, furious at being taxed for the defence of a distant frontier, rose in rebellion and marched on London. Daubeny's troops had to be recalled for the defence of the capital, and though Henry defeated the rebels at Blackheath on 17 June, he shrank from shedding more blood—or spending more money.[3] James had already, through Lord Hume and the Earl of Angus, informed Henry's representatives of the terms on which he would refrain from attacking England. Henry snatched at the opportunity; on 5 July he instructed Richard Fox, Bishop of Durham, the ablest diplomat in England, to offer a cessation of hostilities if James surrendered Perkin and sent Angus, Hume, and the Bishop of Moray as ambassadors to England. If James refused to surrender Perkin, Fox was to ask that the ambassadors should be sent, that James should come to England for a personal interview with Henry, and that hostages should be given for a proper observance of the treaty. If, however, James refused to make any advance on the terms offered by Angus and Hume, Fox was to accept them.[4]

Henry's readiness to agree with his adversary quickly prompted that adversary to smite his other cheek. On 21 July 1497, while minstrels played her "doune the gait", Mons Meg was dragged from Edinburgh Castle[5]; at the beginning of August, along with other great guns that had been kept in readiness at Hume and

---

[1] *C.T.S.*, VOL. I, pp. 306, 308, 310, 320, 323, 328, 331, 334, 335, 337-9, 342, 343, 345.

[2] Polydore Vergil, *Historia Anglica*, VOL. II, p. 1517; Hall, p. 476.

[3] Polydore Vergil, *Historia Anglica*, VOL. II, pp. 1518-25; Hall, pp. 477-80.

[4] *L. and P. Richard III and Henry VII*, VOL. I, pp. 104-9.

[5] *C.T.S.*, VOL. I, p. 348.

Coldingham,[1] she was thundering against Bishop Fox's castle of Norham. For a week, while his light horsemen ravaged the Bishop's lands, James remained before Norham, directing the siege by day, and playing cards with De Ayala at night. "How so be it he did noo hurt to that Castell."[2] Then, hearing that the Earl of Surrey, at the head of an army of 20,000 men, was only two days' march distant, he abandoned the siege and returned to Edinburgh, to learn that Surrey had crossed the Tweed on 15 August, and was "prostrating and defacing" castles and towers in the neighbourhood of Berwick.[3] Reassembling his disbanded troops, he marched to within a mile of Ayton Castle, which, on 17 August, Surrey had summoned to surrender. The captain of the castle had refused, declaring that he was confident of being relieved within twenty-four hours, whereupon Surrey, in the words of King Henry, "laid ouir ordynaunce to bete It wyth all, and soo bett that place with owir gunnys ffrom ij of the clok tyll v at afftyr none that they beyng withyn the Castell were ffayn to yolde". James made no attempt to relieve the castle; only after it had been razed to the ground on the following day did he send two heralds to Surrey with the suggestion that the fate of Berwick should be decided either by a general engagement between the two armies, or by a fight "hand ffor hand" between their two leaders. Surrey, King Henry informed the Lord Mayor of London, answered "lyke a wyse man and hardy knygth" that "thowth the town of Berwyk was owyrs the which he cowde not putt In pledge withouth owir assent, yit he wold putt his body therunto, the which was more precious unto hym than all the tounys of the world".[4]

The Earl prepared for battle, but the King "ffled shameffully and sodeynly with all his company". He had reverted to the tactics of Bruce, and allowed the Scottish climate to fight his

[1] C.T.S., VOL. I, pp. 326, 338, 339, 346.

[2] C.T.S., VOL. I, p. 350; Polydore Vergil, *Historia Anglica*, VOL. II, pp. 1525-6; Hall, p. 480.

[3] C.T.S., VOL. I, pp. 350-1; Polydore Vergil, *Historia Anglica*, VOL. II, p. 1529; Hall, p. 481.

[4] Henry VII to J. Tate, Lord Mayor of London, 28 Aug. 1487, inserted in Guildhall MS Great Chronicle of London, fols. 258[v]-9.

battles for him; after only five days in Scotland, the English army, "vexid grevously all that tyme with contynuell Rayn and cold wedyr", its ranks filled with sick and dying men, withdrew to Berwick. No threats or persuasions, not even the knowledge that they had been paid a fortnight in advance, Henry complained bitterly, could keep them together, much less make them invade Scotland a second time.

Henry was furious when he heard that Surrey's army had melted away. "Noo lytill dyfficulte it is", he wrote to the Lord Mayor on 28 August, "to have soo convenable a tyme for the subduyng of the scottis as this was."[1] But he knew how to curb unprofitable passion; on 5 September he empowered the Bishop of Carlisle, Sir Thomas Dacre, William Warham, Master of the Rolls, and Henry Wyatt—or any two of them, Warham always being one—to treat with James or his commissioners.[2] De Ayala, who was looked on as remarkable because he could hear the word "Scotland" pronounced without losing his temper,[3] continued to play cards with the King and to point out the madness of his foreign policy. He had squandered the meagre resources of his kingdom, he had even been forced to coin his great gold chain,[4] and he had nothing to show in return, not even military glory, for he had failed to capture the one considerable fortress that he had attacked. If he had not prevailed against an England distracted by rebellion, how could he hope to withstand an England reunited and clamorous for revenge?

Such arguments, we may guess, De Ayala and his own sager counsellors, like Elphinstone, put before him. The Spanish ambassador was present at Ayton when, on 30 September 1497, Elphinstone, accompanied by Andrew Forman, Prior of Pittenweem, Sir Patrick Hume of Fastcastle, and Master Richard Lawson, met Fox, Warham, and John Cartington, and with them concluded a treaty for a seven years' truce. De Ayala was not

[1] Great Chronicle of London, fols. 259^{r-v}.
[2] Cal. Doc. Scot., VOL. IV, No. 1636.
[3] Cal. of State Papers, Spain, VOL. I, No. 204; Londoño and the Sub-Prior of Santa Cruz to Ferdinand and Isabella.
[4] C.T.S., VOL. I, p. 314.

satisfied; he persuaded James to make him his ambassador extra-ordinary at the English court, and with Warham negotiated a revision of the treaty which altered its duration from seven years to one year after the death of the survivor of the two sovereigns. On 13 December 1497 King Henry gave his assent to the amended treaty, and agreed to submit all disputes arising out of the recent troubles to the arbitration of Ferdinand and Isabella. Finally, on 10 February 1498, James ratified the treaty.[1]

[1] *Cal. of State Papers, Spain*, VOL. I, No. 186; *Cal. of State Papers, Venice*, VOL. I, Nos. 759, 760; Polydore Vergil, *Historia Anglica*, VOL. II, pp. 1528-9; Hall, p. 482. Abstract of treaties, *Cal. Doc. Scot.*, VOL. IV, No. 1644; text, *Foedera*, VOL. XII, pp. 673-80.

IV

THE THISTLE AND THE ROSE

1498-1503

A
T the beginning of February 1498, James had ratified the treaty for a peace which, even if Henry predeceased him, would endure for his whole lifetime and a year after his death; before the end of June he was swearing "by sweet Saint Ninian" that he found nothing more uncertain than peace with England.[1]

The trouble had begun at Bishop Fox's own castle. One day in the early summer of 1498[2] a small body of armed horsemen appeared opposite the Castle of Norham, gazed about them as if they were reconnoitering its defences, and disappeared as silently as they had come. They were probably only thoughtless youths, drawn by mere curiosity, but when they reappeared on the following day, the defenders of the castle were convinced that they meant mischief, and challenged them. Stung by the accusation that they had come as spies, the Scots returned taunt for taunt, whereupon the English sallied out and attacked them. The Scots resisted for a time, but they were outnumbered, and when many of the party had been wounded and a few slain, they rode off, to carry back to Scotland their tale of English perfidy.[3]

A twelvemonth earlier this would have meant instant war, but James, in the words of the Spanish ambassador, had seen "the ears of the wolf"[4]; though he at once sent Marchmont Herald to

---

[1] Hall, p. 487; Polydore Vergil, *Historia Anglica*, VOL. II, p. 1537.

[2] "Two or three months ago"; De Puebla to Ferdinand and Isabella, 25 Aug. 1498, *Cal. of State Papers, Spain*, VOL. I, No. 221.

[3] Hall, p. 487; Polydore Vergil, *Historia Anglica*, VOL. II, p. 1537.

[4] *Cal. of State Papers, Spain*, VOL. I, No. 221.

England[1] with a demand for redress and a declaration that if it were not granted he would not consider himself bound by the treaty, his letter was "full of compliments and courtesy, as though he had been a son writing to his father".[2] Henry replied that as he had no hand in the Norham affair, he did not consider that the treaty had been broken. He would enquire into the business himself, and, if his subjects were to blame, he would see that they were punished.[3]

This over-discreet reply did not satisfy James. On 28 August he despatched Lyon King-of-Arms with letters to Henry and De Ayala. But for his love of peace and his oath, he declared to De Ayala, he should be inclined to deal with the recent intolerable outrages by the sword rather than by prayers. He appealed to De Ayala, since it was he who had negotiated the truce, to advise his emissary and support him should he meet with opposition.[4]

De Ayala's intervention was hardly necessary. Henry did not want war, and Fox felt that, since his servants had undone what their master's diplomacy had effected, it was his duty to work for peace. He wrote to James begging him to act with mildness and humanity, according to his gracious custom, even though he might have taken offence at the fault committed by the garrison of Norham. The appeal to James's chivalrous nature was successful: he invited the Bishop to come to Scotland for a further discussion, and at the beginning of November they met in the Abbey of Melrose.[5]

Fox knew that much hung on the interview: how much, for all his insight and experience, he could not guess. To James, however, as to Macbeth, had been vouched the vision of a line of kings "that twofold balls and treble sceptres carry". If he married the elder daughter of King Henry, it was not improbable that some day a King of Scots might become King of England

---

[1] Hall, p. 487.

[2] *Cal. of State Papers, Spain*, VOL. I, No. 221.

[3] Hall, p. 487; Polydore Vergil, *Historia Anglica*, VOL. II, pp. 1537-8.

[4] *Cal. of State Papers, Venice*, VOL. I, No. 769.

[5] *Cal. of State Papers, Venice*, VOL. I, No. 776; Hall, p. 487; Polydore Vergil, *Historia Anglica*, VOL. II, pp. 1538-9.

as well. It was not impossible that he himself might be that King. In 1498 there were only three lives between the Princess Margaret and the English throne. It is true that in the previous summer he had taken no notice of Henry's proposal that he should marry the Princess, regarding it as a device to delay his invasion of England. Now he was not so sure. He had complete confidence in De Ayala, who, like his master and mistress, wanted to see peace between England and Scotland assured by the marriage of the King of Scots to an English princess. There remained one question—would the alliance with England invalidate the older alliance with France? It could be shelved: though Charles VIII died in April 1498, his successor, Louis XII, had not as yet sent an ambassador to solicit a renewal of the alliance.[1]

So, after he had discussed the affray at Norham and agreed to overlook it, James dismissed all the company except Fox. To him he revealed the true purpose of the meeting. He wished an enduring peace with England, to be secured by a treaty of friendship. Such a treaty he would be ready to sign if Henry would give him the hand of his daughter Margaret. He would send ambassadors speedily to negotiate a marriage, if Fox could assure him that they would not be asking what would certainly be denied. Fox gave a non-committal answer, which left the King with a hope that his proposals would be favourably considered, and departed to report the matter to Henry.[2]

"The news," says Polydore Vergil, "delighted Henry in a wonderful degree, for there was nothing dearer to him than peace".[3] But he did not close at once with James's offer. Private affection for a time vanquished policy. His daughter was only nine years old, and both his wife and his mother were opposed to the marriage. The King of Scots, he knew, was a lusty bachelor of twenty-five, notorious for his gallantries; he probably did not know that James had won a new mistress, Janet Kennedy, the daughter of Lord Kennedy, from her old lover, the Earl of

---

[1] There is no evidence for a renewal of the alliance between 1491 and 1512. See Register House MSS, Treaties with France, Nos. 20 and 22.

[2] Hall, pp. 487-8; Polydore Vergil, *Historia Anglica*, VOL. II, p. 1539.

[3] Polydore Vergil, *Historia Anglica*, VOL. II, p. 1539.

Angus.[1] Some of Henry's advisers, too, disliked the project. They saw, just as clearly as James did, that it might bring England under the rule of a Scottish prince. Henry reassured them. If such a union took place, he argued, it would be an accession, not of England to Scotland, but of Scotland to England, since the greater would always draw the less, as England had drawn Normandy under her sway.[2]

His arguments failed to convince the youthful Thomas More, who spoke so persuasively against the King's demand for three fifteenths—about £90,000—to meet the cost of his daughter's wedding, that the Commons cut the sum down to £40,000, part to be reserved to meet the wedding expenses of Prince Arthur. The King, furious that "a beardless boy had disappointed all his purpose", punished More, who "having nothing could lose nothing", by thrusting his father into the Tower.[3]

On 8 September 1499 Henry ratified a treaty, concluded at Stirling on 20 July, for a truce to last for the joint lives of the two sovereigns, and a year after the death of the survivor,[4] and three days later he commissioned Fox to negotiate a marriage between Margaret and James.[5]

Fox made it clear that the marriage must be delayed for some years. James declared his willingness to wait till Margaret was of marriageable age, but insisted on having the dowry that he would have received had he married a Spanish infanta. Henry, though alarmed by the rumour that James might after all marry the daughter of the Emperor Maximilian, would promise him only half of what he demanded.[6] One obstacle he removed, however, when on 28 July 1500 he obtained a papal dispensation to enable the marriage to take place. For James and Margaret stood within the prohibited degrees of kinship, both being descended from a

[1] R. Scac. S., VOL. XII, pp. xliii–xliv.

[2] Polydore Vergil, Historia Anglica, VOL. II, pp. 1539–40.

[3] William Roper, The Lyfe of Sir Thomas Moore, knighte, ed. E. V. Hitchcock, London 1935, pp. 7–8, 110.

[4] Foedera, VOL. XII, p. 722; Cal. Doc. Scot., VOL. IV, No. 1657.

[5] Foedera, VOL. XII, p. 729; Cal. Doc. Scot., VOL. IV, No. 1658.

[6] De Puebla to Ferdinand and Isabella, 11 Jan. and 16 June 1500, Cal. of State Papers, Spain, VOL. I, Nos. 249, 268.

common great-great-grandfather, John Beaufort, Marquis of Dorset.[1]

Though in the next twelve months there was much coming and going of ambassadors and heralds between the Scottish and the English courts, it was not till 8 October 1501 that James commissioned the Archbishop of Glasgow, the Earl of Bothwell, and Andrew Forman, Bishop-elect of Moray, to act as his ambassadors at the English court, with power to contract a marriage with the Princess Margaret in his name, and to negotiate a treaty of perpetual peace.[2] The King had been compelled to set his own house in order. His brood of illegitimate children could be removed from Stirling Castle at a few hours' notice, and lodged in the town till the Queen had departed,[3] but he would find it more difficult to conceal his mistress, who had made the Castle her home. He had solved the problem a few weeks earlier, when he bestowed the Castle of Darnaway on the Lady Janet on condition that she remained unmarried, and softened the blow of her banishment by granting the Earldom of Moray to her infant son.[4] A few days after his ambassadors had departed, he succeeded in combining a house-warming in Darnaway with a visit to the shrine of St Duthac in Tain.[5]

While the King lingered in Darnaway, hawking in the brief November days, playing cards in the long evenings, the Scottish ambassadors, accompanied by a hundred horsemen, rode into London. They were welcomed at Bishopsgate by a company of English lords and "jolly gallants", who escorted them through Cornhill and Cheapside to their lodging in Smithfield.[6] They found the city in holiday mood, for nine days earlier, on 15 November, Prince Arthur had married Katharine of Aragon, and

---

[1] *Foedera*, VOL. XII, p. 765.

[2] *Foedera*, VOL. XII, pp. 776-9; *Cal. Doc. Scot.*, VOL. IV, Nos. 1675, 1676.

[3] *C.T.S.*, VOL. II, ed. J. Balfour Paul, Edinburgh 1900, p. 445.

[4] *R. Scac. S.*, VOL. XII, pp. xlv-xlvi; *R.M.S.*, VOL. II, No. 2585 (1 June 1501), Nos. 2586, 2587 (12 June 1501).   [5] *C.T.S.*, VOL. II, pp. 125-7.

[6] Contemporary chronicle B. M. Cotton MS, Vitellius A.XVI, printed in C. L. Kingsford, *Chronicles of London*, pp. 154-263; extracts in William Dunbar, *Poems*, ed. David Laing, Edinburgh 1834, VOL. I, pp. 273-5. Guildhall MS, Great Chronicle of London, fol. 291^v.

though the conduits no longer ran with wine, though "curious velvets, beautiful satins, and pleasant silks" no longer decked the houses, there were still tournaments in the Palace of Westminster by day, and "noble and costious banquets" at night.[1] On 26 November they witnessed a "goodly Justes", where the Marquis of Dorset vanquished the Duke of Buckingham, though he "bare hym full valiauntly, and broke many Speris".[2] They had soon to attend to more serious business: on 28 November King Henry issued a commission to the Archbishop of Canterbury, the Earl of Surrey, and Fox, now Bishop of Winchester, to treat with them on all matters regarding the marriage of the King of Scots and the Princess Margaret.[3]

Whatever the ambassadors might have thought of their present surroundings, one at least of their attendants was dazzled by the glittering pageantry and overwhelmed by the evidence of wealth which London displayed. As William Dunbar, unbeneficed clerk, gazed at its river crowded with ships and barges, at its bridge piled high with houses, at the walls and gates which guarded it, at its multitude of churches with their sweet-sounding bells, it seemed to him that he must rank London as "of townes A *per se*". At a dinner given by the Lord Mayor to the ambassadors in Christmas week, he rose from his seat at a side table, and wrote a poem in praise of this "sweet paradise precelling in pleasure", London, "the floure of Cities all". Nor was his host forgotten—

> Noo lord of parys, venyze, or fflorance
> In dygnyte or honour gooth to hym nyy.
> He is exempler, loodster, and Guy,
> Pryncypall patron, and Rose orygynall,
> Above all Mayrys as mastyr most worthy.
> London, thow art the fflowr of Cytees all.

The parsimonious but politic Henry rewarded "the Rhymer of Scotland" with £13.6.8.[4]

---

[1] Hall, pp. 493, 494.   [2] Kingsford, *Chronicles of London*, p. 252.
[3] *Cal. Doc. Scot.*, VOL. IV, No. 1678.
[4] Dunbar, *Poems*, ed. Laing, VOL. I, pp. 273–5; Kingsford, *Chronicles of London*, pp. 253–5; Guildhall MS, Great Chronicle of London, fols. 292–4.

The Guildhall MS version of the "Balade" "London thow art of Townys a per se", which does not appear in any edition of Dunbar, is given in the appendix.

Dr W. M. Mackenzie in *The Poems of William Dunbar*, pp. 240-1, throws doubt on Dunbar's authorship of the poem. "Now on 20th December, 1501", he writes, "an entry occurs in the Scottish *Accounts of the Lord High Treasurer* of a payment to Master William Dunbar of £5 'quhilk wes payit to him efter he com furth of England'. This is plainly the amount of pension due to him at the previous Martinmas, and the entry would suggest that this was the later day of payment, and that Dunbar by that time was therefore back in Scotland, in which case he could not have been at the Lord Mayor's dinner or been the writer of the poem." But the entry in *C.T.S.*, VOL. II, p. 95 "Item, to Maister William Dunbar, quhilk wes payit to him eftir he come furth of Ingland . . . v. li" is not dated; the money may therefore have been paid at any time between 20 Dec. 1501, the latest preceding date, and Whitsunday (15 May) 1502, the earliest subsequent date. The passage in B.M. Cotton MS Vitellius A.xvi "sittyng at dyner one of the said Scottis givyng attendaunce upon a Bisshop Ambassadour the which was Reported to be a Prothonotary of Scotland and servaunt of the said Bishopp made this Balade folowyng" confirms Dr Mackenzie's doubts. "We have no other notice", he writes, "of Dunbar as a 'Protonotary'. . . . It is more difficult to account for him as a servant of Bishop Blacader of Glasgow, who is the 'Bishop Ambassador' referred to." These doubts are shared by Dunbar's latest biographer, Dr J. W. Baxter, in his *William Dunbar, a Biographical Study*, pp. 88-91, who, though he recognises that Andrew Forman was both the protonotary and the bishop ambassador referred to, comes to the amazing conclusion that the chronicler thought him to be the author of the poem. "The authority of the English chronicler, who plainly states that the poem in honour of London was made by the protonotary, who was certainly Andrew Forman, can scarcely be overturned without the support of very much better evidence than has been advanced. The evidence so far as it exists is quite definite and is against Dunbar's authorship." But if the unpunctuated passage quoted in evidence by Dr Baxter means anything at all, it means, not that the author was a protonotary giving attendance upon a bishop ambassador, but a Scot who was in attendance on a bishop ambassador reputed to be a protonotary, and who was a servant of the said bishop. Other evidence exists, however, of which both Dr W. M. Mackenzie and Dr J. W. Baxter seem to have been unaware. This interpretation is supported by the corresponding description of the Christmas festivities in the Guildhall Library MS: "In the Crystmesse weke ffollowyng the mayer had to dyner my lord Chaunceler, whom accompanyed the ffornamyd Scottysh ambassadours wyth many othyr honorable men. In tyme of which dyner a Scottysh preyst Syttyng at oon of the syde tablys made thys Balade here undyr ffoluyng" (fol. 292ᵛ). No title or author's name is given, but there is a marginal gloss "A Scottys Balad: Shaa maior" (fol. 293).

On 24 January 1502 the negotiations were brought to a successful conclusion. According to the marriage treaty the Princess was to be conducted to Lamberton Kirk, at Henry's expense, on or before 1 September 1503, and her marriage was to take place within the next fifteen days. As a marriage gift she was to receive on or before 1 July 1503 lands and castles having an annual rental of £2,000 sterling or £6,000 Scots. She was to have her own suite of twenty-four English attendants. Her husband was to maintain her at his own expense in the state befitting the wife of a king and the daughter of a queen, and in addition was to grant her an allowance of £1,000 Scots every year. Henry, for his part, was to pay as her dowry 30,000 angel nobles—equivalent to £10,000 sterling or £30,000 Scots—in three yearly instalments, but if the Princess died without issue before the period of three years had elapsed, he was to retain the unexpended balance of the sum.[1]

On the following day, in the palace of Richmond, before the King and Queen and a multitude of prelates and nobles, the Lady Margaret, "wittandly and of deliberate mind, having twelve Yeares compleat in Age", pledged herself to take the King of Scots for her husband, while the Earl of Bothwell, speaking as procurator, took her as wife and spouse for his sovereign, and vowed that he would forsake all other for her during his natural life—a vow which it was easier for Bothwell to make than for James to keep. "That don, the Trompetters standing on the Leds at the Chamber End, blew upp, and the lowd Noise of Minstrells played, in the best and most joyfullest manner."[2] At the same time the marriage was announced by a preacher at St Paul's Cross, and a *Te Deum* sung in the Cathedral. That night bonfires blazed throughout the city, and beside twelve of the biggest of them hogsheads of Gascon wine were set, "the which wyne was not long in drynkyng".[3]

---

[1] *Foedera*, VOL. XII, p. 797; *Cal. Doc. Scot.*, VOL. IV, No. 1680.
[2] Narrative of John Young, Somerset Herald, in Leland, *Collectanea*, VOL. IV, pp. 258-62.
[3] Kingsford, *Chronicles of London*, p. 255; Dunbar, *Poems*, ed. Laing, VOL. I, pp. 273-5; Great Chronicle of London, fol. 294.

Bacon, contemplating these festivities more than a century later, when the union that the King's counsellors dreaded had actually taken place, saw in this outburst of popular rejoicing the expression of "a secret instinct and inspiring (which many times runneth not only in the hearts of princes, but in the pulse and veins of people) touching the happiness thereby to ensue in time to come".[1] What Henry and the sager English statesmen welcomed at this period, however, was not the prospect of the union of the two countries at some remote and uncertain date, but the immediate elimination of every possible cause of war between them. For when the representatives of the two sovereigns signed the marriage treaty, they also signed a treaty for a perpetual peace, and an indenture providing for the suppression of disorder on the Borders. It seemed to be a "quite unwreckable, most impeccable, water-tight, fireproof" treaty. It provided for a good, real, sincere, true, entire, and firm peace, band, league, and confederation on land and sea, to endure for ever. Neither prince was to make, or allow war to be made, or advise or favour any war against his ally, or to harbour rebels against his ally, or give safe-conducts to his subjects except at his request. If any king or prince, or any person of lower rank should disturb the kingdom or possessions of either of the two contracting parties, his ally was required, should he be asked, to come to the help of his ally with such forces as he should stipulate, and at his expense. The contracting parties also bound themselves to advise and help each other without fraud or deceit, in spite of any other treaties to the contrary that they might have made with other rulers. Berwick was neither to be attacked by the Scots, nor made a base from which attacks on Scotland could be launched. The Emperor, the Kings of France, Spain, Denmark, and Portugal, the Archduke of Austria, the Dukes of Ferrara, Savoy, Gueldres, and Cleves, the Doge of Venice, and the Hanseatic League, were to be invited within eight months to become parties to the treaty. It was agreed, however, that as long as he did not actually invade England, the King of Scots could, without breaking the treaty,

---

[1] Bacon, *History of the Reign of King Henry VII* in *Works*, edd. J. Spedding, R. L. Ellis, and D. D. Heath, vol. VI, London 1858, p. 216.

help in the defence of the territory of any of these princes who might happen to be at war with England, while the King of England was equally at liberty to help an ally threatened by the Scots. Similarly, violence done to the Scots by the English on land or sea, river or lake without the cognisance of their respective monarchs, would not in itself be regarded as a breach of the treaty. The offended party, if a Scot, was required to lodge his complaint with the English Warden of the Marches, if an Englishman, with his Scottish counterpart. If the Warden neglected or refused to give him satisfaction, he could then complain to his own sovereign who would straightway write to his ally demanding redress. Even if redress were not granted, no breach of the treaty would ensue, but the prince whose subjects had been injured would be entitled within six months to issue letters of reprisal against all those dwelling on the Border, if the offence were committed on land, or against all harbours and creeks used by the malefactors, if it had been done at sea.

The death of either James or Margaret before the day fixed for Margaret's arrival in Scotland was not to invalidate the treaty. Future sovereigns were to renew it within six months of their accession. In the meantime, it was to be confirmed by both sovereigns taking their oath on the Gospels within three months of the marriage. Finally, before 1 July 1503, each sovereign was to ask the Pope for letters approving and confirming the treaty, and for a declaration that he would excommunicate the prince who broke it or allowed it to be broken, and would lay his kingdom under an interdict.[1]

The most important clause in the treaty stipulated that if an Englishman killed a Scot on the Borders, the English Warden of the Marches must arrest him, produce him at the next Warden Court, and, if he were found guilty in accordance with Border law and custom, hand him over to the Scottish Warden, who would be entitled to sentence him to death. It was a clause which James invoked nine years later, against the Lord High Admiral of England.

[1] Treaty in *Foedera*, VOL. XII, p. 793; *Cal. Doc. Scot.*, VOL. IV, No. 1681. Indenture in *Foedera*, VOL. XII, p. 800; *Cal. Doc. Scot.*, VOL. IV, No. 1682.

Before the end of February 1502 the ambassadors returned to Edinburgh; on 2 April Prince Arthur died.[1] There were now only two lives between the bride of the King of Scots and the English throne. Fresh doubts assailed King Henry: though James had accepted him as an ally, he had not promised to forsake all other, so on 27 June 1502 he requested his future son-in-law to repudiate, or at least to refrain from confirming, the ancient league with France. James assured his "richt dere and entierly belovit fader" that the confirmation would not be "skaithfull nor prejudiciale" to either of them. With this answer Henry had to be content.[2]

France was not the only old love whom James found it difficult to forsake; at the end of June he met Margaret Drummond in Falkland,[3] and for a time, it seemed, both his new mistress and his bride were forgotten. According to a tradition long current in the Drummond family, the King's advisers feared that this flaming up of an old passion might put the English marriage in jeopardy.[4] The danger, if danger there had been, was speedily removed. Before the end of the year Margaret Drummond died suddenly,[5] poisoned, it was whispered, by some who feared that the King would never marry as long as she lived. With her perished two of her sisters. All three were buried in the choir of Dunblane Cathedral, beneath three great blue stones, which may be seen to this day. Though there is probably no truth in the legend that James had set his heart on marrying her, but had been forced to yield to the opposition of the nobles, who wished him to marry an English princess, and of the clergy, who declared

[1] *Foedera*, VOL. XIII (1712), p. 54; *C.T.S.*, VOL. II, p. lvi.

[2] *Foedera*, VOL. XIII, p. 12, gives the text of James's letter of 12 July, which contains an abstract of Henry's letter of 27 June, and dates it 1502. Bain prints both an abstract of James's letter and the full text (*Cal. Doc. Scot.*, VOL. IV, No. 1728 and App. I, No. 37), but assigns the letter conjecturally to 1503.

[3] *C.T.S.*, VOL. II, p. 152.

[4] Hon. William Drummond, afterwards Viscount Strathallan, *The Genealogy of the most noble and ancient House of Drummond*, 1681, privately printed Edinburgh 1831, pp. 138-9.

[5] "The preistis that singis in Dunblane for Margret Drummond" received their first quarter's fee on 10 Feb. 1503. *C.T.S.*, VOL. II, p. 358.

QUEEN MARGARET TUDOR

Daniel Mytens (after an earlier portrait)   *Holyrood Palace*

that the lovers stood within the forbidden degrees of kinship,[1] it is certain that he did not regard her as a mere light of love. He ordered dirges to be sung for her in Edinburgh,[2] and year after year he feed two priests to say masses in Dunblane Cathedral for the repose of her soul.[3]

On 10 December 1502 before Henry's commissioners, Sir Thomas Darcy and Henry Babington, professor of theology, James swore by the Gospels and the canon of the Mass that he would faithfully observe the treaties.[4] At once he regretted his action; when he examined the form of the oath more carefully he observed that Henry was styled King of England and France. He insisted on the word "France" being erased, and on a declaration that he had not noticed it at first and had deliberately deleted it being witnessed and recorded in a notarial instrument.[5] In Edinburgh a week later he ratified the two treaties,[6] and also a declaration that he had sworn to observe them, and would never ask the Pope to release him from his oath.[7] But there was another hitch. Darcy, it would seem, resented the denial of the style "King of France" to his master, and refused to accept the treaties. So, although the ratifications of the treaties were exchanged on 20 December, it was Lyon King-of-Arms who took the copies signed by King James to the English court.[8] From Westminster Lyon towards the end of March passed to Rome to obtain the papal confirmation of the treaties.[9] A few days later the Bishops of Worcester and Hereford set out on the same errand.[10] They were successful: on 6 June Pope Alexander VI issued a bull reciting and confirming the treaties of peace and marriage.[11]

[1] Drummond, *Genealogy*, p. 139.

[2] On 29 Jan. 1503. *C.T.S.*, VOL. II, p. 248.

[3] *C.T.S.*, VOL. II, pp. 358, 372, 388, 410, 418, 436, 451.

[4] *Foedera*, VOL. XIII, p. 43; *Cal. Doc. Scot.*, VOL. IV, No. 1690.

[5] *Foedera*, VOL. XIII, pp. 43-7; *Cal. Doc. Scot.*, VOL. IV, Nos. 1691, 1692.

[6] *Foedera*, VOL. XIII, pp. 48-50; *Cal. Doc. Scot.*, VOL. IV, Nos. 1693, 1695.

[7] *Foedera*, VOL. XIII, p. 50; *Cal. Doc. Scot.*, VOL. IV, No. 1694.

[8] *Foedera*, VOL. XIII, p. 52; *Cal. Doc. Scot.*, VOL. IV, No. 1697; *C.T.S.*, VOL. II, p. 352.   [9] *C.T.S.*, VOL. II, pp. 361, 365.

[10] *Cal. Doc. Scot.*, VOL. IV, No. 1701.

[11] *Cal. Doc. Scot.*, VOL. IV, No. 1719.

The death of Queen Elizabeth at the beginning of February,[1] the death of James's brother, John, Earl of Mar, a month later[2] did not delay the preparations for the marriage. The accounts of the English Keeper of the Great Wardrobe[3] and the Scottish Lord High Treasurer bear witness to the anxiety of each monarch that his own—and his neighbour's—subjects should be fully aware of the importance of the occasion. As early as September of the previous year messengers had been despatched from Edinburgh to warn the gentlemen of the southern shires to provide themselves with festal attire "agane the mariage".[4] In the Castle the buzz of the armourer's lathe,[5] the clang of metal upon metal, proclaimed that fifteen armourers, who had arrived at the beginning of the year, were now hard at work.

The armourers came from France[6]; from Middelburg in Flanders came merchants bringing with them the chairs of state, the tapestries, the silver plate, velvets, satins, damasks, taffetas, furs, and cloth of gold, which the King had commissioned them to buy in Bruges.[7] The plate, the chairs, and the tapestries, including "ane pece of Hercules, ane pece of Marcus Corianus, tua pecis of Susanna sewit togiddir, ane covir for ane bed of Susanna, ane pece of Salamon"[8] were destined for his new palace of Holyroodhouse, where he was even now hurrying on the construction of a chapel and a forework or barbican.[9] To the plenishing of the palace, too, went some of the velvet and cloth of gold. Red and "purple-blue" velvet, costing £369, was used for the hangings of the Queen's chamber, seventy-seven and a quarter ells of cloth of gold, costing £386.5.0 were required for the canopy and curtains of her bed of state; there was cloth of gold to the value of more than £200 in each of the canopies of state provided for herself and her husband,[10] and for fourteen

[1] Hall, p. 497.   [2] *C.T.S.*, VOL. II, p. 366.
[3] *Cal. Doc. Scot.*, VOL. IV, App. I, No. 36.
[4] *C.T.S.*, VOL. II, p. 341.   [5] *C.T.S.*, VOL. II, p. 343.
[6] *C.T.S.*, VOL. II, pp. 281, 374.   [7] *C.T.S.*, VOL. II, p. 228.
[8] *C.T.S.*, VOL. II, p. 214.   [9] *C.T.S.*, VOL. II, pp. 269-74.
[10] *C.T.S.*, VOL. II, p. 214. A pound Scots at this time was worth only one third of a pound sterling.

cushions, some of blue and red velvet, some of crimson and cloth of gold, the Treasurer had to disburse £172.7.0.[1] But most of the rich stuffs went to adorn the persons of the King and the members of his household. The King, for example, had provided himself with two gowns of cloth of gold lined with fur, each costing more than £600[2]; of his eleven pages five were to wear with their new tawny satin doublets and crimson hose coats half of cloth of gold and half of blue velvet, and six coats of blue damask or of blue velvet only[3]; his master cook was presented with a gown of velvet lined with fur, a doublet of crimson satin, and black hose,[4] and his horse was caparisoned with cloth of gold at a cost of £63.[5]

If the cloth of gold and silver plate came from Flanders, the Queen's crown at least was home-made—fashioned by John Currour, an Edinburgh goldsmith, from eighty-three coins which the Treasurer handed over to him.[6]

Even the prodigal King became alarmed at the costliness of the preparations for the marriage. He resolved to rectify his financial position, not by cutting down his expenditure, but by discovering the philosopher's stone. The quest began in February, in Bishop Elphinstone's lodging, where he had installed a furnace and bellows for some anonymous alchemist, and provided him with five pounds of quicksilver.[7] It continued all through March, in Stirling Castle, where the alchemist, equipped with "ane pair of gret bellyis", mixed and beated the quicksilver, litharge, borax, and aquavitae which the King had bought for him,[8] and it seems to have ended before 1 June, when "Quinta Essencia" the alchemist, who ten weeks earlier had received a fee of eighteen pounds, was given a beggarly eighteen shillings.[9]

Long before this the restless monarch had galloped off to the south-west, to greet his old mistress, Janet Kennedy, in Bothwell Castle,[10] and to fleet the time with a new one, the "L.A." and

[1] C.T.S., VOL. II, p. 214.
[2] C.T.S., VOL. II, p. 208.
[3] C.T.S., VOL. II, pp. 209-10.
[4] C.T.S., VOL. II, p. 208.
[5] C.T.S., VOL. II, p. 214.
[6] C.T.S., VOL. II, p. 206.
[7] C.T.S., VOL. II, p. 359.
[8] C.T.S., VOL. II, pp. 360-2.
[9] C.T.S., VOL. II, pp. 362, 374.
[10] C.T.S., VOL. II, p. 366.

"M.L.A." of certain discreet entries in the Treasurer's Accounts.[1] Meanwhile, on 4 May, Henry had ratified the marriage treaty.[2] At the end of the third week of May the King hurried back to Edinburgh to receive Lord Dacre and the Dean of St Paul's, who with two other commissioners had come north to take seisin of the lands assigned to the young Queen.[3] On 24 May he issued letters patent, granting to his bride Ettrick Forest and Newark Castle, the Earldom of Dunbar, but not its castle, and the lordship of Cockburnspath, the palace and lordship of Methven, the castle and lordship of Doune, the palace and shire of Linlithgow, and the castle and shire of Stirling,[4] and on 6 June, after the English envoys, acting as attorneys for the young Queen, had visited the various castles and burghs and taken seisin of them, he confirmed the grant.[5]

July had come; the stage was set. In the courtyard of Holyroodhouse the workmen were still hammering together "eastland boards" to make stands for the spectators of the tournaments.[6] Sir Thomas Galbraith, chaplain and illuminator, had left his parchments, and was gilding the royal arms over the new fore yett[7]; in some corner of the palace William Dunbar was meditating a laureate ode. Not till the end of the month did the King return to his capital.[8] He had been flitting about the country despatching messengers—to the Earl of Morton and the Master of Angus to remind their ladies that they must receive the Queen, to the Countess Marischal and Lady Glamis with similar reminders,[9] to the several sheriffdoms to warn the nobles and gentlemen there "agane the Queenis cumming"[10] and to England to find whether the bride and her retinue were near the border. His impatience did not keep him from seeking consolation in the

[1] C.T.S., VOL. II, pp. 370, 380.   [2] Cal. Doc. Scot., VOL. IV, No. 1703.

[3] C.T.S., VOL. II, p. 372.

[4] Foedera, VOL. XIII, p. 62; Cal. Doc. Scot., VOL. IV, No. 1706.

[5] Foedera, VOL. XIII, p. 66 (Cal. Doc. Scot., VOL. IV, No. 1709); p. 68 (No. 1711); p. 69 (No. 1710); p. 70 (No. 1712); p. 71 (No. 1713); p. 73 (No. 1714); p. 74 (No. 1718).

[6] C.T.S., VOL. II, pp. 273-4.   [7] C.T.S., VOL. II, pp. 383, 416.

[8] C.T.S., VOL. II, p. 381.   [9] C.T.S., VOL. II, p. 379.

[10] C.T.S., VOL. II, pp. 380-1.

arms of his latest mistress.[1] For once Dunbar was not amused:
he inserted a direct rebuke to his master in his courtly epithalamium:

> And sen thow art a king, thow be discreit;
>   Herb without vertew thow hald nocht of sic pryce
> As herb of vertew and of odor sueit;
>   And lat no nettill vyle, and full of vyce
>   Hir fallow to the gudly flour-de-lyce;
> Nor latt no wyld weid, full of churlicheness,
> Compair hir till the lilleis nobilness:
> Nor hald non odir flour in sic denty
>   As the fresche Rois, of collour reid and quhyt;
> For gife thow dois, hurt is thyne honesty;
>   Considdering that no flour is so perfyt,
>   So full of vertew, plesans and delyt,
> So full of blisfull angeilik bewty,
> Imperiall birth, honour, and dignite.[2]

On the eighth of the month, at Colly Weston, King Henry bade
farewell to his daughter.[3] He had done all that he could to make
his subjects sensible of the greatness of her destiny; he had committed her to the care of the Earl of Surrey, Lord Treasurer of
England, and his countess, had arranged for companies of nobles
and gentlemen to escort her over the various stages of her journey,
and had ordered the sheriffs of every county and the mayors of
every town through which she was to pass to receive her in a
fashion befitting her new dignity. The Queen, as we may now
call her, richly dressed, rode on a palfrey, which she usually exchanged for a horse litter when she entered a town of importance.
Behind her rode her ladies with their squires, followed by heralds,
minstrels, and trumpeters, and by the Master of the Horse with
his attendants, whose duty it was to clear a space about the
cavalcade so that all might see her. With the company went
James's ambassador, the Bishop of Moray.[4]

We need not follow her progress through Grantham, by way

---

[1] C.T.S., VOL. II, pp. 382, 384.
[2] "The Thrissil and the Rois", ll. 134-47.
[3] Young's narrative in Leland, Collectanea, VOL. IV, p. 265.
[4] Leland, Collectanea, VOL. IV, pp. 266-8.

of Newark, Doncaster, and Pontefract, to York: it is all set down in the narrative of Young, the Somerset Herald, who accompanied her. "Through all the goode Townes and Villages wher she past," he tells us, "all the Bells were rong dayly. And by the Way cam the Habitants of the Countrey for to see the noble Company, bryngyng grette Vessells full of Drynk, and gyffing the same to them that Nedde had of it, saying, that if better they had had, better they should have brought." When she drew near to York on 15 July she was met by the Earl of Northumberland, robed in crimson velvet "more like a prince than a subject,"[1] accompanied by his own herald and master of the horse, and followed by a great company of velvet-clad knights, the harness of whose horses glittered with gold and silver. She rode into the city to the sound of "Trompetts, Mynstrells, Sakebowtts, and High Wods [i.e. hautbois or oboes] retentyssynge", to be received by the Mayor and aldermen, "honnestly arayd in Gownys of Scarlatte", and conducted through the crowded streets to the Minster. All the bells in the city rang that evening, making "grett Melodie for to here", and when she dined in the Archbishop's palace on the following night "Trompetts and other Instruments rang to the Auncyenne Manere, lasting the said Dynner". Much the same scenes were enacted in Durham, Newcastle, and Berwick, which she entered on 29 July.[2]

On 1 August, at the head of a brilliant company, she was borne in her litter to Lamberton Kirk, where she was received by the Archbishop of Glasgow and the Earl of Bothwell on bended knees, and conducted to a tent which the King had ordered to be prepared for her. With Blacader and Bothwell came a great company of lords and gentlemen who in their "apparel and ryche jewels and massy chaynes" far outshone the Englishmen.[3]

Northumberland the Magnificent rode off, having "maid his Devor at his Departynge of Gambads and Lepps", and the Queen, separated from her retinue, was conveyed down precipitous paths to a lonely and gloomy fortalice—Fast Castle, the Wolf's Craig of *The Bride of Lammermoor*. From Fast Castle, over country so

---

[1] Hall, p. 498.   [2] Leland, *Collectanea*, VOL. IV, pp. 268-79.
[3] Leland, *Collectanea*, VOL. IV, pp. 279-81.

rough that in places roads had to be specially made for the wagons and carriages, she went by Dunbar—where "they schott Ordonnaunce for the Luffe of hyr"—and Haddington to the castle of Dalkeith, which she reached on 3 September.[1]

And now King James, his light loves banished, his dead mistress thrust from his mind, resolved to see his bride. Arraying himself in crimson velvet and cloth of gold, but leaving his beard untrimmed, he sallied out from Edinburgh at the head of a cavalcade of nobles and prelates, galloped into the courtyard of the castle, and was escorted to her room. She met him in the doorway at the head of her retinue. Whether he was charmed or not by "the freshest queen of flowers", James set himself to charm the frightened child, and win her affection. He bowed low before her, kissed her, and after he had kissed her ladies and welcomed the Earl of Surrey, led her aside and talked to her for a long time. It was noted as a sign of his regard for her that he remained uncovered all through the conversation. After supper the minstrels struck up, and the Queen and the Countess of Surrey danced to their music. The King rode back through the darkness to Edinburgh, "varey well countent of so fayr Metting". The Queen had less cause for content: that night her palfreys were burned alive in a fire which broke out in the castle.[2]

She was moved to Newbattle, from which a procession of dignitaries, including the Archbishop of York, set out to meet the King. But James "flying as the Bird that syks hyr Pray", avoided them, slipped into the castle, and, with one or two attendants, made his way to her chamber, where he found her playing cards. While they were talking, the procession of dignitaries returned. Then followed low reverences and courteous speeches, music and dancing. The Queen and the Countess danced a basse dance,[3] Sir Edward Stanley sang a ballad to his own accompaniment on the clavichord, and the King himself showed his skill on both clavichord and lute. After he had kissed the Queen—and all her ladies—he leaped on horseback without putting foot into the

[1] Leland, *Collectanea*, VOL. IV, pp. 281-2.
[2] Leland, *Collectanea*, VOL. IV, p. 283; *C.T.S.*, VOL. II, p. 385.
[3] A stately dance, in which the feet were glided, not lifted.

stirrup, and "incontynent ... sporred, follow who myght", back to Edinburgh.[1] Two more evenings passed in the same fashion,[2] and then, on the morning of 7 September, the Queen, dressed in cloth of gold and black velvet, set out in her litter for Edinburgh. Before she left Dalkeith she was presented with three palfreys, sent by the King to replace those that had been burned; she had hardly gone a mile when another messenger met her with a tame hart, also from the King, and proposed that it should be coursed; when she was half-way between Dalkeith and Edinburgh the King himself appeared, mounted on a bay horse caparisoned with cloth of gold, "rennynge as he wolde renne after the Hayre". Behind him rode the three ambassadors who had negotiated the marriage treaty, Blacader, Forman, and Bothwell, followed by a great company of horsemen "in Jaketts of Cloth of Golde, of Velvett, and of Damaske, figured of Golde and of many Colours". The King galloped up to the Queen's litter, leapt from his horse and kissed her, and then, after talking to her for a little, mounted another charger, caparisoned in crimson and gold, without putting foot in the stirrup. He had meant to ride through his capital on it, with the Queen perched behind him, but the horse grew restive, and he was forced to dismount and share one of the palfreys with her.[3]

The first of the pageants designed for the Queen's entertainment was staged on a stretch of greensward about half a mile to the south of the city. Here two knights, mounted and clad in complete armour, fought for the love of a lady, first with lances, then with swords, till the King rode up, calling "*Paix!*" and parted them. As the royal party approached the city, they were met not only by crowds of burgesses and country folk in holiday attire, but by two sombre processions, of brown-robed Franciscan and black-robed Dominican friars. The King and his bride kissed the relics which the friars proffered, then, to the sound of trumpets, they passed under a turreted gatehouse of painted wood. From a window above the arch leant an angel, who presented

[1] Leland, *Collectanea*, VOL. IV, pp. 283-4.
[2] Leland, *Collectanea*, VOL. IV, pp. 284-6.
[3] Leland, *Collectanea*, VOL, IV, pp. 286-7.

the keys of the city to the Queen, while in the turrets other angels sang joyously,[1] perhaps those verses which have the authentic ring of Dunbar:

> Now fayre, fayrest off every fayre,
> Princess most pleasant and preclare,
> The lustyest one alyve that byne,
>   Welcum of Scotland to be Quene!
>
> Younge tender plant of pulcritud,
> Descendyd of Imperyalle blode;
> Freshe fragrant floure of fayre hede shene
>   Welcum of Scotland to be Quene![2]

Another poet was waiting to welcome her within the gate—Gavin Douglas, Provost of the Collegiate Church of St Giles, bringing with him, not an ode, but an arm of the saint, "the wiche was presented to the Kynge for to kysse, wherof he did as before, and began to syng *Te Deum Laudamus*".[3]

To the sound of bells the procession wound up the narrow crowded West Bow, under houses hung with tapestry, to the Mercat Cross, which had been newly painted. Wine spouted from a fountain nearby, distracting the attention of the spectators from a stage on which were presented three oddly selected episodes—the Judgment of Paris, the Annunciation, and the Marriage of the Virgin. Thence the company rode down the High Street to the Nether Bow Port, where on four thrones sat the Four Virtues—Justice, Force, Temperance, and Prudence, triumphant over Nero, Holofernes, Epicurus, and Sardanapalus, who writhed at their feet, and on to the Abbey of Holyrood, where the King's brother, the Archbishop of St Andrews, with the Bishops and Abbots of Scotland, arrayed in their richest vestments, stood waiting to receive the Queen.[4]

On the following day, 8 August 1503, in the church of

---

[1] Leland, *Collectanea*, VOL. IV, pp. 288-9.

[2] B.M. Appendix to Royal MSS, No. 58, fol. 15ᵛ. Anonymous: first ascribed to Dunbar by David Laing. Dunbar, *Poems*, ed. Laing, VOL. I, pp. 280, 301.

[3] Leland, *Collectanea*, VOL. IV, p. 289. Douglas became Provost of St Giles' before 11 March 1503.   [4] Leland, *Collectanea*, VOL. IV, pp. 289-91.

Holyrood Abbey, the marriage, so long debated, so momentous in its results, was at last celebrated. Though a substantial fragment of James's palace of Holyroodhouse still remains, it is impossible at this time of day to determine the whereabouts of the Great Chamber where the King, sitting under a canopy of blue and gold, with his prelates on his right hand and his nobles on his left, received Henry's ambassadors. The cloisters through which the wedding guests filed from the palace to the church have long since been swept away; the nave of the great church is roofless, its windows empty, its bare walls black with grime; of the choir, where the King and his bride knelt together on their cushions of cloth of gold, only the wall foundations and the stumps of columns are left. It is difficult to imagine the scene when the great piers still rose unbroken to "the high embowed roof", and when the autumn sunlight, streaming through the unshattered glass, glittered on the sculptured figures of saint and angel, and added a richer dye to silks and damask, to velvet and cloth of gold. In the north aisle, beside the font, the Queen stood between the Archbishop of York and the Earl of Surrey. A portrait preserved at Compton Wynyates helps us to see her as she was then—a short, lumpish girl with heavy features and a sullen, or frightened, expression. Her hair hung loose beneath the crown that Currour had made for her; the train of her robe of white damask, embroidered with gold and lined with crimson velvet, was carried by the Countess of Surrey. Behind her stood the lords and ladies who had come with her from England, each pair of English ladies accompanied by two Scottish ladies of high degree. Next the Archbishop of Glasgow, followed by Elphinstone and the other prelates, filed slowly into the choir. Last came the King, preceded by Lord Hamilton, bearing the sword of state, and accompanied by his brother, the Archbishop of St Andrews, and followed by the great officers of the Crown with their insignia, and a lengthy procession of lords and knights, many of them wearing gold chains over their robes. No artist has limned their features, they are only shapes in a ghostly pageant, names in the *Scots Peerage*. Contemporary portraits, however, have made us familiar with the appearance of James, with the broad forehead, large eyes, high cheekbones, and lean, pale face shadowed by a mass of straight reddish hair that gave him the look more of a poet than of a king. That day he was decked like a king; over his crimson hose and doublet of cloth of gold he wore a loose jacket of crimson and black, and over this again a robe of white damask, embroidered with gold. On his head he wore a bonnet of black velvet, in which there glowed a single great ruby.

The King and his bride advanced under the rood-screen to the choir, where the Archbishop of Glasgow performed the marriage ceremony. Immediately afterwards the Archbishop of York read the papal bulls permitting the marriage. Then followed the Litany, and Mass; before the Canon was recited the Queen was anointed, and presented with her husband's sceptre.[1]

The wedding ushered in five days of revelry, which were long remembered. The festivities began with a great dinner in the palace, when to the sound of trumpets, and music provided by "Mynstrolls of many Sortes", the Queen was served, first with "a wyld Borres Hed gylt, within a fayr Platter", then with fifty or sixty other dishes, including roast crane, swan, and a jelly decorated with the arms of Scotland and England.[2] Of the minstrels of many sorts the King seemed to admire those who played most vigorously: he rewarded "five lowd menestrales" with the sum of twenty-eight pounds.[3] After dinner there was music and dancing and a display of conjuring within the palace, while without bonfires blazed in the streets.[4] On the following day two different entertainments were offered: an acrobat gave a display of rope-dancing in the palace courtyard, to the delight of the King and his guests,[5] who watched him from the windows, and the Countess of Surrey and her daughter clipped the King's beard. They were well rewarded, the Countess with fifteen ells of cloth of gold, and Lady Grey with the same quantity

[1] Leland, *Collectanea*, VOL. IV, pp. 291-4.
[2] Leland, *Collectanea*, VOL. IV, pp. 294-6; Guildhall MS Great Chronicle of London, fols. 300ᵛ-1, where the names of 52 dishes are given.
[3] *C.T.S.*, VOL. II, p. 387.
[4] Leland, *Collectanea*, VOL. IV, p. 296.
[5] Leland, *Collectanea*, VOL. IV, p. 297; *C.T.S.*, VOL. II, p. 387.

of gold-embroidered damask.[1] Next day, after Mass, the King
gave the accolade to forty-one knights, then, turning to the
Queen, said, "These are your knights." This ceremony inaugur-
ated three days of jousting in the palace courtyard, which Surrey,
sitting apart with the Earl of Bothwell, watched with a cold,
professional eye. The festivities ended on Sunday, 13 August,
when after Mass James created Lord Hamilton Earl of Arran,
Lord Graham Earl of Montrose, and Lord Kilmaurs Earl of
Glencairn. After the King's guests had dined and watched a
morality enacted by three guisers, they danced a few dances and
then filed through the cloisters to be present at evensong. "And
that doon, every Man went his Way."[2]

"Which of us has his desire, or having it, is satisfied?" Already
the Queen had written a letter of bitter complaint to her father.
Surrey and Forman managed everything, she declared; they put
the King's pleasure before her own, and browbeat her Chamberlain. "God send me comford to hys pleasur," she continued,
"and that I and myne that ben lefftt her with me be well entretid.
. . . I would I wer wyt your Grace now . . . our Lord han you
en ys kepyng. Wrytyn wyt the hand of your humble douter
Margaret."[3] Already the King was meditating a visit to the
shrine of St Duthac in Tain, and to another shrine, at Darnaway.[4]
His overgenerous hospitality—he spent £2,200 on wine alone[5]—
had failed to dazzle his southern guests. They sneered at the rude
profusion which they witnessed, and "returned into their countrey, gevynge more prayse to the manhoode, than to the good
maner and nurture of Scotlande".[6]

[1] *C.T.S.*, VOL. II, p. 314.

[2] *C.T.S.*, VOL. II, pp. 385-9; Leland, *Collectanea*, VOL. IV, pp. 296-300.

[3] *Original Letters illustrative of English History*, ed. Sir H. Ellis, 1st series,
London 1824, VOL. I, pp. 41-3.

[4] He left for Tain at the end of September, and seems to have visited
Darnaway early in October.

[5] *R. Scac. S.*, VOL. XII, p. 181.

[6] Hall, p. 498.

V

SCOTLAND IN 1503

JAMES was now the son-in-law of Henry VII, and the heir, twice removed, to the crown of England. Already, having brought his kingdom to comparative peace and comparative prosperity, he had begun to play a part in European affairs. In the previous year, at the prayer of his uncle, King John, whose queen had been captured by the rebellious Swedes, he sent two ships and two thousand men to Denmark. We shall see him, in 1505, protesting to another kinsman, Charles, Duke of Gueldres, against his too hospitable reception of Edmund de la Pole, nephew of Edward IV and pretender to the English throne.

But his realm was only comparatively peaceful: he could not as yet give rein to his ambition, and realise his dream of imposing peace upon the rest of Europe, and leading the armies of Christendom against the Turk. After the war on the Borders came to an end, he had been forced to lead more than one expedition to the Western Isles. As we shall see, the reversal of his policy of conciliation in 1498, signalised by the wholesale revocation of charters which he had granted a few years earlier to the former vassals of the Lord of the Isles, had created wide-spread discontent, which before the end of 1503 was to flare up into open rebellion.

But when it came, the rebellion would affect only the fringes of his kingdom; we shall not find, as in the reign of James II, a rebellious island magnate acting in concert with a Douglas or an Earl of Crawford. For one thing, there could be no question of the King's popularity. His very faults—his extravagance, his love of display—endeared him to a people who, in the words of Pedro de Ayala, were "vain and ostentatious by nature", spending "all they have to keep up appearances".[1] He was the epitome of the

---

[1] *Cal. of State Papers, Spain*, VOL. I, No. 210.

Scotland of his day: every one of his subjects saw in him something to admire, something that he would copy if he could.

Though much more than his father he was "given to Buildings and trimming up of Chappels, Halls, and Gardens,"[1] his subjects did not object. Military necessity, they recognised, dictated the rebuilding of the frontier fortress of Dunbar,[2] and the building of new, or the repair of old castles at Inverness,[3] Tarbert,[4] and Loch Kilkerran in Kintyre.[5] It was not military necessity that dictated the building of the new palace of Holyroodhouse. The foregate or barbican, the chapel, the great hall, the gallery—a long, corridor-like apartment, then a novel feature in a great house—had been built before the arrival of Queen Margaret,[6] but it was not till 1505 that the Tower—probably the present north-west wing of the Palace—was completed.[7] Edinburgh Castle had for the time ceased to be a royal residence, and was used instead as an arsenal and store. Here the national archives were kept; here was the treasure house with the crown jewels and the King's scanty reserves of bullion. "He is not able to put money into his strong boxes," said de Ayala.[8]

By the addition of two towers and a barbican James made Stirling a more formidable stronghold; he also made it a pleasanter place to live in. He completed the decoration of a new palace, "the Kingis hous", within its walls, and surrounded it with orchards and gardens.[9] The south side of Linlithgow Palace— the chapel, the hall adjoining, and the long galleries with their square-headed "Tudor" windows, were also built by his orders.[10]

---

[1] Drummond of Hawthornden, *History of the Lives and Reigns of the five James's, Works*, p. 61 (of James III).

[2] *C.T.S.*, VOL. I, pp. 323, 328, 330-1, 334-5, 337-9, 342-3, 345, 351, 355, 357, 359, 364, 368, 389.   [3] *C.T.S.*, VOL. I, p. 376.

[4] *C.T.S.*, VOL. I, p. 215; *R. Scac. S.*, VOL. XI, p. 162.

[5] *C.T.S.*, VOL. I, p. clxv; *R. Scac. S.*, VOL. XI, p. lxv.

[6] *C.T.S.*, VOL. II, pp. 87, 269, 273.

[7] *C.T.S.*, VOL. III, Edinburgh 1901, pp. 84, 85, 87.

[8] *Cal. of State Papers, Spain*, VOL. I, No. 210.

[9] *C.T.S.*, VOL. I, pp. 276, 277, 278, 279, 280, 281, 282, 283, 284, 286, 291, 297, 303, 306, 307, 322, 323, 336, 355, 364, 367, 370, 372, 377, 384, 386, 387, 389, 390; VOL. II, pp. 81-5, 269-81.   [10] *C.T.S.*, VOL. I, pp. 195, 204.

Gardens were laid out, beehives bought, orchards planted, and the whole enclosed by a "dyke".[1]

Masons were busy at Falkland too, where in 1501 the erection of the new palace was begun beside the old castle.[2] Falkland was to be, not a fortress, but a hunting lodge, set in the centre of a game preserve provided with "stanks" or fishponds,[3] and a "deir fald" for captive deer.[4] Falkland served the royal table at Holyroodhouse with delicacies like swans and wild boars. It supplied, too, the deer which were coursed in the King's Park. They were caught in nets and conveyed to Edinburgh in a litter.[5] The monarch who coursed tame deer regarded foxes as vermin: on one occasion he paid six and sixpence for a trap "to sla foxes in the park of Faukland".[6]

In some of the more distant royal castles too, a new hall or "palace" was added to the old towers—at Methven in 1496,[7] at Lochmaben in 1504,[8] and at Dingwall in 1507.[9]

Gifts of "drinksilver" to the masons at the royal palaces testified to the King's interest in their work. Usually he gave them a shilling or two each, but on one occasion he rewarded the masons of Linlithgow for the successful "pendin of thre voutis" —construction of three vaulted roofs—with three unicorns or fifty-four shillings.[10] Characteristic too, of the King's consideration for his less fortunate subjects was his payment of fourteen shillings "to ane masoun in Faukland that wes pit fra the werk".[11]

Though the Treasurer might shake his head over the expenditure on building of sums that were vast in proportion to the King's actual resources—over six hundred pounds, for example, was spent on Linlithgow in 1490,[12] between two and three thou-

---

[1] *C.T.S.*, VOL. I, pp. 176, 195, 380.
[2] *C.T.S.*, VOL. II, pp. 87-9; VOL. III, pp. 82, 295, 298.
[3] *C.T.S.*, VOL. II, p. 461.
[4] *C.T.S.*, VOL. II, pp. 424, 425; VOL. III, pp. 171, 298.
[5] *C.T.S.*, VOL. II, pp. 120, 407; VOL. III, pp. 171, 172, 181, 348, 356, 410, 411, 414, 415.
[6] *C.T.S.*, VOL. III, p. 171.   [7] *C.T.S.*, VOL. I, p. 276.
[8] *C.T.S.*, VOL. II, p. 278.   [9] *R. Scac. S.*, VOL. XII, p. 516.
[10] *C.T.S.*, VOL. I, p. 181.   [11] *C.T.S.*, VOL. II, p. 128.
[12] *C.T.S.*, VOL. I, pp. 195, 204.

sand pounds on Stirling in 1501,[1] over eight hundred pounds on Falkland in 1505[2]—James's subjects were roused only to emulation. It was not only in the royal castles that a new "palace" or hall was added to the older tower, and in the burghs the prosperous merchants were building houses fit to receive the King himself. But, except for the introduction here and there—for example in the St Leonard's College Chapel in St Andrews—of the square-headed late Perpendicular window, there was nothing new in the architectural fashions of James's reign. Though some of his masons were Frenchmen, their work does not reveal that flowering of medieval strength into Renaissance grace displayed at Blois or Amboise; there is rather, as in the chapel of Linlithgow Palace with its five tall lancet windows, a reversion to an earlier style.

Much of what James built has been altered out of recognition; much has disappeared. The Falkland that we know today—a French château miraculously set down in Fife—is indeed James's palace, but remodelled by the foreign craftsmen imported by his successor. The Palace in Stirling Castle is an attempt at the same miracle made by their heavy-handed Scottish imitators. Of the Palace of Holyroodhouse only the tower remains; the rest was burned down by Cromwell's soldiers in 1650; the foirwerk or barbican escaped only to be pulled down by a progressive burgh council a hundred years later. His Linlithgow indeed survives, but roofless, with unglazed windows, and naked walls.

Its walls were often bare, its windows empty of glass, and its halls and galleries deserted even in James's time, for, as he never spent more than a few weeks in any of his palaces, he did not deem it necessary to have them completely furnished. When, with his household of almost one hundred persons, he moved from Edinburgh to Linlithgow or Stirling, plate, tapestries, beds, and even glass windows were brought from the *garde meuble* in the Castle or from Holyroodhouse, "tursit" in carts or on pack-horses, and sent before him.

Wherever else his restless spirit might drive him, he spent the greater part of the year in Edinburgh, Stirling, and Linlithgow.

[1] *C.T.S.*, VOL. II, pp. 81-2.   [2] *C.T.S.*, VOL. III, p. 82.

He usually returned to one of them for Christmas, Linlithgow in the earlier years of his reign,[1] and afterwards Edinburgh,[2] though in Melrose in 1496,[3] Aberdeen in 1497,[4] and Arbroath in 1502[5] his minstrels and guisers disturbed the peace of monastery or bishop's palace. Lent sometimes found him in Stirling, not in the Castle, but in the convent of the Observantine friars, dressed in the brown robe of their order. Before his marriage he usually remained in Stirling till Easter was over, though sometimes, obedient to the admonition of Dunbar, he hastened from Stirling "quhair nowdir plesance nor delyt is" to Edinburgh "the mirry toun".

It was not mere restlessness that made the King move from Edinburgh to Linlithgow, from Linlithgow to Stirling, and from Stirling back again to Edinburgh. His household, which included grooms and clerks, ushers and cup-bearers, turnspits, kitchen varlets, cooks, and an "archcook", keepers of the napery, the candles, and the coals, a barber, a tailor, a cutler, a buyer of fish and a dresser of poultry and capons, amounted in all to about one hundred male and female servants. Many of them were of gentle birth: in 1499 his carver was the Master of Gray,[6] his cupbearer the Master of Hume,[7] his pantler Sir Patrick Crichton,[8] and his Master of the Stables Sir Adam Hepburn.[9] Sir Archibald Edmonston was keeper of the wine-cellar,[10] and his son, James Edmonston, principal keeper of the King's silver plate.[11] Their wages were modest: with one exception none of them had more than twenty merks a year; four merks was a more usual figure, and the kitchen varlets had to be content with two. But some of

---

[1] C.T.S., VOL. I, pp. 99-101 (1488), 171 (1490), 183-4 (1491), 257, 267 (1495).

[2] C.T.S., VOL. I, p. 239 (1494); VOL. II, pp. 129 (1501), 257 (1502), 411-2 (1503), 470-1 (1504); VOL. III, pp. 358-9 (1506); VOL. IV (Edinburgh 1902), p. 180 (1511).   [3] C.T.S., VOL. I, pp. 308-9.

[4] C.T.S., VOL. I, p. 374.   [5] C.T.S., VOL. II, p. 352.

[6] R. Scac. S., VOL. XI, pp. 163, 246, 257.

[7] R. Scac. S., VOL. XI, pp. 206, 246, 257.

[8] R. Scac. S., VOL. XI, pp. 202, 246, 255.

[9] R. Scac. S., VOL. XI, pp. 97, 341.

[10] R. Scac. S., VOL. XI, pp. 161, 246, 255.   [11] Ibid.

I

them could count on substantial money gifts at Christmas or Easter in addition to the customary gifts of clothing, and none of them had any need to spend a penny on food or lodging. They had free quarters in the palace, and lived on the provisions that had been piled up in the great vaulted storerooms underneath. At a time when the King's tenants paid their rents mainly in kind, and—transport being difficult and dear—delivered them at the nearest royal castle, it was easier for the King and his household to make the round of the places where the provisions had been stored than for the provisions to be brought to them. There was another reason; King and court fled from the pestiferous odours that invaded a royal palace when it was occupied by a large company for more than two or three weeks, and returned only when the choked garderobe flues had been cleared out and fresh rushes strewn in all the rooms. For the sanitation of a sixteenth-century palace was far inferior to that of a thirteenth-century monastery. The King, however, possessed at least one bath—a "pipe" or barrel bought for three shillings, and sawn down into the requisite shape at the cost of another three.[1]

But restless as he was, determined to "fill the unforgiving minute", De Ayala described him as a wonderful linguist, able to speak Latin, French, German, Flemish, Italian, and Spanish, in addition to "the language of the savages who live in some parts of Scotland and on the islands", a student of the Bible and other devout books, as well as of profane histories, of which he had read many, both in Latin and in French.[2] The diplomatic De Ayala certainly exaggerated the King's intellectual accomplishments even more than he did the size and population of his country: Buchanan came much nearer the truth when he described James as *ingenio quidem acri, sed vitio temporis ab literis inculto*[3]—of keen but uncultivated intelligence. His purchase in 1503 of some score of books,[4] mostly philosophical and theological works, has been cited as proof of his devotion to scholarship,

---

[1] *C.T.S.*, VOL. II, pp. 112, 439.

[2] *Cal. of State Papers, Spain*, VOL. I, No. 210.

[3] Buchanan, *Rerum Scoticarum historia*, BK. XIII, in *Opera omnia*, ed. Ruddiman, VOL. I, p. 255.   [4] *C.T.S.*, VOL. II, pp. 359–64.

but most of them were destined for the Observantine Friary, not for the royal library.

His gently born subjects, who watched him shooting with the long bow,[1] the cross bow,[2] and hand-culverin,[3] playing a vigorous game of tennis,[4] or the less strenuous "lang bowlis",[5] saw in him nothing of the scholar or recluse. Better than books, he loved horses and dogs. He was a fearless horseman, capable of riding from Stirling to Aberdeen, and thence to Elgin, in one day; capable, too, of mastering the most vicious animals. He treated a foreign dog-fancier, Jean Caupene, the "John de Cawpanis" of the Treasurer's Accounts, as if he had been an ambassador, maintained him, with his servants and dogs, and gave him two hundred pounds and a letter of recommendation to Louis XII when he returned to France.[6] But more than dogs or horses he loved hawks. Once, while he was still in his teens, he paid one hundred and eighty pounds for a single hawk,[7] and though he never repeated this youthful folly, he spent considerable sums every year, either in buying hawks, or in rewarding those who brought hawks as gifts to him, or in defraying the expenses of falconers sent into the remotest mountains and islands of his realm to capture hawks and bring them to the mews at Craigforth or Inchkeith. His falconers accompanied him on almost all his journeys—even his pilgrimages to the shrines of St Duthac or St Ninian.

We can imagine the King, mounted on his white courser, with hawk on wrist, riding home through the gathering darkness. We

[1] *C.T.S.*, VOL. I, pp. 333, 352; VOL. II, pp. 438, 450; VOL. III, pp. 154, 339; VOL. IV, pp. 327, 334.

[2] *C.T.S.*, VOL. I, pp. 92, 175, 181, 194, 345, 352; VOL. II, pp. 102, 359, 446, 449, 452, 457, 466, 475; VOL. III, pp. 183, 196, 204, 362, 373, 374, 375; VOL. IV, pp. 85, 90, 326, 327, 343, 415.

[3] *C.T.S.*, VOL. I, pp. 122, 181, 350; VOL. IV, pp. 97, 98, 101, 102, 103, 105, 106, 111, 112, 115, 121, 122, 129, 130, 132, 317.

[4] *C.T.S.*, VOL. I, pp. 275, 277, 360, 386, 389; VOL. II, pp. 150, 152, 153.

[5] *C.T.S.*, VOL. I, p. 332; VOL. II, p. 112; VOL. III, p. 392.

[6] *C.T.S.*, VOL. II, pp. 204, 205, 207, 305, 306, 360, 363, 365, 368, 373, 377, 378, 380, 383, 394, 395, 396, 397, 398, 400, 401, 409; VOL. III, pp. 35, 92, 95, 147, 154, 162, 163.   [7] *C.T.S.*, VOL. I, p. 95.

can imagine him entering the great hall of the palace—Linlithgow, it may be—and to the sound of trumpets washing his hands in a silver basin which a henchman—a youth of gentle birth—presents to him, and seating himself at the supper table. It was placed on a dais a few inches high, strewn, like the rest of the floor, with bent grass, though under the King's feet a lyare or rich carpet was placed. Behind him blazing logs were piled high on a great stone fireplace; the firelight reddened the linen tablecloth, and gleamed on the escutcheons in the timber roof, on the windows set high up in the walls, and on the silver plate, platters, goblets, bowls, and saltfats, placed for use on the table or for display on the carpeted shelves of the "copburd". He could see on the walls to right and left of him the familiar tapestries that had been brought from Holyroodhouse, and at the other end of the hall the minstrels' gallery, and beneath it the screens, the partition of carved wood through which the servants passed to kitchen and buttery. On the high table and the tables between it and the screens, candles, set in prickets or spiked candlesticks, cast a fitful light on the faces of the guests.

> Of capounis and Cunningis they had plentie,
> With wyne at their will, and eek Vennyson;
> Birdis bakin in breid, the best that may be.

And so the King ate, without the help of a fork, the meat which the Master of Gray carved for him, or "wauchtit at the wicht wyne", harsh as well as strong, made palatable only by the addition of sugar and spices. Sometimes he would break off to speak to Elphinstone or another grave Lord of Council, or to watch the antics of Currie the fool and his wife, Daft Ann, or to listen to his quartette of Italian minstrels. But he did not linger long at the table. "I have never seen a man so temperate in eating and drinking out of Spain", said De Ayala. "Indeed," he added, "such a thing seems superhuman in these countries".[1] And James seems to have despised the rere-supper, or late evening meal as much as those contemporary moralists who denounced it with ferocious gusto.

[1] *Cal. of State Papers, Spain*, VOL. I, No. 210.

Before he left the supper table he washed his hands a second time—the absence of forks from the royal table made this necessary. After supper he employed various devices for abridging the tedious hours. He diced or played cards or backgammon, usually for small stakes. Sometimes he called for music. He had his own musicians, trumpeters, drummers, and fiddlers, in addition to the four Italian minstrels, but he was always ready to listen to and to reward a stranger, be he singer, harper, or fiddler. Dancers, like the mysterious "Wantonness", and acrobats were always made welcome. Sometimes he would watch guisers, three or four actors from his own household or from the burgh, perform a farce on a platform erected before the screens. Sometimes,

> Quhene that the nycht dois lengthin houris
> With wind, with haill, and hevy schouris

he would sit with his courtiers about the fire to listen to the stories told by professional or semi-professional raconteurs, like "Watschod the tale tellare", or "Widderspune the foulare that tauld tales and brocht foules to the King".[1]

Such were his ordinary diversions, shared with his familiar friends and the half-dozen laborious officials, members of his Secret Council, who were always in attendance on him. Even when he went to Kintyre in the summer of 1498 Elphinstone, the Lord Privy Seal, Sir Robert Lundy, the Treasurer, Master Richard Murehede, the Secretary, and Master Walter Drummond, Clerk of Rolls, Register, and Council, accompanied him.[2] But Christmas, when the great lords were summoned to "the Kingis Yole", demanded something more ambitious, and, knowing this, singers, fiddlers, harpers, tumblers, and dancers flocked to the palace.

The invasion began on 6 December—St Nicholas Day—when the choristers from the adjacent abbey, one of them disguised as a bishop, the rest as demons, burst into the palace, roared parodies of the psalms which they were accustomed to chant reverently in church, and refused to leave till they had obtained a handsome

[1] C.T.S., VOL. I, pp. 307, 326, 330, 378.
[2] R.M.S., VOL. II, No. 2436.

gratuity from the King.[1] Soon after the departure of the St Nicholas Bishop and his imps the rule of the Abbot of Unreason began.[2] One of the less dignified members of the royal household, often Alexander Kers, the cook, was chosen to be master of revels that were sometimes too boisterous for even the robust taste of the time. As Christmas drew nearer, new liveries were issued not only to the "Abbot",[3] but to the remainder of the King's servants "against Yule".[4]

Christmas Day was ushered in by the clerks of the chapel singing carols at the door of the King's chamber.[5] One of these carols still survives—Dunbar's beautiful *Rorate coeli desuper*. A little later the King, accompanied by his great officers of state and his heralds and pursuivants, attended High Mass and made his Christmas offering.[6] On his return to the palace the heralds cried "*Largesse*" before him and obtained the customary gift.[7] Then followed the Christmas dinner, when the tables were spread

> With all divers dainties dicht daintily,
> Cerculit with silver seemly to seen.

Music, dancing, and card-playing occupied much of the time between the long and elaborate meals.[8] Contrary to his usual practice the King played for high stakes; he often lost seventy pounds in one night; sometimes he exhausted the Treasurer's supply of ready money and was reduced to borrowing a few pounds from one of the ushers.[9]

Though by the accepted method of computation the New

---

[1] *C.T.S.*, VOL. I, pp. 239, 307, 370; VOL. II, pp. 128, 349, 409, 410; VOL. III, pp. 175, 176, 356.

[2] *C.T.S.*, VOL. I, pp. 270, 327; VOL. II, pp. 111, 432; VOL. III, p. 127.

[3] *C.T.S.*, VOL. II, p. 320.

[4] *C.T.S.*, VOL. I, pp. 191-4, 231-5; VOL. III, p. 299.

[5] *C.T.S.*, VOL. I, pp. 102, 129, 174.

[6] *C.T.S.*, VOL. I, pp. 100-1, 126, 171, 173-4, 239, 308, 374.

[7] *C.T.S.*, VOL. I, pp. 100, 126, 174, 184, 308, 374; VOL. III, p. 359.

[8] *C.T.S.*, VOL. I, pp. 184, 308; VOL. II, p. 353.

[9] *C.T.S.*, VOL. I, pp. 100, 308, 374, 375; VOL. II, pp. 130, 131, 132, 352, 353, 354, 411, 413, 414, 471; VOL. III, pp. 177, 359, 361; VOL. IV, pp. 91, 92, 93, 401, 402.

Year did not begin till 25 March, 1 January was styled New
Year's Day. Already, a full century before the Reformation, it
overshadowed Christmas in the mind of the ordinary Scotsman,
as it did till less than a generation ago. It was the recognised day
for the giving of presents to kinsfolk and servants. On New
Year's Day 1507, for example, the King presented one of the
Queen's ladies with a golden rosary, costing over seventy pounds.
To another he gave a jewelled image of St Michael, to a third a
gold chain. The Queen was the recipient of a jewelled "serpent's
tongue", (a fossil, supposed to be a test of poison), but the
Treasurer's Accounts give no hint as to the destination of "ane
hert of gold . . . quhilk he gaif away" at the same time.[1] The
chief cook and the master of the wine-cellar received their accustomed "basin silver", and none of the "divers menestrales, schaw-
maris, trumpetis, taubronaris, fithelaris, lutaris, harparis, clars-
charis, piparis" who crowded the palace at this season went unrewarded away.[2]

Plays, sometimes enacted by "guisers" from the town, helped
to speed the long nights of early January. Not till 6 January,
Uphaliday or Twelfth Night, did the Christmas festivities come
to an end. In the morning the King attended Mass and made an
offering of gold, frankincense, and myrrh.[3] Later in the day he
abdicated for a few hours in favour of another monarch, the
King of the Bean,[4] who might be one of his own trumpeters.
In the evening a morrice dance, performed by guisers in parti-
coloured dresses decked with bells, brought "the daft days" to
an end.

There were pageants and plays again on Fastern's E'en—
Shrove Tuesday—dances in which gallants

> Kest up gamountis to the skyis
> That last came out of France,

[1] C.T.S., VOL. III, pp. 359-60.
[2] C.T.S., VOL. I, pp. 174, 184, 309; VOL. II, pp. 130, 353, 412, 472; VOL. III,
pp. 177, 360; VOL. IV, pp. 92, 402.
[3] C.T.S., VOL. I, pp. 127, 240; VOL. II, p. 69; VOL. III, p. 268.
[4] C.T.S., VOL. I, pp. 127, 184; VOL. II, pp. 131, 354, 485.

and tournaments in which the combatants fought with pointless lances and "battle-axes of tree".[1]

After his marriage the King always hurried back to Holyrood before the end of Lent, and there distributed the customary Maundy alms to his bedesmen on Skire Thursday.[2] There were as many of them as he was years old, and each received, in addition to a penny for every year of the King's life, a blue gown, and a wooden cup and platter—the insignia of his calling of licensed beggar. As at Yule, the doors of the palace were open to the great lord and the strolling minstrel; as at Yule, the King, followed by a train of courtiers resplendent in new-bought velvets and taffetas, on Easter Sunday attended Mass and made his offering[3]; as at Yule, the heralds cried "*Largesse*" before him when he returned to the great hall of the palace,[4] and as at Yule, neither they, nor the multitude of lutars, harpers, fiddlers and pipers, went unrewarded away.[5]

As the King spent his days, so did his great nobles—Bothwell, Angus, Huntly, Crawford, and their fellows—save that they read less and hunted more. Like him they moved from castle to castle, where, as in the royal palaces, the new hall was added to the old tower; like him, they spent the heavy nights playing at cards and dice, and listening to songs and stories; like him, they willingly suffered invasion by guisers and minstrels at Christmas and Easter.

Even if he could, King James would not have stayed put. In the year 1504, for example, he left Edinburgh for Falkland in the middle of January.[6] There his days were spent in hunting and hawking, his nights in playing cards and listening to the music of the lute, till on 29 January he rode to St Andrews to be present at the burial of his brother, James, Duke of Ross and Archbishop of St Andrews, who had died a fortnight before.[7] At the begin-

[1] *C.T.S.*, VOL. II, pp. 202, 386, 476, 477; VOL. III, pp. 182, 183.
[2] *C.T.S.*, VOL. II, pp. 71, 78, 249, 259.
[3] *C.T.S.*, VOL. I, pp. 132, 171, 198, 241, 326, 387; VOL. III, pp. 57, 289; VOL. IV, pp. 40, 186, 438.
[4] *C.T.S.*, VOL. I, pp. 132, 176, 241, 326, 387; VOL. IV, pp. 112, 340.
[5] *C.T.S*, VOL. I, pp. 132, 176, 326-7; VOL. IV, p. 340.
[6] *C.T.S.*, VOL. II, p. 415.
[7] *C.T.S.*, VOL. II, p. 417.

ning of February he was back in his capital, playing golf with the Earl of Bothwell and watching "the gysaris of Edinburgh that daunsit in the Abbey".[1] On 13 February he was in Stirling[2]; on the 24th he lodged in Biggar at the house of Bessie Bertram[3]; and on the 25th he reached Dumfries, where he was entertained by a "crukit vicar that sang" and by the burgh pipers.[4] On 4 March he set out for Edinburgh, leaving behind him the cook's boy, who had broken his leg; but James, with that consideration for the misfortunes of others which endeared him to his subjects, left money to meet his expenses, including his surgeon's fee.[5] He would do as much for a complete stranger: a few days later he saw a man standing disconsolate beside his dead horse, and comforted him with a gift of fourteen shillings.[6] Parliament met in Edinburgh from 11 to 20 March[7]; when it was prorogued, the King went to Stirling, where he was overwhelmed with gifts of pike for his Lenten fare.[8] He returned to Edinburgh for Easter, which that year fell on 7 April.[9] In the middle of April, and again in the middle of May, he visited Dumbarton to inspect the ships that were about to sail for the Isles.[10] He left fourteen shillings for the pipers of Dumbarton,[11] and on his way back to Edinburgh distributed the same sum to "the seik folkis at the toun end of Strivelin". "Ane blind man be the gait" got fourteen pence.[12]

On 3 June he visited the Isle of May in "the litill bark callit the Colomb", and heard the clerks of his chapel say mass in the deserted priory.[13] He was rowed to Anstruther,[14] and next day he heard mass in both Crail and St Monans.[15] A few days later he accompanied the Queen, and twenty-four carts containing her dresses, to Linlithgow, where on Corpus Christi Day he witnessed a play.[16] Leaving his Queen at Linlithgow he rode off, first to Bothwell to spend a few days with his mistress, then to Whithorn, where he ordered a requiem mass to be sung for Eleanor Jones,

[1] C.T.S., VOL. II, p. 418. [2] C.T.S., VOL. II, p. 419.
[3] C.T.S., VOL. II, p. 420-1. [4] C.T.S., VOL. II, pp. 421. [5] Ibid.
[6] C.T.S., VOL. II, p. 423. [7] A.P.S., VOL. II, pp. 239-54.
[8] C.T.S., VOL. II, p. 426. [9] Ibid.
[10] C.T.S., VOL. II, pp. 428, 434. [11] Ibid. [12] Ibid.
[13] C.T.S., VOL. II, p. 437. [14] Ibid. [15] Ibid.
[16] C.T.S., VOL. II, pp. 437-8.

one of the Queen's ladies in waiting.[1] He rode back by Glenluce, Ayr, and Paisley to Linlithgow, which he reached at the beginning of July,[2] only to give orders for the immediate conveyance of his baggage, which included a white peacock, to Stirling.[3] Here he spent less than a fortnight; on 24 July he was back in Edinburgh.[4] But not for long: he was planning a raid, in conjunction with Lord Dacre, the English Warden of the West March, on the turbulent inhabitants of Eskdale. It was an odd combination of picnic and punitive expedition: he took with him falconers, minstrels, and his master cook; on 14 August he paid fourteen shillings to the minstrels of Dumfries: the same sum he paid three days later to "the man that hangit the thevis at the Hullirbus", with the addition of eightpence "for ane raip to hing thaim in".[5]

A day or two later he reached Canonby in Eskdale, to find gifts of venison and wine from Lord Dacre and the Bishop of Carlisle waiting for him.[6] On 21 August he watched the hanging of another batch of thieves, and listened to two Englishwomen who sang in his tent.[7] From Canonby he went to his own castle of Lochmaben, where for two nights he played cards with Lord Dacre.[8] His mind was now set only on hawking: he lingered at Lochmaben till the middle of September, sometimes listening to the singing of "the crukit vicar of Drumfreis",[9] and then went on to Dunfermline, where he was joined by the Queen, who had come from Stirling with thirty-five carts.[10] He was at Falkland on the 27th,[11] and on the 30th he bestowed twenty-eight shillings on a student in St Andrews.[12]

Winter was approaching, and he had not yet paid his annual visit to the shrine of St Duthac in Tain. He rode back to Dunfermline to take his leave of the Queen,[13] and then, accompanied by a poet, three falconers, four Italian minstrels, a Moorish

[1] C.T.S., vol. II, pp. 439–40, 442.
[2] C.T.S., vol. II, p. 443.   [3] C.T.S., vol. II, pp. 444–5.
[4] C.T.S., vol. II, p. 448.   [5] C.T.S., vol. II, pp. 452–3.
[6] C.T.S., vol. II, p. 454.   [7] Ibid.
[8] C.T.S., vol. II, p. 455.   [9] C.T.S., vol. II, pp. 455–8.
[10] C.T.S., vol. II, pp. 458–9.   [11] C.T.S., vol. II, p. 459.
[12] C.T.S., vol. II, p. 460.   [13] C.T.S., vol. II, p. 461.

drummer, and a horse laden with silver plate,[1] he set out on his pilgrimage. He did not lack entertainment on the way: in Perth it was provided by a "sowtar lutar"[2]; in Dunottar a "chield playit on the monocordis" to him[3]; in Aberdeen the burgh pipers performed, and in Elgin, Forres, and Darnaway maidens danced before him.[4] He reached Tain on 22 October,[5] halted again at Darnaway on his homeward journey,[6] and on 8 November was back again in Falkland, having travelled from Aberdeen by Coupar Angus and Perth.[7] Meantime the Queen had remained in Dunfermline, unmoved by the rumours that the pest had broken out in the burgh, and by her husband's orders to take refuge in Lindores Abbey.[8] James did not join her at once, but visited Stirling and Linlithgow, where he was saddened by the sight of "the seik folkis at the toun end".[9] He was in Holyrood, playing cards, on 18 November[10]; a few days later he crossed the Forth to escort the Queen from Dunfermline to the capital.[11] He meant to spend Yule there, but he could not rest. Before the end of the month he was in Whitekirk, listening to "twa wemen that sang"[12]: on 9 December he played backgammon at Samuelstoun,[13] and on the 18th he was hawking at Melrose.[14] He returned to Holyrood for Christmas, to find that the chambers had been hung with "the arres clathes fra Linlithgow", and that "the silver weschale quhilk wer in Strivelin" glittered in the hall.[15]

His restlessness might betoken an unstable temperament, but it served him well: it brought him into contact with every class of his subjects, in every part of his kingdom, and enabled them to recognise and admire not only his "young adventurousness", his zest for new experience, but also his sympathy, his generosity, and his strong sense of justice, evident in little things as in great. The "puir wif on the gait that criit on the King" did not cry in

---

[1] C.T.S., VOL. II, p. 462. [2] Ibid.
[3] C.T.S., VOL. II, p. 463. [4] Ibid.
[5] C.T.S., VOL. II, p. 464. [6] Ibid.
[7] C.T.S., VOL. II, p. 465. [8] C.T.S., VOL. II, p. 463.
[9] C.T.S., VOL. II, p. 466. [10] C.T.S., VOL. II, p. 467.
[11] C.T.S., VOL. II, pp. 468-9. [12] C.T.S., VOL. II, p. 469.
[13] Ibid.   [14] C.T.S., VOL. II, p. 470.   [15] Ibid.

vain; the man whose corn was trodden down by the King's horses was compensated in full. In his turn the King gained a knowledge of his country which few of his counsellors possessed.

There was less wood and more water than in the Scotland of today. Marshes and reed-fringed pools, the haunt of the heron, crane, and bittern, covered what is now fertile cornland; Edinburgh itself—the Lislebourg of French travellers—was almost encircled by a ring of lochs, most of which have long since been drained. Trees and hedges were as scarce as in Dr Johnson's time: the medieval Scot had felled and burned recklessly, and had neglected to plant; his castle usually rose stark above the unenclosed tilth or pasture. In 1504 Parliament declared that "the wod of Scotland is uterlie distroyit", and called upon every lord and laird to make deer parks, fish ponds, rabbit warrens, and dovecotes on his estates, and to plant, in addition to hedges and orchards, an acre of timber.[1] But the country was not wholly bare: there were still great forests of Scots fir in some parts of the Highlands, and though all the woods of Fife barely sufficed to build one ship, that ship was the *Michael*, from its great size the envy of neighbouring monarchs. There was a superabundance, too, of "firthis" or "holtis"—thickets of hawthorn and sloe, like the one in which the disconsolate Robin of Henryson's poem kept "his herd under a heuch . . . in dolour and in care".

In all probability the fields were not as empty of people as they are today. As the King rode out from his castle—it might be Darnaway—in the early morning, he would hear the Grenge —the home farm—awake to another day's work. Gavin Douglas has described the scene:

> Tyte on hys hynys gaif the grief ane cry,
> Awaik on fut, go till our husbandry;
> And the hyrd callis furth apon hys page,
> Do dryve the catall to thar pasturage:
> The hynys wife clepis up Katheryn and Gill;
> Za, dame, said thai, God wait, with ane gude will.[2]

[1] *A.P.S.*, VOL. II, pp. 242, 243.
[2] Gavin Douglas, *The Aeneid of Virgil translated into Scottish Verse*, ed. G. Dundas, Edinburgh 1839, VOL. II, p. 851 (Prologue to spurious BK. XIII).

He would rejoice, like Henryson, to see the peasants working in the fields:

> Sum makand dyke, and sum the pleuch can wynd,
> Sum sawand seidis fast frome place to place,
> The Harrow is hoppand in the saweris trace;
> It wes greit Ioy to him that lufit corne,
> To see thame laubour, baith at euin and morne.[1]

But, according to De Ayala, they did not work too hard, and much of their labour was misdirected. "The corn is very good," he said, "but they do not produce as much as they might because they do not cultivate the land. Their method is the following: they plough the land only once when it has grass on it, which is as high as a man; then they sow the corn, and cover it by means of a harrow. Nothing more is done till they cut the corn. I have seen the straw stand so high after harvest that it has reached my girdle."[2]

Most of the farms were small. For example the Crown lands at the Grange of Bothkennar in Stirlingshire, which extended to only thirty-five bovates, or 455 Scots acres, were divided among twelve tenants, who held them on a three years' lease, and paid a rent of sixteen shillings, one boll of wheat, two bolls and two pecks of barley, and two capons for each bovate.[3] At one time the holdings on the same estate might be uniform in size, but that time was long since past; though half the Bothkennar farms were approximately two bovates in extent, one was as large as five and a half bovates, and one as small as one bovate. One half of the lands of Ardit, in Fife, to take another example, were divided equally between two tenants; another two had a twelfth part each, and the remaining five a sixteenth each.[4] Here, as in most places, the tenants were required to pay a "grassum" when their three years' lease was renewed, and to render *servitia et cariagia consueta*—put in an occasional day's work on the demesne,

---

[1] Fable of the Swallow and the other birds, in *Poems*, ed. G. Gregory Smith, Edinburgh 1906-14, VOL. II, p. 128.

[2] *Cal. of State Papers, Spain*, VOL. I, No. 210.

[3] *R. Scac. S.*, VOL. XI, p. 409.

[4] *R. Scac. S.*, VOL. XII, p. 640.

and supply carts and horses or draught oxen on certain specified occasions.

The tenants had in addition to help one another at seedtime and harvest. As a rule, they were too poor to hire servants; their farms supported only a few head of cattle. The medieval plough, which required a team of eight or ten oxen and two men, a "caller" to guide it, and a "gadman" to attend to the team, forced co-operation upon the most individualistic of peasants.

Though small farms were rare, large farms, where the labour was supplied by cottagers, each occupying a cotland, were by no means uncommon. The demesne, the "grange" of the sixteenth century, the "mains" or home farm of a later day, was usually kept undivided by the laird, and worked mainly by cottars under the supervision of his grieve. On the Grange of Darnaway, which was farmed in steel-bow,[1] there were in 1502 five plough-men, a shepherd, and a bowman or cowherd, all of whom were paid, not in coin, but in oatmeal. The five ploughs were drawn by fifty oxen, and there were in addition fifty-one cows and calves, one bull, and seven score sheep on the farm. Eleven and a half stacks of oats, five of bere, and two and a half of wheat stood in the stackyard. At the other end of the scale we find the cotlands or *cotagia*, holdings of an acre or two occupied by labourers and craftsmen, whose dwellings formed the "cot toun" which might later become the nucleus of a burgh of barony.

De Ayala was not the only critic of the Scottish farmer. The Lothian-born John Major, looking at the Scottish scene through the eyes of one who had dwelt long in France, noticed that though there was abundance of stone, the farmhouses were small, like cottages, and unshaded by trees, that there were no hedges round the orchards, and that the land was unmanured. This negligence and improvidence he attributed to uncertainty of tenure. Neither the scanty and dwindling band of "kindly" or customary tenants —corresponding more or less to the English copyholders—nor the multitude who held the land on leases of from three to five years —more often three than five—had established any title to the

---

[1] i.e. the tenant leased stock and implements as well as land, and undertook to give them up undiminished when his lease expired.

land which they cultivated. From the landlord's refusal to renew the lease, and the old rental books show that such refusals were frequent, they had no appeal. It is little wonder that the more spirited of them laid violent hands upon their supplanters. "If a landlord let to another the holding of a quarrelsome fellow," said Major, "him will the evicted man murder as if he were the landlord's bosom friend." If lands were let in perpetuity, Major maintained, negligence and violence would disappear, both landlord and tenant would grow richer, and the tenants would build "fair dwellings that should be an ornament to the country".[1]

It would seem that Major was preaching to the converted. As far back as 1457 Parliament had recommended the King to "give example to the lave" by letting his own lands in feu farm[2] —in other words, letting them in perpetuity, free from the more onerous feudal casualties, in return for a fixed rent, to be paid every year, and a composition for the new infeftment, exactly specified in the feu charter, to be paid by the holder, and by each of his successors when he entered into possession of the land.

Numerous charters of feu farm were granted by James II in the closing years of his reign, but his successor seems to have overlooked this method of augmenting his revenue. In 1504, however, Parliament reaffirmed and amplified the statute of 1457, permitting the King "to sett all his propir landes, baith annext and unannext, in few ferme . . . swa that it be not in diminution of his Rentale, grassoumes, nor all vther dewites".[3] A second statute extended this permission to "everilk lord, barrone, and Frehaldar, spirituale or temperale".[4] In spite of this legislation, royal grants of charters in feu farm were comparatively rare for a year or two; then in 1508, with the King's growing awareness of the financial implications of a spirited foreign policy, they begin to crowd the pages of the Register of the Great Seal. For the grant of land in feu farm meant both an increased rental, and the immediate payment of a lump sum to the superior.[5]

---

[1] Major, *History of Greater Britain*, pp. 30-1.
[2] *A.P.S.*, VOL. II, p. 49.   [3] *A.P.S.*, VOL. II, p. 244.   [4] Ibid.
[5] To take two examples from Crown lands in Fife: Ardit was set in feu farm in 1509. One half was, as before, divided equally between two tenants;

The change did little to improve the lot of the poorer tenants. That the laird should now hold his land of the King or some other great landowner in feu farm did not necessitate his departure from the ancient practice of letting it on short leases to his own tenants. When he did let it in feu farm the occupants were often unable to pay the increased rental, and found their holdings let over their heads to the cadet of some noble house. As Sir David Lindsay wrote thirty years later,

> . . . now begins ane plague amang them new,
> That gentill men thair steadings taks in few.
> Thus man thay pay great ferme or lay thair steid.
> And sum ar plainlie harlit out be the heid,
> And ar distroyit without God on them rew.[1]

If we are to believe Major, the staple diet of the Scottish peasant consisted of oatmeal bannocks, baked on an iron girdle, or on the hearth[2]; but he had his gaudy days, when his diet was more varied. In *The Complaynt of Scotland*, written about the middle of the sixteenth century, we read of a shepherd's feast, at which the rustics, each equipped with "ane horne spune in the lug of there bonet", consumed "ky mylk & youe mylk, sueit mylk and sour mylk, cuirdis and quhaye, sour-kittis, fresche buttir ande salt buttir, reyme, flot quhaye, grene cheis, kyrn mylk"; but to this intolerable deal of milk they had "na breid bot ry caikis and fustean skonnis maid of flour". The names of the songs that they sang at this festival remain to tantalise us—"Be yon

the other half, previously divided among seven, was now divided among four. The money rent leaped from £8.6.8. to £29.6.8., without any diminution of the annual payments in kind, while the grassum, £26.13.4., became a composition of new infeftment—£29.6.8. R. Scac. S., VOL. XIII, pp. 610, 623. Le Casche, near Auchtermuchty, previously divided among twelve tenants, paying a rent of £8.1.4., 5 chalders of oats, and 2 chalders, 8 bolls of barley, 72 poultry, and a grassum of £6.13.4., was in 1509 granted in feu farm to the brother and the second son of Sir William Scott of Balweary, at an annual rent of £24.6.8., with the payments in kind as before and a fee of £24.6.8. for the new infeftment, on condition, however, that they did not remove any of the existing tenants. R. Scac. S., VOL. XIII, pp. 614, 621.

[1] *Ane Satyre of the Thrie Estaitis*, in *Works*, ed. D. Hamer, VOL. II, p. 249.
[2] Major, *History of Greater Britain*, pp. 7-11.

woodside", "Late, late, on evenings", "Broom, broom on hill",
"The Frog cam to the mill door", and the names of the dances
which they danced, when "euyrie ald scheipherd led his vyfe be
the hand, and euyrie yong scheipherd led her quhome he luffit
best". But we have no contemporary record of their regimen
on ordinary working days, no inventory of the scanty plenishing
of the dwellings—turf hut or "clay biggin" which they inhabited.

Inventories of the furniture in the smaller castles, however,
are common enough. We know that in the castle of Darnaway
in 1505 there were, besides the spits, caldrons, pots, pans, and
other kitchen implements, forty-seven plates and dishes of pewter,
twelve trenchers, six candlesticks, six pieces of tapestry, five
cushions, two beds with red and green canopies, two bolsters,
six feather mattresses, a folding table, three forms and settles, and
one chair.[1] The plastered walls of the chambers which were not
hung with tapestry were probably adorned with frescoes, such
as one sees in Huntingtower today.

If the King lodged, as he sometimes did, in the house of a
wealthy burgess, he would find as much comfort there as in the
castle which he had quitted. There would be only one chair in
the hall, it is true, but no castle had more; the floors would be
covered with rushes, but so were the floors of his own palace.
The rooms were dark, for the raftered roofs were low, and the
windows small, and as a rule only the upper half of the window
was glazed; the lower half was closed by a wooden shutter. It
was such a "schot wyndo" that Gavin Douglas[2] "onschet" to
perceive "the mornyng, bla, wan, and har". But the wooden
ceilings were painted in gay colours and tapestry hung on the
walls of the principal rooms; costly plate glittered on the "copburd", and a fire of logs burned in the great stone fireplace, above
which were carved the arms of the master of the house, if he
were armigerous, or the monograms of himself and his wife.
Before such a fire, at a table on which there was more silver than
pewter, the burgess and his cronies would set themselves

[1] R. Scac. S., VOL. XII, p. 673.
[2] Prologue to Aeneid, BK. VII, 1839 edn., VOL. I, p. 380.

K

With mychty drink and metis confortyve
Agane the stern wyntir for to stryve.[1]

The bedchamber would probably be empty except for the bed; at most it would contain a chest for holding clothes, but the bed would be canopied and curtained with cloth of arras, and the occupant would sink into an enormous feather mattress, while he

Warpit my hed, kest on clathis thrynfald
Fortil expell the peralus persand cald.[2]

The merchant's house, like the laird's castle, was built over a vaulted basement which contained the kitchen and storerooms. As in the castle, the main entrance was on the first floor. Access to it was gained sometimes by a forestair projecting into the street, sometimes by a pend or covered passage leading from the street to a courtyard or garden behind the house. For, as we can see from an early sixteenth-century prospect of St Andrews, behind almost every house, except in the very heart of the town, stretched a long and narrow garden close.

The appearance of these substantial stone houses, some of them miniature castles, "with battlements, machicolation, and all other manner of defence and munition necessar for safety and profit", filled with costly plenishing from Flanders, was only one indication of the increase in the wealth and prestige of the Scottish burghs.

The thirty-nine royal or free burghs were of all sorts and sizes, from Edinburgh, "*A per se*" among the cities of Scotland, to purely agricultural communities like Lauder,[3] where, according to the burgesses themselves, trade had entirely ceased, or petty seaports like Crail, Cullen, or Inverkeithing, which exported a few lasts of herring, and paid a pound or two to the King's customs. But certain privileges were common to them all. The burgesses of Crail, like those of Edinburgh, could choose their magistrates without interference from King or Bishop. They could discuss burgh politics in the head courts which met thrice

---

[1] *op. cit.*, VOL. I, p. 379.   [2] Ibid.
[3] *R.M.S.*, VOL. II, No. 2679.

yearly, after Christmas, after Easter, and after Michaelmas; their disputes were settled, their offences against law and order punished in the burgh court, which met in the Tolbooth once a fortnight. Should they be summoned to appear before the Sheriff or the Justiciar, they could be repledged—that is, they could object to the royal court as incompetent and insist on being tried in the burgh court.

According to a statute of 1504, only "the grete counsale of the tovne" could admit a new burgess.[1] It was no longer necessary for him, however, to be in possession of a house and a rood of land within the burgh: a payment of one pound made one a burgess of Edinburgh, while eighty loads of stones or a chalder of lime sufficed at Peebles.[2] The right of possessing a market cross and market place, of exacting tolls, of holding weekly markets and annual fairs, was enjoyed by many towns, such as St Andrews and Glasgow, which were not royal burghs; but only royal burghs were allowed to engage in foreign trade,[3] or to send commissioners to Parliament.

This last right was seldom exercised by the smaller and more remote burghs. While Edinburgh and Stirling were represented in every Parliament that met in the reign of James IV, and Linlithgow, Dundee, Haddington and Ayr in every Parliament but one, the commissioners from Elgin, Forres, Inverkeithing, Peebles, Renfrew, Rothesay, and Rutherglen appeared in only one Parliament, and half-a-score of burghs did not trouble to send commissioners at all.

The financial burdens imposed on the royal burghs were light. Apart from the customs dues, levied on exports of hides, wool, woolfells, woollen cloth, salt, coal, and fish, and collected by the customers, there were the burgh mails, made up, in theory, of the annual rent of fivepence which each burgess had been compelled to pay to the King, the fines exacted by the burgh

[1] *A.P.S.*, VOL. II, p. 245.

[2] *Charters and Documents relating to the Burgh of Peebles, with extracts from the records of the Burgh A.D. 1165-1710*, ed. W. Chambers, Edinburgh 1872, p. 193.

[3] To this rule Glasgow was a partial exception. See W. M. Mackenzie, *The Scottish Burghs*, Edinburgh 1949, p. 78.

courts, and the petty customs—tolls levied on goods brought to fair or market. But in the fourteenth century each burgh had succeeded in commuting these variable payments for a fixed annual sum. The terms varied in accordance with the ability of the burgh to drive a bargain—Aberdeen paid almost three times as much as Perth, which paid more than twice as much as Edinburgh—but in most cases they were distinctly advantageous to the burgh. In addition, the burghs were expected to provide a fifth of any grant of money which Parliament made to the Crown.

The burgh mails were paid to the Chamberlain. The time was past when in every royal burgh he held the Chamberlain's Assize, in which every detail of the administration of the burgh was exhaustively investigated, but he still presided over the infrequent meetings of the Court of the Four Burghs, a body containing representatives of Edinburgh, Stirling, Linlithgow, and Lanark, in which matters affecting the interests of all the royal burghs were considered. But long before the end of the fifteenth century Linlithgow and Lanark were surpassed in wealth and influence by towns like Perth, Dundee, and Aberdeen. Parliament, recognising this, had decreed in 1487 that representatives of all the royal burghs should meet once a year at Inverkeithing to provide and "trete apoun the welefare of merchandise, the gude Rewle and statutes for the commoun proffit of borowis".[1] The statute, like most of the acts of the 1487 Parliament, remained a dead letter, but in 1491 the later Convention of Royal Burghs was again foreshadowed by a meeting of representatives of Edinburgh, Aberdeen, Perth, Dundee, and Haddington, to discuss the sending of a trade mission to the Archduke of Austria.[2] The Court of the Four Burghs, however, continued to function. It met in Edinburgh on 10 November 1500 to give a ruling on the perennial question of "craftsmen using merchandise",[3] and in 1503 the commissioners from Lanark twice rode from Edinburgh

[1] *A.P.S.*, VOL. II, p. 179.
[2] *Records of the Convention of the Royal Burghs of Scotland*, VOL. I, ed. J. D. Marwick, Edinburgh 1870, p. 504.
[3] *op. cit.*, pp. 505–6.

to attend it, and were twice paid thirty-two shillings for their expenses.[1]

Almost equalling the royal burghs in prestige, far surpassing all but the largest of them in wealth, were burghs of regality like St Andrews, Glasgow, Arbroath, and Dunfermline. Within the limits of his regality the archbishop, bishop or abbot, as lord of the regality, enjoyed powers equal to those of the King. Through his bailie he exercised as extensive jurisdiction as the sheriff in civil cases and the justiciar in criminal cases; his vassals could be repledged from either sheriff court or justice aire. It was the lord of the regality who appointed the bailie, who, however, tended in practice to become a hereditary dignitary; in Arbroath the bailie was always an Ogilvy of Airlie, in St Andrews a Learmonth of Dairsie. In St Andrews, too, the bailie of the regality was also provost of the burgh; in Glasgow the burgh council waited upon the Archbishop a few days after Michaelmas to request him to nominate two bailies from a list of eight burgesses which they presented to him; but though the practice might vary, the principle was the same—no burgh official could be appointed without the approval of the lord of the regality. To him came the fines exacted in the burgh courts, the tolls levied in the burgh market; he enjoyed the privilege too, of exporting wool, hides, and fish free of customs duty.

Most of the burghs of regality were destined to become royal burghs, but though a commissioner from St Andrews was present in James's first Parliament, no change in their status was made in his reign.

The royal burghs were loud in their complaints against those who violated their monopolies of local or foreign trade. In 1506, for example, the burgesses of Montrose complained to the King that they had suffered heavy losses, and the King's customs had been defrauded by the export of wool, hides, and salt fish from Stonehaven and Gourdon, and also by the trafficking in these goods carried on every day at the churches of Fordoun, Fetteresso, and Fettercairn. The King stopped this leakage in his customs by

---

[1] *Extracts from the Records of the Royal Burgh of Lanark*, ed. R. Renwick, Glasgow 1893, p. 13.

granting a charter to the burgh authorising the provost, bailies, and burgesses to seize the offending goods, keep one half of the money which was obtained from their sale, and remit the other half to the Exchequer.[1] A similar complaint from Aberdeen five years later was answered by the grant of a similar charter.[2]

This restriction of trade to a comparatively small number of burghs, most of them situated on the coast, caused grave inconvenience to those who lived at some distance from a market. The country folk in the neighbourhood of Peebles, for example, found that they were forbidden to "mak ony merchandis or by ony pennyworthis bot within the merkat placis of the burgh" under pain of the forfeiture of their wares.[3] They might traffic with chapmen or pedlars, but the chapmen ran the risk of having their goods confiscated: in 1503 the King empowered the Sheriff of Wigtown and the aldermen and bailies of the burgh to seize the goods of "chepmen and al utheris" who should "tak apoun hand to by, sel, nor regret in ony wise walx, irne, ter, fustiane, braid claith or narow, salt, wyne, hide, woll, skyn, martis and victalis".[4] As Bishop Elphinstone pointed out in pleading the cause of Rayne, there was "no convenient place providing entertainment for man and beast between the burghs of Aberdeen and Elgin, where the lieges travelling there could be accommodated".[5]

It is not surprising, therefore, that in the reign of James IV there should have been a great increase in the number of burghs of barony. Altogether twenty-four were granted charters—four, Old Aberdeen,[6] Rayne, Fordyce,[7] and Clatt,[8] at the instance of Bishop Elphinstone. The charter granted in 1493 to Rayne "lying between the burghs of Aberdeen and Elgin", constituted it "a free burgh of barony in perpetuity" and gave the inhabitants "full power and liberty to buy and sell in the said burgh, and that there should be burgesses, bailies, and other officers in the said

---

[1] *R.M.S.*, VOL. II, No. 3017. [2] *R.M.S.*, VOL. II, No. 3628.
[3] *Registrum secreti sigilli regum Scotorum, The Register of the Privy Seal of Scotland* (hereafter referred to as *R.S.S.*), VOL. I, ed. M. Livingstone, Edinburgh 1908, No. 596. [4] *R.S.S.*, VOL. I, No. 927.
[5] *R.M.S.*, VOL. II, No. 2132. [6] *R.M.S.*, VOL. II, No. 1910.
[7] *R.M.S.*, VOL. II, No. 2492. [8] *R.M.S.*, VOL. II, No. 2588.

burgh, and that the said bishop and his successors should have the power to elect the said bailies".[1] The burgh was to have a market cross, and was to be allowed to hold a market every Monday, and a fair in the week beginning with St Lawrence's Day (10 August).[2] With the right to hold markets went the right to exact tolls. Other charters of erection of burghs of barony are in the same terms: the burgesses were allowed to hold fairs and markets, but were not allowed to engage in foreign trade, and their officials were chosen for them by the lord of the barony, lay or ecclesiastic.

One or two of King James's charters conferred new privileges on existing burghs of barony. In the charter of new infeodation which he granted to the burgh of Dunkeld in 1513, the confirmation of ancient rights was followed by the grant to the bishop, his steward and baron-bailie, and their successors, the right to arrest and punish all thieves, robbers, "sorners", rebels at the horn for slaughter and similar crimes, and all other notorious criminals within the said barony,[3] because Dunkeld, being situated in the Highlands, was a place where criminals and malefactors congregated.

In theory, the royal burghs had a uniform constitution. Down to the year 1469 the alderman or provost, the bailies, and other burgh officials had been elected at the Michaelmas head court, which was attended by the whole body of burgesses. In that year, however, Parliament decreed that "because of great . . . contensione yeirly for the chesing of the samyn throw multitud and clamor of commonis", no official or member of the burgh council should remain in office for more than one year, and that "the Aulde counsail of the toune sall cheiss the new counsail, in sic novmyr as accordis to the toune. And the new counsail and the aulde of the yeir before, sall cheiss all officiaris pertenyng to the toune as Alderman, bailyes, Dene of gild, and utheris officiaris. And that Ilka craft sall cheiss a persone of the samyn craft that sall have voce in the said electioune of the officiaris."[4] The risk of an altogether inexperienced council assuming office was removed by an act passed in 1474, which stipulated "that thair salbe of the

[1] *R.M.S.*, vol. II, No. 2132.   [2] *R.M.S.*, vol. II, No. 2445.
[3] *R.M.S.*, vol. II, No. 3852.   [4] *A.P.S.*, vol. II, p. 95.

aulde consale of the yer before foure worthy personis chosin yeirly to the new consale at their Entre to syt with thame for that yeir, and haue power withe thame to do Justice".[1]

But theory and practice did not coincide: there were still royal burghs which had bailies, but neither provost nor burgh council, where the burgesses were content, when the need arose, to appoint an assize or inquest—an *ad hoc* committee of eight or twelve—and to dissolve it when the need was past. At Lanark business such as the serving of heirs, the appointment of burgh officials, and the administration of the Common Good, which in a large burgh would have been handled by the council, was dealt with either by an inquest or by the "balyeis and communite".[2] The Burgh Records of Peebles show that the change from the old system to the new did not take place till 2 March 1504, on which day the two bailies and whole community of the burgh met in the Tolbooth, and "ordanit that thair salbe xxiiij of the best nychtburis of the towne chosing and sowrne to soit one acctions belangand the vtilite and comoun profit to the towne". They were to control the burghal revenues and property; no payment was to be made from the common good by bailies or burgh treasurer, unless it had been authorised by at least eight of the twenty-four. To this new council the old name of "douzaine" was given. "Gyf thair be ony feit to ony comoun werk," it was decreed at Peebles, "it salbe befor the balyeis and the dosane, and thai sal . . . tak sekir souerte for the complettin of the werk."[3] Such "comoun werk" might include "the kepyn of the knok"— the keeping of the town clock—for which the burgesses of Lanark paid two merks yearly,[4] or watching the cattle of the burgesses, for which Will Brown in Lanark was paid at the rate of ninepence for each beast, and a sheaf of corn from each household.[5]

It will be observed that the record of this constitutional change in the burgh of Peebles makes no mention of certain personages

[1] *A.P.S.*, VOL. II, p. 107.
[2] *Extracts from the Records of the Royal Burgh of Lanark*, p. xxviii.
[3] *Charters and Documents relating to the Burgh of Peebles*, p. 199.
[4] *Extracts from the Records of the Royal Burgh of Lanark*, p. 12.
[5] *op. cit.*, p. 6.

who figure in the 1469 Act—the Alderman, the Dean of Gild, and the representatives of the crafts. As yet only the larger burghs deemed it necessary to have a provost, as the Alderman was now called—a civic dignitary who would preside at the head courts, represent the burgh in Parliament, and lead its armed forces to battle; the smaller burghs found their two or four bailies sufficient.

Only the larger burghs, too, had a Dean of Gild. The sovereigns who granted their first charters to the Scottish burghs in the twelfth and thirteenth centuries, or confirmed and amplified them in the fourteenth century, envisaged these burghs as primarily trading communities. The most important element in the burgh, the only element that really counted, consisted of the merchants or traders, to whom was reserved the right of dealing in wool, hides, and other staple goods, and of engaging in foreign trade. It was assumed that these traders would organise themselves into a Gild under a Dean; in the new charter, for example, which Robert the Bruce granted to Dundee in 1327,[1] he allowed the burgesses to have their Gild Merchant. But in many burghs no gild merchant seems ever to have been constituted. In others it seems to have disappeared as a separate entity: "gild brother" and "burgess" had become synonymous—Henryson's Town Mouse, it will be remembered, "was Gild brother and made ane fre Burges"[2]—and while there might be a Dean of Gild, he was elected at the same time and in the same manner as the other burgh officials. Even in towns like Ayr, where the Gild had maintained its separate existence, it had become, as it were, a function of the burgh: the Gild Court met in presence of the Provost and the Dean of Gild. In Edinburgh, however, we still see a clear line of demarcation between the gild brother and the ordinary burgess: a stranger could become a burgess on payment of a fee of £3; he had to pay an additional £5 if he wished to become a gild brother. The eldest son of a burgess paid 6s. 8d. for his "burgesry" and 13s. 4d. for entrance to the gild; the second son

[1] *Charters, Writs and Public Documents of the Royal Burgh of Dundee 1292-1880*, ed. W. Hay, Dundee 1880, pp. 9-11.

[2] Henryson, *Poems*, ed. G. G. Smith, VOL. II, p. 14.

paid 13*s.* 4*d.* and £1 respectively.[1] Even in Edinburgh, however, no one could be made a gild brother without the consent of the burgh council; even in Edinburgh the representatives of the craftsmen had a voice in the election of the Dean of Gild. Not till the opening years of the reign of James's successor did the merchants of burghs like Edinburgh and Dundee attempt to reorganise the Gild and take the election of the Dean into their own hands.

This action, unsuccessful in the case of the Dundee merchants, was only one episode in a struggle between merchants and craftsmen which began long before James's accession and continued long after his death. The early years of the fifteenth century had witnessed the formation, among the craftsmen of certain burghs, of associations termed craft-gilds, or crafts, or trades. This movement was perhaps encouraged by an Act of Parliament, passed in 1425, which ordained "that in ilk tovne of the realme of ilk sindry craft usyt therein be chosyn a wyss man of that craft . . . the quhilk sallbe haldyn Dekyn or maister".[2] Apparently the merchants were alarmed, for the Act was revoked in the following year.[3] The revocation was of no avail: in 1469 Parliament admitted that the representatives of the various crafts were entitled to vote in the election of Provost, Bailies, and Dean of Gild.[4]

But the crafts felt that they required additional safeguards if their claim to exact fines and fees from their members, and to exclude incompetent practitioners from the exercise of their mystery was not to be challenged. As usual, the first move was made in Edinburgh: on 18 February 1474 the ten members of the Hatmakers' Craft secured from the Burgh Council a special seal of cause or charter ratifying their statutes.[5] Before the accession of James IV four other Edinburgh crafts had successfully petitioned the Council for similar charters—the Wrichts and Masons in 1475,[6] the Websters or Weavers in 1476,[7] the

---

[1] *Extracts from the Records of the Burgh of Edinburgh*, ed. J. D. Marwick (hereafter referred to as *Edinburgh Records*), VOL. I, Edinburgh 1869, pp. 112-3.

[2] *A.P.S.*, VOL. II, p. 8.   [3] *A.P.S.*, VOL. II, p. 13.

[4] *A.P.S.*, VOL. II, p. 95.   [5] *Edinburgh Records*, VOL. I, pp. 26-8.

[6] *Edinburgh Records*, VOL. I, pp. 31-2.   [7] *Edinburgh Records*, VOL. I, pp. 33-4.

Hammermen in 1483,[1] and the Fleshers in 1488.[2] Five more crafts followed their example in James's reign: the Coopers in 1489,[3] the Waulkers and the Tailors in 1500,[4] the Barbers and Surgeons in 1505,[5] and the Cordiners in 1510.[6]

The length of apprenticeship and the entrance fee varied from craft to craft; a mason, for example, paid 6s. 8d. and a barber £5, but a threefold purpose—the maintenance of a high standard of workmanship and the safeguarding of the material and the spiritual interests of their members, was common to all. We may take the Cordiners' Seal of Cause as typical. It was granted, among other reasons, "for augmentatioun of divine seruice at the altar of Crispine and Crispiiane situat within the College Kirk of Sanct Geill". Before a youth could enter on his seven years' apprenticeship he was required to pay a fee of 6s. 8d. When he completed his apprenticeship he could not "sett up buith"—open a workshop—unless he had been found "sufficient habill and worthi . . . and admittit thairto first be the sworne maisteris of the said craft, and maid freman and burgess of the said burgh". He had in addition to pay an "upsett" or entrance fee of four merks—two if he was the son of a burgess—which was applied "to the reparatioun and vphaldin of divine seruice at our said altar". He was expected also to attend "quarter comptis"—the quarterly meetings of the craft—to pay a penny a week for the maintenance of the ornaments of the altar, and to "sustene the priestis meit theirof as cummis about". Should he fail in any of these duties, he rendered himself liable to a fine of two pounds of wax, and the same penalty was imposed on him if he harboured the apprentice of a fellow craftsman.

Not all craftsmen were members of a craft; several seals of cause mention the servants or "feit men"—journeymen receiving a weekly wage, and paying a halfpenny a week for the maintenance of the altar of the craft in the parish church. But no definite line of demarcation could be drawn between employer and em-

---

[1] *Edinburgh Records*, VOL. I, pp. 47-9.   [2] *Edinburgh Records*, VOL. I, pp. 54-6.
[3] *Edinburgh Records*, VOL. I, pp. 57-8.
[4] *Edinburgh Records*, VOL. I, pp. 80-1, 81-2.
[5] *Edinburgh Records*, VOL. I, pp. 101-4.   [6] *Edinburgh Records*, VOL. I, pp. 127-9.

ployed: the master, like the village tradesman of the present day, would often get along without either journeyman or apprentice; the "feit man" knew that, with ordinary luck, he could pay his "upsett" and become a master.

Hours of work were long. The masons repairing St Giles' began at the stroke of five in summer, and worked till seven in the evening. In winter they had to work "quhill day licht be gane".[1] But holidays were frequent, though the demand for holidays with pay furnished Parliament in 1493 with one argument for the suspension of all deacons of craft for a year. Nor were the meetings of the crafts always solemn affairs: we may suspect that when the Barbers and Surgeons of Edinburgh insisted that each new member should provide "ane dennar to the maisteris of the said craftis at his admissioun and entres amangis ws"[2] they were following a practice already firmly established among the lowlier crafts. And when the festival of their patron saint came round, masters, servants, and apprentices must have been conscious of a tie stronger than contiguity or material interest as they marched in procession to the parish church with banner displayed, or knelt in the chapel which they had adorned and cared for to hear mass said by their own chantry priest.

Meantime the merchants, from whose ranks the representatives of the burghs in Parliament were drawn, continued to view with suspicion the crafts whose existence they had reluctantly sanctioned. In 1493 they persuaded Parliament, as we have seen, to suspend all deacons of craft for a year, on the ground that the statutes which they had made were "contrair the commone proffet", and might lead to "convocatioun and rysing of the kingis liegis", and also prohibited the levy of the weekly penny for the maintenance of the altar "quhilk is great skaith to the commoun profit".[3] But the weekly penny was still paid. They resented any encroachment by the craftsmen on their monopoly of foreign trade. On 10 November 1500 the Court of the Four Burghs declared that the Acts of Parliament of 1467 and 1487, forbidding craftsmen to "use merchandise or sail in merchandise"

[1] *Edinburgh Records*, VOL. II, p. 61.
[2] *Edinburgh Records*, VOL. I, p. 103.   [3] *A.P.S.*, VOL. II, p. 235.

must be strictly observed,[1] and on 8 January 1501 the King ratified
their decree.[2] Three years later they secured from Parliament an
act, aimed both at the craftsmen and at the great lord who might
seek to dominate the burgh, forbidding anyone to "have Jurisdiction within burgh bot thai usis merchandice within the said
burgh".[3] Only if a craftsman renounced his craft could he "use
merchandise" or hope to sit on the burgh council. Poverty or
pride in their professional skill would forbid most craftsmen to
make the sacrifice, but some of them did make it: when on
29 November 1508 the craftsmen of Edinburgh waited on the
Provost and Bailies with a request that six or eight of them should
be admitted to "the daylie counsale of the toun", they found
"ane pairt of the craftismen of the toun" sitting with the Council.
They had to be content with an assurance that the privileges which
they already enjoyed would be respected, and that the question
of representation on the Burgh Council would be raised in the
next Parliament.[4] If it was raised, no record of debate or decision
remains; not till the reign of James VI did Parliament definitely
sanction the admission of craftsmen to the burgh councils.[5]

The fifteenth-century Scot, like his nineteenth-century de-
scendant, "was born to dissension as the sparks fly upwards". In
Edinburgh the perpetual "cryis of carlingis and debaittis" offended
the ears of the poet,[6] and moved the Burgh Council to declare
that anyone convicted of "flyting and scaldrie" should be made
to stand at the Mercat Cross till four in the afternoon.[7] In
Aberdeen too, scolds lifted up their voices: on 16 June 1490, the
Burgh Court decreed that "Christane Lilburne sall cum in presence
of the alderman, balyeis, and the haile court, and on her kneis ask
Schir Johne Streweling forgifnes for the strublance of him under
silence of nycht, openly glammerand him, saiand scho sald ger
banys the said Schir John out of this toune, quhilk the said Schir

[1] *Records of the Convention of the Royal Burghs of Scotland*, VOL. I, p. 505.
[2] *Edinburgh Records*, VOL. I, pp. 88-9.
[3] *A.P.S.*, VOL. II, p. 244.   [4] *Edinburgh Records*, VOL. I, pp. 118-9.
[5] *A.P.S.*, VOL. III, ed. T. Thomson, London 1814, p. 363.
[6] William Dunbar, *Poems*, ed. J. Small, Edinburgh 1884-93, VOL. II, p. 261.
[7] *Edinburgh Records*, VOL. I, p. 97.

John wald nocht haf sustenit for jc crounis, and atour for part assithment of the said blasfemmy, the said Cristian sall com on Sonday nixt to the hie altar in Sanct Nicholes kirk, and proffer j lib. of wax in hir hand to the said Schir John, at hie mestim, in presons of the hail pepill."[1]

Words were often followed by deeds: the more law-abiding burgesses fought out their quarrels in the courts, with the result that the Burgh Council of Edinburgh, overwhelmed by "the greit multitude of pleyis," declared that everyone brought before it who lost his case would be fined eight shillings.[2] Others laid hands even on the magistrates and their statutes. On 20 October 1500 William Paterson and Patrick Lawson were found guilty of "invading" Bailie Todrig "with cruell wawpouns and drawin swordis", and were sentenced to "be had to the trone and their handis to be straken throch".[3] On Hogmanay of 1502 the same penalty was meted out to a certain Harvy for "ryving of the actis of the toun and lychtlying of the officeris".[4] In October 1511 the Council advised the Bailies to take one or two servants with them when they went to the fish market and places like it "sua that the baillies be nocht destitute in tyme of neid".[5] And there was always the fear that a brawl between two individuals might swell into a murderous riot. In 1494 the Burgh Council of Edinburgh, mindful of "the dyvers and mony barganis and tulyeis that hes bene committit in tymes bygane into this toune vpoun the Hie Streitt, and throw the quhilkis thair hes bene sindrie slauchteris", ordered every merchant and craftsman to provide himself within eight days with a sword or axe, a salade, gloves of plate, and, if possible, a brigandine, or jack, and to keep them beside him in his booth, so that he might come at once to the aid of the provost and bailies if need arose, "throw the quhilk guid rewle may be had bayth day and nicht, and the honour of the toun observit and kepit".[6] Four years later the burgesses who had neglected to

[1] *Extracts from the Council Register of the Burgh of Aberdeen 1378–1570*, ed. J. Stuart (hereafter referred to as *Aberdeen Register*), VOL. I, Aberdeen 1844, p. 46.
[2] *Edinburgh Records*, VOL. I, p. 98.
[3] *Edinburgh Records*, VOL. I, p. 86. [4] *Edinburgh Records*, VOL. I, p. 96.
[5] *Edinburgh Records*, VOL. I, p. 135. [6] *Edinburgh Records*, VOL. I, p. 68.

provide themselves with "defensabill gear" were warned that they must either pay a fine of twenty pounds or stand in the stocks for three days and then be banished the burgh.[1]

But the noisy procession that, on the first Sunday in May, with banners displayed, marched through the streets of Edinburgh to the beat of drum and the roar of cannon, had no designs against the good rule or honour of the burgh. They were douce craftsmen, who were returning from the Boroughmuir, armed with branches of the birch tree, that they might, in obedience to immemorial custom, "bring hame summer to the toun"; and the mock prelate who directed, or misdirected, their movements, the Abbot of Unreason or of Narent, was not an irresponsible buffoon, but a burgess, sometimes even a bailie, appointed by the Council to supervise the municipal plays and pageants. Sometimes he "joked wi' deeficulty", and begged to be relieved of an office which required him "to mak sportis and jocositeis in the toun", when he was used to "hiear and gravar materis". In Aberdeen he was styled the Abbot of Bon-Accord, and was assisted by a Prior.[2] But, perhaps as a result of the closer connection with England, which affected both Scottish poetry and Scottish architecture at this time, the Abbot in the early years of the sixteenth century became Robin Hood, and his assistant Little John,[3] and in Aberdeen at least, the burgesses who brought in summer were expected to array themselves as foresters in green and yellow, "with bowis, arrowis, brass, and all uther convenient thingis".[4]

The "Abbot" also acted as pageant master on Corpus Christi Day, when the craftsmen in their best attire marched solemnly through the town behind the banners of their respective crafts, and when certain of their number impersonated characters in sacred history. In Lanark, for example, Our Saviour, the Three Kings of Cologne, St Martin, and St George and the Dragon, were all represented. Lanark was probably content with a procession; in the larger burghs there was almost certainly both a

---

[1] *Edinburgh Records*, VOL. I, p. 73.   [2] *Aberdeen Register*, VOL. I, p. 59.
[3] *Edinburgh Records*, VOL. I, p. 176; *Aberdeen Register*, VOL. I, p. 440.
[4] *Aberdeen Register*, VOL. I, p. 438.

procession and a play, performed either in the churchyard, or in the playfield of the burgh. In Edinburgh the Hammermen, clad in complete armour, with their drums beating and their four banners displayed, rode immediately before the Sacrament in the procession. One was dressed for the part of King Herod, two were doctors, and other five or six represented King Herod's knights. We are told nothing, however, about the position of the other crafts in the procession or the scenes which they enacted in the play. In Aberdeen the craftsmen in their best array marched two and two behind the banners decorated with the insignia of their crafts. The Fleshers came first, then the Barbers, the Skinners, the Cordiners, the Tailors, the Websters and Waulkers, and the Baxters. Last, forming an escort to the Sacrament, came the Hammermen, among whom were included smiths, masons, slaters, and wrights. Each craft had to "furnish a pageant". The Fleshers "tormented" St Sebastian, the Barbers St Lawrence, and the Skinners St Stephen. The legends of St Martin, St Nicholas, St John, and St George were enacted by the Cordiners, the Litsters or Dyers, the Websters, and the Baxters respectively. The Coronation of the Virgin was entrusted to the Tailors, the Crucifixion to the Hammermen, and the Resurrection to the Wrichts, Masons, Slaters and Coopers.[1] If we are to judge from an inventory of "the grayth of the Corpus Christi procession" preserved in the Burgh Records, the Dundee programme was even more ambitious. The pageant master had at his disposal sixty crowns, six pairs of angels' wings, three mitres, Christ's coat, hose, and gloves, three great crosses, St John's coat, St Thomas's spear, a cross for St Blaise, St Katherine's wheel, St Andrew's cross, "a saw, a ax, a rasour, a guly knyff, a worm of tre, the haly lamb of tre", St Barbara's castle, Abraham's hat, and twenty-three heads of hair.

Aberdeen had also a Candlemas procession and play, an "alde and lovabile consuetud", for the better observance of which the Burgh Council issued regulations in January 1505. The craftsmen were instructed "to observe and keipe the said procession, als honorabily as thai can; And thai sale, in order to the Offering in

[1] *Aberdeen Register*, VOL. I, pp. 451-2.

Iames the fourt
Befor his Rovne.
1489 He marved
Mardaret eldest dochter
of Henri the seventh

JAMES IV AND QUEEN MARGARET

The Seton Armorial   *Winton Castle*

By permission of Sir David Ogilvy, Bt.

the Play, pass tua and ij togidr socialie". Quarrels about preced-
ence had disturbed the procession in 1503. Only certain crafts
were expected to furnish players—"the cordinaris, the Messing;
wobstaris and walcaris, Symeon; the smyths [and] goldsmiths, iij
Kingis of Cullane; the litstaris, the Emperour; the masons, the
Thre Knichtis; the talyors, our Lady, Sanct Brid, and Sanct
Elene; and the skynners, the Tua Bischopis." The penalty for a
breach of any of the rules was a fine of forty shillings, which was
to be applied to "St Nicholas werk"—the completion of the great
parish church.[1]

On St Nicholas' Day another "auld rite and loveable consue-
tude" was observed in Aberdeen, when every man in the burgh
who was able to bestride a horse decked himself in his bravest
attire and rode through the town behind Robin Hood and Little
John, "quhilk was callit in yers bipast Abbat and Prior of Bon-
acord".[2]

Not only in Aberdeen, but in almost every Scottish burgh the
day began and ended with music. In Edinburgh, a few months
before James came to the throne, "all honest persounis of substance" were required to contribute to the support of the three
burgh pipers, by taking it in turn to supply them with either a
day's work or a day's wages.[3] The band were "mercenary persons", however, who refused to exert themselves for threepence
a day. Dunbar complained that they played only two tunes:
"Now the day daws", and "Into June".[4]

The garlanded horsemen riding out to bring home summer,
the banners and processions and pageants of Corpus Christi Day,
the boy bishop and his "deevilots", the guisers and dancers who
made the Daft Days dafter still, seem to belong to a Scotland
more studious of the art of living cheerfully, more skilful in
making its own pleasures, fonder of music and colour and pageantry, than the Scotland of today. One contrasts the "Blyth
Aberdeen", or "Edinburgh the merry toun" of Dunbar's poems

[1] *Aberdeen Register*, VOL. I, pp. 432-3.
[2] *Aberdeen Register*, VOL. I, pp. 439-40.
[3] *Edinburgh Records*, VOL. I, p. 52.
[4] Dunbar, *Poems*, ed. Small, VOL. II, p. 262.

with the douce and dismal burghs of the late sixteenth century, and bewails the change wrought by Calvin and Knox. But one forgets the long months of drudgery that separated these rare festivals. One forgets, too, that the joyless Scot existed long before Calvin, the Scot who was bored by processions and pageants, and had to be bullied into a pretence of merrymaking. The Burgh Council of Aberdeen, for example, warned absentees from the St Nicholas Day cavalcade that they would lose any tack, pension, or office of profit which they held of the burgh, and in addition be "secludit, removeit, and uterlie expellit".[1]

But there were times, even when the country was at peace, when no thoughtful Scot could look about him and see any cause for cheerfulness, when the noise of both mirth and contention ceased in every town, and when even the bright and tranquil spirit of Henryson was darkened. "Is it Thy will, O Lord of Heaven", he asks, when the pest was raging in Scotland,

> That we should thus be hastily put down,
> And die as beasts?[2]

In March 1498 the pest appeared in Swanston, Currie, and other places in the neighbourhood of Edinburgh. The Burgh Council at once announced that any person from an infected area who tried to get into the town would be put to death, and anyone who tried to shelter him would be banished and have all his goods burned.[3] In May the town gates of Aberdeen were repaired and "lokit with lokis and keis" against suspicious persons.[4] In November the Burgh Council of Edinburgh, alarmed at the "perilous seiknes of pestilence now rissin in the east pairtis and lairglie spreid", tightened up its regulations governing the admission of strangers to the burgh,[5] and in April 1499 it forbade anyone to shelter any refugee from the pestilence town of Haddington under pain of death.[6]

For a time it seemed that the precautions were to be effective,

---

[1] *Aberdeen Register*, VOL. I, p. 440.
[2] "Ane prayer for the Pest", in *Poems*, ed. G. G. Smith, VOL. III, p. 162.
[3] *Edinburgh Records*, VOL. I, p. 72.   [4] *Aberdeen Register*, VOL. I, p. 66.
[5] *Edinburgh Records*, VOL. I, p. 74.   [6] *Edinburgh Records*, VOL. I, p. 76.

but before midsummer the pestilence arrived in the capital. A great silence fell on the city; schools were closed, children were forbidden to wander about the streets, merchants might not set up their booths, or hold markets at the gates of the burgh. In November "bearers and cleansers" were appointed by the Council and paid at the rate of twelvepence a day, "becaus thair lawbouris ar heavy and dayngerous".[1] The first four seem to have succumbed; in February 1500 five others were appointed to carry on their perilous and loathsome task "quhill God provide remeid".[2] October came, and found the Council issuing instructions for the boiling of infected clothing and the fumigation of infected houses,[3] but by this time the pestilence seems to have spent its force.

Earlier in the year the Provost of Aberdeen had judged it necessary to put his affairs in order before he made a journey to Berwick, as "the quyntray was dangerfull throw this plage of pestilence".[4] But the pest did not find its victims only in the burghs: it invaded, among other places, the parish of Caputh in the diocese of Dunkeld. The Bishop visited the afflicted and caused the sacraments of the Church to be administered to them. "Next day", continues his biographer, "he blessed water, dipped a bone of St Columba in it, and sent it by his chancellor for them to drink. Many drank it and recovered. But one insolent fellow replied to the chancellor 'Why does our bishop send us water to drink? I wish he had sent me instead a pot of his best ale'. But he, along with the others who did not drink the water, died of the pest, and thirty of them were buried in one grave."[5]

Two years later the pest returned to Scotland, if indeed it had ever departed. In May 1502 the Burgh Council of Edinburgh issued orders "that nane of certane townes suspect of pest repair heir nor be harbereit",[6] and in August it forbade anyone to speak to an infected person, or to "be fundin passand on the hie gaitt after ix houris in the nycht without a byrning lycht or a rationabill

[1] *Edinburgh Records*, VOL. I, pp. 76-7.   [2] *Edinburgh Records*, VOL. I, pp. 77-8.
[3] *Edinburgh Records*, VOL. I, pp. 84-6.   [4] *Aberdeen Register*, VOL. I, p. 68.
[5] Myln, *Vitae*, p. 43; translated in *Rentale Dunkeldense*, ed. Hannay, p. 313.
[6] *Edinburgh Records*, VOL. I, p. 93.

caus" under pain of banishment or branding on the cheek.[1] Two years later, in October 1504, we find the gates of Edinburgh being guarded against persons and goods coming from infected places.[2] The precautions were useless; before the beginning of July in the following year the pest had reappeared in the capital. This time the Burgh Council came near to discovering the real cause of the trouble: on 4 July 1505 it entrusted the public bellman, Thomas Glendinning, with the "purgeing and clengeing of the hie streitt . . . of all maner of muk, filth of fische and flesche, and fulyie weit and dry".[3] In spite of the exertions of Thomas and his two assistants the foul smells remained; three months later the Council forbade any person to melt tallow in houses fronting the High Street, "for till eschew the dishonesty and euil disposit savour thairof", and issued instructions "that the furrouris and skynneris dicht nor schaik their skynis on the hie gaitt, nor hing thame on the forestairis, for till eschew the evil sauour thairof, and the inhonesty that follows thairupon".[4] But these sanitary measures were confined to one street, the wynds and vennels still stank to heaven. And so, though the pest seems to have disappeared from Edinburgh in the autumn of 1505, it returned seven years later, to add a new anxiety to a country poised on the brink of war, and to hang on the flanks of the army that marched to its doom at Flodden.

> Use derth, o lord, or seiknes, and hungir soir,
> and slak thy plaig that is so penetryfe.
> The pepill ar perreist: quha ma remeid thairfoir,
> bot thow, o lord, that for thame lost thy lyfe?
> Suppois our syne be to the pungetyfe,
> Oure deid ma nathing our synnis recompens.
> Haif mercy, lord, we ma nocht with the stryfe:
> Preserve us fra this perrelus pestilens.[5]

---

[1] *Edinburgh Records*, VOL. I, p. 96.   [2] *Edinburgh Records*, VOL. I, p. 100.
[3] *Edinburgh Records*, VOL. I, p. 105.   [4] *Edinburgh Records*, VOL. I, p. 107.
[5] R. Henryson, "Ane prayer for the Pest", in *Poems*, ed. G. G. Smith, VOL. III, p. 163.

VI

RELIGIOUS LIFE

THE great Scottish lord of the time of James IV, when the hour of his death approached, no longer thought, as his thirteenth-century ancestor had done, of winning the favour of heaven by founding a monastery—or augmenting its endowments; he tried to win it and perpetuate his memory in earth in another way, by founding, as an Earl of Crawford had done in the great new church of the Blessed Virgin in Dundee, a chapel where mass would be said in perpetuity for the souls of himself and his kin, or by enlarging and beautifying some humble country church, and staffing it with a "college" of secular priests. In 1504, for example, John, first Lord Semple, founded a collegiate church at Lochwinnoch to the glory of God and the Blessed Virgin, in honour of the choir of saints triumphant, for the salvation of the King and Queen, their ancestors and descendants, also for his own salvation and for that of his wife and of their ancestors and descendants. The church was to be staffed by a provost and six chaplains, who every day, at the end of high mass, were to go to the tomb of the founder and his wife, and there sing the *De profundis* and pray for the welfare of their souls and the souls of all their kinsfolk. The music of the organ, the voices of boy choristers were to give a beauty and dignity to the ritual that was hard to compass in the ordinary country church, served by a single priest.

In their display of religious zeal, however, most of King James's subjects were outdone by their sovereign. De Ayala noted that he ate no meat on Wednesdays and Fridays, that he would not mount a horse on Sunday, even to go to mass, and that before transacting any serious business he heard two masses.[1]

[1] *Cal. of State Papers, Spain*, VOL. I, No. 210.

Nothing was allowed to interfere with his annual pilgrimage to the remote shrines of St Ninian and St Duthac. When Holy Week came round, he retired to the Observantine Friary which he had caused to be built in Stirling, and shared the fasts and vigils of the friars. To this day the church of Ladykirk, on the bank of the Tweed opposite Norham, stands as a witness to his gratitude for an escape from drowning.

As it seemed to be with the sheep, so it seemed to be with the shepherds. Of Bishop Elphinstone one who knew him well wrote: "If we should think of one who for his virtue, or something more excellent than virtue, merited immortality, of one who at every stage of his life, his innocent youth, his glorious manhood, his blameless old age, displayed modesty, piety, honour and sanctity, who did nothing unworthy of a Christian, we at once think of Bishop William. . . . The sweet name of Jesus was never absent from his mind, and day and night, waking or aroused from sleep, he had it ever on his lips."[1] Another contemporary writer, who has left us pen-portraits, not only of the Bishop, but of the Dean and every one of the canons and vicars-choral in Dunkeld Cathedral, has no ill and much good to say of them. Bishop George Brown, after he had surmounted his financial worries, "gave his whole mind to good works".[2] The Dean was "a shining example to all secular deans in the kingdom; a strong tower against which the enemies of the Church cannot prevail . . . in the time of famine he causes porridge to be distributed to all the poor who may come, a good helping to each."[3] The sub-chanter was "devout, courteous, and kindly, and very entertaining company".[4] One canon was "noble by birth, but much more noble by his wisdom and eloquence",[5] another was "spiritually minded in all things, learned, with a profound knowledge of canon law and a strong sense of justice . . . unwilling to listen to scurrility or scandal, but delighting in decent jests when

---

[1] Boece, *Vitae*, pp. 110-1.
[2] Myln, *Vitae*, p. 29; *Rentale Dunkeldense*, ed. Hannay, p. 304.
[3] Myln, *Vitae*, p. 55; *Rentale Dunkeldense*, ed. Hannay, p. 320.
[4] Myln, *Vitae*, p. 61; *Rentale Dunkeldense*, ed. Hannay, p. 324.
[5] Myln, *Vitae*, p. 63; *Rentale Dunkeldense*, ed. Hannay, p. 326.

he dined".[1] The vicars-choral were equally talented and virtuous —"modest, honourable, skilled in music", or "devout and ingenuous, always speaking as his heart dictated", or "a hater of sloth, careful of his furniture, a keen gardener". One of the clerics, the writer admits, is naturally short-tempered, but, he adds, "with a very kind heart".[2]

From the evidence of another sixteenth-century writer it would appear that the monastery, like the cathedral, was a home of primitive virtue. Ferrerius gives an engaging description of the arrival of the youthful Thomas Crystal at the monastery of which he was many years later to become abbot. As soon as he entered the nave of the abbey church of Kinloss, he fell on his knees before the Rood, and prayed that he might be permitted to accomplish some mighty work for the Church universal and for the community in which he was to be enrolled. When he looked up he saw that the image of the Saviour was smiling on him, and he knew that his prayer would be answered.[3] Both as monk and abbot he toiled "with oars and sails" for the good of his monastery, refusing all offers of advancement to a richer benefice, "preferring the poverty and peace" of Kinloss. He repaired the monastery buildings, built up a serviceable library, and improved the rations of the monks. "What shall I say of the bread?" his biographer wrote, "The monks had been accustomed before to eat 'broad bread', that is, an oatmeal cake baked on a girdle over the fire; now, through the kindness and care of Abbot Thomas, each brother was issued daily with thirty-two ounces of wheaten bread."[4]

But even in these panegyrical biographies written by Ferrerius, Myln, and Boece—none of them a critic of the established order —one encounters disconcerting admissions that point to an almost universal decay of faith and morals. Abbot Thomas was indeed

[1] Myln, *Vitae*, p. 64; *Rentale Dunkeldense*, ed. Hannay, pp. 326-7.

[2] Myln, *Vitae*, pp. 68-70; *Rentale Dunkeldense*, ed. Hannay, pp. 329-31.

[3] Ferrerius, *Historia abbatum de Kynlos, una cum vita Thomae Chrystalli abbatis*, (hereafter referred to as Ferrerius, *Historia de Kynlos*), ed. W. D. Wilson, Edinburgh 1839, pp. 62-3.

[4] Ferrerius, *Historia de Kynlos*, pp. 66, 70, 77, 79.

a conscientious and industrious administrator, a skilled musician, respecting at least the learning which he did not possess, but he succeeded an abbot who, in the words of Ferrerius, "would have been pious enough if he had not yielded to the pleasures of the flesh, and to love." He was excessively fat, more easy-going than his predecessor—"a man somewhat too harsh, who often, being troubled with black bile, fell into a fury that was indistinguishable from madness".[1]

Under the rule of Thomas Crystal Kinloss does seem to have been a model community, but when he became abbot in 1500 he found "religion fainting and all but dead", and failed to revive it till he had expelled "certain diseased sheep from his flock".[2] Even manslaughter had not been unknown in the monastery: Ferrerius reports the case of a monk who beat a boy to death in the cloister. He was unfrocked, but, accompanied by another monk, he went to Rome, where he received absolution.[3] Finally, Ferrerius pays his hero this significant compliment: "he was so munificent to his kinsfolk, that he may not inappropriately be compared to the bishops of the greatest dioceses."[4] It was the universal practice among the Scottish prelates. The saintly Bishop of Aberdeen, in the words of Boece, bestowed "broad lands and benefices" on many of the family of Elphinstone,[5] and the number of Browns on Myln's list of the canons of Dunkeld Cathedral[6] shows that Bishop Brown too considered it his duty to push the fortunes of his kinsfolk.

A more damaging compliment was paid by Myln to another of the cathedral clergy—"since he has been made a canon, he has been rarely reported absent".[7] Non-residence was too common to cause remark, though occasionally a reforming bishop or dean would try to grapple with the evil. On 4 October 1488 the Dean and Chapter of Moray ordered all absentee canons to resume

[1] Ferrerius, *Historia de Kynlos*, pp. 34, 35.
[2] Ferrerius, *Historia de Kynlos*, pp. 69-70.
[3] Ferrerius, *Historia de Kynlos*, p. 33.
[4] Ferrerius, *Historia de Kynlos*, p. 80.   [5] Boece, *Vitae*, p. 100.
[6] Myln, *Vitae*, pp. 59, 60; *Rentale Dunkeldense*, ed. Hannay, pp. 523, 524-5.
[7] Myln, *Vitae*, p. 68; *Rentale Dunkeldense*, ed. Hannay, p. 329.

residence under pain of forfeiture of one-seventh of their prebend. A month later it was reported that ten canons, including the subchanter, "had not bothered to obey". They were declared contumacious, and a seventh part of the prebend was divided among the canons who had remained in residence. Evidently the defaulters did not all return to their manses in the chanonry, for on 8 May 1489 a general convocation of canons declared that absentees who failed to return within three months and forty days would lose a third of their prebend, and that if they stayed away for a year they would be deprived of their benefices altogether till they gave satisfaction. Leave of absence, however, might be obtained "to study letters, or for other honourable causes".[1]

But the Bishop or Dean might himself be an absentee. Of the Dean of Glasgow, for example, it was recorded in 1501 that he "does not make residence", while Elphinstone himself was often absent from his diocese for months at a time. In such cases the explanation was not sloth or negligence: both were busy public servants; the Dean, Richard Murehede, had been Clerk Register, and was now the King's Secretary; while Elphinstone was Keeper of the Privy Seal, and a Lord of Council. In Scotland, as in every other kingdom in Europe, the civil service was, of necessity, recruited mainly from the clergy, the only educated class in the community, and was paid, as a rule, not by pensions charged against the revenues of the Crown, but from the fruits of benefices secured by the royal influence. It was not his piety, but his knowledge of canon and civil law gained at Paris and Orleans, and his experience in the administration of it gained as Official of Glasgow and of Lothian, that made Elphinstone Bishop of Aberdeen.

Elphinstone never forgot his duty to his diocese; other royal servants never troubled to set foot within the church or monastery to which they had been appointed. Patrick Paniter, for example, who succeeded Murehede as Secretary in 1505, obtained, at the instance of the King, a dispensation from Pope Julius II absolving him for two years from taking holy orders,

---

[1] *Registrum episcopatus Moraviensis*, ed. Innes, pp. 259-66.

though he was already perpetual vicar of Kilmary.[1] The dispensation was renewed for another two years in 1507, and again in 1509,[2] though he was now Archdeacon of Moray, and when in 1513 the King secured for him the Abbey of Cambuskenneth, he also secured a dispensation from assuming the monastic habit till another two years had elapsed.[3]

"Benefices are nocht leill devydit," wrote William Dunbar, "Sum men hes sewin, and I nocht ane."[4] He had substantial grounds for his complaint: cases of clerics holding more than two benefices were not uncommon. The benefices might be incompatible: the Bishop of Moray was also Abbot of Dryburgh and Prior of Pittenweem; the Bishop of Caithness was Abbot of Kelso and of Ferne. It is easy to multiply examples: in 1510 the King petitioned Pope Julius II to allow his Treasurer, George Hepburn, Bishop of the Isles, to hold the Abbeys of Arbroath and Iona *in commendam*, "that his authority and nobility of race may bind that uncivilised people in devotion to the Church".[5] Still, except from those who were left out in the division of the spoil, no murmur of complaint was heard: it was universally assumed that when a benefice was granted *in commendam* the sole duty of the commendator was to collect its revenues.

Unfortunately, it was not only useful public servants who benefited by the manipulation of ecclesiastical patronage: in 1504 James bestowed the Abbey of Tungland on a mysterious "French leech", John Damian,[6] who "causet the King believe that he ... wold make fine golde of uther mettall, quhilk science he callit the quintassence; quhairupon the King maid greit cost, bot all in vaine".[7] Even the failure of his attempt to fly from Stirling to France with "ane paire of wingis" and Dunbar's savage descrip-

---

[1] *L. and P. Richard III and Henry VII*, VOL. II, p. 222; *R.S.S.*, VOL. I, No. 1365.

[2] *Letters and Papers, Foreign and Domestic, of the Reign of Henry VIII*, catalogued by J. S. Brewer, 2nd edn. revised and enlarged by R. H. Brodie (hereafter referred to as *L. and P. Henry VIII*), VOL. I, London 1920, PT. I, No. 208.

[3] *L. and P. Henry VIII*, VOL. I, PT. I, No. 1757; PT. II, No. 2155.

[4] "Of the warldis instabilitie", in *Poems*, ed. Small, VOL. II, p. 227.

[5] *L. and P. Henry VIII*, VOL. I, PT. I, Nos. 502, 548.

[6] *C.T.S.*, VOL. II, p. 422.   [7] Lesley, pp. 76 Sc., 331-2 L.

tion of it[1] did not lose him the royal favour. The King evidently accepted his explanation "that thair was sum hen fedderis in the wingis, quhilk yarnit and covet the mydding and not the skyis"[2]: he tried to secure a pension of two hundred ducats for him from the fruits of the abbey when he resigned it in 1509, lest he be oppressed by poverty. James had already made a more scandalous use of his influence: in 1497 he secured for his brother, James, Duke of Ross, a youth of eighteen, the Archbishopric of St Andrews, rendered vacant by the death of Archbishop Schevez.[3] That his brother could not be consecrated, lacking as he did twelve years of the canonical age, did not trouble the sensitive but supple conscience of the King; always in desperate straits for money, he snatched at the chance of diverting into his own coffers the revenues of the second richest benefice in Scotland. Before the end of the year he made his brother commendator of the wealthy Abbey of Holyrood; in 1500 he added Dunfermline Abbey, the richest benefice in Scotland, to his "cleik of kirkis", and in 1502 Arbroath Abbey, equal in value to St Andrews. The premature death of the Archbishop in 1504 did not make the King abandon his policy; he secured the Archbishopric for the eldest of his illegitimate children, Alexander Stewart,[4] a boy of eleven, who had been prepared for a clerical career by the gift of the Archdeaconry of St Andrews at the tender age of nine. A certain restiveness, however, had apparently manifested itself among the Scottish prelates; in spite of the exertions of his father, five years had to pass before the boy archbishop was informed that "Dunfermline recognised its new master", and it was not till 1512 that he became commendator of the Priory of Coldingham.

When the key positions in the Scottish Church were thus filled according to royal policy or royal caprice, unimpeded by the papal Curia except when a higher bidder appeared in Rome,

---

[1] "The Fenzeit Freir of Tungland", in *Poems*, ed. Small, VOL. II, pp. 139-43.
[2] Lesley, pp. 76 Sc., 331-2 L.
[3] For James, Duke of Ross, see Herkless and Hannay, *Archbishops of St Andrews*, VOL. I, pp. 165-209.
[4] For Alexander Stewart, see Herkless and Hannay, *op. cit.*, VOL. I, pp. 215-66.

no improvement in clerical morals could be expected. The parish priest could have no compunction about sharing his manse with a mistress and a brood of children, when he knew that the bishop's palace sheltered similar guests, and suspected that the archdeacon reproved sin only for the sake of the fines that he could exact from the sinner. As a monk of Cambuskenneth put it: "Evil prelates, who do not enter by the door of the sheepfold, or even by the window, choose men like unto themselves, and encourage them, not to chastity of life or mortification of the body, or grief for sins, but to the vain glory of this world, and to insane pleasures."

The ordinary Scotsman seems to have regarded the ecclesiastical system as one which could not be changed, which could only be accepted and endured. The young gallant might chuckle over the adventures of the Friars of Berwick; the anonymous author of the *Thre Prestis of Peblis* might urge that only with the restoration of the capitular election of bishops would the Church regain its ancient spiritual power; from his lecture room in the Sorbonne John Major might deliver the opinion that the custom of non-residence was destitute at once of justice and common sense, or suggest that it was not absolutely necessary for a bishop to have a train of fourteen servants—the ordinary Scotsman believed, like the truant sacrist of Lindores, that "the Abbey bell wad aye be gotten rung". But some criticism there must have been, criticism directed not merely against the working of the system, but against the doctrinal foundations on which it rested, else Walter Kennedy would not have written:

> The schip of faith, tempestuous wind and rane
> Dryvis in the see of Lollerdry that blawis.[1]

Once, if we are to believe John Knox, the murmur of the coming tempest reached the ears of the King himself. In 1494 thirty men and women, known as the Lollards of Kyle, were brought before the King and his Council at the instance of Blacader, Archbishop of Glasgow. They included George Campbell of Cessnock, later Sheriff of Ayr, Adam Reid of Barskimming or Starwhite, and other persons of consequence in Kyle and

[1] "The Praise of Aige", in Dunbar, *Poems*, ed. D. Laing, VOL. II, p. 90.

Cunningham, some of them familiar friends of the King. The chief of the thirty-four charges against them were that they had asserted that worship of "the sacrament of the kirk" is idolatry, since, "after the consecration in the Messe, thare remanes braid, and that thair is nott the naturall body of Christ"; that the Pope was not the successor of St Peter "but where he [Christ] said 'Go behynd me, Sathan'"; that neither masses nor papal indulgences could profit souls in Purgatory; that every faithful man or woman is a priest, while "thei which ar called principallis in the Church ar thevis and robbaris"; that images and relics were not to be worshipped; that prayers should not be offered to the Virgin; and that priests should be allowed to marry. "The accusatiouns of the Bischop and his complices was verray grevouse," says Knox, but "the ennemies in the end war frustrat of thair purpoise", thanks to the good-natured monarch's admiration of Reid's verbal dexterity. When the Archbishop said with a sneer "Reid, believe ye that God is in heaven?" he replied "Not as I do the sacraments seven". "Adam Reid, what say ye?" exclaimed the astonished King. Reid explained that he believed God to be both in heaven and on earth. "But thou and thy faction", he continued, turning to the Archbishop, "declare by your works, that either ye think there is no God at all, or else that he is so shut up in heaven that he regards not what is done in the earth . . . else thou should not make thyself checkmate to the King, and altogether forget the charge that Jesus Christ the Son of God gave to his apostles, which was, to preach his evangel, and not to play the proud prelates, as all the rabble of you do this day. And now, Sir," he said, turning to the King, "judge ye whether the bishop or I believe best that God is in heaven." A brisk exchange of texts followed, but it was cut short by the King. "Wilt thou burn thy bill?" he asked Reid. "Sir, the bishop and ye will," was the bold reply. "With these and the lyik scoffis", concludes Knox, "the Bischop and his band war so dashed out of countenance, that the greatest part of the accusatioun was turned to lawchter."[1]

[1] John Knox, *History of the Reformation*, BK. I, in *Works*, ed. D. Laing, VOL. I, Edinburgh 1846, pp. 7-12.

The ignorance of the rank and file of the clergy was another source of weakness to the Scottish Church. A retentive memory and a pleasant voice was all that was required of a candidate for the priesthood. Of that model abbot, Thomas Crystal, it is related that he was taught Latin by a monk of Culross Abbey, but when his parents saw that he outdistanced all the other scholars, urged by their friends, they removed him with overmuch haste from the grammar school, and set him to study music. It was a wise decision: his voice, *canora et crispans*, gained him the friendship of many great dignitaries, and three abbots invited him to enter their monasteries as a novice. His formal education ended with his twelve months' novitiate in Kinloss Abbey, during which his studies seem to have been confined to the memorising of psalms, hymns, and canticles, and "other things of that kind".[1]

Many of the Scottish clergy had not even entered a grammar school; all that they knew they had learned from the sang scule attached to the cathedral, abbey, or collegiate church in which they had been choristers. The master of the sang scule was expected to have a knowledge of Gregorian chant, plainsong, and pricksong, and to impart it to the boys. He was expected, in some places at least, to teach them to read, but he was not expected to give them the meaning of the Latin which they were required to sing. Many candidates for the priesthood were even more lightly equipped. "The bishops admit . . ." declared John Major, "men who are quite unskilled in music, and they ought at least to understand the Gregorian chant."[2] Those who went to a grammar school usually left at the age of fourteen, when they had mastered their "Donat" or Latin Grammar, read a little Livy and Ovid, and learned to write and speak a Latin that was serviceable, if far from Ciceronian. Almost every Scottish burgh had its grammar school, located usually in a single hired room in a private house, and taught by a single master, appointed sometimes, as in Arbroath, by the Abbot, sometimes, as in Aberdeen, by the burgh council, but usually by the bishop of the diocese.

At the beginning of James's reign the young scholar had two

---

[1] Ferrerius, *Historia de Kynlos*, pp. 61-2.
[2] Major, *History of Greater Britain*, p. 30.

Scottish universities to choose from, St Andrews and Glasgow. The chances were that he would avoid Glasgow, "a university poorly endowed, and not rich in scholars", with a teaching staff of two regents or professors, and make for St Andrews, with its student population of over a hundred. Here he found that he could not be a *martinet*, flitting from a house in the town to the lecture hall *in vico*—in South Street, the St Andrews equivalent of the *Vicus stramineus* of Paris—unless he was abjectly poor, or the son of a burgess of St Andrews; he had to live either in the Paedagogium, which was almost as old as the University, or in the College of St Salvator, founded by Bishop Kennedy in 1450. Both the Paedagogium and St Salvator's maintained a complete staff of masters or regents, capable of supplying the quantum of Aristotelean science and philosophy necessary for the degree of Master of Arts. The student began by studying logic, proceeding by the way of the *Universals* of Porphyry or the *Summulae* of Petrus Hispanus to Latin versions of the *Topics* and *Prior* and *Posterior Analytics*. Half way through his second year he "determined", and celebrated the successful passage of this stage of his career by giving a feast, which might cost as much as ten pounds, and by presenting gloves to various university officials. In Lent he went forward to Responsions, and if he satisfied the two regents who were his opponents in debate, he was admitted as bachelor. In the second half of his course he studied natural science, geometry, metaphysics, and ethics, again as presented by Aristotle or by his medieval scholastic interpreters. Towards the end of his fourth year he had to undergo first the *temptamen*, in which, seated on the Black Stone in the examination hall, he was cross-questioned by four *temptatores*, and second, the *examen in cameris*, in which, as a member of a *camera* or group of half-a-dozen candidates, he displayed his prowess in debate. He could now claim his *licentia ubique docendi*, and, should he choose to provide another ten-pound feast, with caps and gloves of good quality for the expectant examiners, go on to take his Master's degree. Often he preferred to remain a simple licentiate.

Though a faculty of theology had been in existence since the earliest days of the University, few Masters of Arts were willing to qualify for the degree of Bachelor of Theology by remaining in residence till they had reached the age of twenty-five, and fewer still embarked on the additional five years' course of study, teaching, and discussion which led to the doctorate. At Glasgow the faculty of canon law maintained a precarious existence, but both universities catered almost exclusively for the student of Arts; the aspiring theologian or canonist usually left them for Paris or Orleans.

Even within the Faculty of Arts reform was needed. Students were admitted who were too young and without an adequate grounding in Latin; their introduction to logic had to be delayed till they had acquired enough Latin to enable them to follow the lectures and discussions, with the result that metaphysics was crowded out altogether. In St Andrews one innovation of doubtful value had indeed been made: the students who came up in the same year were piloted through the whole of their course by the same regent. There was no escape: for four years the scholar must listen to the same teacher; for four years the teacher lectured to the same half-dozen or half-score of red-robed scholars.

The university, like the grammar school, was still regarded primarily as a seminary for youths destined for the Church, to be attended by the Laird's younger son, who might already be provost of a collegiate church or rector of a parish, but to be avoided by his elder son, who would succeed him as sheriff. But the famous Education Act of 1496 revealed a new conception of the functions of school and university—to train members of the ruling classes for the exercise of the duties appertaining to their station. The eldest sons of all "barronis and frehaldaris that ar of substance" were to attend a grammar school from the age of nine at the latest, till they "have perfite latyne", and then proceed to the "schools of art and Jure", where they were to remain for three years. The country would then be provided with an adequate supply of competent amateur judges, "throw the quhilkis Justice may reigne universalie throw all the realme".[1]

None knew better than Elphinstone that there was no "school of jure", no faculty of civil law, in either of the existing univer-

[1] *A.P.S.*, VOL. II, p. 238.

BISHOP WILLIAM ELPHINSTONE

By permission of the University of Aberdeen   *Marischal College, Aberdeen*

sities. He was distressed, too, at the low level of education in his own northern diocese, "separated from other parts of the kingdom by arms of the sea and lofty mountains, inhabited by men rude, ignorant of letters, and almost barbarous", living at so great a distance from a university "that they cannot devote themselves to study, nay rather, are so ignorant that by no means can men be found fitted to preach the Gospel to the people of these regions, or even to administer the sacraments of the Church". Through the good offices of the King he obtained from Pope Alexander VI a bull, dated 10 February 1495,[1] authorising the establishment of a *studium generale* in the burgh of Old Aberdeen, with faculties of arts, theology, canon law, civil law, and medicine. Knowing that poverty had crippled the University of Glasgow, he waited till he had negotiated the transfer of the revenues of the derelict Hospital of St Germain, within the diocese of St Andrews, and of various parish churches, to his new foundation[2] before he summoned Hector Boece from Paris to be its principal. Five years later, in 1505, he completed his scheme by the building of a college, dedicated to St Mary *in nativitate*, but styled soon afterwards King's College.[3]

Thus Scotland, with a population approximately one-tenth of that of England, had now three universities to England's two. But though, in the words of its first principal, "from the University of Aberdeen there went out in a short time many men trained in theology, canon law and civil, and very many trained in philosophy",[4] it may be doubted if the founder had not missed a great opportunity. If only Elphinstone had succeeded Schevez, he might have increased the endowments of St Andrews, revived its moribund faculty of canon law, inspired it with some of his own passion for learning, and given Scotland a university which would have ranked, if not with Oxford or Cambridge, at least with Orleans or Poitiers. As it was, Scotland still failed to hold the ambitious student. Although he might have listened in Aber-

[1] *Fasti Aberdonenses, Selections from the Records of the University and King's College of Aberdeen 1494-1854*, ed. C. Innes, Aberdeen 1854, No. 1.
[2] *Fasti Aberdonenses*, ed. Innes, Nos. 4-17.
[3] *Fasti Aberdonenses*, ed. Innes, No. 46.   [4] Boece, *Vitae*, p. 91.

M

deen to lectures on theology and canon law "after the fashion of Paris", and on civil law "after the laudable fashion of Orleans", as a rule he avoided substitutes and crossed the seas to France.

The King would have approved of his choice. He sent his illegitimate son, Alexander, the young Archbishop of St Andrews, to Padua, where in 1508 he met "that cunning clarke . . . the splendour and ornament of our age", Erasmus of Rotterdam. Erasmus was engaged as his tutor, and went with him to Siena early in the following year. "I lived with him at one time in Siena," wrote Erasmus, "and trained him in the maxims of rhetoric and of Greek letters. . . . At one and the same time he was studying the lawyers . . . he had lessons in rhetoric and would declaim on a prescribed theme, exercising both the pen and the tongue. He was learning Greek and rendered his daily portion at the stated time. In the afternoon he would turn to music, the monochord, the pipe, the lute; sometimes, too, he would sing."[1]

Alexander returned to Scotland in 1510. If he had ever formed any plans for the introduction of Greek into the university of which he was chancellor, they perished with him at Flodden, but he was successful in carrying out a more modest reform. On his return to St Andrews he had been shocked at the state of the Paedagogium, now, in his own words "through lack of endowments and of learned men almost extinguished . . . and in ruins", and he proposed to "endow it and erect it into a college" to the glory of God, the defence of the faith, and the increase of learned men.[2] This scheme he abandoned, however, when he found that the Prior, John Hepburn, anxious about the supply of adequately trained clergy for the cathedral, was proposing to divert the buildings and revenues of the semi-derelict Hospital of St Leonard to the purposes of a completely new college. In 1512 the Archbishop and the Prior co-operated in the foundation of the College of St Leonard, in which twenty poor clerks, students of arts, and

[1] Erasmus, *Adages*, Chil. II, Cent. v, in *Opera omnia*, ed. Leclerc, VOL. II, Louvain 1703, p. 544, cited in Herkless and Hannay, *Archbishops of St Andrews*, VOL. I, p. 262.

[2] J. Herkless and R. K. Hannay, *The College of St Leonard*, Edinburgh 1905, p. 89.

six students of theology, were to be maintained. Conditions of admission were made more stringent than at the Paedagogium and St Salvator's: students had to be at least fifteen years of age, certified by the Sub-Prior and a canon of the Cathedral, "as these examiners would avoid the vengeance of God", to be skilled in writing and to have an adequate knowledge of Latin and the Gregorian chant.[1]

It may be argued that the activities of Elphinstone, Alexander Stewart, and Hepburn resulted only in the creation of new facilities for acquiring the old learning, of schools untroubled by the restless, enquiring spirit of the Renaissance, ready to put everything to the test of experiment. The founding of a chair of medicine in Aberdeen, to be held by a layman,[2] may seem to point in another direction, but the mediciner was instructed to lecture after the fashion of the school of Paris—in other words, to stick to first principles and to avoid any suspicion of empiricism. But the passion for investigation and experiment affected the Court, if it did not touch the universities; it moved the King to buy drugs,[3] and books on alchemy,[4] and to subsidise the Abbot of Tungland's researches.[5] One would like to believe Pitscottie's story that "the king gart tak ane dum woman and pat hir in Inchekeytht and gaif hir twa young bairnes in companie . . . to knaw quhat langage thir bairnes wald speik quhene they come to lauchfull aige",[6] but unfortunately there is something like it in Herodotus. One may claim King James however, on the strength of a letter which he sent to the surgeons and barbers of Edinburgh on 13 October 1506,[7] as the founder of the famous school of medicine in that city. The letter confirmed the seal of cause, which the Burgh Council had granted to the craft on 1 July of the preceding year.[8] Henceforth no one could practise as a sur-

[1] op. cit., p. 146.   [2] Fasti Aberdonenses, ed. Innes, No. 46.
[3] C.T.S., VOL. I, pp. 23, 24; VOL. II, pp. 34, 100, 365, 410; VOL. III, pp. 205, 380; VOL. IV, pp. 125, 135, 283, 313, 354, 406.   [4] C.T.S., VOL. IV, p. 92.
[5] C.T.S., VOL. II, pp. lxxvi-lxxviii, 62, 63, 138, 140, 357, 359, 360, 361, 362, 363, 374, 393, 402, 403, 404, 407, 416; VOL. III, pp. 46, 158, 182, 183, 188, 330, 353, 379; VOL. IV, pp. 76, 77, 79, 80, 83, 85, 86, 90, 91, 92, 96, 99, 101, 102, 104, 137, 283, 287.   [6] Pitscottie, VOL. I, p. 237.
[7] R.S.S., VOL. I, No. 1343.   [8] Edinburgh Records, VOL. I, pp. 101-4.

geon and barber in the burgh unless he had been "dilegentlie and avysitlie examinit" by the masters of the craft. He had to satisfy his examiners that "he knows anotamell, nature and complexion of every member humanis bodie, and inlykewayes he knaw all the vaynis of the samyn, that he may mak flewbothomell in dew tyme, and als that he knaw in quhilk member the signe hes domination for the tyme", for, it is explained "every man aucht to knaw the nature and substance of every thing that he werkis, or ellis he is negligent". Even the apprentices and feed servants had to be able to read and write. The entrance fee was stiff—five pounds—"with ane dennar to the maisteris of the saidis craftis at his admissioun". In return, he shared in certain privileges—"anis in the yeir ane condempnit man efter he be deid to mak anatomell of, quhairthrow we may haif experience", and a monopoly of the sale of whisky in the burgh.

There is evidence too, that some university teachers regarded Latin not simply as a clue to the labyrinth of scholastic philosophy, but as a key to the garden of the Muses. The appearance of lectures on poetry and rhetoric points to a revival of the study of literature for its own sake. Hector Boece, brought from Paris to Aberdeen to teach theology, sought to imitate Livy in his *Scotorum Historia*, blending history, legend, and vain imagination in stately periods. But of all who studied or taught in the Scottish universities in the reign of James IV, the one who conforms most closely to our conception of a Renaissance scholar is Gavin Douglas, the third son of "Bell-the-Cat". In his boyhood, like most youths of gentle birth, he had been a page in some noble household—"[I] spekis as I lernyt quhen I was page,"[1] he confessed in 1512—but he seems also to have known the inside of a grammar school, and to have formed no very high opinion of the level of grammar school Latinity. His own translation of Virgil, he declared.

> sal be reput a neidfull wark
> To thame wald Virgill to childryn expone . . .
> Thank me tharfor, maisteris of grammar sculys
> Quhar ye syt techand on your benkis and stulys.[2]

[1] Prologue to *Aeneid*, BK. I, 1839 edn., VOL. I, p. 6.
[2] Postscript to *Aeneid*, VOL. II, p. 907.

He matriculated at St Andrews in 1490, and left it, probably to continue his studies at the University of Paris, in 1494. He returned to become first, Rector of Prestonkirk, and after 1501, Provost of the Collegiate Church of St Giles in Edinburgh. He displayed the same passionate admiration for Chaucer—"principall poet but peir, heavenlie trumpat"—and for Virgil—"Vesper, and the day starne at morow, thou Phoebus, lychtnar of the planetis all". He translated Ovid's *De remedio amoris*, and he knew Horace's *Ars poetica*. For aids to the study of Virgil he used the *Commentaries* of Servius, and the "grete volume clepit *Saturniad*" of Macrobius. He was familiar with more recent literary criticism, with the works of Italian Renaissance scholars like Poggio, Lorenzo Valla, and Cristofero Landino, and he got much of his mythological lore from the "Περὶ γενεαλυγίας *deorum*" of Boccaccio. Philosophy he left behind him in St Andrews—

> Betuix *genus, sexus, and species*
> Diuersite in our leid to seik I ces;
> For *obiectum* and *subiectum* alssua
> He war expert couth fynd me termys tua,
> Quhilkis ar als ryfe amangis clerkis in scuylle
> As evir fowlis plungit in laik or puyll.[1]

He found matter more to his liking in the histories of Caesar, Livy, and Suetonius, and in the *De civitate Dei* of St Augustine. Finally, his statement that Henry, Lord St Clair,

> . . . with gret instance, divers tymys seir,
> Prayt me translait Virgill or Homeir,[2]

would indicate that he had some knowledge of Greek, where or from whom acquired no one can tell.

Till 1508 the Scottish scholar was dependent on the presses of England and the continent for his supply of printed books; till 1508 no Scottish author had experienced the felicity of seeing his own works in print. On 15 September 1507, however, the King had issued a letter under his privy seal stating that as Walter Chepman and Andrew Myllar, burgesses of Edinburgh, had at his request "takin on thame to furnis and bring hame ane prent [printing-press] with al stuf belangand tharto and expert men to

---

[1] Prologue to BK. I, VOL. I, p. 15. [2] Prologue to BK. I, VOL. I, p. 6.

use the samyne, for imprenting within our realme of the bukis of
our lawis, actis of parliament, croniclis, mess bukis and portuus
[breviaries] efter the use of our realme, with additiouns and
legendis of Scottis sanctis now gaderit to be ekit thairto . . . and
to sell the sammyn for competent pricis", he forbade anyone to
take manuscripts out of the country "to ger imprint the samyne
in utheris cuntreis to be brocht and sauld agane within our realme
to caus the said Walter and Androu tyne thare greit labour and
expens".[1]

Chepman, who was a prosperous Edinburgh merchant, probably supplied the capital, and Myllar, who had been a printer
in France, the practical knowledge. Their venture was supported,
if indeed it had not been inspired, by Elphinstone, who, dissatisfied
with the various haphazard modifications of the Sarum Use, had
collected the material for new service books "efter our awin
Scottis use". The new service books, the royal letter continues,
were to be used throughout the kingdom as soon as they had been
printed and distributed, and "na maner of sic bukis of Salusbery
use" were to be imported and offered for sale.

In February 1509 appeared the *Pars hyemalis* of Elphinstone's
Aberdeen Breviary; in June 1510 the *Pars aestivalis*. "*Laus Deo
cuius gratis finis adest presenti opusculo.*" The books were no "*opus-
cula*" but noble volumes, as pleasant to look at as the manuscript
service books which they were meant to displace.

Nor were they the first printed matter to issue from Chepman
and Myllar's press. The National Library of Scotland possesses a
volume made up of eleven slender booklets—"The Porteous of
Nobleness", "The Knightly Tale of Golagros and Gawaine",
"The Tale of Sir Eglamour of Artoys", "The Golden Targe",
"Ane Buke of Gude Counsale to the King", "The Maying and
Disport of Chaucer"—really Lydgate's "Complaint of the Black
Knight", "The Flyting of Dunbar and Kennedy", "The Traitie
of Orpheus", "The Ballade of Lord Barnard Stewart", "The Twa
mariit Wemen and the Wedo", and "A Gest of Robyn Hude".
"The Twa mariit Wemen and the Wedo" and "Robyn Hude"
seem to have been printed on the continent, the former probably

<hr/>

[1] R.S.S., VOL. I, No. 1546.

by a printer in Rouen who had already done work for Myllar. The remainder were "imprentit in the south gait"—now the Cowgate—of Edinburgh, in or about the year 1508, for though six are undated, "The Maying and Disporte of Chaucer" is dated 4 April 1508, "Golagros and Gawaine" 8 April 1508, and "The Porteus of Nobleness" 20 April 1508. To the same year probably belongs a more ambitious venture—an edition of Blind Harry's *Wallace*, of which only a few leaves of a single copy have survived.

Legends of the saints, tales of knightly adventure, imitations of Chaucer—the books printed by Chepman and Myllar revealed a Scotland which for all its intellectual activity was still untouched by the spirit of the Renaissance. They included, it is true, a version of the legend of Orpheus and Eurydice, by Robert Henryson, schoolmaster in Dunfermline, but Henryson's version owed more to Boethius and Nicholas Trivet than to any classical author. Eurydice is carried off by a fairy; Orpheus follows her, not to the Hades of Vergil, where

Umbrae ibant tenues simulacraque luce carentum

but to a medieval hell, where beside Herod and Pilate, Ahab and Jezebel,

> . . . fand he mony pape and cardinal,
> In haly kirk quhilk dois abusion,
> And bischopis in thair pontificall . . .
> Abbotis and men of all religion.[1]

The naivete, studied or unstudied, which charms one in the *Fables* and *Robene and Makyne*, jars in this attempt at high tragedy. Orpheus meets his lost love in Hades:

> Quod he "my lady lele, and my delyt,
> Full wa is me to se yow changit thus;
> Quhare is thy rude [complexion] as rose wyth chekis quhite,
> Thy cristall eyne with blenkis amorouse,
> Thi lippis rede to kis diliciouse?"
> Quod scho "as now I dar noucht tell, perfay;
> Bot ye sall wit the cause ane othir day".[2]

[1] Henryson, *Poems*, ed. G. G. Smith, VOL. III, p. 50.
[2] Ibid.

He wins her back, only to lose her again.

> Thus chydand on with lufe, our burn and bent,
> A woful wedow homewart is he went.[1]

This couplet ends the story, but not the poem; the four hundred lines of narrative are followed by almost three hundred lines of moral, in which the poet explains that Orpheus signifies "the part intellective Of mannis saule", and that Eurydice "is our affection Be fantasy oft movit up and doun".[2]

If in *Orpheus* the schoolmaster jostles the poet, in the *Moral Fables* the poet comes to terms with the schoolmaster and converts him into an ally: from a schoolbook, Walter the Englishman's translation into Latin verse of Aesop's *Fables*, he draws the material for the majority of his thirteen delightful little animal stories. For others he takes the French *Roman de Renart* or Caxton's *Historye of Reynard the Foxe*. True, he propitiates the schoolmaster by attaching a *moralitas*, as elaborate as it is irrelevant, to each of them, but once he has made this concession, he lets nothing distract him from his task of telling a story, and setting his birds and beasts to converse in amusing and seeming-natural speech. And he knows his business: he can retell a twenty times told fable so that it seems entirely fresh and new, so that the sophisticated reader finds himself praying that the valiant wether will outface the wolf, and rejoicing in the unexpected escape of the Uponlandis Mous from the claws of Gilbert the Cat. He looks out on the animal world, and finds that it is an exact counterpart to the world of men, but his animal characters are animals, nicely observed, not types and abstractions, or human beings tricked out in feathers or fur. "Upon ane tyme", he writes

> Ane lytill mous come till ane Rever syde;
> Scho micht not waid, hir schankis wer sa schort,
> Scho culd not swym, scho had na hors to ryde;
> Of verray force behovit hir to byde,
> And to and fra besyde that Rever deip
> Scho ran, cryand with mony pietuous peip.[3]

In vain the *moralitas* explains that the mouse is the soul of man;

---

[1] *op. cit.*, VOL. III, p. 54.   [2] *op. cit.*, VOL. III, p. 56.
[3] "The Taill of the paddok and the mous", *op. cit.*, VOL. II, p. 206.

for us she remains a real mouse, the central figure in a moving little tragedy. For the poet's heart goes out to the weak and foolish, the victims of injustice and cruelty, whether they be mice or sheep, or little birds hovering above the fowler's snare, or "the puir commons, that daily are oppressed be tyrant men". But he never allows his sympathy or indignation to blur his vision or deaden his sense of humour: his animal villains, like their victims, are exactly observed and nicely discriminated, though amused pity has now given way to amused contempt.

He has set his birds and beasts in a Scottish landscape. Sometimes, like a coloured miniature in the black letter of a psalter or book of hours, a vivid little description of some rural scene will diversify the narrative. It may be a picture of the "cadger, with capill and with creillis" laden with herring, or of the ploughman, struggling with an unruly team of oxen, or of an old man and his wife preparing linen—

> The Carl pullit the Lyne,
> Rippillit the bollis, and in beitis set,
> It steepit in the burn, and dryit syne
> And with ane Bettil knokkit it and bet,
> Syne swingillit it weill, and hekkillit in the flet;
> His wyfe it span, and twynit it in to threid.[1]

As it is with his *Moral Fables*, so it is with his *Robene and Makyne*. This Scottish version of a French *pastourelle* is no copy, but something fresh and original. The faithless Robin of the French poems becomes a slow-moving, matter-of-fact Lowland rustic, the forsaken Marion or Mariot a strong-willed young woman, dowered with a sense of humour and a nippy tongue. So it is too with the *Testament of Cresseid*, a continuation of Chaucer's *Troilus and Criseyde*. According to Sir Francis Kinaston, who translated *The Testament* into Latin verse in the time of Charles I, "Mr Henderson wittily observing, that Chaucer in his 5th book had related the death of Troilus, but makes no mention of what became of Cresseid, he learnedly takes on him in a fine way to express the punishment and end due to a false inconstant whore". There is more to it than this. Henryson had the wit to

---

[1] "The swallow and the other birds", *op. cit.*, VOL. II, p. 134.

see that Chaucer's heroine was not a mere "false inconstant whore". The schoolmaster may scold; the poet relents:

> I sall excuse, as far furth as I may,
> Thy womanheid, thy wisdome and fairness;
> The quhilk Fortoun hes put to sic distres
> As hir pleisit, and nothing throw the gilt
> Of the.[1]

His Cresseid is a frail and pitiful figure, as helpless in the toils of fate as the feeble little creatures in the *Fables*.

There is much in *The Testament* that Chaucer would have been proud to call his own, and some things that are beyond even his reach. Henryson's description of the dazzling and chilling splendour of the wintry skies, of the "greit cald" which drove him to the fireside and Chaucer's poem, is a fitting prelude to the apparition of

> Cupide the King ringand ane silver bell,
> Quhilk men micht heir fra hevin unto hell,[2]

and to the awesome pageant of the angry gods. Saturn pronounces the doom of the fickle Cresseid

> Thy greit fairnes, and all thy bewtie gay
> Thy wantoun blude, and eik thy goldin Hair
> Heir I exclude fra the for evermair,[3]

and Cynthia adds the "sentence diffinityue"

> Quhair thow cummis, Ilk man sal fle the place;
> This sall thow go begging fra hous to hous,
> With Cop and Clapper lyke ane Lazarous.[4]

So the proud beauty becomes a leper, dwelling "into yone Hospitall at the tounis end". Then comes the poignantly beautiful description of the last meeting of the lovers. Troilus, riding home victorious from a sally against the Greeks

> Neir by the place can pas
> Quhair Cresseid sat, not witting quhat scho was.
>
> Than upon him scho kest up baith her Ene,
> And with ane blenk it came into his thocht

---

[1] *The Testament of Cresseid, op. cit.*, VOL. II, p. 6.
[2] *op. cit.*, VOL. II, p. 8.   [3] *op. cit.*, VOL. II, p. 14.   [4] *op. cit.*, VOL. II, p. 15.

That he sumtime hir face befoir had sene;
Bot scho was in sic plye he knew hir nocht;
Yit than hir luik into his mynd it brocht
The sweit visage and amorous blenking
Of fair Cresseid, sumtyme his awin darling.[1]

The tragic power of this scene owes nothing to Chaucer's example. Nor could Chaucer have bettered the moving simplicity of the lines which should have ended the poem:

Lo, fair Ladyis, Cresseid, of Troyis toun,
Sumtyme countit the flour of Womanheid,
Under this stane, lait Lipper, lyis deid.[2]

In his sanity, his balance, his power of getting outside himself, of thinking and feeling with the diverse creatures of his fancy, in his avoidance of mere virtuosity and literary ostentation, Henryson resembles the author of *Troilus* and *The Canterbury Tales* more closely than does that vehement, self-centred poet who has been styled the Scottish Chaucer. While the personality of Henryson eludes us, William Dunbar is the most clearly defined of all the shadowy figures that haunted the court of King James. He was a member of a cadet branch of the noble family of which the Earl of March was the head, born in 1460, according to the assertion of his friend and rival Walter Kennedy that he was "consavit in the grete eclips" of that year. He was destined for the church—for a bishopric, his kinsfolk fondly hoped—

I wes in yowthe, on nureise kne
Cald dandillie, bischop, dandillie.[3]

He entered St Andrews University, "determined" in 1477, paid his licentiate's fees in 1479, and became Master William Dunbar. The four years at St Andrews are followed by a period of twenty-one years about which official records are silent, but from his rival's jocular slanders in *The Flyting of Dunbar and Kennedy* and his own jesting confessions in *How Dumbar was desyred to be ane Freir* we can hazard a guess at some of his activities. He became a vagabond scholar, of the tribe of François Villon, bearing "ane tume purs", and wrapped in "ane threid bair goun". He sought

---

[1] *op. cit.*, VOL. II, p. 20.   [2] *op. cit.*, VOL. II, p. 24.
[3] *Poems*, ed. W. M. Mackenzie, p. 43.

to remedy his "consumption of the purse" by various devices, hawking pardons for food and drink in every parish "Fra Etrike Forest furthward to Dunfrese", leaving a Scotland that had become too hot to hold him, and wandering through England and Picardy in the disguise of a Franciscan friar, to beguile the faithful by his eloquence. In France he changed his brown robe for the trappings of a pilgrim, complete with staff and cockleshells, but his pilgrimage took him no farther than Paris.

At the age of thirty his talents had gained him nothing better than some unspecified minor post in the King's service. He seems to have been one of the clerks who sailed with Bothwell in the *Katherine* when he went as ambassador to France in 1491. If Kennedy is to be believed, he was so sea-sick that the captain ordered him to be put ashore on the Bass. He certainly visited Denmark, possibly in 1492, when Lord Ogilvy went as ambassador to King John, and brought home with him the horrible memory of the "Densemen on the rattis"—Danish rebels tortured on the rack. On 15 August 1500 the King granted him a pension of £10 a year for life, or till such time as he obtained a benefice of the annual value of £40.[1] At the end of the following year, as we have seen, he accompanied the Scottish ambassadors to London, and was present at the dinner which the Lord Mayor gave to them in Christmas week, where, rising from his place at a side table, he recited "London, thou are of cities *A per se*". He was now "The Rhymer of Scotland", as the English records style him, turning out with equal ease and art a stately epithalamium on the occasion of the royal marriage, and vivacious records of the King's amorous adventures and wild repentances. He seems to have speedily gained the friendship of the young Queen, and took it upon himself to rebuke his sovereign for his neglect of "that sweit meik Rois". Not that his concern was entirely altruistic; if only the King were a more considerate husband, the poet declared,

> than weill war me,
> But benefice I wald nocht be;
> My hard fortoun wer endit than.[2]

[1] *R.S.S.*, VOL. I, No. 563.   [2] *Poems*, ed. J. Small, VOL. II, p. 218.

On 17 March 1504, having at last taken priest's orders, he celebrated his first Mass, in the presence of the King, who made an
offering of seven French crowns.[1]

Though no longer "half-fed, half-mad, half-sarkit", though
to his pension were added gowns from the royal wardrobe and
an occasional gift of money,[2] the poet was still unsatisfied. Sometimes he lashed with savage gusto the charlatans and illiterate
rustics who had passed him in the race for preferment—

> Twa curis or thre, hes upolandis Michell
> With dispensationis in ane knitchell,
> Thocht he fra nolt had new tane leif—[3]

sometimes he broods over the freaks of fortune or of the royal
judgment that left him, for all his gentle birth and rare talents,
unprovided even with "ane kirk scarce coverit with hadder",
until, to his embittered mind, the world seems wholly false and
deceitful:

> The sugurit mouthis, with myndis therfra,
> The figurit speiche with faceis tua,
> The plesand toungis, with hartis unplane,
> For to considder is ane pane.[4]

He does not share Henryson's compassion for the weak and
the oppressed; the only injustice that really moves him is the
injustice inflicted on himself; were that rectified, he hints, he
would not be so ready to spy out and proclaim abuses:

> Had I rewarde amang the laif,
> It wald me sumthing satisfie,
> And less of my malancolie,
> And gar me mony falt ouerse,
> That is now brayd befoir myn E.[5]

The benefice never came his way, but in November 1507 his
pension was doubled,[6] and in August 1510 it was raised to £80 a
year[7]—more than twice the sum that Hector Boece received as

[1] *C.T.S.*, VOL. II, p. 258.
[2] *C.T.S.*, VOL. III, pp. 154, 181, 331, 361; VOL. IV, pp. 106, 127, 249-50.
[3] *Poems*, ed. Small, VOL. II, p. 106.
[4] *op. cit.*, VOL. II, p. 226.   [5] *op. cit.*, VOL. II, p. 222.
[6] *C.T.S.*, VOL. IV, p. 69.   [7] *R.S.S.*, VOL. I, No. 2119.

Principal of Aberdeen University. Notes of payments to him occur in the Treasurer's Accounts till May 1513; after that date there is no mention of him in record. For aught we can tell, the poet may have marched in the King's company to Flodden, and perished beside the pupil of Erasmus.[1]

Dunbar was our first professional man of letters, one who gloried in the name of makar, who did not want to be anything else, who craved a benefice because it would enable him to write and "live in some disport". Nothing vexes him more than the temporary loss of his skill—when,

> To dyt, thocht I begowthe to dress,
> The sentence lay full evill till find,
> Vnsleipit in my heid behind,
> Dullit in dulness and distres[2]

except perhaps the knowledge that an inaccurate text of his poems has been put into circulation, because someone

> fulle dismemberit hes my meter,
> And poysound it with strang salpeter,

and

> Hes indorsit myn indytting
> With versis off his awin hand vrytting.[3]

Often, it is true, he shows resentment because his poetry is not a marketable commodity—

> Jok, that wes wont to keip the stirkis,
> Can now draw him ane cleik of kirkis
> With ane fals cairt in to his sleif
> Worth all my ballatis under the birkis,
> Excess of thocht dois me mischief,[4]

sometimes he draws comfort from the thought that

> Als lang in mynd my wark sall hald . . .
> But wering, or consumptioun,
> Roust, canker, or corruptioun,

---

[1] If, however, it was he who wrote "Ane Orisoun, quhen the Gouernour past in France", attributed to him in the *Maitland Folio Manuscript*, ed. W. A. Craigie, Edinburgh 1919-27, VOL. I, pp. 210-1, he must have survived Flodden by at least four years.   [2] *Poems*, ed. Small, VOL. II, p. 254.
[3] *op. cit.*, VOL. II, p. 210.   [4] *op. cit.*, VOL. II, p. 106.

As ony of thair werkis all,
Suppois that my rewarde be small.[1]

He is not a scholar; he mistakes Apollo for a goddess, and confounds the persons of "Pallas and prudent Minerva". Unlike Gavin Douglas, he is completely uninterested in the rediscovery of classical literature; to him Chaucer is still the "rose of rhetoris all", the master craftsman whose work must be sedulously imitated. He too, must tell how, on a morning in May, he wandered into a garden, fell asleep, and dreamed a dream. But when he has told how the Golden Targe of Reason failed to protect him against the assaults of Dame Venus and her train, he confesses that his variation on a theme of Chaucer has varied for the worse:

> Thy fresch anamalit termes celicall
> This mater coud illumynit have full brycht:
> Was thou nocht of oure Inglisch all the lycht.[2]

He is too modest: he handles his outmoded theme with dexterity and assurance, and gives it a freshness and lively grace. But we cannot say of any of Dunbar's poems, as Dryden said of *The Prologue*, "Here is God's plenty. We have our fore-fathers and great-grand-dames all before us." He is not sufficiently interested in his fellow-men. Time and again, it is true, he paints in telling strokes the motley throng of seekers after royal favour—

> Fenyeouris, fleichouris, and flatteraris;
> Cryaris, craikaris, and clatteraris . . .
> Monsouris of France, gud clarat-cunnaris . . .
> Schulderaris, and schowaris, that hes no schame,[3]

but hatred and contempt distort his vision, and he produces caricatures instead of portraits.

Once, however, he matches himself with the Chaucer of *The Canterbury Tales*: his *Twa Mariit Wemen and the Wedo* is a masterpiece of the same order as *The Wife of Bath's Prologue*. But Dunbar handles the sordid theme in his own way: he revives for the last time the cumbrous unrimed alliterative verse, the oldest measure in the language, and uses it with consummate art, makes

---

[1] *op. cit.*, VOL. II, p. 221.   [2] *op. cit.*, VOL. II, p. 10.
[3] *op. cit.*, VOL. II, p. 221.

his three lovely women utter their amoral confessions against a background of enchanting beauty, and his savage humour, his contemptuous interest in the whole business of sex, bears a closer resemblance to the inverted Puritanism of Aldous Huxley than to the genial humanism of Chaucer.

It is difficult to realise that the author of this poem, and of the even more frankly naturalistic *In Secreit Place*, also wrote, in addition to one or two conventional love poems, the tender and reverent *In Prais of Wemen*:

> Sen scho hes borne him [Christ] in her halines,
> And he is well and grund of all gudnes,
> All wemen of us suld haif honoring,
> Service and luve, aboif all uthir thing.[1]

It is equally difficult for some critics to see how the author of a blasphemous parody of the requiem mass should have written those triumphant Christmas and Easter hymns, or that meditation on the Passion, with its refrain "O mankind, for the love of thee". It may be, as one of his editors thought,[2] that the meditative and religious poems were written when the extravagant and erring poet was sobered by age and experience. But we have no assurance that it was so; we know that he could pass from the macabre horror of *The Dance of the Sevin Deidly Synnis* to the crude excremental humour of its sequel *The Soutar and Tailyours War*, and from that to the light-hearted banter of the postscript *Amends to the Telyouris and Soutaris*. The astounding contrasts in the themes of his verses probably signifies nothing more than an unusual responsiveness to the mood of the moment. Resentment or resignation, black despair or ribald mirth—they are of equal value as stuff for his poetry.

For all his disconcerting diversity of moods and themes, his mind ranges within comparatively narrow limits. He is a virtuoso and there are times when we are tempted to think of him as nothing more, careless of what his theme may be as long as it gives him an excuse for working out a pattern of beautifully sounding words.

But he is more than "a reed through which every wind is

---

[1] *op. cit.*, VOL. II, p. 171.   [2] J. Small. *op. cit.*, VOL. I, p. lxix.

blown to music". He feels fiercely and intensely; he strings some
verses round the commonplace "None may assure in this world",
then suddenly his imagination catches fire, and he sees the race
of man *sub specie aeternitatis*:

> Quhat help is thair in lordschipis sevin,
> Quhene na houss is bot hell and hevin,
> Palace of licht, or pitt obscure,
> Quhair youlis ar with horreble stevin?
> In to this world may nane assure.
>
> *Ubi ardentes animae*
> *Semper dicentes 'Ve! Ve!'*
> Sall cry Allace! that wemen tham bure.
> *O quante sunt iste tenebre!*
> In to this warld may none assure.[1]

Into a metrical exercise, a conventional love poem written
"Quhone he list to feyne" come the magic lines

> My deathe chasis my lyfe so besalie
> That wery is my goist to fle so fast.[2]

He heralds one of his savage attacks on the charlatan Abbot of
Tungland with a line of haunting beauty, "Lucina shining in
silence of the night".[3] Out of the reflection that death comes to
all, out of the remembrance of a Latin tag used by Lydgate,
comes the sombre and disturbing splendour of *The Lament for the
Makaris*—

> Onto the ded gois all Estatis,
> Princis, Prelotis, and Potestatis,
> Baith riche et pur of all degre;
> *Timor mortis conturbat me.*[4]

"Out of three sounds he makes, not a fourth sound, but a star."
This is his peculiar glory; no other Scottish poet is so sensitive to
the magic of words; no other Scottish poet is master of such a
range of subtle musical effects.

From the long catalogue in *The Lament for the Makaris* of
poets lately dead it has been concluded that Dunbar and Henryson
were only two out of a crowd of poets equally gifted. The

[1] *op. cit.*, VOL. II, p. 102.   [2] *op. cit.*, VOL. II, p. 245.
[3] *op. cit.*, VOL. II, p. 149.   [4] *op. cit.*, VOL. II, p. 48.

N

trouble is that while *The Lament* gives a long list of poets whose poems are unknown, the collections made in the second half of the sixteenth century—the Bannatyne and Maitland MSS—contain scores of poems to which neither author nor date can be assigned. One would like to know which of the makars enumerated by Dunbar was the author of the spirited and amusing *Freiris of Berwick*, an old *fabliau* fashioned into a realistic story of contemporary life. And who wrote the delightful lines—

> Be glaid al ye that luvaris bene
> For now hes May depaynt with grene
> The hillis, valis, and the medis
> And flouris lustely upspreidis.
> Awalk out of your sluggairdry
> To heir the birdis melody
> Quhois suggourit nottis loud and cleir
> Is now ane parradice to heir?[1]

Gavin Douglas in *The Palice of Honour* ranked "greit Kennedie" with "Dunbar yit undeid",[2] but apart from his contribution to *The Flyting of Dunbar and Kennedy*, in which he draws on a vocabulary of vituperation as extensive as that of his opponent, there is nothing in the scanty poetical remains of "Guid Maister Walter Kennedy" to show that he was more than a competent writer of moral verse.[3]

Gavin Douglas is heavier metal. As we have seen, benefices, for which the needy clerk clamoured in vain, came early to the son of the Earl of Angus: his dedication of *The Palice of Honour*, completed in 1501, to the King "quhais micht may humbill thing avance", was followed by his elevation to a position of ease and dignity. As Provost of St Giles he had the money to procure books and the leisure to read them. Of both he made good use —excessive use, in the opinion of one of the religious gilds. On 27 February 1511 he admitted that he had neglected to celebrate the Mass of the Holy Blood, and bound himself, along with the

[1] *Bannatyne Manuscript*, ed. W. Tod Ritchie, Edinburgh 1928-34, VOL. III, p. 301.
[2] Gavin Douglas, *Palice of Honour*, ed. J. G. Kinnear, Edinburgh 1827, p. 28.
[3] Five poems by Walter Kennedy are printed in David Laing's edition of Dunbar's *Poems*, VOL. II, pp. 89 ff.

other prebendaries, to have it celebrated every Wednesday, under penalty of a fine to be paid to the confraternity.[1] In January 1512, at the request of his kinsman, Henry, Lord St Clair, he began his translation of the *Aeneid* of Virgil. In spite of interruptions, the work proceeded rapidly: the Prologue to Book VII was written at the beginning of the following winter; Book XII was begun in May 1513; the Prologue to Book XIII—a supplement added by Mapheus Vegius—was written in June, and on the feast of St Mary Magdalene, 22 July 1513, he could declare

> Now is my wark all fynyst and compleit . . .
> The bettir part of me salbe upheld
> Abufe the starnys perpetualy to ryng,
> And heir my nayme remane, but enparyng . . .
> Thus up my pen and instrumentis full yore [ready]
> On Virgillis post I fix for evirmore.[2]

Ambition, perseverance, extensive reading, the command of an enormous vocabulary, keen interest in the technique of versification—Douglas had them all. But that confidence which carried him through to the end of "the lang desparit wark" made him incapable of self-criticism and impatient of criticism by others. He makes a parade of his learning, piles epithet on epithet in his reluctance to discard any of the words that he has so diligently collected, and for all his experiments in versification, seldom achieves a musical line. He thinks that if he increases the detail in his picture he increases its verisimilitude, if he doubles the number of figures in it he doubles its effectiveness. So in his allegory he must have hundreds of characters—

> Ptholomeus, Ipocras, Socrates,
> Empedocles, Neptenabus, Hermes,
> Galien, Averroes and Plato,
> Enoch, Lameth, Job, and Diogenes,
> The eloquent and prudent Vlisses,
> Wise Josephus and facund Cicero,
> Melchisedech with uther mony mo.
> Thair voyage lyis throw out this wilderness;
> To the Palice of Honour all they go,[3]

---

[1] *Edinburgh Records*, VOL. I, p. 130.   [2] "Conclusio" to *Aeneid*, 1839 edn., VOL. II, p. 912.   [3] *Palice of Honour*, 1827 edn., pp. 5-6.

and the Palace is a bewildering confusion of

> Pinnakillis, fyellis, turnpekkis mony one,
> Gilt birneist torris, quhilk like to Phebus schone,
> Skarsment, reprise, corbell, and battellingis.[1]

His second allegorical poem, *King Hart*,[2] a version of the Everyman theme, is less ambitious and more effective. It is a well-planned tale, which moves swiftly to the inevitable close, unencumbered by superfluous displays of erudition.

The most astonishing of all his works is his translation of Virgil's *Aeneid*, the first translation of a great classical author—if we except Chaucer's translation of Boethius—to be attempted by a Scottish or English writer. One cannot but applaud the courage with which Douglas hacks and smashes his way through the dryad-haunted Virgilian woods, his valiant attempts to hammer his stubborn Scots into the semblance of Virgil's smooth and stately Latin. He is not deficient in scholarship—he seldom mistakes his author's meaning. He is not deaf to the music of the Virgilian hexameter, but, hearing it, he is unable to reproduce it in his own tongue. Thus

> *Sunt lacrimae rerum et mentem mortalia tangunt*

becomes

> Thir lamentable takins passir befor
> Our mortale myndis aucht to compassion steir,

and Dido's famous

> *Non ignara mali miseris succurrere disco*

> Thus, nocht misknawand quhat pane is ennoy to dre,
> I lernyt to help all tholis aduersryte.

Though he often lapses into something very like doggerel, there are times when he rises to the height of Virgil's great argument. Compare his rendering of Book II, ll. 355-60:

> Swa, with thir wordis, the yong menis curage grew,
> That in the dyrk like ravennus wolfeis, on rawis,
> Quham the blynd fury of thar empty mawis
> Dryvis furth of thar den to seik thar pray,
> Thair litil quhelpis left with dry throtis quhil day;

[1] *op. cit.*, p. 46.
[2] *Poetical Works*, ed. J. Small, Edinburgh 1874, pp. 85-120.

> So, throw the wapynnys and out fays went we
> Apon the deid ondowtit, and wald not fle.
> Amyd the cite we held the master streit;
> The dyrk nycht hyd ws with cloys schaddowis meit,

or of Book VI, ll. 268-81 beginning

> Thai walking furth sa dyrk, oneth thai wyst
> Quhidder thai went, amyd dym schaddowys thar,
> Quhar evir is nycht, and neuir lyght dois repar,
> Throwout the waist dongion of Pluto kyng,
> Thai voyd boundis, and that gowsty ryng:
> Siklyke as quha wald throw thik woddis wend
> In obscure licht, quhen moyn may nocht be kend,

with the Latin originals, and one must admit that the distance between them is not so great, that in fact the verses of the sixteenth-century Scot reveal a keener joy in sturt and strife, a deeper sense of the horror of the shade.

In the Prologues to the thirteen books he discourses at length on a variety of topics—on the art of translation, on fitting style to the matter, on the character of the happy warrior, and on Love—

> Quhou schort quhile doith hys fals plesance remane!
> Hys restles blys how sone takis the flicht!
> Hys kyndnes alteris in wraith within a nycht:
> Quhat is, bot torment, all his langsum fayr,
> Begun with feir, and endyt in despair?[1]

In the Prologue to Book IV, the pious ecclesiastic is at war with the poet: he sees in Dido's love for Aeneas only "brutal appetite ... and wild dotage"; in the Prologue to Book VI, however, he protests that the Book which follows is not what it seems to be

> Al full of leys or auld ydolatryis ...
> ... bot gaistis and elrich fantasyis,
> Of browneis and bogillis ful;

that, on the contrary, it confirms the teachings of orthodox theology—

> Quhat cristyn clerk kouth hym haue consalit bettir,
> Al thocht he was nevir catholyk wight?

[1] Prologue to *Aeneid*, BK. IV, 1839 edn., VOL. I, p. 183.

demands the poet. The churchman answers at the end of a long hymn—a creed rather—which forms the Prologue to Book X.

Most of the Prologues "date"; two, however, do not, and are secure of a place in any anthology of Scottish verse. Much has changed in four hundred and fifty years, but our Scottish weather has not. There are few passages in the poems of the Scottish Chaucerians that bring us nearer to those laid in earth more than four centuries ago than the description of a night and morning in winter, in the Prologue to Book VII.

> In this congelit sesson scharp and chill,
> The callour ayr, penetratyve and puyre,
> Dasyng the blude in every creatur,
> Maid seik warm stovis, and beyn fyris hoyt,
> In dowbill garmont cled, and wily coyt . . .
> A schot wyndo onschet a litill on char,
> Persavyt the mornyng bla, wan, and har,
> With clowdy gum and rak ourquhelmyt the ayr,
> The fulye stythly, hasart, rouch, and hair;
> Branchis bratlyng, and blaknyt schew the brays,
> With hirstis harsk of waggand wyndill strays;
> The dew droppis congelit on stybbil and rynd,
> And scharp hailstanys, mortfundeit of kynd,
> Hoppand on the thak and on the causay by:
> The schot I closit, and drew inwart in by,
> Chyvirrand for cold, the season was so snell.[1]

To this he opposes, in the Prologue to Book XIII, the unearthly beauty of the long June days, when the sunset melts imperceptibly into the sunrise:

> I see the poill, and eik the Ursis brycht,
> And hornyt Lucyne castand bot dym lycht,
> Becaus the symmyr skyis schayn sa cleyr . . .
> Yondyr dovn dwynys the evyn sky away,
> And vpspryngis the brycht dawyng of day
> Intill ane other place nocht far in sundir,
> That to behald was plesans, and half wondir.
> Furth quynchyng gan the starris, one be one,
> That now is left bot Lucifer allone.[2]

---

[1] Prologue to BK. VII, VOL. I, pp. 379, 380.
[2] Prologue to spurious BK. XIII, VOL. II, pp. 846, 847.

Flodden marked the end of this brief efflorescence of Scottish poetry, if indeed it was not the direct cause of its premature decay. Henryson, it is true, had been dead for half-a-dozen years; Douglas had already resolved to give up poetry, and "on grave materis luke"; Dunbar had left his youth far behind, but the young poets who would have carried on the torch probably lay dead beside the young scholar of whom Erasmus demanded "What hadst thou to do with fierce Mars . . . thou that were destined for the Muses and for Christ?"[1]

[1] Erasmus, *Adages*, Chil. II, Cent. V, in *Opera omnia*, ed. Leclerc, VOL. II, p. 544, cited in Herkless and Hannay, *Archbishops of St Andrews*, VOL. I, p. 262.

VII

HIGHLANDS AND ISLANDS

THE troubles in the Western Isles were far from finished when James left them, apparently reduced to his obedience, in the summer of 1495. Before another twelvemonth had passed, Bute was devastated by a body of Islesmen. The government tried to secure the co-operation of the Island chiefs in the maintenance of order: on 3 October 1496 the Council declared that any summons issued before 26 April 1497 against any person dwelling in the Lordship of the Isles was to be accepted and executed by the chief of his clan. If the chief failed to execute the summons, proceedings would be taken against him as if he were "the principale party defendour" in the case.[1] On the same day the Council set on record that in the presence of Argyll five of the chiefs—MacLean of Duart, MacIan of Ardnamurchan, Allan MacRuari of Moidart, Ewen Allan, son of Lochiel, and Donald Angus, son of Keppoch—"be the extensione of thare handis" had promised, under a penalty of five hundred pounds, to refrain from inflicting scaith on one another.[2]

Of the two possible claimants to the Lordship of the Isles, one, Donald Owre, the grandson of John of the Isles, had been for some years in the King's service. In 1494 foodstuffs had been delivered to him for the provisioning of the castle at Tarbert,[3] and the Treasurer's Accounts record money payments made to him and his servants in the three following years.[4] The other, Alexander of Lochalsh, made a second attempt at rebellion. He invaded Ross, apparently in 1497, but was defeated by the Munroes and Mackenzies at Drumchatt, and compelled to return to the Isles. Soon afterwards, while attempting to organise

[1] *Acts of the Lords of Council in Civil Causes*, VOL. II, p. 41.   [2] Ibid.
[3] *C.T.S.*, VOL. I, p. 244.   [4] *C.T.S.*, VOL. I, pp. 273, 342, 380, 381.

another invasion, he was killed in Oronsay by MacIan of Ard-namurchan.[1]

In the north, too, trouble threatened. In January 1498 Far-quhar MacIntosh was summoned before the Lords of Council,[2] but he failed to appear. It was probably soon after this that, along with MacKenzie of Kintail, he was warded in Edinburgh Castle.

Early in March 1498, after an absence of three years, the King visited the Isles in person. He sailed from Ayr, touched at Arran, inspected his new castle at the head of Loch Kilkerran—now Campbeltown Loch—and the castle at Tarbert, and returned to Ayr after a week's absence.[3] At Duchal Castle, on 16 March, he executed the General Revocation[4] which was expected of every Scottish sovereign when he reached the age of twenty-five. By this Act all charters which he had previously granted, including those granted to the former vassals of the Lord of the Isles, were rendered null and void. The letters which he sent to the Isles a few days later by Lord Gordon's man[5] probably informed the island chiefs of the change in their legal status; they were now tenants at the King's pleasure.

For the time being, however, James did nothing to disturb them; he sought, rather, to strengthen his influence over them by displaying a more lively interest in their concerns. On 1 April, for example, he petitioned the Pope to sanction the erection of the Abbey Church of Iona into a cathedral for the Bishop of the Isles. He visited his castle of Kilkerran again in May,[6] and returned to it in June for a stay which lasted for two months. He bestowed favours on those chiefs who had given signs of their loyalty: Alexander MacLeod of Dunvegan, as a reward for his faithful service, and on the understanding that he would put his galleys at the King's disposition whenever he required them, was granted lands in Lewis and Skye, along with the office of Bailie of Trouterness in Skye.[7] He even bestowed them twice over: barely a fortnight later Argyll's brother-in-law, Torquil

[1] Gregory, *History of the Western Highlands and Isles of Scotland*, pp. 92-3.
[2] *Acts of the Lords of Council in Civil Causes*, VOL. II, pp. 94-5.
[3] *C.T.S.*, VOL. I, pp. 381, 382.   [4] *C.T.S.*, VOL. I, p. 383.   [5] Ibid.
[6] *C.T.S.*, VOL. I, pp. 390, 391.   [7] *R.M.S.*, VOL. II, No. 2420.

MacLeod of Lewis, was also constituted Bailie of Trouterness.[1]

This policy of personal supervision was abandoned before it had been well begun. The King's visits to the Isles ceased; on 22 August 1499 the royal castle of Tarbert was put into the keeping of the Earl of Argyll, who was also entrusted with the maintenance of order in the King's lands in Knapdale.[2] On 22 April 1500 the King issued a commission to the Earl of Argyll and five others, empowering any three of them, as long as Argyll was one of the three, to "set" all the lands in the Lordship of the Isles except Kintyre and Islay, for a term of three years.[3] Three days later the change from direct rule to government by deputy was completed, when the King made Argyll Lieutenant General within the boundaries of the old Lordship of the Isles, Kintyre and Islay excepted, with power to rule and govern the King's lieges, make statutes, ordinances and regulations for their government, to capture, chastise, and "justify" rebels, to raise the royal standard against rebels, besiege and storm their strongholds and dwellings, and grant remissions.[4] These delegated powers he was to enjoy for a period of three years.

When on the death of his father in the summer of 1501 Alexander, Lord Gordon, became third Earl of Huntly, similar powers were conferred on him. On 11 August letters were directed to him, authorising him to receive in the King's name all "bandis and oblissingis" of earls, lords, barons and their kinsmen north of the Mounth, using force if necessary, and empowering him to collect the King's rents in Lochaber, and to raise the lieges against any person who should resist him.[5]

Already the island chiefs were growing restless; they could not fail to notice that Argyll granted remissions only to his own clansmen, and they must have suspected that he would use the authority delegated to him for his own aggrandisement at their expense. His own brother-in-law, Torquil MacLeod of Lewis, seemed to be meditating rebellion; in November he was ordered to appear before the Lords of Council. As he paid no heed to

[1] *R.M.S.*, VOL. II, No. 2424.   [2] *R.S.S.*, VOL. I, No. 413.
[3] *R.S.S.*, VOL. I, No. 513.   [4] *R.S.S.*, VOL. I, No. 520.
[5] *R.S.S.*, VOL. I, Nos. 722-3.

the summons, he was outlawed, and his lands declared forfeit to the Crown. He was still at liberty on 21 March 1502, when the King issued a commission to Huntly, Lord Fraser of Lovat, and William Munro of Fowlis, or any two of them, Huntly being one, empowering them to let the King's lands in Lochaber and Mamore for a period of five years "to gud trew, and sufficient men for the plenysing thairof and expelling of trespassouris and brokin men furth of the sammyn". They were also empowered to let the lands which had belonged to the outlawed chief, and were advised that preference should be given to "gud trew men, being afald in our soverane lordis opinion, for thair gude trewe service to be done in plenising of the said landis and persewing of the said Torquell".[1]

In the same month MacKenzie of Kintail and Farquhar MacIntosh escaped from prison.[2] MacKenzie, however, was killed, and MacIntosh recaptured before 3 April. James showed his relief by giving a messenger twenty shillings to take the news to his mistress at Darnaway.[3] He had reasons, too, for doubting the loyalty of Donald Owre, whom the Islesmen regarded as the lawful heir of the last Lord of the Isles, though King and Parliament maintained that he was the illegitimate son of an illegitimate son. James imprisoned him for a time, then granted him a respite and released him.

> Off the falis fox dissimvlatour,
> Kynd hes every thieff and tratour;
>> Eftir respyt
>> To wirk dispyt
>> Moir appetyt
>>> He hes of natour

was Dunbar's comment on the King's misplaced generosity. Persuaded probably by Torquil MacLeod, he decided to make good by the sword his claim to the Lordship of the Isles. MacLeod secured for him the support of many of the disaffected chiefs, including MacLean of Lochbuie, MacLean of Duart, and Ewen Allanson of Lochiel. Bute was burned and harried so thoroughly

---

[1] *R.S.S.*, VOL. I, No. 792.   [2] *C.T.S.*, VOL. II, pp. xcii, 141, 145.
[3] *C.T.S.*, VOL. II, p. 143.

that for three years the tenants were excused the payment of their rents to the King.[1] In the Lordship of the Isles, those who had professed loyalty to the King were "attacked and destroyed in warlike manner". To a royal summons to surrender his protégé MacLeod responded by handing him over to MacLean of Duart, then, descending upon Badenoch at Christmas, burned and ravaged far and wide.[2]

The seriousness of the situation was recognised by the Parliament which met in Edinburgh on 11 March 1504. It expressed its approval of Huntly's undertaking to besiege the castles of Eilean Donan at the head of Loch Alsh, and Strone on Loch Carron, "quhilkis ar rycht necessar for the danting of the Ilis", and to occupy them after they were captured. It recommended that the King should send a ship and guns to help in the siege operations,[3] and agreed to consult Huntly about the building of a new castle at Inverlochy.[4] It was understood that the King would discuss with Argyll the strengthening of the existing castles at Dunaverty and Loch Kilkerran.[5]

Parliament was strangely slow to identify the real authors of the rebellion. Of all the rebels, it summoned only MacLean of Lochbuie, MacLean of Duart, and Ewen Allanson of Lochiel to answer the charge of treason, and it found guilty only the two last.[6] Torquil MacLeod and MacLean of Lochbuie it included among the eight chiefs to whom, on 19 March, it directed letters exhorting them to invade and pursue the two traitors, and "harry, destroy, and burn their lands", half of which would go to the captor of the traitors if he delivered them to the King.[7]

The chronic restlessness in the Highlands and Islands Parliament attributed to "the great abusion of Justice . . . for lacke and faulte of Justice aires, justices and scheriffes" because of which "the people are almost gane wilde". It ordained, therefore, that there should be Justices depute—a Sheriff for the North Isles, who would hold his court in Dingwall or Inverness, and another for the South Isles, administering justice at Tarbert or Loch Kilkerran.

---

[1] R. Scac. S., VOL. XII, pp. 247, 248.   [2] A.P.S., VOL. II, p. 263.
[3] A.P.S., VOL. II, p. 240.   [4] A.P.S., VOL. II, p. 248.   [5] Ibid.
[6] A.P.S., VOL. II, pp. 241, 247-8.   [7] A.P.S., VOL. II, p. 248.

The inhabitants of Bute, Arran, the Cumbraes, Knapdale, and Kintyre were to go to the justice aire at Ayr or Rothesay; the inhabitants of that part of Cowal which was not within the lordship of Argyll were to go to the aire at Dumbarton, and malefactors from Lochaber and Mamore would stand their trial at Inverness. It further proposed that the inhabitants of Argyll, "quhen the Kingis grace pleiss", should come to Perth, "sa that everilk heland man, and lauland man may cum and ask to have Justice".[1] Recognising that the "greit lak and falt of Justice" in Caithness and Ross, "quhair throw great enormitie and trespasse hes growen in thay partis", was due to the excessive size of the sheriffdom of Inverness, Parliament further ordained that there should be a Sheriff of Ross, who should administer justice from Tain or Dingwall, as he thought fit, and a Sheriff of Caithness, sitting in Dornoch or Wick.[2]

Finally, it advocated a greater respect for the law. All the King's subjects, especially those living in the Isles, must be ruled "be our Soverane Lordis awin Lawes, and the commoun Lawes of the Realme and be nane uther Lawes". Even the King was brought to admit that his over-hasty granting of remissions had been largely responsible for "the great inconvenientis of slauchter movit and happenit ilk day mair and mair", and to promise that he would give no remissions for premeditated murder.[3]

It had been decided that while Huntly attacked the rebel strongholds on the mainland, a fleet should sail from Dumbarton to besiege the remote castle of Cairn na Burgh, in the Treshnish Isles to the west of Mull. Though in the middle of April the King spent three days visiting various ships in the fleet,[4] he did not sail with it. Sir Andrew Wood was in charge of it till 11 May, when his command was transferred to the Earl of Arran.[5] Though the Treasurer's Accounts contain numerous references to the wine and meal, guns and gunstones supplied to the fleet, though the despatch of Robert Barton and Hans, the King's German gunner, to Cairn na Burgh on 6 May[6] seemed to show that the

---

[1] *A.P.S.*, VOL. II, pp. 241, 249.   [2] *A.P.S.*, VOL. II, pp. 241-2, 249-50.
[3] *A.P.S.*, VOL. II, p. 250.   [4] *C.T.S.*, VOL. II, p. 428.
[5] *C.T.S.*, VOL. II, p. 433.   [6] *C.T.S.*, VOL. II, p. 431.

reduction of the castle had been more difficult than was expected, no account of the siege operations has been preserved. The fleet returned to Dumbarton before the end of June,[1] having apparently accomplished its task.

Nothing is known of the result of Huntly's expedition. But it was plain that the rebellion had not been crushed; on 7 June MacLean of Lochbuie, MacQuarrie of Ulva, and MacNeill of Barra were summoned by Parliament to stand their trial for treason[2]; on 17 August one of the King's ships was sent back to the Isles, where it remained on patrol till 27 December.[3]

Though another fleet was fitted out in Dumbarton in the spring of 1505,[4] though the armament of the ships was increased by guns taken from Edinburgh Castle, it had to be diverted to Arran, where a band of rebels, headed by one Walter Stewart, were holding the Earl's own castle. The return of the fleet to Dumbarton at the end of July ended naval operations for that year.

In the meantime, letters had frequently been exchanged by the King and MacIan of Ardnamurchan. In November MacIan appeared at court, attended by a tail of three servants and a priest. The tactful monarch showered favours upon them: to the three servants he gave "bridle silver" to the amount of three pounds for three horses which they delivered to him,[5] to the priest a gown of French tawney,[6] and to MacIan himself scarlet hose, white shoes, and a gown of damask lined with white fur,[7] and on 25 November he followed up this last gift with the grant of a charter confirming him in the possession of certain lands in Islay and Jura, Ardnamurchan and Sunart, with Mingary Castle in Ardnamurchan, and the office of Bailie of the crown lands in Islay.[8]

The King now realised that his most dangerous opponent was Torquil MacLeod, who sat secure in his stronghold at Stornoway. On 15 December he summoned him to stand his trial for treason-

[1] C.T.S., VOL. II, pp. 442, 443.
[2] A.P.S., VOL. II, p. 255.   [3] C.T.S., VOL. II, p. 475.
[4] C.T.S., VOL. III, pp. 136, 138.   [5] C.T.S., VOL. III, p. 172.
[6] C.T.S., VOL. III, p. 103.   [7] Ibid.   [8] R.M.S., VOL. II, No. 2895.

able help given to Donald Owre, for attacking and destroying the lieges in the Isles to make him Lord of the Isles, for handing him over to Lauchlan MacLean of Duart in defiance of the royal command, for invading Badenoch, for deforcing the King's officers, and for "divers robberies, arsons, rapes, and homicides".[1]

The messenger to whom the summons was entrusted reported that as he could not arrest the criminal, and as "there was na furth to me till his dwelling-place", he had to read it at the Mercat Cross of Inverness. MacLeod did not appear to stand his trial, which took place in Edinburgh on 3 February 1506, in presence of the King. He was found guilty, and sentenced to lose life, land, and goods.[2]

In the meantime some of the rebels were beginning to lose heart. The chiefs of Ulva and Barra seem to have made their peace with the King before the end of 1505, and in January 1506, through the instrumentality of Argyll in some cases, respites were granted to various chiefs and clansmen.[3] On 22 March Inverlochy was handed over to Huntly: on 10 June Argyll, acting as the King's Lieutenant in the West, issued instructions to MacIan of Ardnamurchan for the better government of the districts entrusted to him. He was to hold bailie courts four times a year, and to cause "all thevis, pikaris, and sornaris that oppress the cuntre . . . menslaaris . . . and comon tulyeouris" convicted at them "to be punyst in all gudlie hast but favouris". He was to hold courts at fifteen days' notice at other times of the year to deal with complaints of "slauchter, sornyng, and oppression", and cause "all sornaris and oppressouris of the Kingis leigis . . . and all utheris idill personis that wirkis nocht nor has nocht to live upon of thar awin to be expellit and put furth . . . or ellis caus tham to wirk and labour for thair living". At the same time, by persuading MacLean of Lochbuie and MacLean of Duart that MacIan was not out to aggrandise himself at their expense, Argyll secured their adherence to the royal cause. In the presence of Argyll and six other commissioners MacIan, "the haly evangelist tuichit", exchanged assurances with the two MacLeans that both parties

[1] A.P.S., VOL. II, p. 261.   [2] A.P.S., VOL. II, pp. 263-4.
[3] R.S.S., VOL. I, Nos. 1197, 1208.

should be "harmless and scaithless" in their persons and goods till 1 May 1507, and promised that he would submit his dispute with MacLean of Lochbuie to the arbitrament of the King and his Council. In the far north, too, the chief of the clan MacKay was ready to co-operate with the royal forces.

Not till midsummer had passed were operations against the last rebel stronghold begun. As before, a small fleet, based on Dumbarton, co-operated with the land forces under the Earl of Huntly; at the end of June John Smollett, burgess of Dumbarton, sailed to the Isles to make contact with William Brownhill's ship,[1] and at the same time William Brown passed "with his schip to fure the Erle of Huntly in the Ilis".[2] As before, guns had to be taken from Edinburgh Castle; as before, expert foreign gunners went with them to the Isles.[3] But though we know that in July the King presented Huntly with a sword,[4] that on 29 August, while hunting in Balquhidder, he gave twenty-eight shillings "to ane man that com . . . with tithingis of the Lewis",[5] that on 3 September MacLean of Lochbuie's harper was with the King at Inchcailloch, and received nine shillings from him,[6] that a week later a ship called the *Raven* was sent to Lewis,[7] we know nothing about the actual siege of Stornoway Castle or the date and manner of its capture. It must have fallen early in October, for by the middle of the month the guns that had been used to batter down its walls were back in Edinburgh Castle.[8]

The rebellion was over. It is true that Torquil MacLeod had escaped, and remained at large till his death five years later, but Donald Owre was captured and lodged in Stirling Castle,[9] and before the end of the year pardoned rebels like MacLean of Lochbuie were exchanging gifts with the King.[10] Those chiefs who had served the King well did not go unrewarded; MacIan received a fresh charter confirming him in the possession of lands in Islay and Jura,[11] and Hugh MacKay of Strathnaver, "for his

[1] *C.T.S.*, VOL. III, p. 200.   [2] Ibid.   [3] Ibid.
[4] *C.T.S.*, VOL. III, p. 206.   [5] *C.T.S.*, VOL. III, p. 338.
[6] *C.T.S.*, VOL. III, p. 339.   [7] *C.T.S.*, VOL. III, p. 340.
[8] *C.T.S.*, VOL. III, p. 350.   [9] *C.T.S.*, VOL. III, pp. lxxxii, 415.
[10] *C.T.S.*, VOL. III, p. 355.   [11] *R.M.S.*, VOL. II, No. 2895.

good service in resisting and attacking the rebels" was granted for the time of his life the lands in Assynt and Cogeach that had belonged to Torquil MacLeod.[1]

The one who profited most by his loyalty was Huntly. On 8 September 1507 the King granted him lands which had formerly been held by Margaret, the sister of Alexander of Lochalsh, who had "applyit and subjectit hir persone, landis, and gudis, quhether in lauchfull mariage or atherways we knaw nocht", to one of the confederates of Torquil MacLeod[2]; on 13 September he was empowered to set the lands of Glengarry and Invergarry to the existing tenants for the space of five years,[3] and on 13 December he was given similar powers over the inhabitants of Knoydart.[4] On 16 January 1509 he was made hereditary Sheriff of Inverness, with the power to create sheriffs depute for Caithness, Ross, and Lochaber,[5] as was laid down in the Act of 1504. At the same time he was granted the castle of Inverness, with the lands pertaining to it. These lands, of the annual value of 102 marks, were Crown property, and should not have been alienated. James, however, undertook to make Parliament authorise the transaction, which it did a few weeks later.[6]

That the King thought of maintaining his authority in the Highlands and Islands by planting castles at strategic points is shown by his despatch of masons and carpenters to Lewis in 1506[7] to repair the captured castle of Stornoway, by the instructions which he gave to Huntly to build a "towr and strenth with barmkyn" at Inverlochy before Martinmas 1507,[8] and by his grant of a charter in December 1509 requiring John Grant of Fruchy to build a stone tower surrounded by a wall "for a defence against the attacks of robbers and malefactors" at Urquhart on Loch Ness.[9]

[1] *R.M.S.*, VOL. II, No. 3202.   [2] *R.S.S.*, VOL. I, No. 1532.
[3] *R.S.S.*, VOL. I, No. 1543.   [4] *R.S.S.*, VOL. I, No. 1582.
[5] *R.M.S.*, VOL. II, No. 3286.   [6] *R.M.S.*, VOL. II, No. 3286n.
[7] *C.T.S.*, VOL. III, p. 349.   [8] *R.S.S.*, VOL. I, No. 1668.
[9] *R.M.S.*, VOL. II, No. 3990. But his grant of Stornoway Castle to Malcolm MacLeod of Lewis, the brother of the exiled Torquil, in 1511 (*R.M.S.*, VOL. II, No. 3578), and his unfailing acceptance of Huntly's repeated excuses for delaying the building of Inverlochy (*R.S.S.*, VOL. I, No. 2279), seem to reveal a

o

In reality James left the Highlands and Islands pretty much as he had found them, with their old feuds unappeased, with the gulf between the "wild Scot" and the civilised Scot as wide as it had ever been. The solitary instance of the Hebridean clerk who received a grant of Crown lands in Skye that he might study law at the university and practise law in the Isles, like the solitary instance of the Lowland Scottish priest in the diocese of Dunkeld who heard confessions in Gaelic, cannot be taken to mean that there was any closing of the gulf in James's day. Proximity, indeed, seemed to increase ill will. The town of Dunkeld, as we have seen, according to the charter of new infeodation granted in 1513, just because it was in the Highlands, was so crowded with "transgressors and malefactors . . . thieves, robbers, sorners, rebels at the King's horn for slaughter and other crimes", that the Bishop and his officers had to be empowered to deal with them on the spot, instead of sending them to the justice aire at Perth. And punished they were, without mercy. When the good Bishop Brown, the son of a burgess of Dundee, lay on his death-bed, he remembered a Highlander called MacKay whom he had seen lately dangling from the gallows, and remarked complacently: "Praise God! I shall now die in a better fashion than that fellow who was hanged with beard unkempt."[1]

In short, the structure of Celtic Scotland had not been materially altered by James's activities. Parliament might propose measures for the more effective administration of justice in the Highlands and Islands; it could not ensure their execution: not till the middle of the seventeenth century, for example, did Ross and Caithness become separate sheriffdoms. Without an adequate revenue—James judged it wise not to renew the special tax for the campaigns in the Isles after 1497—without a standing army, with an insignificant navy, the King was compelled to play off clan against clan, to call in two of his most powerful subjects to carry out his work of pacification on their terms and in their way. He could not be expected to see that the peace which they secured

belief that the Isles had been sufficiently daunted, and that he was called upon to play a part on an ampler stage.

[1] Myln, *Vitae*, pp. 51-2; *Rentale Dunkeldense*, ed. Hannay, p. 318.

for him would last no longer than his own lifetime, and that his policy of short cuts and improvisations had expedited the process by which, in the seventeenth century, the clan Campbell became as dangerous to its neighbours and to the monarchy as the clan Donald had been in the fifteenth.

VIII

THE ROAD TO FLODDEN

No stait in erd heir standis sickir;
As with the wynd wavis the wickir,
(So) wavis this worldis vanite;
Timor mortis conturbat me.

THE death of Henry VII in April 1509 did nothing to disturb the friendly relations between the two countries. The youthful Henry VIII exchanged courteous letters with his brother-in-law,[1] and before the year was out both monarchs had confirmed the treaty of perpetual peace.[2] Any risk of a revival of the old Scottish friendship with France leading to a breach of the new friendship with England seemed to be removed by the treaty between England and France, made in March of the following year.[3]

King James, now in his thirty-seventh year, seemed to have lost all appetite for military glory and to be content to stay at home and cultivate his garden, still thorny and tangled enough in places, in spite of his twenty-one years' care. There was the Borders, for example. Had not stories of innocent travellers waylaid and slain made the King, at the head of a great body of horsemen, ride out from Edinburgh through the darkness of a winter's night till he came to the Water of Rule? Had he not, sitting in the Tolbooth of Jedburgh, pronounced sentence of death

---

[1] James IV to Henry VIII, 11 June 1509, acknowledging letter from Henry, *L. and P. Henry VIII*, VOL. I, PT. I, No. 69.

[2] Henry on 29 Aug. (*L. and P. Henry VIII*, VOL. I, PT. I, No. 153; *Foedera*, VOL. XIII, p. 267); James on 28 Nov. (*L. and P. Henry VIII*, VOL. I, PT. I, No. 252; *Foedera*, VOL. XIII, p. 267).

[3] 25 March 1510. *L. and P. Henry VIII*, VOL. I, PT. I, No. 406; *Foedera*, VOL. XIII, p. 270; *Cal. of State Papers, Spain*, VOL. II, London 1866, No. 36.

on the malefactors, brought before him with ropes round their necks—a judgment that kept the Borders quiet for the remainder of his reign.[1]

In vain Louis XII tried to lure him into foreign adventures; to the French King's request for four thousand experienced foot soldiers, to be sent by sea to Genoa or Savona,[2] James replied by asking Louis how many men he wanted and begging Louis to regard him as a kinsman and a brother, on whom he could rely in his hour of need.[3] James's harassed and bewildered uncle, King John of Denmark, was fobbed off with similar evasive courtesies when he appealed for help against the rebellious Swedes and their allies, the Lübeckers: he received neither the 2,000 men whom he demanded in July 1509,[4] nor the flotilla of four ships which he begged for in December.[5] James's lust for adventure seemed to be satisfied now by the mimic warfare of the tournament, when, disguised as a savage knight of the woods, he flashed into the lists and hurled his more youthful opponents to the ground; he seemed to look for no battlefield beyond the tilt-yard.[6]

All this was only seeming; despite his thirty-six years, James was younger than the realist of eighteen who sat on the English throne; the middle-aged monarch was no wary, disillusioned statesman, but a moonstruck romantic, whose eyes were ever at the ends of the earth. When his nobles, clad in their glittering tilting armour, gay with crest and embroidered surcoat and painted shield, rode into the lists, he thought himself a second King Arthur. Arthur's task—to war with the heathen—would

[1] Lesley, pp. 81-2 Sc., 339 L.; *C.T.S.*, VOL. IV, p. xxiii.

[2] 10 July 1507. *Flodden Papers, Diplomatic Correspondence between the Courts of France and Scotland 1507-1517*, ed. Marguerite Wood, Edinburgh 1933 (hereafter referred to as *Flodden Papers*), pp. 1-4.

[3] *Epistolae Jacobi Quarti, Jacobi Quinti et Mariae Regum Scotorum eorumque tutorum et regni gubernatorum; ad Imperatores, Reges, Pontifices, Principes, Civitates et alios ab anno 1505 ad annum 1545*, Edinburgh 1722-4 (hereafter referred to as E.R.S.), VOL. I, pp. 83-5.

[4] 46th *Report* of the Deputy Keeper of Public Records, London 1886, APP. II, p. 54.

[5] *L. and P. Henry VIII*, VOL. I, PT. I, No. 285.

[6] In the summer of 1508. Lesley, pp. 78 Sc., 334 L.

be his task too. It was perhaps as a dedication to this task that he
sent Robert Barton, shipmaster—and, some said, pirate—to offer
a costly ship of silver at the shrine of his patron saint at Compos-
tella in Spain.[1] For "the Crusade against the Infidel", to every
other sovereign in Europe, to the Pope himself, a useful phrase
in the jargon of diplomacy, was to James something far different:
he saw himself in the near future, leading a great fleet to the
shores of Palestine, and then, at the head of the united forces of
Christendom, advancing, sword in hand, against the Turk.

For this enterprise he must have ships, and so his agents werr
busy in almost every maritime country in Western Europe, buying timber and cordage,[2] and all the woods in Fife were laid low,
while the gilding of the new-built *Margaret* glittered in the Pool
of Airth,[3] and the wrights in the royal dockyard at Newhaven
toiled at a greater ship than the *Margaret*—the greatest ship in all
Europe, it was said. He must have competent sea-captains, men
skilful and daring like the Bartons, and if they sometimes mingled
a little piracy with their legitimate transactions, he must not
alienate them by scrutinising their deeds more closely. And he
must have a base nearer Palestine than Leith or Dumbarton—
Marseilles perhaps, or even Venice.

The other princes of Europe did not share his enthusiasm;
they were more eager to fly at each others' throats than to combine against the Turk. Venice had long been the bulwark of
Christendom against the Infidel, but in 1508 the Pope joined with
Louis XII, Maximilian and Ferdinand, King of Aragon, to form
the League of Cambrai, that the Republic might be forced to
give up those portions of its territory to which the allies laid
claim. The League was only too successful; the resounding victory gained by the French at the Battle of Agnadello, in May
1509, made Julius pause; in his haste to humiliate Venice he had
established the French more firmly than ever upon the soil of

---

[1] *C.T.S.*, VOL. IV, pp. 40-1: "The secund day of Maij [1508], payit to Robert
Bertoun, quhilk he laid doun for ane schip of silvir weyand xxxj½ unce, quhilk
he offerit for the King in Sanct James in Spanze."

[2] *C.T.S.*, VOL. IV, pp. 46, 47, 289, 294-5, 296, 373.

[3] *C.T.S.*, VOL. IV, pp. 68, 114, 131.

Italy. Julius did not hesitate: the alien must be driven north of the Alps; at the beginning of 1510 he removed the interdict which he had pronounced against the Republic "all the more willingly", as he explained to James, "since we believe that the Doge and Republic of Venice, through the situation of their territory and the facilities they have for assembling a fleet, may be of the very greatest service to the cause of Christendom".[1]

Soon the Pope and His Most Christian Majesty were at war. In the early summer of 1510 Julius seduced 10,000 Swiss mercenaries from their temporary allegiance to France by offering them higher rates of pay and sent them against the territories of the pro-French Duke of Ferrara. He tried, for a time in vain, to detach the shifty Ferdinand from his alliance with Louis and Maximilian. In September Louis retaliated by convoking a synod of the French clergy at Tours, which declared that the King was justified in making war against Julius, and threw down the gauntlet to the Pope by urging the summoning of a General Council, to meet at Pisa in the autumn of the following year. October found the implacable and indomitable Julius at Bologna, besieged by the French and in imminent danger of capture.

Meantime the Pope's letter had started a fantastic train of thought in the mind of the King of Scots; the Venetians had money, they had ships and a great harbour; but they had no one to command their forces, for they had recently lost their Captain General, the Count of Pitigliano. What was to hinder—but let Andrea Badoer, the Venetian Ambassador in London, continue the story.

On 20 April Badoer informed his Government that he had had several conversations with a Scottish priest who enjoyed the confidence of King James; indeed it was when he had visited London at an earlier date as a Scottish ambassador that Badoer first got to know him. The priest declared that his master was the friend of Venice; "the friend of France", Badoer suggested. The priest replied by asking how much the Republic had paid the Count of Pitigliano. King James would make an excellent

[1] *L. and P. Henry VIII*, VOL. I, PT. I, No. 372; James IV, *Letters*, ed. R. L. Mackie, No. 300.

commander, he hinted, and added that he would like to see Venice.[1]

Badoer was impressed. Ten days later he assured his Government that James could bring ten thousand fighting men and a hundred and fifty ships to the aid of the Republic and—here the purpose of these mysterious conversations is revealed—after he had accomplished what was required of him by the Republic, he would, without cost to Venice, lead the forces under his command against the Turk.[2] On 11 May he returned to the charge: his theme was now James's valour and covetousness of honour,[3] and a month later he reminded the Signory that James was still eager to lead the Venetian forces to battle.[4] It was all in vain, on 9 September the Doge and Senate informed him that they had conferred the command on one of their prisoners of war, the Marquis of Mantua, captured in the previous summer and now released at the special request of the Pope.[5]

These negotiations, the success of which would have brought James into conflict with France, seem to have been carried on with the approval of the English Government. When in November 1510 the Archbishop of York, the English ambassador in Rome, stated that Henry was willing to enter into a league with the Pope and the Venetians against France, he added that the King of Scots, a valiant man, would be a good commander-in-chief for the Venetian expedition.[6]

The failure of his Venetian scheme did not daunt the versatile James. If Venice was closed to him Marseilles must serve; he

[1] *Cal. of State Papers, Venice*, VOL. II, London 1867, No. 63; *L. and P. Henry VIII*, VOL. I, PT. I, No. 434.

[2] *Cal. of State Papers, Venice*, VOL. II, No. 66; *L. and P. Henry VIII*, VOL. I, PT. I, No. 450.

[3] *Cal. of State Papers, Venice*, VOL. II, No. 66; *L. and P. Henry VIII*, VOL. I, PT. I, No. 455.

[4] *Cal. of State Papers, Venice*, VOL. II, No. 73; *L. and P. Henry VIII*, VOL. I, PT. I, No. 493.

[5] *Cal. of State Papers, Venice*, VOL. II, No. 81; *L. and P. Henry VIII*, VOL. I, PT. I, No. 570.

[6] *Cal. of State Papers, Venice*, VOL. II, No. 90; *L. and P. Henry VIII*, VOL. I, PT. I, No. 617.

would send an ambassador to his old ally, Louis of France, to ask for his co-operation. He had wit enough to see, however, that the crusade could not be even begun, let alone carried to a successful conclusion, as long as Louis was at variance with the Pope. If James desired to be the champion of Christendom, he must first reconcile the Pope and the Most Christian King.

James did not shrink from the task: on 22 October 1510 he wrote to his successful rival, the Marquis of Mantua, asking him if he thought that a Crusade had any chance of success, and informing him that he had despatched the Bishop of Moray to France to effect a reconciliation between Louis and the Pope and Venice "so that one army drawn from all nations may be turned against the enemies of Christ".[1] Soon Forman had landed in France and was making his way to the Château of Blois. Like his master, Forman had his dreams, but they were not dreams of great fleets sailing eastward to Constantinople or Alexandria. He saw himself grasping the archiepiscopal staff, or—why not— decked in the purple of a Cardinal. Forman reached Blois before the end of December and submitted a lengthy questionnaire to the French King.[2] His master wanted to know how many ships and men-at-arms Louis would furnish for a Crusade, and how the men-at-arms should be equipped and paid—*car vous entendes telles choses mieulx que homme vivant*: how much money he would contribute and where and how he would pay it, in what year and month he would be ready; whether he thought the Infidels should be attacked by land or sea, and where the expedition should disembark, at Alexandria or at Constantinople. His master asked for this information because he wanted to know how much he should ask from other princes but "always the greatest hope which he had in the world touching that affair" was in the French King.

Louis professed sympathy but avoided a direct answer to

[1] *E.R.S.*, vol. I, p. 128; *L. and P. Henry VIII*, vol. I, pt. I, No. 598.

[2] "The calculation, demand, and the King of France answers thereupon," *Flodden Papers*, pp. 6-10. It is undated, but a clause in the instructions given by Louis XII to Forman on 17 Jan. 1512 (*Flodden Papers*, pp. 17-19) seems to indicate that it was presented when Forman first arrived in France.

James's questions. To the ambassador's appeal that he should compose his quarrel with the Pope, he answered that he could do nothing without the consent of his ally, Maximilian.[1] Louis saw, however, that the supple Scot would make a useful go-between, now that Julius refused to see any of his ambassadors. When Forman set out for Italy on 29 December 1510,[2] he left not only as the ambassador of Scotland but as the ambassador of France.

Letters announcing Forman's arrival at Rome appear to have reached James about the beginning of February 1511.[3] James redoubled his efforts for peace. Julius would admit no Frenchman to his presence[4]; he might, however, listen to the half-French, half-Scottish Duke of Albany. James wrote to Louis, urging him to send Albany[5]; he wrote to Albany, commissioning him to act with Forman as Scots ambassador[6]; he wrote to Julius[7] and to Maximilian[8] explaining that Albany was his representative. He wrote in addition to the Duke of Savoy,[9] to the King of Hungary,[10] to three several Cardinals,[11] and to the whole College of Cardinals.[12] It was all in vain; though Albany went to Bologna before the middle of March, taking with him proposals for a peace, Julius flatly refused to see him.[13]

Forman had better luck; not only did Julius admit him to his presence, he communicated to him the terms on which he would consent to make peace with France. On 5 May, while the French ambassador, the Bishop of Paris, waited uneasily at Piacenza, Forman laid before Julius the answers of Louis to his demands.[14] Julius rejected the proposals, but professed great admiration for the bearer of them, "He has shown and he shows", Julius wrote to James on the following day, "such trustworthiness, prudence, diligence and nimble wit, that he has pleased us in no uncertain fashion, and he seems worthy of promotion to a much more exalted rank." He added that he proposed "*favente*

---

[1] *L. and P. Henry VIII*, VOL. I, PT. I, No. 708.   [2] *op. cit.*, No. 649.
[3] *op. cit.*, No. 685.   [4] *op. cit.*, No. 720.   [5] *op. cit.*, No. 684.
[6] *op. cit.*, No. 688.   [7] *op. cit.*, No. 684.   [8] *op. cit.*, No. 690.
[9] *op. cit.*, No. 691.   [10] *op. cit.*, No. 694.   [11] *op. cit.*, Nos. 687, 697.
[12] *op. cit.*, No. 702.   [13] *op. cit.*, No. 720.   [14] *op. cit.*. No. 756.

Altissimo" to make Forman a cardinal at the next creation.[1]

But Forman was destined never to wear a Cardinal's hat. In June 1511, something happened that drove the mediator into the arms of France and filled the mouth of the peacemaker with threats of war.

Of the Scottish sea-captains and merchant venturers none stood higher in the favour of King James than the three brothers, John, Robert and Andrew Barton, shipowners and shipmasters of Leith. It was John Barton who, in the autumn of 1507, took the young Archbishop of St Andrews to the continent[2]; it was John Barton who now commanded the *Margaret*.[3] Twice at least the King had visited Robert Barton's house[4]; it was Robert, too, who presented the silver ship at the shrine of St James.[5] To Andrew, the eldest of the three, the King gave in 1510 lands in Fife valued at 222 marks of the new extent.[6] But James had already bestowed on the brothers a more valuable and more dangerous gift.

Of the extent of the Bartons' legitimate trade the Treasurer's Accounts and Andrew Halyburten's Ledger give ample evidence. Piracy, they knew, was more profitable, if more perilous than legitimate trade. Could they have the profits without the risks of piracy? They believed that they could.

Thirty years earlier a ship, commanded by their father, John Barton, had been captured by some Portuguese vessels after a struggle in which some of the crew were killed. When repeated appeals to the King of Portugal had failed to secure redress, James III had been persuaded to issue letters of marque, which had been renewed by James IV at the beginning of his reign. Since then the letters of marque had been repeatedly suspended, but in 1506 the brothers raked up the thirty-year-old grievance. James was sympathetic: on 20 November he renewed the letters,[7] and in July 1507 he sent Rothesay Herald to the Portuguese Court to announce that they were again in force.[8]

---

[1] *E.R.S.*, VOL. I, p. 138; *L. and P. Henry VIII*, VOL. I, PT. I, No. 760.
[2] *C.T.S.*, VOL. IV, p. 72.   [3] *op. cit.*, p. 346.   [4] *op. cit.*, pp. 108, 131.
[5] *op. cit.*, pp. 40-1.   [6] *R.M.S.*, VOL. II, No. 3511.   [7] *E.R.S.*, VOL. I, pp. 91-3.
[8] *L. and P. Richard III and Henry VII*, VOL. II, p. 276; *C.T.S.*, VOL. IV, p. 106.

Trouble soon followed. Before the end of the following year Robert Barton found himself a prisoner, in danger of his life, in —of all places—the friendly town of Veere.[1] He had captured a Portuguese ship and had been clapped into jail at the suit of some Portuguese merchants. James protested vigorously to Maximilian[2] and to Margaret of Savoy, Governor of the Netherlands[3]; the Lady of Veere and the Bailiff of the town, Henry de Borssalia, used their influence on behalf of the prisoner,[4] and Robert was released. Undeterred by his brother's ordeal, John Barton borrowed his ship, the *Lion*, captured a Portuguese vessel, and helped himself to goods on board, without stopping to enquire about the nationality of their owners. But one was an Englishman, a second was, or said he was, a Frenchman, and a third a Fleming. As a result John was, in December 1509, sued by the aggrieved owners, but the Lords of Council deferred their decision till they should have heard evidence from the Councils of Bruges and Middelburg, the Parlement of Rouen, the Admirals of La Rochelle and of Harfleur and Honfleur.[5]

Next came a protest from Emmanuel of Portugal, delivered in June 1510 by his ambassador Edward Ferdinandi,[6] which made James suspend the letters of marque for a season. For a time the Bartons seem to have transferred their attentions from the ships of Portugal to those of Lübeck. On 28 December 1509 John of Denmark asked James to allow Andrew Barton and his brothers to serve him in their own ships[7]: in May 1510 he issued a letter of protection to Andrew for a ship which he had captured, laden with pepper,[8] and in September he issued letters patent declaring

---

[1] *L. and P. Richard III and Henry VII*, VOL. II, pp. 274-5; *E.R.S.*, VOL. I, p. 111.   [2] *L. and P. Richard III and Henry VII*, VOL. II, pp. 274-6.

[3] *E.R.S.*, VOL. I, pp. 111-2.   [4] *L. and P. Henry VIII*, VOL. I, PT. I, No. 188.

[5] *Acts of the Lords of Council in Public Affairs 1501-1554*, ed. R. K. Hannay, Edinburgh 1932, App., p. lxiv; Register House MSS, Acta Dominorum Concilii, VOL. XXII, fol. 67.

[6] Emmanuel of Portugal to James IV, 18 Sept. 1509 (*E.R.S.*, VOL. I, pp. 103-4; *L. and P. Henry VIII*, VOL. I, PT. I, No. 171); James IV to Emmanuel of Portugal, 21 June 1510 (*L. and P. Henry VIII*, VOL. I, PT. I, No. 504).

[7] *L. and P. Henry VIII*, VOL. I, PT. I, No. 285.

[8] 46th *Report* of the Deputy Keeper of Public Records, App. II, p. 55.

that spoil taken from the enemies of Denmark by Robert had been taken under his commission.[1]

Andrew found it difficult to be content with legitimate gains. In March 1511 Aloysius Bonciannus, an envoy from Margaret of Savoy, appeared in Edinburgh to lodge a complaint with the Council. Andrew Barton had captured a Breton ship and had taken from it goods belonging to certain merchants of Antwerp. No explanation was volunteered by Andrew, for Andrew judged it prudent to absent himself from the Court, whereupon the Lords of Council, understanding "that the said And(ro) is to depart hastely furth of the realms to the partis beyond se" summoned him to appear within sixteen days.[2] On 1 April Aloysius appeared before the Lords of Council, but Andrew did not. The Lords of Council, however, were no longer sympathetic: to the complaints of Aloysius they replied that "if he or any uther wald gar tak the said party, that is to say Andro Bartyn, justice sald be ministrat". With this reply the ambassador had to be content, though he protested that he "doutit the said Andro's departing and that perell was thair intill".[3]

Barton had probably returned to Denmark for a season, for King John had again asked James for a loan of Barton and his ships.[4] Then, with incredible levity, James renewed the letters of marque.[5] Barton sailed southward in the *Lion*, accompanied by a smaller vessel, the *Jenny Pirwin*, and, in the words of Hall, "saiying that the kyng of Scottes, had warre with the Portingales, did rob every nacion, and so stopped the kynges stremes, that no merchauntes almost could passe, and when he took thenglishmenes goodes he said they wer Portyngales goodes, and thus he haunted and robbed at every haven's mouthe."[6] The plundered merchants, instead of complaining to the Scottish Lords of Council or to the Warden of the Marches, appealed to King Henry.

[1] 46th *Report* of the Deputy Keeper of Public Records, App. II, p. 55.
[2] Register House MSS, Acta Dominorum Concilii, VOL. XXII, fol. 78.
[3] Register House MSS, Acta Dominorum Concilii, VOL. XXII, fol. 112.
[4] 46th *Report* of the Deputy Keeper of Public Records, App. II, p. 55.
[5] *E.R.S.*, VOL. I, pp. 120-1; *L. and P. Henry VIII*, VOL. I, PT. I, No. 828.
[6] Hall, p. 525.

According to the Treaty of 1502, which he had confirmed in
1509, Henry should first have asked the King of Scots for redress;
then, if he obtained no satisfactory answer from James at the end
of six months, he should have issued letters of marque. Henry
preferred speedier methods: he ordered the Admiral of England,
Sir Edward Howard, and his brother, Lord Thomas Howard, to
deal with Barton at once. The Howards hastily equipped two
ships and put to sea in June 1511, determined to seek out and
destroy "the King's enemy".

When Lord Thomas was lying in the Downs, temporarily
separated, by stress of weather, from his brother, he caught sight
of the *Lion* making for Scotland. He gave chase at once and
overhauled her. But Andrew, "brass within and steel without",
refused to strike his flag; he answered cannonade with cannonade,
and in the lulls of the firing his opponents could hear him blowing
his whistle to encourage his men.

> "Ffight on my men," sayes Sir Andrew Bartton,
> "These English doggs they bite soe lowe;
> Ffight on ffor Scotland and Saint Andrew
> Till you heare my whistle blowe."[1]

Even when the ships had crashed together, even when the
decks of the *Lion* were swarming with English sailors, the battle
continued. Not till Andrew, mortally wounded, was made
prisoner did the remnant of his crew surrender to the English.

Meantime the Admiral had sighted, pursued and overtaken
the *Jenny Pirwin*. With the same wild valour with which, two
years later, he boarded the galley of Prégent de Bideux, he flung
himself on board "the barque of Scotland". The Scots fought "as
hardy and well-stomaked men", but with no better success than
their comrades in the *Lion*. They were all killed or captured.

The two prize ships were brought into Blackwall on 2 August,
and the crews lodged in the "place" belonging to the Archbishop
of York.[2] The news of Barton's death infuriated James. His great

---

[1] Ballad of Sir Andrew Barton: *The English and Scottish Popular Ballads*,
ed. Francis James Child, VOL. III, Boston 1888, p. 342.

[2] Hall, p. 525; see also Lesley, pp. 82 Sc., 339 L.; *Cal. of State Papers, Venice*,
VOL. II, No. 119; *L. and P. Henry VIII*, VOL. I, PT. I, Nos. 854, 855.

sea-captain had been treacherously slain, but he comforted himself with the thought that for such an outrage the Treaty of 1509 provided a remedy. If an Englishman killed a Scot within the English Marches, the English Warden of the Marches had to arrest the murderer, produce him at the next Warden Court, and, if he was convicted by the laws of the Marches, hand him over to the Scottish Warden. James invoked the Treaty, and drew on himself the undying animosity of the Howards by demanding that they should appear before the Warden Court.[1]

Henry first made his position secure by sending the Bishop of Winchester and some of the Council to interview the Scottish captives. Fox soon persuaded them to admit that they were pirates "who had deserved to die by the law and to be hanged at the low water mark". A priest who was among the captives cried, "My lords, we appeal from the King's justice to his mercy." "Then", said Fox, "you shall find the King's mercy above his justice" and ordered them to leave the country within twenty days, and to pray for the King. Henry then sent James the insolent answer that it did not become one prince to accuse another of breaking a Treaty simply because he had done justice on a thief or pirate, and that if he had shown justice instead of mercy Barton's men would have been as dead as Barton himself.[2]

How James would take the rebuff was uncertain: though he announced that he was sending six commissioners, including the Earl of Argyll, Lord Drummond, and the Justice Clerk to meet Dacre and Sir Robert Drury at the next Warden Court, though on 26 July safe-conducts were issued to them,[3] Badoer reported that English troops were moving north.[4] Henry and his advisers were taking no risks: on 29 July John Cutt and Richard Gough were instructed to review the garrisons and see to the defences of Carlisle, Norham and Berwick,[5] and on 16 August Thomas Lord Darcy was appointed captain of Berwick.[6] For a time it seemed

---

[1] Hall, pp. 525, 558.   [2] Hall, p. 525.
[3] *L. and P. Henry VIII*, VOL. I, PT. I, No. 833(65).
[4] On or after 25 July. *Cal. of State Papers, Venice*, VOL. II, No. 117; *L. and P. Henry VIII*, VOL. I, PT. I, No. 854.
[5] *L. and P. Henry VIII*, VOL. I, PT. I, No. 827.   [6] *op. cit.*, No. 845.

as if Henry would not stop at defensive measures; the Howards almost prevailed upon him to declare war. But Wolsey and Fox laboured for peace,[1] and at the beginning of November persuaded him to send the patient and much experienced Nicholas West to the Scottish Court. West was authorised to treat of the pardon and remission of all quarrels between the subjects of James and the subjects of Henry.[2] West set out, but went no further than York. Though Henry was resolved to continue the negotiations, he had not put away all thought of war with Scotland. In the summer he had sent 1,000 English sailors and some artillery to the Low Countries to assist Margaret of Savoy in her campaign against James's kinsman and ally the Duke of Gueldres[3]; on 17 December he asked that his artillery should be returned, as it would be required in his operations against the Scots.[4]

If James refrained from making war on England before the end of 1511 it was not because he wanted peace. He wanted war; he was throwing all his energies, all the resources of his kingdom into preparations for war; his great new ship, the *Michael*, now floated on the waters of the Forth[5]; ships from Flanders were bringing guns and gun metal into Leith[6]; guns were being fashioned in the new forges in Edinburgh Castle by artificers imported from France.[7] But he was not ready yet: there were too many obstacles in his path. One indeed he had removed: on 30 July he shelved the dispute with Portugal by informing the Procurator of the King of Portugal at Antwerp that he had forbidden reprisals, and that he would send commissioners to Bruges to settle the matter.[8] Another, far more serious, remained—the treaty with England, a breach of which would inevitably bring him under the ban of excommunication. He tried to get round

[1] *L. and P. Henry VIII*, VOL. I, PT. I, No. 880.

[2] *L. and P. Henry VIII*, VOL. I, PT. I, No. 969(2), (7).

[3] *L. and P. Henry VIII*, VOL. I, PT. I, No. 825; *Cal. of State Papers, Venice*, VOL. II, No. 116.   [4] *L. and P. Henry VIII*, VOL. I, PT. I, No. 992.

[5] *C.T.S.*, VOL. IV, pp. lv, 313.

[6] *C.T.S.*, VOL. IV, pp. lxxii-lxxiii, 278, 286, 302.

[7] *C.T.S.*, VOL. IV, pp. 276-8.

[8] *E.R.S.*, VOL. I, pp. 120-1; *L. and P. Henry VIII*, VOL. I, PT. I, No. 828. The dispute was not settled till 1563: *A.P.S.*, VOL. II, p. 544.

THE GREAT MICHAEL

Reconstructed model in the Royal Scottish Museum, Edinburgh

Photo: The Scotsman Publications Ltd.

it; on 5 December he complained to Julius that the peace which now obtained was more dangerous than war, as Henry, in spite of his oath, allowed, and even ordered, James's subjects to be killed or imprisoned. He must assume, therefore, that both Henry and he were liberated from their oaths, and that the Treaty was now annulled. Julius refused to be drawn, and maintained an ambiguous silence.[1]

Above all, James had wit enough to see that he could not make war on England single-handed; he must have allies. Where was he to find them? Not among his kinsmen. From his uncle of Denmark he could expect only appeals for help; his cousin, the Duke of Gueldres, had been driven from his Duchy in the last campaign. There remained his "good brother, friend and confederate", the King of France. Louis had no desire for a war with England. Neither the capture of Bologna in May, nor a dangerous—almost a mortal—illness in the summer of 1511, had weakened the Pope's implacable hatred of him. In July, by summoning a General Council to meet at the Lateran in April 1512, Julius made the Council of Pisa, before ever it had met, a schismatic assembly.[2] In September he told Forman, whom Louis had sent to him a second time, that Louis must abandon all attempts against Venice, and surrender Bologna and Ferrara.[3] Knowing that denunciations would not move Louis, he set about the building up of a great confederation hostile to France; on 4 October 1511 he put his signature to a treaty of alliance with Spain and Venice.[4] This was only a beginning; this Holy League, he hoped, would soon include England and the Empire.

Ten days later Louis heard of this League "*si deshonneste, si presomptueuse et si arrogante, faicte en grant dommage de la crestiente et grant deshonneur de tous roys crestiens*".[5] He did not suspect that

---

[1] E.R.S., VOL. I, pp. 122-4; L. and P. Henry VIII, VOL. I, PT. I, No. 974.

[2] L. and P. Henry VIII, VOL. I, PT. I, No. 816.

[3] L. and P. Henry VIII, VOL. I, PT. I, No. 870; Louis XII to James IV, 8 Nov. 1511, Flodden Papers, p. 12.

[4] Cal. of State Papers, Spain, VOL. II, No. 56; L. and P. Henry VIII, VOL. I, PT. I, No. 889.

[5] L. and P. Henry VIII, VOL. I, PT. I, No. 902. The quotation is from the letter of 8 Nov., Flodden Papers, p. 14.

P

Henry was a party to the Holy League, and that the English ambassador, Cardinal Bainbridge, had refused to sign only because his commission had not yet arrived,[1] and he seems to have remained ignorant for some weeks both of Henry's admission to the League on 13 November,[2] and of the treaty concluded on 17 November,[3] by which Henry and Ferdinand each undertook to send 6,000 men into Aquitaine before the end of April 1512, to bring it once more under the sway of England. On 8 November he wrote to James, denouncing the alliance of the Pope, Spain and Venice, but praying him to keep on friendly terms with the King of England.[4] He had sent Forman a third time to the Pope, but his offer to surrender Bologna and Ferrara if Julius would withdraw from the League was treated with the same contempt as before,[5] and at the beginning of December 1511 Forman returned to Blois.[6]

Louis was growing anxious. He saw that in the impending struggle he must have an ally more reliable than the slippery Maximilian. Why not the King of Scots? He seemed really to believe in his mad project of a crusade—could not that be used as a bait? And if the King of Scots, why not his uncle, the King of Denmark? At the end of December 1511 or the beginning of January 1512 Louis despatched Dr Peter Cordier to Scotland. Already he had begun to be suspicious of Henry; Cordier was instructed to promise James that in the event of an English invasion of France, Louis would help him to conquer England. On

[1] *Cal. of State Papers, Spain*, VOL. II, No. 56.

[2] *L. and P. Henry VIII*, VOL. I, PT. I, Nos. 939, 969(40); *Cal. of State Papers, Spain*, VOL. II, No. 58.

[3] *L. and P. Henry VIII*, VOL. I, PT. I, No. 945; *Cal. of State Papers, Spain*, VOL. II, Nos. 59, 60.

[4] Louis XII to James IV, 8 Nov. 1511, *Flodden Papers*, pp. 10-17.

[5] *L. and P. Henry VIII*, VOL. I, PT. I, No. 1020; *Cal. of State Papers, Venice*, VOL. II, No. 143.

[6] The material for this and the following paragraph is from the very detailed account of the mission of Cordier, based on his own report, in P. W. Becker, *De rebus inter Ioannem et Christianum II Daniae reges, ac Ludovicum XII et Iacobum IV Galliae Scotiaeque reges a. MDXI-MDXIV actis*, Copenhagen 1835. The Scottish part of his mission is described in pp. 29-34.

29 January James sent the French ambassador to Denmark, equipped with a silver ewer and basin.[1] In the letter of commendation which Cordier carried with him James explained to his uncle that the ambassador had told him of the League of the Pope, Spain and Venice, of the perfidy of Julius, of the disaster threatening Christendom and of the Council which Louis had summoned to avert it. He announced that he had summoned his prelates and nobles to advise him about the sending of representatives to the Council, and urged John to act in concert with him.[2] That Louis was still uncertain about Henry's attitude is evident from the instructions which he gave to Forman on 17-18 January 1512. Before he returned to Scotland Forman was to seek an audience with Henry. He was to urge both monarchs to sink their differences—"si le roy d'Ecosse ne le fait . . . le roy [Louis] le prendra tresmal"—and combine to support Louis against the Pope.[3] To James he was to give the long-delayed answer to his questions about a crusade—a promise of a tithe, to be levied on every part of the French territories, a year after peace had been made with the Pope, and in addition as many cavalry and infantry as he might require, a good supply of guns and ammunition, and all the ships necessary for the transport of his men.[4]

In his brief stay at the English Court, Forman must have learned, if he did not know already, that Henry had ranged himself on the side of the enemies of France. He went to Scotland a little after the middle of February 1512[5] with his mind made up. There must be no reconciliation with England; the ancient league with France, never actually denounced by James in spite of his promises to Henry VII, must be confirmed, and that confirmation

---

[1] C.T.S., VOL. IV, p. 328.

[2] E.R.S., VOL. I, p. 129; L. and P. Henry VIII, VOL. I, PT. I, No. 1039. James had summoned, not his Parliament as Brodie says, but his Council—"prelatos nostros et barones."

[3] Louis XII, instructions to the Bishop of Moray (1), Flodden Papers, pp. 17-19.

[4] Louis XII, instructions to the Bishop of Moray (2), Flodden Papers, pp. 19-26.

[5] L. and P. Henry VIII, VOL. I, PT. I, No. 1076; VOL. II, PT. II, London 1864, p. 1454.

must be only the first step to the active co-operation of the two princes. Louis would see that the advocate of a pro-French policy did not lack his reward.

To Edinburgh there came also, in the early days of March, Octavian Olarius, with a letter from the Pope commanding James to join the Holy League, or at least to abstain from helping France,[1] and Leonardo Lopez, the Spanish Ambassador in London, with a letter from Ferdinand to the same effect.[2] James had ears only for Forman; he had eyes only for the visionary crown and the phantom fleets and armies promised by King Louis. Already on 29 February, he had issued a summons to the nobles and prelates[3]; with them he sat in council to listen to Forman's story, and on 6 March he decided to offer to renew the ancient League.[4]

The draft treaty which Unicorn Pursuivant carried with him when he left Scotland on 10 March 1512[5] was simply a copy of the 1491 treaty,[6] itself a copy of a copy, deriving ultimately from the treaty made by Robert II of Scotland and Charles V of France in 1371.[7] It contained ten articles: (1) The King of Scots and the King of France bound themselves to support each other against the King of England in peace and war. (2) If war broke out between either King and the King of England, his ally was to make war at once on England with his whole power, if he could do so without breaking an existing truce. (3) Each prince promised to punish as a traitor any of his subjects who should help England. (4) Neither King would receive rebel subjects of the

[1] C.T.S., VOL. IV, pp. 334-5. The letter was written on 6 or 7 Jan. 1512: L. and P. Henry VIII, VOL. I, PT. I, No. 1014.

[2] The letter, according to L. and P. Henry VIII, VOL. I, PT. I, No. 1108, and E.R.S., VOL. I, pp. 131-3, was written on 6 Nov. 1511 and delivered on 8 Jan. 1512. According to L. and P. Henry VIII, VOL. I, PT. I, No. 1108(2) (Add. MS 324) it was delivered on 8 March. The latter seems to be the correct date; a Spanish ambassador was in Edinburgh in March 1512: C.T.S., VOL. IV, p. 336.

[3] C.T.S., VOL. IV, p. 333.

[4] L. and P. Henry VIII, VOL. I, PT. I, No. 1089; Flodden Papers, p. 45.

[5] C.T.S., VOL. IV, p. 335.

[6] Register House MSS, Treaties with France, No. 20.

[7] Register House MSS, Treaties with France, No. 2.

other. (5) If either made a truce with England, his action did not bind his ally unless he had first obtained that ally's consent. (6) Neither King was to make a peace with England unless his ally was included. (7) Neither King was to interfere in any dispute about the succession of his ally's kingdom. (8) The Treaty was to be confirmed by the Pope; neither King would ask to be absolved from it, and (9) even if that absolution were granted it would be deemed invalid. (10) Each King promised to swear on the Gospels that he would observe the Treaty.[1]

Scarcely had Unicorn sailed when, on 12 March, De la Motte arrived in Scotland.[2] He had apparently been sent to announce that France was threatened with an English invasion, and to find out what Scotland and Denmark would do if the invasion took place. A few days later Octavian Olarius departed,[3] taking with him a letter in which James solemnly lectured the Pope. Louis must be handled gently—persuaded to return to his allegiance—instead of being driven to worse crimes by a display of vindictive hatred. James would try to get him to give up Bologna and Ferrara, and disarm the Council of Pisa, but only if warlike measures against him were abandoned.[4] His reply to Ferdinand was equally spirited; he urged the Catholic King not to draw the sword against a Catholic warrior, but to conserve the whole strength of Christendom for a great crusade.[5]

The magnificent post-dated cheque with which his ally had presented him did not altogether satisfy James. When De la Motte left for France on 25 March[6] he took with him a confidential letter in which James told Louis that as his marriage had already made him heir to the childless Henry and as an open break with England would destroy all hope of his peaceful succession to the English throne, he expected his ally not to abandon him in his struggle for the English crown, or at least not to make

---

[1] *Flodden Papers*, App. II, pp. 143-8.   [2] *C.T.S.*, VOL. IV, p. 336.
[3] On or a little before 16 March. *C.T.S.*, VOL. IV, pp. 334-5.
[4] *E.R.S.*, VOL. I, pp. 135-7; *L. and P. Henry VIII*, VOL. I, PT. I, No. 1100.
[5] *E.R.S.*, VOL. I, pp. 131-3; *L. and P. Henry VIII*, VOL. I, PT. I, No. 1108.
[6] *C.T.S.*, VOL. IV, p. 337. James rode with the Ambassador to Dumbarton, and visited him while his ship lay becalmed there.

peace without his consent. Further he asked Louis to send him not only money, provisions and guns, but troops of all arms, and suggested that the pension of 50,000 crowns which he paid to Henry might be usefully diverted from his enemy to his ally.[1]

The French King's answer to these demands was presented to James by the Bishop of Ross on 21 April 1512. Louis agreed to support James in any rightful claim against England or any other power, and to conclude no agreement with James's enemies without his consent, unless he was included in the agreement. Though he wanted James to send some ships to France as quickly as possible he urged James to make his main effort on land *"pour faire destourner le roy d'Angleterre de la guerre contre le roy trescrestien"*. He could give James neither men nor munitions; the money paid to Henry was not a pension, it was a repayment of sums advanced by England to the Bretons, and paid by them to their Duchess, the Queen of France. The King of Denmark, who had first raised the question of the pension, and his son the Viceroy of Norway, should be informed that Louis would never forsake James, *"en quelque fortune que ce soyt, prosperite ou adversite"*, so that the four princes might be as one and form a perpetual and inviolable alliance.[2]

But the treaty was not yet confirmed. On 24 May De la Motte received further instructions from Louis at Blois,[3] and in the following month he sailed into the harbour of Ayr at the head of a fleet of captured merchantmen and fishing boats, which he straightway sold to the inhabitants of the burgh.[4] On 18 June he delivered to James a copy of the treaty from which the clause in the second article relating to existing truces with England had been deleted, on the ground that it would stultify the whole treaty.[5] James accepted the change, but introduced modifications of his own when he signed the treaty on 10 July 1512: the fifth article became a simple undertaking that neither of the contracting

---

[1] James's letter has not been preserved: his demands, however, are recapitulated in the instructions of Louis to the Bishop of Ross, *Flodden Papers*, pp. 38-43.

[2] *Flodden Papers*, pp. 38-43.   [3] *Flodden Papers*, pp. 44-7.

[4] *L. and P. Henry VIII*, VOL. I, PT. I, No. 1262; *C.T.S.*, VOL. IV, p. 350.

[5] *Flodden Papers*, p. 46.

parties would make a truce with the King of England without his partner's consent, and the sixth disappeared altogether.[1] If we are to believe the report of John Anislow, the Captain of Norham, he also wrote to Louis protesting that unless he got the pension already paid to Henry he would be unable to invade England.[2]

On the following day De la Motte left for France in William Brownhill's ship, escorted by the ships of Robert Barton and David Falconer.[3] The English were on the lookout, however; Falconer's ship was "drownit" and Falconer himself made prisoner.[4] Barton and Brownhill, to Falconer's disgust, did not wait to fight.[5] The modified treaty was finally confirmed by Louis at Blois on 12 September 1512.[6]

Meantime both Louis and James had been searching feverishly for allies. Louis had lost Maximilian, who had concluded a truce with the Pope and Venice in April.[7] Something, they still hoped, might be got from John of Denmark—from John of Denmark who on 11 February had written to Henry asking if he might have one of the ships taken from Andrew Barton, as it had been presented to him by James,[8] and on 12 February had sent to James his customary appeal for help against the Swedes and their allies, the men of Lübeck,[9] and from whom Cordier had got nothing more than a promise that he would send ambassadors to the Pope, to suggest that he should convoke a General Council somewhere in Germany.[10] On 22 April Carrick Pursuivant was despatched to the Danish Court with letters to the King and Queen announcing

[1] *L. and P. Henry VIII*, VOL. I, PT. I, No. 1287.

[2] Anislow to Ruthal, 11 Sept. 1512, *L. and P. Henry VIII*, VOL. I, PT. I, No. 1380.

[3] *C.T.S.*, VOL. IV, pp. 297, 352.

[4] *L. and P. Henry VIII*, VOL. I, PT. I, No. 1298.

[5] *L. and P. Henry VIII*, VOL. I, PT. I, No. 1380.

[6] Register House MSS, Treaties with France, No. 23.

[7] *Cambridge Modern History*, VOL. I, p. 136.

[8] *L. and P. Henry VIII*, VOL. I, PT. I, No. 1056.

[9] 46th *Report* of the Deputy Keeper of Public Records, App. II, p. 55.

[10] John of Denmark to Louis XII, 11 April 1512, Becker, *De rebus inter Ioannem et Christianum II . . . ac Ludovicum XII et Iacobum IV . . . actis*, pp. 100-2. *L. and P. Henry VIII*, VOL. I, PT. I, No. 1140, a very brief abstract, gives the date incorrectly as 12 April.

the birth of a prince—afterwards James V—twelve days before.
He was also instructed to explain to King John the desire of Louis
that Scotland and Denmark should support him in his appeal
from the Pope to the Council of Pisa. He was also to announce
that Henry had mobilised a fleet and an army which might be
turned against Scotland at any moment, and that Ferdinand proposed to join his ally in a descent on France. Louis therefore
wanted to know what Scotland and Denmark would do if France
were invaded, just as James wanted to know what Denmark would
do if Scotland were invaded. In conclusion, Carrick was to say
that James, to put France under an obligation to both Scotland
and Denmark, had decided to renew the old alliance: he therefore
prayed that his uncle would conclude truces with his enemies,
keep his fleet and army ready for service and announce as soon as
possible what help he was ready to give.[1]

King John, less accustomed to give than to receive, replied
with an announcement that he had made truces with the Swedes
and the Lübeckers, and a vague promise that he would send help
to James if he asked for it.[2] James did not want vague promises:
on 28 May he sent Carrick back again to discover the exact number of ships and men and the exact amount of money that the
King was prepared to send to Scotland if it was invaded, and on
what conditions he was prepared to help France.[3] He repeated
his appeal on 7 August,[4] after two months had passed without
any news of Carrick, but he got from his uncle nothing more
definite than a complaint that certain Scots—names unknown—
had plundered certain Danish ships.[5]

Clearly little was to be expected from Denmark, and with
every month the French King's need increased. The Italian campaign of 1512, after a glorious opening had ended in disaster.
The French had captured Ravenna on 11 April, but the death of
Gaston de Foix in the moment of victory left them without a

[1] E.R.S., VOL. I, pp. 141-2; L. and P. Henry VIII, VOL. I, PT. I, No. 1155.
[2] E.R.S., VOL. I, pp. 143-4; L. and P. Henry VIII, VOL. I, PT. I, No. 1211.
[3] E.R.S., VOL. I, pp. 148-50; L. and P. Henry VIII, VOL. I, PT. I, No. 1212.
[4] E.R.S., VOL. I, pp. 165-7; L. and P. Henry VIII, VOL. I, PT. I, No. 1330.
[5] E.R.S., VOL. I, pp. 167-8; L. and P. Henry VIII, VOL. I, PT. I, No. 1523.

capable commander, and before the end of June they had been hustled north of the Alps. The fear of invasion hung over France itself: on 24 April Lancaster Herald announced to Louis that his master had decided to support the Pope, and was preparing to send an army to France[1]; at the beginning of June Sir Edward Howard escorted an army commanded by the Marquis of Dorset to Fuenterrabia, then, doubling back, plundered the coasts of Brittany.[2] All through the summer, the English troops lay inactive before Bayonne, waiting for the Spanish army that was to co-operate with them in the conquest of Guienne.[3] Jean d'Albret, King of Navarre, knew that Guienne was not Ferdinand's real objective; he had already sent ambassadors to negotiate a treaty with France, but on the very day on which the treaty was concluded, his kingdom was invaded by a Spanish army under the Duke of Alva.[4] He fled to France; Louis could do nothing for him. It was true that Dorset's army, wearied out with disease and inactivity, mutinied and went home,[5] but the ignominious end of the Guienne campaign really augured ill for France. Henry had learned his lesson. He would depend no more on shifty allies; when next an English army crossed the sea he would lead it himself.

The odds against Louis were mounting up: on 19 November Maximilian joined the Holy League.[6] The Pope, the Empire, England, Spain and Venice were now arrayed against him. Next year, if he sent his armies southwards into Italy to regain his lost towns and provinces he would expose the northern part of his kingdom to invasion by the armies of Henry and the Emperor. Weakly obstinate, he could not bring himself to cut his losses; he resolved that his armies must march into Italy in 1513 as they

[1] *L. and P. Henry VIII*, VOL. I, PT. I, Nos. 1157, 1169.

[2] *L. and P. Henry VIII*, VOL. I, PT. I, Nos. 1216 (*Cal. of State Papers, Spain*, VOL. II, No. 174), 1260, 1268.

[3] *L. and P. Henry VIII*, VOL. I, PT. I, Nos. 1319, 1320.

[4] *L. and P. Henry VIII*, VOL. I, PT. I, Nos. 1375, 1376.

[5] *L. and P. Henry VIII*, VOL. I, PT. I, Nos. 1475 (*Cal. of State Papers, Venice*, VOL. II, No. 211), 1487.

[6] *L. and P. Henry VIII*, VOL. I, PT. I, No. 1486 (i) and (ii); *Cal. of State Papers, Spain*, VOL. II, Nos. 73-6.

haď done in 1512, only this time the King of Scots must invade England and so keep at home, or bring home, the English troops destined for the invasion of France.

So far the treaty of perpetual peace had remained—technically —inviolate: Henry was still James's "Derrest Bruther and Cous- ing". Neither James nor Henry wanted immediate war: James, willing to wound, was afraid to strike till he had allies to strike with him; Henry, maturing schemes of French conquests, did not want to be distracted by an unprofitable war with Scotland. On 15 April 1512, after receiving a declaration from James that he was willing to keep the peace if Henry would give way in the dispute about captured ships,[1] he commissioned West and Dacre to go to Scotland as ambassadors.[2] They arrived in Scot- land about the end of April and left before the middle of June,[3] having got from James nothing beyond a promise that he would send ambassadors to England for further discussions. James, they thought, wanted peace; his subjects were eager for war.[4]

His subjects seemed to think that an attack on the Scottish coasts would follow the departure of the ambassadors; messages were sent to the coasts of East Lothian and Fife to keep a lookout for English ships,[5] and in Aberdeen trenches were dug and guns hastily put in position "to the resisting of our auld ennemeys of Ingland".[6]

The only Englishman who crossed the border at this time was Dacre's servant, Beverlaw, who on 13 July delivered to James a letter from Henry containing the disconcerting news that Louis had recognised his protégé, Richard de la Pole, the younger brother of the imprisoned Earl of Suffolk, as King of England.[7] James told Dacre that he did not believe the story,[8] and in letters which he despatched on 18 July he tried to embarrass Henry by demanding a safe-conduct for six members of his Council, with

[1] L. and P. Henry VIII, VOL. I, PT. I, No. 1147.
[2] L. and P. Henry VIII, VOL. I, PT. I, Nos. 1142, 1170 (14), (15).
[3] L. and P. Henry VIII, VOL. I, PT. I, Nos. 1261, 1268.
[4] L. and P. Henry VIII, VOL. I, PT. I, No. 1268.
[5] C.T.S., VOL. IV, p. 352.
[6] Aberdeen Register, entry under 18 June 1512, VOL. I, p. 83.
[7] L. and P. Henry VIII, VOL. I, PT. I, No. 1297.　　　　[8] Ibid.

an escort of a hundred horsemen, Scots, French or Italians, which would entitle them to pass through England "without any search, arrest or trouble" any time in the next twelve months, and by offering to send Forman as an ambassador to Henry—and to other princes.[1] He also, with studied tactlessness, informed Henry that he could not support the candidate whom Henry had recommended for the archdeaconry of Dunkeld—John Carwenale, Queen Margaret's English chaplain. Carwenale's claim was contested by a cousin of the Bishop, who, James explained, "is auld and cummys notht to court, and geve we did to him or his cousing . . . by resoun and law, it wald be rumorit and allegit the cause of his deid, albeit he decessit of age".[2]

Dacre forwarded the correspondence with a covering letter to Henry on 20 July. He told Henry that musters were going on all over Scotland, but added that James and his Council seemed disposed to be friendly and begged him not to treat Falconer as a pirate.[3]

In answer two letters were despatched at the end of July. In the first Henry informed James that, though he could not make peace with France without the consent of his allies, he was willing to receive Forman.[4] The second professed to be a confidential letter for Dacre's eye alone, but Dacre was instructed to convey it, with a show of secrecy, to the King of Scots. It contained an unequivocal declaration that while Henry would welcome Forman as an ambassador to England, he would not allow him to cross to France, nor would he grant a safe-conduct to the six Scottish dignitaries with their bodyguard of one hundred horsemen Scots, French or Italians—including perhaps De la Motte himself. He would restore a Scottish ship which his people had captured, if the Scots would restore the English ships which they had captured. He regretted that in time of peace his allies should join with his enemies to attack English merchantmen. When the Scots attacked his people successfully, he complained, they called

[1] *L. and P. Henry VIII*, VOL. I, PT. I, Nos. 1294, 1299; Pinkerton, VOL. II, p. 76n.
[2] *L. and P. Henry VIII*, VOL. I, PT. I, No. 1300.
[3] *op. cit.*, No. 1302.   [4] *op. cit.*, No. 1314.

themselves the French King's subjects; when they were captured in company of Frenchmen, then they were King James's subjects, which much perplexed him. "To break with our brother", Henry concluded, "we never purposed ne intended to do; and to permit our subjects to be robbed without redress we may not suffer." A declaration that the execution of the captured Falconer was to be postponed, was enclosed in a separate scroll, to be used by Dacre as he thought fit.[1]

The rumour of musters north of the Border[2] caused more perturbation at Portsmouth, where the King was, than at Carlisle. The Earl of Surrey must go northwards with a commission to array the forces of Yorkshire, Lancashire, Northumberland, Cumberland and Westmorland[3]; at the beginning of August the Keepers of the King's Wardrobe issued to him a banner with a St George's cross, a standard embroidered with a red dragon, and four banners with the royal arms for four trumpeters.[4] The Bishop of Durham, too, suddenly anxious for the safety of his frontier stronghold, despatched 200 sheaves of arrows and 100 bows to Norham Castle.[5]

The English Warden refused to be perturbed; he duly met the Scottish Warden at Cornhill on 5 August[6]; on the 17th he suggested to Henry that as it was evident from James's letters that he intended no immediate break, it would be politic to overdrive the time till the corn was housed and the stubble was eaten bare, and invasion made impossible for that year. The payment of four or five thousand angels to the King, the Scottish Treasurer had told him, might solve all problems. It would be honourable to pay the Queen's legacy, he added; the sum was small.[7] Neither Dacre's letter nor the letter which the Captain of Norham sent to Ruthal on 11 September,[8] with the news that the height of war was over in Scotland, could reassure Henry's advisers. On 18 September, Queen Katharine informed Cardinal Bainbridge that the Scots had declared war and had attacked Berwick, and that Surrey had gone north at the head of 30,000 men, to treat

[1] L. and P. Henry VIII, VOL. I, PT. I, No. 1315.   [2] op. cit., No. 1302.
[3] op. cit., No. 1365 (3).   [4] op. cit., No. 1317.   [5] op. cit., No. 1323.
[6] op. cit., No. 1302.   [7] op. cit., No. 1342.   [8] op. cit., No. 1380.

the King of Scots as Ferdinand had treated the King of Navarre.[1] When she wrote Surrey had already reached Pontefract.[2] Here he stayed for a month, waiting for the news that the Scots had crossed the Border. But Dacre had been right; the news never came, and on 15 October the great guns which had been sent to Pontefract[3] from the Tower of London rolled back along the road to the south. On 9 November Badoer reported to his Government that Surrey had returned and that the dispute with Scotland seemed to be well-nigh adjusted.[4]

[1] *L. and P. Henry VIII*, VOL. I, PT. I, No. 1391.
[2] *L. and P. Henry VIII*, VOL. I, PT. I, No. 1450.
[3] *L. and P. Henry VIII*, VOL. I, PT. I, No. 1475.
[4] *Cal. of State Papers, Venice*, VOL. II, No. 211.

IX

THE EVE OF FLODDEN

O N St Andrew's Eve 1512, when a great gale from the east screamed and roared up the Forth, the people of Leith heard, in a lull of the storm, the sound of guns. A strange ship had battled its way in from the open sea and now strained at its anchor not far from the shore. The news soon spread: in Edinburgh the alarm bell was rung for three hours on end, and every burgess hurriedly buckled on his unaccustomed armour. It was a false alarm; there was no rash and insolent Howard on board, but De la Motte, with a store of fair words and large promises.

The French ship dragged its anchor and was driven right up to Blackness, where the great *Michael* lay. The King rowed out through the storm to his new ship, and there he received the ambassador, who presented him with the final version of the treaty,[1] signed by Louis, and thanked him, on behalf of his master, "for the great affection and love" which he had shown.

De la Motte had been sent to do more than exchange polite speeches and deliver gifts of wine, cannon, cloth of gold, and gunpowder. He brought the King, according to Dacre's letter of 10 December, 30 tuns of wine, 8 lasts of gunpowder, 200 gunstones of iron, 8 serpentines of brass for the field, and some plate. To the Queen he gave eight lengths of cloth of gold.[2] He was to represent to James—so his instructions ran—that it was now necessary to diminish the arrogance of the English, who had joined with the Pope and with Ferdinand, the contriver of "a faction very dangerous to Christendom which he called the Holy League", and to do his utmost against "*ladite dampnee secte scis-*

---

[1] *Flodden Papers*, pp. 47-52; Register House MSS, Treaties with France, No. 23.　　　　[2] *L. and P. Henry VIII*, VOL. I, PT. I, No. 1504.

matique". To encourage James in this enterprise he was empowered to offer a subsidy of 50,000 francs, good pieces of artillery, and a supply of ammunition, and to promise that when the strife in Christendom was over Louis would help his ally, as if his ally were himself, in his "holy voyage and enterprise" against the Infidel.[1]

To Edinburgh also there came at the end of the year[2] the leisurely Octavian Olarius with a letter from the Pope written on 1 July, exhorting James to an "expedition against these most pestilent Turks", an expedition which would be possible only if he persuaded Louis to make his peace with the Church.[3] Octavian had made the journey from Rome to Edinburgh by way of Aberdeen, probably because he wanted to consult Elphinstone, the weightiest opponent of James's new policy, before he presented himself at the Scottish Court.[4] He had made his journey in vain; his letter lay unheeded while James watched De la Motte's servants dance the morrice dance,[5] or rode in company with De la Motte to the shrine of St Ninian at Whithorn.[6]

It was a sorrowful Yule that year, disturbed by rumours of war and news of pestilence. When on 7 January wappenschaws were ordered in all burghs and sheriffdoms,[7] the pest had already made its appearance in Stirling. Before the end of the month messengers were riding from burgh to burgh, both north and south of the Forth, with the King's proclamation of 17 January, threatening with death anyone sick of the plague who sought to come to kirk or market or to mix with his healthy neighbours in any other way, and anyone who tried to import infected goods into the realm.[8]

[1] *Flodden Papers*, pp. 53-6.   [2] *C.T.S.*, VOL. IV, p. 402.
[3] *E.R.S.*, VOL. I, pp. 156-9; *L. and P. Henry VIII*, VOL. I, PT. I, No. 1271.
[4] *C.T.S.*, VOL. IV, pp. xxiii, 399.
[5] On 5 and 16 Dec., *C.T.S.*, VOL. IV, pp. 399, 400.
[6] On 17 Dec., *C.T.S.*, VOL. IV, p. 400.   [7] *C.T.S.*, VOL. IV, p. 402.
[8] *C.T.S.*, VOL. IV, p. 404. The text of the proclamation is given in *Edinburgh Records*, VOL. I, pp. 139-41. Other clauses, calling for the slaughter of all stray cats and dogs, and the cleansing of wynds and gutters, and prohibiting the placing of middens at the entrance to burghs, show a knowledge of at least the rudiments of sanitation.

James did not accept the omen. On 12 January he wrote another letter to the King of Denmark, already, though James did not know it, nearing the end of his perplexities. It was carried by a youth of noble birth, Magnus Belde, nephew of the Chancellor of Denmark, who had been educated at the Scottish Court.[1] James represented that an English invasion of France would be followed inevitably by an English invasion of Scotland, indeed there was a chance that the English, warned by the experience of the previous year, might invade Scotland and leave France alone. Fear of invasion had driven him to renew the old defensive alliance with France. He therefore begged his dearest uncle to despatch the Danish fleet to Scotland, and to encourage his own subjects and the merchants of the Hanse towns to send provision ships.[2]

It is doubtful if King John ever saw this appeal. He died on 21 February 1513. Three months later, on 17 May, King James, hooded and gowned in black, knelt beside his black-robed Queen in the choir of the Church of Holyrood, while the priests sang a requiem for the soul of King John.[3] Black was the proper wear; the Danish King's death destroyed all hope of Scotland obtaining help from Denmark.

Meantime the seas had become dangerous for French and Scottish ships; it was not till 14 February that De la Motte and James Ogilvy embarked on the *Petite Louise*, commanded by the stout-hearted Philippe Russel.[4] The letters which they bore contained the momentous announcement that James intended to invade England at midsummer.[5] With them went Octavianus Olarius,[6] carrying with him a letter written two days earlier[7] and articles drawn up on the previous day.[8] James protested to the Pope that he had laboured for peace, but the Henry's refusal of safe-conducts to his ambassadors had made him labour in vain.

---

[1] C.T.S., VOL. IV, p. 402.
[2] L. and P. Henry VIII, VOL. I, PT. I, No. 1564; E.R.S., VOL. I, pp. 169-73.
[3] C.T.S., VOL. IV, pp. 422, 439.
[4] L. and P. Henry VIII, VOL. I, PT. I, No. 1645.
[5] Flodden Papers, p. 71.
[6] L. and P. Henry VIII, VOL. I, PT. I, No. 1645.
[7] L. and P. Henry VIII, VOL. I, PT. I, No. 1615.
[8] L. and P. Henry VIII, VOL. I, PT. I, No. 1624.

THOMAS HOWARD

EARL OF SURREY, SECOND DUKE OF NORFOLK

By permission of His Grace the Duke of Norfolk   *Arundel Castle*

Then followed the tale of sunk ships and slaughtered seamen, and of vain demands for redress. He was helpless, he complained; if he resorted to force, Henry by his insinuations would make Julius act against him. Thus the letter; in the articles he added a request that Julius would not believe any extraordinary reports about him until he had heard his case or pass any sentence against him.

He was too late. Already Julius lay on his deathbed; already, yielding to the counsels of Cardinal Bainbridge, he had sent to England letters monitory and a bull executorial, denouncing excommunication against the King of Scots.[1] Not for two months, however, did James learn of the doom hanging over him.

On 21 February 1513 Julius II died; on 10 March he was succeeded by Giovanni de' Medici, who assumed the name of Leo X. The change of Pope brought no immediate change of policy. Soon, however, there were defections from the Holy League; on 8 February Louis commissioned Odet de Foix to negotiate with Spain,[2] and a month later the Venetians, no longer comfortable in a league which now included their implacable enemy, Maximilian, entered into an alliance with France.[3] On 1 April a truce for one year, to include the allies of the contracting parties if they so desired, was concluded by the representatives of Louis and Ferdinand.[4]

Meantime in the Castle of Edinburgh Robert Borthwick with thirteen workmen toiled all day, and sometimes all night, fashioning brazen cannon.[5] At Newhaven the shipwrights were busy, cleaning and tallowing the hulls of the King's three ships, repairing the damaged hull of the *Margaret* by candlelight, and fitting the *Margaret* and the *Michael* with new masts.[6] On 20 March the King added to his navy a French ship—"the barque of Abbeville"—which he bought for three hundred pounds.[7]

[1] *L. and P. Henry VIII*, VOL. I, PT. I, No. 1735.

[2] *L. and P. Henry VIII*, VOL. I, PT. I, No. 1611; *Cal. of State Papers, Spain*, VOL. II, No. 85.

[3] *L. and P. Henry VIII*, VOL. I, PT. I, No. 1703.

[4] *L. and P. Henry VIII*, VOL. I, PT. I, No. 1736; *Foedera*, VOL. XIII, p. 350; *Cal. of State Papers, Spain*, VOL. II, No. 91.

[5] *C.T.S.*, VOL. IV, pp. 508, 509.

[6] *C.T.S.*, VOL. IV, pp. 462-74.　　　　[7] *C.T.S.*, VOL. IV, p. 475.

Q

James was certainly preparing for war, as Dacre informed Henry on 24 February, but rumour magnified the extent of his preparations. According to Dacre there were no fewer than eighty workmen in the Castle—in reality there were never more than twenty[1]—manufacturing guns, gunpowder, lance-staves, and arrow-heads of a new pattern, and in addition to the *James* and the *Margaret*, which the King visited daily at Newhaven, there were at Leith thirteen large ships with three tops, ten smaller ships, and a captured English ship, while a sixty-oar galley was being built to serve as a tender to the *Great Michael*.[2]

Henry did not need this warning; already, on 18 February, he had commissioned Dacre and West to treat with the King of Scots for a settlement of the differences between the two countries.[3] West went north equipped with a bull executorial and letters monitory from the Pope to James and Forman and to the King of Denmark, and with a commission for abolition from Henry. On 13 March he wrote from Berwick that the Scots would keep the peace if Henry would grant their ambassadors safe-conducts and allow their merchandise safe passage by sea. Henry was not convinced; this demand for free passage for merchant ships, he told West on the 20th, might be a device for getting the Scottish fleet over to France unmolested. The English had sustained three times as much damage as the Scots, and ought to be recompensed accordingly. However he advised West to settle as many claims as possible, and wipe out the residue by abolition. If the Scots required extreme justice for attempts done at sea which could not be settled by the law of the borders—a reference to the death of Andrew Barton is probably intended here—he should suggest a general abolition or amnesty.[4]

West had already left Berwick. Dacre did not accompany him. He seems to have reached Edinburgh on Sunday, 20 March,[5]

---

[1] *C.T.S.*, VOL. IV, p. 510. The number rose to 20 in May.

[2] *L. and P. Henry VIII*, VOL. I, PT. I, No. 1645.

[3] *L. and P. Henry VIII*, VOL. I, PT. I, Nos. 1627, 1662(32); *Foedera*, VOL. XIII, PP. 333, 347.   [4] *L. and P. Henry VIII*, VOL. I, PT. I, No. 1690.

[5] The substance of what follows, to the end of the final paragraph on p. 235, is taken from West's despatch to Henry of 1 April, an abstract of which is printed in *L. and P. Henry VIII*, VOL. I, PT. I, No. 1735.

the day on which Unicorn Pursuivant and John Barton came
from France in a ship laden with gunpowder, cannonballs, and
wheat. Unicorn and Barton, who brought the news of the Pope's
death, at once hurried off to Stirling, where, as was his custom
in Holy Week, James had shut himself up in the convent of the
Observantine Friars. As the King's conscience would not permit
him to see an English ambassador till Easter was past, West decided to remain in Edinburgh till Wednesday the 23rd, passing
the time by exchanging none too polite letters with Forman,
who declared that he would have been a Cardinal if Henry had
not withheld his safe-conduct. He reached Stirling on Thursday;
on Good Friday he attended service in the Chapel Royal and
after the sermon was called to the traverse or enclosure where
the Queen sat. "If I were now in my great sickness," she cried
when she read the letters from her brother which West gave to
her, "this were enough to make me whole."

The King he did not see till Sunday. James summoned the
ambassador into his presence just before High Mass, told him that
the Pope was dead and promised him an interview on the morrow.
That night he dined with the Queen, told her that Henry meant
to go to France in person, and implored her to try to keep
Scotland out of the war. She replied by demanding her legacy.
West told her that she might have it if her husband promised to
keep the peace, but the entrance of James cut the conversation short.

The knowledge that a sentence of excommunication was
hanging over him, that West had with him the letters monitory
and the bull executorial had already given James food for Lenten
meditation. He did not want to break with the Pope; in spite of
repeated requests from Louis he had not sent representatives to
the schismatic Council of Pisa. Forman must go on his travels
again, must get a more definite promise of help from Louis and
persuade the new Pope to withhold confirmation of his predecessor's sentence. On Good Friday (25 March), he commissioned
Forman to appoint or revoke the appointment of cardinals or
others as protectors of Scotland at the Court of Rome.[1] Between
Good Friday and the end of the month he wrote a letter to the

[1] *L. and P. Henry VIII*, VOL. I, PT. I, No. 1706.

Pope, and a "remonstrance" to the King of France. In the first he notified Leo that he had again commissioned Forman to go to Rome to promote the cause of peace.[1] In the second he told Louis that he had declared "open war by land and sea" to the English ambassadors, although they had promised that if he kept the peace, King and Parliament would declare him heir to the English crown in the event of Henry's dying without children. There was not a word of truth in all this story, which was designed to beguile the niggardly Louis into sending men, money and guns. He asked for 2,000 men with experience of open warfare and siege operations, 200 or 300 men-at-arms, and a good artillery train, with gunners who knew their job. He wanted the French fleet to come to Scotland, instead of the Scottish fleet going to France. Finally he bade Louis remember his promise that if Scotland came to the help of France he would not make peace till he had placed the crown of England upon the head of the King of Scots.[2]

On 31 March Forman sailed for France in John Barton's ship, furnished with fine bread, fed capons, a barrel of salmon which the King had sent, and two puncheons of ale "ordanit for my Lord of Murrays awn drynk".[3] He had looked on James for the last time. When he returned, it would be to a Scotland bereft of its King, stricken by the disaster of which he had been the chief contriver. But what did that matter? The prize for his unswerving fidelity to a foreign King was now almost within his grasp.

Before this, however, on 28 March, the long debate between King James and the English ambassador had begun. West's scheme was to urge James to promise not to invade England. If James gave a definite promise, well and good; if he gave a definite refusal King Henry would know where he stood and could act accordingly. James's scheme was to steer carefully between the "Scylla of Yea and the Charybdis of Nay" and to keep West and his master in ignorance of his intentions. When he was reminded of the Papal bull, James declared that he would send Forman to

---

[1] *L. and P. Henry VIII*, VOL. I, PT. I, No. 1707.

[2] *Flodden Papers*, pp. 72–9.

[3] *C.T.S.*, VOL. IV, p. 474; *L. and P. Henry VIII*, VOL. I, PT. I, No. 1735.

Rome to appeal against it, that if the Pope condemned him un-heard he would never do obedience to him and that if he wanted to make war on England, which he would not do without giving due warning by herald, the Pope should not stop him. West asked drily to whom he would appeal from the Pope. "To Prester John," the King answered—giving the nickname of Pré-gent de Bideux, the famous French corsair.

After dinner, West asked the King point blank if he would keep the peace while Henry was in France. If Henry would do him justice, was the King's answer. West pointed out that commissioners had already been sent to the Borders for the redress of grievances—Lord Conyers and Sir Robert Drury had been appointed in February. That same Sir Robert Drury, James retorted, had declared that the English would snap up every Scottish ship that put to sea. West thereupon proposed that if he feared his claims would not be granted he should accept an act of abolition, and offered him 1,000 marks if he would keep the peace. James protested that he did not need the money, and asked angrily why his wife's legacy had not been paid. It would be paid if he kept the peace, West assured him; if he did not, he would lose both the legacy and his finest towns. The King, more angry than before, declared that he would pay the legacy himself, but his tirade was cut short by the entrance of the Dean of the Chapel Royal, who told him that the friar was waiting to begin his sermon.

On Wednesday, not satisfied with the discussion which he had had with Beaton, Argyll, Paniter, and Sir John Ramsay on the previous day, West made his way uninvited to the chapel where he knew the King was. James saw him, protested that he had been on the point of sending Paniter to him, and began to talk about his crusade. He showed West "a little quayr of iiij sheets of paper sewed together"—the secret articles which Louis had given to Forman in 1512, containing the offer of a fleet and an army one year after peace had been made. "Now," said the deluded monarch, after he had read the articles to West, "now you see wherefore I favour the French King and wherefore I am loth to lose him, for if I do I shall never be able to perform my journey." West said that Louis would never do what he had promised, and pressed for a definite answer. James said he would give it in the afternoon.

The afternoon came, but not the definite answer. At first the King said that West already knew his mind enough, then after some pressure he arrived at the point from which he had started in the morning; he would keep the peace if Henry would do him justice. West now asked to have a promise in writing. James flatly refused. Henry should have no letter of his or new bond to show in France whereby he might lose the French King. West protested that his master only wanted to know how James would behave in his absence. James replied that he would say nothing either of Henry's absence or his presence; to give a more definite undertaking would encourage Henry "to go overrun the French King". West pointed out that Henry would regard such an answer as a refusal, and James protested that he needed nothing more, he already knew his mind well enough. "I know neither you nor your mind," was the biting retort. The King was furious, but in the end promised that if West put his demands in writing he would get an answer in black and white. West accordingly wrote out his requests after he had taken leave of the King and sent them to the Secretary.

Thursday morning came, but no answer. In answer to West's complaints the King said that it would be given in the afternoon. In the afternoon Argyll, Paniter, and Henryson the Justice Clerk came to him—without the answer. No answer, they announced, would be given till they knew what justice would be done by England. The King would not consent to abolition. West might leave next day, if he pleased; the King would send his answer after he had gone. West asked if this was James's final answer, the Scots assured him that it was; he exclaimed angrily that if the Scots gave him no clearer answer it would be considered a negative, that they were trifling with him, and that he might waste a twelvemonth in this way.

On 1 April he was admitted to the Council and got from Argyll the definite assurance that Scotland would keep the peace if England would do the same. West's suspicions were aroused,

however, when Argyll declined to put his declaration into writing; and he repeated Argyll's speech to the King when James
entered the council chamber. His suspicions grew when the King
behaved much as Argyll had done; first saying that Argyll's
answer was his answer for the time, and then flatly refusing to let
West copy out the answer and read it aloud to him. James tried
to allay his suspicions; he took the ambassador aside and told him
that he durst not show too much friendliness to England before
his Council, as the news would be carried to France and he would
lose the French King. He was willing to let King Louis go, however, if King Henry would make the same promises. On this
admission, West advised him to send a substantial ambassador to
England; James drew back at once—it would mean the loss of
the French King.

Later in the day letters from Henry, written on 26 March,
were delivered to the ambassador. They contained a request
"well and lovingly written" for the *Michael*, a declaration that
Scottish ships would not be molested if they did not associate
with French ships, and an announcement that the commissioners
on the Borders had paid compensation for two captured Scottish
ships. West returned to James and laid the letters before him.
James refused to give his great ship to Henry on the ground that
Louis had already demanded her. West expressed the hope that
the French would not get her; James replied "that he wist not".

The Court was now on the point of leaving Stirling; West
would fain have left Scotland; he found the "country so myser
and the people so ungracious" that he wished he were in Turkey,
but his instructions compelled him to stay till he got a definite
"yes" or "no" from James. On Sunday, 3 April, he followed the
Court to Edinburgh; on Monday he went down to Leith to see
what ships were there, and discovered the truth about the great
fleet. There were only nine or ten small ships with tops, only
one of which was rigged for war, and some balingers and crayers.
At Newhaven West saw workmen caulking the seams of the
Margaret and fitting in her maintop. The King did not arrive in
Edinburgh till Monday night. It was easy to see what his thoughts
were; he spent the whole of Tuesday in Leith.

On Wednesday, armed with letters which had been delivered to him the previous day, the ambassador went to Holyrood. He saw the King after Mass and showed him a copy of a letter from the Pope, a letter which made James declare that Henry was fortunate to have such a pope. He did not know that West had kept back a more important document, a threat by Pope Leo to confirm the sentence—to come into effect should James break with Henry—which had been pronounced by Pope Julius.[1] When West again asked for the *Michael*, James tried to overawe the ambassador by telling him that his new ships mounted sixteen big guns on either side—"more great ordenaunce . . . than the Frenshe Kyng ever had at the siege of any town", "which", West wrote, "me thought to be a greate crak".

Two days later Paniter brought West the draft of James's letter to Henry—a repetition of the familiar complaints "and sharpe words of unkyndnesse". West glanced at it and told Paniter that it was now clear that James's intentions were unfriendly: he had been asked to say plainly whether he would observe his oath to keep the peace with England, and he would not answer. Next day (9 April) in a chapel at Holyrood he made a last appeal to James for a definite answer in writing, only to be told that James was afraid to lose the French King and that there was no point in sending a written answer, since Henry said that his words and his deeds agreed not. West argued that the friendship of England was much more important to James than the friendship of France: without the help of England he could not even attempt his crusade. James began to hedge; he protested

[1] "The confirmation of th' acts doon by his predecessor agaynst hym and his realm in case he breyke with your Grace." But it seems to have been a threat to confirm rather than a definite confirmation. Not till 15 Sept., two days before the news of James's death arrived in Rome, did Bainbridge and the Bishop of Worcester persuade the reluctant Leo to fulminate a new bull against James for his breach of the treaty. At this time Leo expressed the belief that the Bishops of Durham and Carlisle had already, acting on the warrant of the bull issued by Julius II, excommunicated the King of Scots (*L. and P. Henry VIII*, VOL. I, PT. II, No. 2276). On 29 Nov. he stated definitely that James had been excommunicated by Bainbridge, empowered by the bull of Julius II (*L. and P. Henry VIII*, VOL. I, PT. II, No. 2469).

that he was still a true friend to Henry and would die rather than see him dishonoured, but Henry would dishonour himself if he tried to hinder the crusade. Though Henry got no flattering words from him, he added, he would find good deeds. At this point the Dean of the Chapel Royal entered and reminded the King that it was past noon, whereupon he took West by the arm and conducted him to a room adjoining. "Sir", said West, "sithe your Grace woll aunswer nor doo non otherwise then ye have said . . . I beseche you gif me license to depart." "With good will," replied the King, and dismissed him after urging him to visit the Queen and the infant Prince at Linlithgow.

On Sunday (10 April) he told the Queen what answer he had received from James. She saw too clearly what it meant; gave him tokens for her brother, Queen Katharine, and the young Princess, and kept silent about her legacy. He returned to Edinburgh on the following day, and on Wednesday, 13 April, set out for Berwick.[1]

He knew now how the land lay, that nothing would make James give a definite undertaking to keep the peace with England should Henry invade France. He knew, too, that the letters which he carried were not calculated to conciliate his master. James wrote that he had spoken to his "derrest fallou . . . quha as scho menis for oure sake gettis notht hir faderis legacy promist in zoure divers lettrez. Ze ma do to zoure awin as ze think best, scho sall have no lose thereof." He and his lieges wanted not abolition, but redress in full; if it was not granted, he threatened, "we intend to advertise you quhairintill it failzeis". The letter concluded with a request, all but a command, that Henry should give up his expedition against the French, who, in any case, were ready for him.[2]

Still, James had refrained from an open declaration of war. He was unwilling to commit himself, West thought, till he had heard from De la Motte, who was known to be on his way to

[1] The account of the second stage of West's mission is based on his despatch of 13 April 1513, in *Original Letters illustrative of English History*, ed. Ellis, VOL. I, pp. 65-75. An abstract is printed in *L. and P. Henry VIII*, VOL. I, PT. I, No. 1775. [2] *L. and P. Henry VIII*, VOL. I, PT. I, No. 1776.

Scotland with biscuits and beer and despatches from King Louis.[1]
As day after day passed without his appearance, James began to
fear that he had been captured, for a great English fleet, commanded by Sir Edward Howard, had sailed over to the coast of
Brittany. But disaster soon overtook it; disease broke out
among the starving crews, and in a confused encounter with part
of the French fleet on 25 April, the Admiral, accompanied by a
single follower, leapt on the deck of the French flagship and was
slain.[2] At the end of the month the whole fleet was back in
Plymouth.[3]

De la Motte did not arrive in Scotland until the middle of
May.[4] On 19 May he presented to James instructions drawn up
on 5 March.[5] Anyone but the infatuated King could have seen
that Louis was giving too little and asking too much. He was
pleased to approve of the proposed Scottish invasion of England
in midsummer, but refused to send money, guns and other munitions to Scotland till the Scottish fleet had joined the French fleet
off the coast of France. He was specially anxious to have the great
ship which De la Motte had described to him, "qui ne s'en treuve
une telle en crestiente".[6]

Meantime Forman had arrived at the French court with the
Remonstrance drawn up at the end of March,[7] and on 8 May
James Ogilvy was despatched to Scotland with an answer.[8]
Louis, as usual, was profuse in polite phrases, but in nothing
more: he asked James to send on his own ships and the expected
fleet from Denmark, or at least, if the Danish ships had not arrived,
to send the Scottish ships according to his promise. As soon as
the Scottish ships arrived they would be fully equipped and
victualled, and 50,000 francs would be delivered to Forman or to
anyone else whom James cared to commission. The ships would
be sent back "selon la disposicion du temps et des affaires", and

---

[1] L. and P. Henry VIII, VOL. I, PT. I, No. 1775.
[2] L. and P. Henry VIII, VOL. I, PT. I, Nos. 1825, 1844.
[3] L. and P. Henry VIII, VOL. I, PT. I, No. 1844.
[4] C.T.S., VOL. IV, p. 411.
[5] Flodden Papers, pp. 66-72.   [6] Flodden Papers, p. 70.
[7] Flodden Papers, pp. 72-9.   [8] Flodden Papers, pp. 79-83.

with them Prégent de Bideux and seven galleys, to be at the disposal of the King of Scots. Something more important followed: he asked James to break with Henry and invade England with the best and biggest army he could raise as soon as Henry had embarked for France. This invasion, he continued, would enable James to recover more easily the realm and crown of England. As for De la Pole, James had only to make his pleasure known, whether he wanted him sent with the fleet, or kept at the French court for useful employment thereafter. Forman had told him that open war was already declared against the English; for this he thanked James with all his heart. He knew that James had refused the reversion of the English crown which Henry's ambassador had offered him; he therefore promised, on the word of a king, that he would never make peace with England without the consent of the King of Scots, and that he would perform fully all that he had sworn to do for him.

On 24 May, a few days before De la Motte returned to France, James made a half-hearted attempt to avert the now imminent war. He wrote to Henry, at the suggestion of Louis, he said, offering to enter into the truce arranged by the Kings of France and Aragon, if Henry would do the same. "And surlie, dearest Brothir," he added, "we think mair lose is to you of youre late admirall, quha decessit to his grete honour and laude, than the avantage micht have bene of the vynnyng of all the Franche galeis, and thair equippage. The saidis umquhile vailyeant Knichtis service . . . war bettir applyt apoun the Innemyis of Crist."[1]

Nothing came of this appeal; probably nothing was meant to come of it. When Ogilvy arrived in Scotland, a day or two at most after De la Motte's departure,[2] James decided to send the fleet to France as soon as it was ready. But the great fleet which had dazzled the imagination of friend and foe had still to be created, and even those ships which he had were far from ready. The Scottish Navy consisted of three ships, undergunned, with skeleton crews,[3] and a fourth ship with apparently no crew at all.

[1] Pinkerton, VOL. II, p. 454; L. and P. Henry VIII, VOL. I, PT. II, No. 1922.
[2] On or about 1 June. C.T.S., VOL. IV, p. 412.
[3] C.T.S., VOL. IV, p. 481.

Guns had to be got on board, skeleton crews brought up to full strength, and private shipowners persuaded to lend their ships to the King. So in the second week of June fifty carts made the journey from Edinburgh to Leith, carrying guns from the Castle to the shore[1]; and between 16 June and 23 June messengers were sent to every part of Scotland to enlist sailors, who were to assemble on 1 July.[2] It was not until 25 June, however, that her guns were ferried over to the *Margaret*,[3] and though at Leith thirty-two workmen toiled day and night, carrying artillery and provisions to the boats, when July came only one quarter of their task had been accomplished,[4] and the mobilisation of the sailors had to be postponed for a week.[5]

France was now in an evil plight; the army which had crossed the Alps in the late spring to reconquer Milan, was, on 6 June, shattered by the Swiss before the walls of Novara. The English transports, protected by the fleet under Lord Thomas Howard, the new Admiral of England, were conveying troops by the thousand into northern France.[6] On 25 June Thérouanne was summoned to surrender[7]; on the 30th King Henry sailed for France, to conduct the siege in person.[8]

Before he left Henry arranged that the Queen was to act as Regent,[9] and that the Earl of Surrey was to be his Lieutenant in the north, with power to raise the armed forces of the six northern counties.[10] Though Fox and the much-experienced Dacre did not believe that James would invade England, Henry was resolved to run no risks—he had heard that in Veere artillery, armour and long spears called "Colin Clouts" were being shipped daily to Scotland. To Surrey, who had come to Dover to bid him farewell, he said, "My Lord, I trust not the Scots, therefore I pray you be not negligent."

[1] *C.T.S.*, VOL. IV, p. 480. [2] *C.T.S.*, VOL. IV, pp. 413-4.
[3] *C.T.S.*, VOL. IV, p. 481. [4] *C.T.S.*, VOL. IV, p. 483.
[5] *C.T.S.*, VOL. IV, p. 414.

[6] *L. and P. Henry VIII*, VOL. I, PT. II, Nos. 1931, 1936, 1949; *Cal. of State Papers, Venice*, VOL. II, No. 252.

[7] *L. and P. Henry VIII*, VOL. I, PT. II, No. 2027.

[8] *L. and P. Henry VIII*, VOL. I, PT. II, No. 2061.

[9] *L. and P. Henry VIII*, VOL. I, PT. II, No. 2055 (46). [10] Hall, p. 555.

"I shall do my duty," replied Surrey, "that Your Grace shall find me diligent, and to fulfil your will shall be my gladness." "May I see him or I die that is the cause of my abiding behind," growled the veteran after Henry had left him, "and if ever he and I meet, I shall do that in me lieth to make him as sorry." He escorted the Queen to London, left for the north on 22 July, and on 1 August was back at Pontefract, his old headquarters.[1]

He left nothing to chance; long before any fighting could take place he summoned the knights and gentlemen who would lead the county levies to a council of war; he moved the artillery, commanded by Nicholas Appleyard, from Durham to Newcastle, and he established a system of posts, so that in the event of invasion relays of horsemen might carry the mobilisation orders within a few hours as far as the Welsh Marches.[2]

James had now gained one other—very uncertain—ally. In the early summer O'Donnell of Tyrconnel, accompanied by his harper, came to Scotland on some mysterious errand.[3] Probably he wanted to involve James in his long-standing feud with the O'Neils of Antrim; probably James hoped that with a little encouragement he might attack one of the English strongholds in Ireland—Carrickfergus for example—and so make trouble for Henry. In any case, by a treaty signed on 25 June James took O'Donnell under his protection, and promised to send him ships and men whenever he asked for them.[4] When he left Edinburgh in mid-July he was followed by two guns, one a great cannon drawn by thirty-six horses, four carts laden with ammunition, twenty workmen, and eight quarriers "for undirmynding of wallis". But the simple Irishman, wiser than James, had apparently no wish to snatch chestnuts from the fire to oblige his ally; when he sailed for Ireland he left the guns behind him.[5]

We would give much to be able to lift the veil of oblivion, and see Scotland as it really was in the summer of 1513, that last summer of a too brief golden age. The curtain rises for a moment, it is true; in the Prologue to Gavin Douglas's translation of the spurious thirteenth book of the Aeneid, we see the woods and

[1] Hall, pp. 555-6.   [2] Hall, p. 556.   [3] C.T.S., VOL. IV, pp. 415-6, 434-5.
[4] R.M.S., VOL. II, No. 3856.   [5] C.T.S., VOL. IV, p. 527.

fields that environed the town of Edinburgh lying dark and silent under the stars.

> Owt ouer the swyre swymmys the soppis of myst,
> The nycht furthspred hir cloke with sabill lyst:
> That all the bewte of the fructuus feld
> Was wyth the erthis umbrage clene ourheld:
> Involuyt in tha schaddois warryn sylde. . . .
> Ontyll a garth under ane greyn lawrer
> I walk onon, and in a sege down sat,
> Now musyng apon this and now on that.
> I se the poill, and eik the Ursis brycht,
> And hornyt Lucyne castand bot dym lycht,
> Becaus the symmyr skyis schayn sa cleir.[1]

Other lights the poet did not see, the light on the shore at Leith, where the boats were being loaded with provisions for the fleet, the riding lights of the ships lying at anchor in the Firth, the glow of the furnaces roaring all night long up in the Castle.[2] There is no note of foreboding here, no word of the pestilence daily creeping nearer to the capital—on 15 June it had reached the village of Dean[3]—or of the clamour in the Council when the young nobles, ignorant of war, tried to shout down the aged Elphinstone when he pleaded for peace, "because like a mad old man, he had spoken stupidly and thoughtlessly against the commonweal, against their sacred treaty and ancient league".[4] Later, those who survived Flodden were to plead that they had been bullied and browbeaten by the King.[5]

James had his way; on 24 July the summons to battle was sent out; the lieges were ordered to assemble at Ellem in Berwickshire.[6] On the 25th[7] the *Michael* and her five companions,[8] the

---

[1] Douglas, *Aeneid of Virgil*, ed. G. Dundas, VOL. II, pp. 846, 847.

[2] *C.T.S.*, VOL. IV, App. II *passim*.   [3] *Edinburgh Records*, VOL. I, p. 141.

[4] Boece, *Vitae*, pp. 104-5.

[5] Ruthal to Wolsey (*Facsimiles of National Manuscripts*, photo-zincographed by Sir H. James (hereafter referred to as *Fac. Nat. MSS*), PT. II, Southampton 1865, No. 5; *L. and P. Henry VIII*, VOL. I, PT. II, No. 2283).

[6] *C.T.S.*, VOL. IV, pp. 416-7.   [7] *C.T.S.*, VOL. IV, p. 417.

[8] The number of ships in the Scottish fleet that sailed for France is uncertain. The Treasurer's Accounts for July, in addition to noting the supplies delivered to the four royal ships, record supplies of provisions for forty days for the crews

King's glittering toys, sailed slowly down the Firth and were lost to view beyond the Isle of May. The fleet was commanded, not by any of James's skeely skippers, but by the inexpert Earl of Arran.

On 26 July came the final break. James sent Lyon King of Arms to order Henry to "desiste fra further invasion and utter destruction of . . . the Most Christien Kyng", else he would do "what thyng we trayest may crast cause you to desist fra persuite of him".[1] A day later another herald was despatched to Paris with the information that the fleet had sailed.[2]

The die was cast. But James was not altogether happy. Octavian Olarius had reappeared with a letter, written on 28 June, in which the Pope expressed his anger at the news that James was preparing to attack England, and hinted that a word from Henry would loose the censures of the Church.[3] At the beginning of August James seems to have accompanied the Queen to Linlithgow. Here, if we are to believe Pitscottie, as he sat in his stall in the Church of St Michael "werie sad and dollarous, makand his divotioun to god to send good chance and fortoun", a stranger thrust past the assembled nobles and bowed low before him. To the bystanders his lofty forehead and bright yellow hair, his great staff, his linen girdle and long blue robe seemed familiar: it was as if the figure of St James had stepped from the painted wall.

The stranger spoke, "Sir King, my Mother has sent me to thee, desiring thee not to pass at this time where thou art purposed,

---

of five other ships—John Barton's barque, the Spanish barque, Brownhill's ship, Chalmers's barque and the "Barque Mytoune". Smaller quantities of provisions were supplied to two other vessels, the *Mary* and the *Crown*. There were therefore at least nine vessels and possibly as many as eleven in the Scottish fleet. The *Michael* was much the largest. She carried 303 mariners and 7 gunners; next came the "Barque Mytoune" with 130, then the *Margaret* and the Barque of Abbeville with 83 and 60. Chalmers's barque carried 60 men, the *James* 56, and the remaining three ships 40 apiece. *C.T.S.*, VOL. IV, pp. 495-504.

[1] Hall, pp. 545-7; *L. and P. Henry VIII*, VOL. I, PT. II, No. 2122.

[2] Louis XII to the Grand Master of Brittany, A. Spont, *Letters and Papers relating to the War with France 1512-1513*, London 1897, pp. 175-7.

[3] *L. and P. Henry VIII*, VOL. I, PT. II, No. 2036.

for if thou does thou wilt not fare well in thy journey . . . further she bade thee not mell with no women." "Be this man had spokin thir wordis to the kingis grace," continues Pitscottie, "the ewin song was neir done, and the king panssit on thir wordis studeing to gif him ane ansuer bot in the meane tyme . . . this man wanischit away . . . as he had bene ane blink of the sone or ane quhipe of the whirle wind."[1]

Buchanan, telling the story in almost the same words, alleges that he had it from the lips of Sir David Lindsay, who was an eyewitness.[2] For once we may believe them; we may believe too that the apparition was a creature of flesh and blood, an actor in an interlude designed to change the purpose of the superstitious King.

On 8 August James rode out on his last pilgrimage to the shrine of St Duthac.[3] Five days later Lyon King-of-Arms arrived in the English camp before Thérouanne and delivered James's defiance to King Henry.[4] The King read it, then turning on the trembling herald cried, "Now we perceive the King of Scots . . . to be that same person whom we ever took him to be . . . for notwithstanding his oath, his promise in the word of King and his own hand and seal, yet now he hath broken his faith and promise to his great dishonour and infamy for ever, and intendeth to invade our realm in our absence, which he durst not once attempt our person being present. . . . Therefore, tell thy master, first he shall not be comprised in any league wherein I am a confederate, and also that I, suspecting his truth (as now the deed proveth) have left an Earl in my realm at home that shall be able to defend him and all his power . . . but thus say to thy master that I am the very owner of Scotland and that he holdeth it of me by homage, and in so much as now contrary to his bounden duty he being my vassal doth rebel against me, with God's help I shall at my return expulse him from his realm, and so tell him."

---

[1] Pitscottie, VOL. I, pp. 258-9.

[2] Buchanan, *Rerum Scoticarum historia*, BK. XIII, in *Opera omnia*, ed. Ruddiman, VOL. I, p. 251.

[3] *C.T.S.*, VOL. IV, p. 419.

[4] *L. and P. Henry VIII*, VOL. I, PT. II, No. 2157.

"I may not say such words of reproach," Lyon answered boldly, "to him whom I owe only my allegiance and faith."

"Wherefore came you hither?" snapped the King. "Will you receive no answer?"

"Yes," replied Lyon. "Your answer requireth doing and no writing; that is, immediately you should return home."

"Well," growled Henry, "I will return to your damage at my pleasure, and not at thy master's summoning."

Later in the day Henry dismissed the Scot with a letter, couched in even more vigorous and incisive language, and a gift of a hundred angels.[1] The letter was never delivered; before Lyon could get a ship to take him from Flanders to Scotland, Flodden had been fought.

[1] Hall, pp. 545-8.

R

X

FLODDEN

Who ever knew Christian king in such a case
As I, wretched creature, that cannot have
In churche, or churchyard, any manner place
Emong Christen people, to lye in a grave:
The earthe mee abhorreth, all men mee deprave;
My frends forsake mee, and have no pity;
The worlde taketh from mee all that he mee gave:
Miserere mei Deus et salva mee.

(*The Mirror for Magistrates*)

WHEN James's ultimatum reached Henry on 19 August fighting had already begun. At the beginning of August Lord Hume and a great force of borderers rode far into Northumberland, burning villages and farm-steadings, and "lifting" cattle and horses. Surrey was far away at Pontefract; he had sent Sir William Bulmer to the Borders, however, with two hundred mounted archers. Bulmer now called out the gentlemen of the north, and with a force which did not amount in all to one thousand men, prepared to intercept the homeward march of the Scots. He concealed his little army among the bushes of broom which grew thick on the plain of Milfield, between the Till and the lower slopes of the Cheviot. The Scots walked into the trap: though they fought like men, according to their opponents, they could not resist the flights of arrows shot without intermission by the unseen archers. It was estimated that five or six hundred of the raiders were slain and more than four hundred made prisoner; all the plunder was recaptured, and though the Warden escaped, he had to leave his banner in the hands of the English.[1] The Ill Raid was the name which the Scots gave to this luckless expedition.

[1] Hall, pp. 555-6.

Of the assembling of the main Scottish army, of the exact date and manner of departure, of the route which it followed before it crossed the Border there is little to be learned from contemporary records. It was probably only a portion of the host which encamped under the "stately and aged" oaks of the Boroughmuir; probably the bulk of the army, like the contingents from Fife and Angus, marched straight to the appointed rendezvous at Ellem in Berwickshire.[1] The darkness sometimes lightens, but only for a moment: we catch a glimpse of a room in Edinburgh Castle, where the Captain's lady sits embroidering the King's coat-armour; we see another woman hurriedly sewing the fringes to the Royal Standard of crimson and gold and to the blue banners of St Andrew and St Margaret; we see a waiting soldier take them from her hands and gallop with them through the darkness after the King.[2] On Friday, 19 August, the Provost and Bailies of Edinburgh, after arranging for the government of the town in their absence, left the council-chamber for the camp[3]; it was probably on the evening of the same day that James rode out from his capital for the last time.

Much more clearly do we see the departure of the artillery. On Wednesday, 17 August, a gang of forty workmen dragged five of the biggest guns from the Castle to St Mary's Wynd— outside the Netherbow Port—where they lay all night with twelve sentinels standing guard over them. On Thursday, dragged by a team of thirty-two oxen attended by eight drivers, the first of the great guns rumbled and creaked down St Mary's Wynd and out into the open country. All through Thursday and Friday the slow procession continued down the High Street and through the Netherbow Port[4]—curtals, culverins, sacres and serpentines, seventeen guns in all,[5] drawn by four hundred oxen;

---

[1] *C.T.S.*, VOL. IV, p. 416.　　　　　[2] *C.T.S.*, VOL. IV, p. 521.

[3] *Edinburgh Records*, VOL. I, pp. 141-2.　　[4] *C.T.S.*, VOL. IV, pp. 515-20.

[5] The names given in the French version of the "Articles of Battle" (Pinkerton, VOL. II, p. 458) and in the "Trewe Encountre" (*Proceedings of the Society of Antiquaries of Scotland*, VII (1866-7), p. 146. The corresponding names in *C.T.S.* are "cannone", "gros culvering", "culvering pikmoyane", and "culvering moyane". A great curtal fired a shot of 60 lb., a culverin a shot of 20 lb., a sacre a shot of 10 lb., and a serpentine a shot of 4 or 5 lb. The "cannon"

gangs of workmen, carrying picks, shovels and drag-ropes; more oxen, pulling a crane, a string of packhorses laden with cannon balls, and a long array of powder-carts. We can follow the procession as far as Dalkeith, where the first casualty of the campaign occurred—one of the draught oxen broke its neck[1]—then we lose sight of it for a time.

Before the last of the guns had been dragged from the Castle, while the King still waited in Holyrood, a strange story was whispered in Edinburgh. It has been preserved in the pages of the credulous Pitscottie. "In this meane tyme . . ." he writes, "thair was a cry hard at the marcat crose of Edinburgh at the houre of midnight proclamand as it had bene ane sowmondis of Plotcok (Pluto), quhilk dosyrit all men to compeir baitht earle, lord, barone, and gentillmen and all honest burgessis withtin the toune, ewerie man specifieit be his awin name to compeir withtin the space of xl dayis befoir his maister quhair it sall happin him to apoynt and be for the tyme under the paine of dissobedience. But quhither thir sowmandis war proclameit be waine persouns night walkeris or dronkin men for thair pastyme, or gif it was but ane spreit as I haue schawin to zow befoir, I cane not tell trewlie."[2]

Nevertheless, nothing could be heard but "Forward!"[3] On 22 August the Scottish army, after advancing down the valley of the Whiteadder, crossed the Tweed, probably by the fords of Graydon and Rutherford, a little below its junction with the Till.[4] A foreknowledge of approaching death seems to have weighed upon the nobles: on 24 August, while the army was encamped at Twizelhaugh, they persuaded the King to make an ordinance that the heirs of any man who should be killed or should die of wounds or disease while with the army, should be exempt from the payment of the casualties of wardship, relief or

of the Scottish list, however, may have been not great curtals but demi-curtals, firing a shot of only 35 lb.   [1] *C.T.S.*, VOL. IV, p. 519.

   [2] Pitscottie, VOL. I, p. 260.   [3] Pitscottie, VOL. I, pp. 261-2.

   [4] For a list of the fords of the Tweed in the sixteenth century see the "View and Survey" of Sir Robert Bowes and Sir Ralph Elleker printed in Hodgson, *History of Northumberland*, PT. III, VOL. II, pp. 194-202.

marriage.[1] It was a statute often invoked in the months after Flodden.

The King's first objective was Norham Castle; Anislow, the Captain, had boasted that he would hold it till Henry himself came from France to relieve it, and for a time it seemed as if he would make good his boast. Though the Scottish guns battered the walls for six days they damaged only the outer defences; the great central tower remained intact; thrice James hurled his inexperienced troops against the fortress, and thrice the storming parties were driven back with heavy loss. But Anislow had been too energetic; at the end of six days he found that he had shot away all his ammunition, and on 28 or 29 August he surrendered.[2] James now advanced slowly up the right bank of the Till, battered down the castle of Etal[3] and captured the castle of Ford,[4] which he made his headquarters. On 4 September he was still at Ford[5]; in a fortnight he had advanced exactly six miles into England.

Pitscottie and Buchanan have censured his inactivity and have alleged that he lingered at Ford because he had fallen in love with the chatelaine, the beautiful Lady Heron, whose husband was a prisoner in Scotland.[6] But to Pitscottie and Buchanan no story is too scandalous to be told against a Stewart king—or queen. It is true that at the prayer of the lady James promised not to destroy her home, but only on condition that she delivered to him, before noon on 5 September, Lord Johnstone and Alexander Hume,

[1] *A.P.S.*, VOL. II, p. 278.

[2] *L. and P. Henry VIII*, VOL. I, PT. II, Nos. 2270, 2279, 2283; Hall, p. 557.

[3] There is no reference to the capture of Etal in any contemporary account, but it lay on James's route from Norham to Ford. It was in "very great decay" in 1542 (Bowes and Elleker's survey, Hodgson, *History of Northumberland*, PT. III, VOL. II, p. 191). Wark may have been captured at this time, as the Scottish chroniclers assert, but its capture is not mentioned in any contemporary account. Bowes and Elleker say it was in great decay as the result of a siege by Albany, but do not mention any earlier siege (*op. cit.*, p. 179).

[4] "A contemporary account of the battle of Flodden", in *Proceedings of the Society of Antiquaries of Scotland*, VII (1866-7), (hereafter referred to as "Trewe Encountre", p. 143.

[5] Ibid.

[6] Pitscottie, VOL. I, pp. 262-4; Buchanan, *Rerum Scoticarum historia*, BK. XIII, in *Opera omnia*, ed. Ruddiman, VOL. I, p. 251.

who were prisoners in England.[1] Such a bargain does not reveal a too ardent lover.

It was not light love that made James hesitate either to attack Berwick, as the English had expected him to do, or to advance farther into England. The succession of wet and stormy days, the pestilence that had followed the army from Scotland, the check before the walls of Norham, had deprived hundreds of his untried troops of their stomach for fighting.[2] Desertion on a large scale had begun while the siege of Norham was still in progress, and as early as 5 September deserters had arrived in Edinburgh in sufficient numbers to arouse the wrath of the Burgh Council.[3] The state of the artillery, too, evidently caused James some anxiety: on 29 August he sent the Treasurer to Edinburgh for draught oxen, ammunition, and wheels for the gun-carriages.[4] He had boasted that he would be in York before Michaelmas[5]: now he recognised that to advance into the heart of England with an army dwindling daily from sickness and desertion would be the maddest of gambles.

Nor did his agreement with Louis necessitate such a risky adventure. The confederate Kings had evidently calculated that the mere presence of a large Scottish army on the wrong side of the Border would be sufficient to draw the whole, or the greater part of the English army from France. And James could tempt it home with impunity, for even if it escaped the united French and Scottish fleets it would arrive in England too late in the year to attempt the long march to the Border. All that was required was a reconnaissance in force, followed by a discreet withdrawal when it produced the desired effect.

In any case the southward road was now barred. Surrey was in the field. On 25 August he learned that the Scots had crossed the Tweed. He at once sent out the prearranged summons, and

[1] Hall, p. 558.

[2] Ruthal to Wolsey (*Fac. Nat. MSS*, PT. II, No. 5; *L. and P. Henry VIII*, VOL. I, PT. II, No. 2283); *E.R.S.*, VOL. I, p. 187.

[3] *Edinburgh Records*, VOL. I, p. 143.

[4] *C.T.S.*, VOL. IV, p. 522.

[5] *L. and P. Henry VIII*, VOL. I, PT. II, No. 2313; *Cal. of State Papers, Venice*, VOL. II, No. 341.

at the head of his own bodyguard he advanced from Pontefract
to York. Through "the foulest day and night that could be",
over roads that had become dangerous torrents—his guide was
all but drowned before his eyes—the "old crooked earle" pushed
on to Newcastle. At Durham he halted to hear Mass in the
Cathedral and to borrow the banner of St Cuthbert from the
Prior. On the 30th he reached Newcastle, where he was joined
by Dacre and other gentlemen of the north with their contingents.

"All that nyghte the wynde blew corragiously", filling Surrey
with fears for the safety of Lord Thomas Howard and of the
contingent he was bringing from France. When the army moved
off to Alnwick on 3 September the Admiral had not arrived, but
on Sunday the 4th he marched in at the head of 1,000 soldiers
and sailors.[1]

Surrey now organised his forces, dividing them into a vanguard and a somewhat smaller rearguard. The command of the
rearguard he meant to keep in his own hands; the vanguard he
entrusted to the Admiral. Both vanguard and rearguard were
again divided into a centre and two wings. The right wing of
the vanguard, including 1,500 men from Lancashire and Cheshire,
many of them dependants of the Stanleys, was commanded by
Edmund Howard, the Admiral's younger brother: the thousand
odd men on the left wing were led by old Sir Marmaduke Constable; in the centre, led by the Admiral himself, the men of the
bishopric of Durham marched under the banner of St Cuthbert.
Fifteen hundred border prickers under Dacre, reinforced by the
men of Bamburghshire and Tynemouth, formed the right wing
of the rearguard; on the left, Sir Edward Stanley led the remainder
of the levies from Lancashire and Durham; in the centre, under
Surrey's immediate command, were the citizens of York, men
from the estates of the Bishop of Ely, Stanley's kinsman, and the
Abbot of Whitby, and Surrey's own retinue of five hundred
trained men, in liveries of green and white.[2] Altogether, Surrey

[1] Hall, p. 557.

[2] Hall, pp. 557-8; "Trewe Encountre", pp. 144-5. Hall and the "Trewe
Encountre" both give 26,000 as the number of Surrey's troops. While Hall
gives only 1,500 to Edmund Howard and a little over 1,000 to Sir Marmaduke

had 20,000 men under his command.[1] Most of them were infantry,[2] armed with bows or with bills[3]—halberds eight feet long, with heavy jagged blades that could be used for cutting or slashing. Dacre's contingent, however, was mounted.[4]

Estimates of the size of the Scottish army range from under 10,000—in Pitscottie—to over 100,000—in Hall. Surrey's determination to force a battle, however, shows that he believed it to be not much larger than his own. That it cannot have been smaller is proved by the silence observed in the one contemporary

Constable, the "Trewe Encountre" makes each of the four wings number 3,000, and assigns 9,000 men to the centre of the vanguard and 5,000 to the centre of the rearguard. The figure for Dacre's cavalry is taken from the version of Tuke's letter to Pace published in Rome not long after the battle and printed in La Rotta di Francciosi a Teroanna novamente facta, La Rotta de Scocesi, Roxburghe Club, London 1825 (hereafter referred to as La Rotta), App., p. 5, and from the "Articles of Battle" ("Account of the Battle of Flodden", in Fac. Nat. MSS, PT. II, No. 2, and "Gazette of the Battle of Flodden" in Pinkerton, VOL. II, App., pp. 456–8, both hereafter referred to as "Articles of Battle"). Dacre himself stated that he had the men from Bamburghshire and Tynemouth (L. and P. Henry VIII, VOL. I, PT. II, No. 2386). The "Trewe Encountre" also assigns to him 1,500 of the Bishop of Ely's men from Lancashire.

   [1] 18,699 in addition to the Admiral's contingent from the fleet. See L. and P. Henry VIII, VOL. I, PT. II, No. 2651(3).

   [2] Mr W. M. Mackenzie (The Secret of Flodden, Edinburgh 1931, pp. 41–2) asserts that the troops travelled on horseback. "It explains", he says, "how the English army with its baggage and artillery could . . . now, between five in the morning and four in the afternoon, do 15 miles to Flodden." But the distance from the English camp to the battlefield was nearer 8 than 15 miles. The reference of Ruthal—"the mervelous grete payn and laboure that they toke in going 8 myles that day [9 Sept.] on fote" (Fac. Nat. MSS, PT. II, No. 4) —and the statement in the "Articles of Battle" that ten thousand more would have been slain if the English had been horsed, finally dispose of Mr Mackenzie's contention.

   [3] Ruthal to Wolsey, Fac. Nat. MSS, PT. II, No. 4.

   [4] Tuke to Pace, La Rotta, App., p. 5: "cum mille quingentes equitibus". The copy of his letter in the Sforza Library, Milan, printed in Cal. of State Papers, Venice, VOL. II, No. 316, and in Calendar of State Papers and Manuscripts existing in the archives and collections of Milan (hereafter referred to as Cal. of State Papers, Milan), VOL. I, ed. A. B. Hinds, London 1912, No. 660, appears to give "with fifty horse".

Scottish account of the defeat.[1] Though losses by sickness and desertion are urged as excuses for the defeat, it is nowhere stated that the Scots were actually inferior in numbers to the English. We may conclude that in spite of the wastage from desertion, the Scottish army still had a superiority, though a very slight superiority, in numbers.

But how if James would not wait to be attacked? As Dacre had already argued, it would pay James to withdraw his forces beyond the Border for a few days, and renew the invasion after the English army had dispersed. To prevent such a move Surrey resolved to appeal from the general to the knight-errant: he sent Rougecroix Pursuivant to tell James that he would be ready to do battle with him on Friday, 9 September, at the latest.[2] Along with Surrey's challenge went a message from the Admiral, nicely calculated to infuriate the King, "In asmuche as the sayde kynge hadde diverse and many tymes caused the sayde lorde too be called at dayes of true, too make redresse for Andrew Barton, a Pirate of the sea . . . he was nowe come in hys awne proper person too be in the Vauntgarde of the felde to Iustifie the death of the said Andrewe, agaynste hym and all hys people, and woulde se what could be layed to hys charge the sayde daye, and that he nor none of hys compaignye shoulde take no Scottshe nobleman prysoner, nor any other, but they shoulde dye if they came in hys daunger, onles it were the kynges awne person, for he sayde he trusted to none other curtesye at the handes of the Scottes."[3]

The double challenge appeared to have had the desired effect. On the morning of Tuesday 6 September, Surrey, who had advanced to Bolton on the previous day, was informed by Islay Herald that James would wait for him till noon on Friday the 9th.[4] Surrey accordingly pushed forward to Wooler Haugh, on the left bank of the Till, at the southern end of the narrow plain

---

[1] *E.R.S.*, VOL. I, pp. 186-9.

[2] "Articles of Battle"; Hall, p. 558; "Trewe Encountre", p. 143; Tuke, (*La Rotta*, App., p. 3; *Cal. of State Papers, Venice*, VOL. II, No. 316; *Cal. of State Papers, Milan*, VOL. I, No. 660).   [3] Hall, p. 558.

[4] "Articles of Battle"; Hall, p. 569; "Trewe Encountre", pp. 143-4.

through which that stream flows northward to join the Tweed.[1] On the left the outlying ridges of the Cheviot loomed grey through the mist and rain. Half a dozen miles in front of him, at the eastern extremity of one of the remoter ridges, Flodden Hill, at that time bare of trees, rose to a height of 509 feet. Somewhere on the slopes of Flodden Hill the Scottish army was posted.[2] James on hearing of Surrey's approach had set fire to Ford Castle,[3] and had moved his forces across the Till to a position like a fortress, protected on one side by a marsh,[4] and "enclosed in thre parties with three great mountaynes, soe that ther was noe

[1] Hall, p. 560; "Trewe Encountre", p. 145.

[2] Hall, p. 560: "uppon the syde of a hyghe mountayne, called Floddon on the edge of Cheuyot"; Polydore Vergil, *Historia Anglica*, VOL. II, p. 1619: "verticem montis quem Floddonem incolae vocant, occupat". It is difficult at this time of day to determine the exact position of the Scottish camp or to identify the "three great mountaynes" of the "Trewe Encountre" and the "great marrische" of Hall's chronicle. Ridpath in his *Border History of England and Scotland*, new edition, Berwick upon Tweed 1848, p. 338, states that the Scottish camp was protected "by a battery of cannon they had erected near the foot of the eastern declivity of the Flodden-hill, bearing full upon the bridge at Ford", and adds in a footnote, "the vestiges of the intrenchment for this battery still remain." But there was no bridge at Ford before the eighteenth century (E. Jervoise, *The Ancient Bridges of the North of England*, London 1931, pp. 3-4) nor have we any proof that the entrenchments which Ridpath saw were sixteenth-century gun emplacements. The rapidity with which the move from Flodden Hill to Branxton Hill was executed on the afternoon of 9 Sept. shows that the Scottish camp cannot have been on the southern side of Flodden Hill, but must have been on the eastern or north-eastern side. In this connection it may be noted that Col. Elliot, who starts with the assumption that the Scots encamped on the southern side of the hill, is forced to postulate an intermediate position, assumed on the evening of the 8th or early on the morning of the 9th, in which the Scots faced not south, but east (*The Battle of Flodden and the Raids of 1513*, Edinburgh 1911). There seems no reason why this intermediate position of Col. Elliot's hypothesis should not really have been James's initial position after he left Ford Castle. From it he could threaten Surrey's flank should the English commander lead his army down the left bank of the Till, while Flodden Hill and Flodden Edge intervened to prevent an attack from the south.

[3] "View and Survey", by Bowes and Elleker, Hodgson, *History of Northumberland*, PT. III, VOL. II, p. 191.

[4] Hall, p. 560.

passage nor entre unto hym but oon waye, wher was laied marvelous and great ordenance of gunnes".[1]

What was Surrey to do? Stay where he was, and watch the
invaders return at their leisure to Scotland? He knew that if he
did not attack soon his army would go to pieces[2]; already the
long marches and short rations were beginning to tell on them,
and, what disheartened them even more, they had drunk all their
beer.[3] On Wednesday the distant rumble of the Scottish artillery[4]
reminded him of the other alternative—to hurl his men against
the guns. No, he must get the Scots down to Milfield, that wide
stretch of level ground that lay to the south-east of Flodden Hill.
On the afternoon of Wednesday 7 September, suspecting that
James would give him the slip,[5] he sent Rougecroix with a letter
accusing him of choosing a position that was like a fortress, and
challenging him to come down to the plain of Milfield, where
the English army would wait for him between twelve and three
the following afternoon.[6]

When the letter was delivered to him on the following
morning, the King was furious. He refused to speak to Rougecroix, but one of his gentlemen brought the herald his answer—
"Show to the Earl of Surrey that it beseemeth him not, being an
Earl, so largely to attempt a great prince. His Grace will take and
hold his ground at his own pleasure, and not at the assigning of
the Earl of Surrey, whom the King, my maister supposeth to deal
with some witchcraft or sorcery, because he procedeth to fight
upon one (and) the same ground."[7]

James could flatter himself that so far he had acted like a prudent commander. By accepting the first challenge he bound
Surrey to fight with him before noon on 9 September; by refusing
the second it seemed that he compelled Surrey to throw his men

[1] "Trewe Encountre", p. 146.

[2] Polydore Vergil, *Historia Anglica*, VOL. II, pp. 1620-1.

[3] Ruthal to Wolsey (*Fac. Nat. MSS*, PT. II, No. 4; *L. and P. Henry VIII*,
VOL. I, PT. II, No. 2283); "Trewe Encountre", p. 147.

[4] Hall, p. 560.   [5] "Trewe Encountre", p. 146.

[6] Summarised in *L. and P. Henry VIII*, VOL. I, PT. II, No. 2239. See also
Hall, p. 560, and "Trewe Encountre", p. 146.

[7] "Trewe Encountre", p. 146; Hall, p. 560.

against an impregnable position. If Surrey fought he would be defeated; if he did not fight the Scots could go home unmolested, with their honour untarnished. Surrey's reading of the situation seems to have been different. James's refusal to leave his position showed that he had not really accepted the first challenge: Surrey was therefore no longer bound by its terms, but was free to attack James when and where he could.

James did not know that the game was already lost; the invasion had completely failed to achieve its object—to draw home either the whole or a considerable part of the English army in France. On the very day that the Scots crossed the Tweed Thérouanne surrendered, and Henry's siege-guns were even now being dragged through Artois to their new positions before the walls of Tournai.

On the morning of Thursday 8 September, Surrey ordered his men to cross from the left to the right bank of the Till. Though from time to time during the day the Scots had caught sight of the long train of armed men winding northwards among the hills, they did not divine Surrey's intention; they thought that he would continue his northward march on the morrow and attempt to draw them home by raiding the Merse. So the Scots made no attempt to intercept Surrey, but contented themselves with burning some small villages on the other side of the marsh which protected their position. Surrey's plan was to lure James from his position by threatening to cut off his retreat.[1] But to get between the Scots and Scotland he must first recross the Till. There were two bridges which the artillery might cross; Etal Bridge, which fell into ruins a few years after Flodden,[2] and Twizel Bridge, about four miles further downstream; though the Till drowned two for the Tweed's one, there were three places where infantry might flounder across; at Heton Mill, for example, about a mile above Twizel Bridge, at Willowford, about half a mile above Etal, and at Sandyford, about half a mile above Willowford. But Etal Bridge and the two fords to the south of it were dangerously near the Scottish position.

---

[1] "Trewe Encountre", pp. 146-7; Hall, pp. 560-1.   [2] Bowes and Elleker in Hodgson, *History of Northumberland*, PT. III, VOL. II, p. 191.

The English encamped that night by the side of Barmoor Wood,[1] about four miles to the north-east of Flodden Hill.[2] While the soldiers shivered on the windswept hillside, a council of war was held in Surrey's tent, at which it was resolved that the whole army should cross the Till at dawn on the morrow, the vanguard and the guns at Twizel Bridge,[3] the rearguard by the ford at Heton.[4]

At five o'clock on the morning of Friday, 9 September, the English marched out from their camp[5]; six hours later the Admiral, according to plan, crossed the Till by Twizel Bridge,[6] while about a mile to the south Surrey's division plashed through the shallows beside Heton Mill.[7] Then both divisions wheeled to the left, and with the wind and the rain in their faces[8] plodded southward across the rolling moorland. Four miles ahead of them a long ridge, which rose to a height of five hundred feet at one point, stretched across their line of march.

The ridge was Branxton Hill, the little church at the foot, with the Norman tower, Branxton Church. One or two features we notice which were hidden from the English in the early stages of their advance—the stream, for example, known then as Sandy-

[1] "Trewe Encountre", p. 147; Hall, p. 561.

[2] Thomas Hodgkin, "The Battle of Flodden", in *Archaeologia Aeliana*, XVI (1894), p. 16.

[3] Hall, p. 561.

[4] "At Mylforde": Hall, p. 561. For the topography of Branxton and its neighbourhood see the article by Hodgkin referred to above and the answer to it by C. J. Bates later in the same volume; also Robert White, "The Battle of Flodden", in *Archaeologia Aeliana*, III (2nd Series, 1859), pp. 197-235, and Rev. Robert Jones, Vicar of Branxton, *The Battle of Flodden Field*, Edinburgh 1864. Hodgkin thinks that Surrey would use at least two of the three fords (*Archaeologia Aeliana*, XVI (1894), p. 23); Jones is convinced that the ford at Heton was impracticable for multitudes of men and horses clothed in armour (*Battle of Flodden Field*, p. 23); Bates, like Col. Elliot, identifies Milford with the ford near Heton Mill (*Archaeologia Aeliana*, XVI (1894), pp. 360-1).

[5] Hall, p. 561.   [6] "Articles of Battle".

[7] Hall, p. 561. In the "Articles of Battle" there is no mention of the fording of the Till by Surrey's division, simply the statement that Surrey followed the Admiral, and crossed afterwards with the rearguard.

[8] Ruthal to Wolsey (*Fac. Nat. MSS*, PT. II, No. 4; *L. and P. Henry VIII*, VOL. I, PT. II, No. 2283).

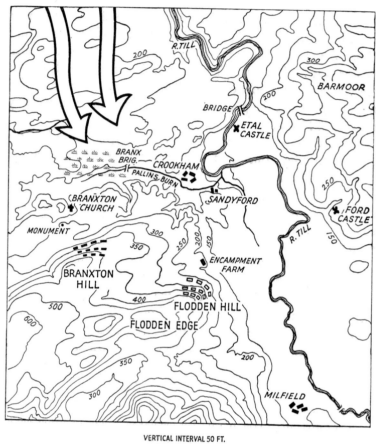

VERTICAL INTERVAL 50 FT.

THE BATTLE OF FLODDEN

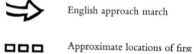

⇒ English approach march

□□□ Approximate locations of first

■■■ and second Scottish positions

For the area as a whole see endpaper

ford, now as the Pallinsburn, which, rising a little less than a mile north-west of the church, flows eastward to join the Till. In itself it was an insignificant obstacle—"but a man's step over"[1]—but the little valley through which it flows was a marsh in dry weather and in wet weather a veritable lake. If Surrey swerved to the east, he would become involved in this morass, unless he could discover the causeway leading to a bridge—Branx Bridge—which in those days spanned the stream.[2] We notice, too, that Branxton Hill does not slope down evenly to the plain; it sinks, then, about a quarter of a mile to the west of the church, it rises again to form a low round hillock, crowned today by the Flodden monument. Local tradition has not preserved its name, though Hodgkin[3] identified it with the Piper's or Pipard's Hill mentioned by Stow[4] as the place of the King's death.

Branxton Hill is the first of a series of ridges which rises fold upon fold till it reaches a height of almost three thousand feet in the Cheviot. At the eastern end of the next ridge, only a mile and a half from the summit of Branxton Hill, is Flodden Hill. The hollow between them is dead ground; any movement of troops across it would be quite invisible to the English.

At what hour James first learned of this surprise wheel to the south it is impossible to say. He seems, however, to have been quick to recognise the peril in which he stood. Surrey had not only got between him and Scotland, he meant to occupy Branxton Hill. The tables would then be turned; to get back to Scotland the Scots would first have to attack a position similar to their own, a position which would be all but impregnable.

James did not hesitate. The trumpets rang out; tents were struck; the rubbish accumulated in the camp was set on fire, making "a great and a marvellous smoke"; teams of men and of oxen hauled the guns from their emplacements, and soon the

---

[1] Hall, p. 561.

[2] Letter of Rev. Robert Jones in *Archaeologia Aeliana*, III (2nd Series, 1859), p. 232.

[3] *Archaeologia Aeliana*, XVI (1894), p. 25. Robert White, however, admits that he could find no tradition identifying it with Pipard's Hill.

[4] John Stow, *Chronicles of England*, London 1580, p. 901.

whole Scottish army, horse, foot and artillery, had been hustled across the hollow, up the southern slope of Branxton Hill and over the ridge to the other side. The Scots halted high on the northern slope of the hill, above the church and the hillock where the monument now stands.[1] Quickly they were arranged in great square and diamond-shaped formations, five of them altogether, each a bowshot distant from its neighbour.[2] The division on the extreme left was commanded by Lord Hume and the Earl of Huntly. Next to it was placed the division led by the Earls of Crawford, Montrose and Errol. Further to the right was ranged the large and splendidly equipped division commanded by the King himself. Here were most of the nobles and the officers of the royal household, the Bishops of Caithness and the Isles, and the King's son, the young Archbishop of St Andrews. Beyond the King's division, on the extreme right of the army, were placed the Highlanders and Islesmen, under the Earls of Lennox and Argyll.[3] The fifth division, commanded by the Earl of

[1] Hall, p. 561; "Trewe Encountre", p. 147.

[2] "Articles of Battle": "part of them quadrant, and some pyke wyse"; in the French version "partie deulx estoient en quadrans, et autres en maniere de pointe". Tuke: "Exercitus Scotorum divisus fuit in quinque ordines", *La Rotta*, App., p. 4. Mr Mackenzie thinks that the pikewise formation was a long, narrow column, like the shaft of a pike (*Secret of Flodden*, pp. 56, 57). The words "en maniere de pointe", however, seem to indicate that the "plumps of spears" were compared not to the shaft but to the lozenge- or diamond-shaped head of the pike. According to Tuke and the "Articles of Battle" five Scottish divisions were engaged; according to Hall, p. 561, and the "Trewe Encountre", p. 147, only four. The explanation is probably that, as Drummond of Hawthornden asserts (*History of the Lives of the five James's*, in *Works*, p. 76), Bothwell's division was kept in reserve in the earlier stages of the battle, but joined the King's division when it advanced to meet Surrey. Hall also states (p. 563) that there were two other divisions which took no part in the battle.

[3] Again there are slight discrepancies in the contemporary accounts. In the "Articles of Battle" and Tuke the commanders are placed in the following order, beginning on the left: Hume; Huntly, Errol and Crawford; the King; Lennox and Argyll. The order in Hall is: Hume; Crawford and Montrose; the King; Huntly, Lennox and Argyll. That Hall is wrong is proved by the letter of 17 May 1514 (*L. and P. Henry VIII*, VOL. I, PT. II, No. 2913; Pinkerton, VOL. II, p. 459) in which Dacre states that he encountered both Huntly and Hume.

Bothwell, seems to have been placed in reserve, behind the great phalanx commanded by the King. Most of the Scots, both gentle and simple, were armed with great spears at least five yards in length, targets, and "great and sharp swords".[1] The horses of the mounted men were sent to the rear. With them went the King's charger, for James was determined to fight in the forefront of the battle, and refused to listen to his nobles, who told him plainly that his business was not to fight, but to direct the fighting, and that as a soldier he was worth no more than one man, while as a general he might be worth a hundred thousand.[2] That they might not lose their footing on the muddy slopes, the Scots threw away their shoes and fought in the vamps of their hose.[3]

James's strategy has often been criticised, but his move from Flodden to Branxton is in no way comparable to Leslie's fatal descent from Doon Hill. It put him in a position stronger than the one which he had abandoned, for even if the English succeeded in picking their way through the morass which guarded it on the north, they would have to clamber up a hillside made slippery by heavy rains before they could close with their opponents. Nor is James's tactical scheme deserving of censure: he evidently meant to break up the English columns by artillery fire as they approached the hill, and then drive forward his squares and wedges of spearmen to sweep them away altogether.

So much of the King's intentions we can guess, but further we cannot go. What hopes and fears and memories agitated his mind in that pause before action, brief but seemingly endless, must for ever remain unknown. The soldiers, like their commander, moved to their doom in silence. The Scots who escaped wanted only to forget; no account of the battle by a Scottish soldier is known to exist. So we must be content to watch the struggle from the English side, to turn our eyes from Branxton Hill to the plain across which the Admiral was urging his weary men.

[1] Hall, p. 561; Ruthal to Wolsey (*Fac. Nat. MSS*, PT. II, No. 4; *L. and P. Henry VIII*, VOL. I, PT. II, No. 2283); "Trewe Encountre", p. 151.

[2] Polydore Vergil, *Historia Anglica*, VOL. II, pp. 1621-2.

[3] "Trewe Encountre", p. 151.

S

At first they moved forward blindly, for the movements of their opponents were concealed from them by the thick cloud of smoke that had drifted from the abandoned camp.[1] It was not till the Admiral's men had crossed the stream—Pallinsburn or Sandyford—which runs through the marshy hollow at the foot of the hill, that the air suddenly cleared, and they saw, only a quarter of a mile away, the great glittering phalanxes of spearmen and the batteries of brazen cannon.[2]

At once the Scottish guns opened fire.[3] And now it seemed that the impetuous valour which had betrayed his brother had also led the Admiral to disaster. He had pushed on ahead of his father, ahead of his own artillery, rolling slowly forward with many pauses over the marshy ground,[4] and now he found himself confronted by a force that far outnumbered his own. There was nothing for it but to halt his men in the dead ground at the foot of the hill, wait for the rearguard, and pray that the Scots would not attack.[5] It was now about half-past four in the afternoon.[6] Giving an attendant his *Agnus Dei*—a medallion which hung on his breast—he ordered him to ride with it to Surrey and bid him bring up his troops at once on the left flank of the vanguard, so that vanguard and rearguard might form a continuous front to the Scots.[7]

Surrey understood the need for haste; at any moment the Scots might descend the hill and overwhelm the vanguard. Somehow or other the guns were extricated and dragged forward, somehow or other the rearguard was hustled across the marshy hollow and the stream—according to a long-lived tradition they crossed by Branx Bridge[8]—and formed up on the left

[1] "Trewe Encountre", p. 147; Hall, p. 561.   [2] Hall, p. 561.

[3] "Trewe Encountre", p. 147; Tuke to Pace (*La Rotta,* App., p. 4; *Cal. of State Papers, Venice,* VOL. II, No. 316; *Cal. of State Papers, Milan,* VOL. I, No. 660).

[4] Tuke: "exercitus Anglorum cogeretur indagare quandam viam paludosam relictis post se tormentis", *La Rotta,* App., p. 4.   [5] "Articles of Battle".

[6] "Between four and five in the afternoon", "Articles of Battle" and "Trewe Encountre", p. 150.

[7] Hall, p. 561; "Trewe Encountre", p. 148; "Articles of Battle".

[8] Letter of Rev. Robert Jones in *Archaeologia Aeliana,* III (2nd Series, 1859), p. 232.

of the vanguard. But not quite in the order that had been agreed upon at the beginning of the week. Dacre's fifteen hundred horse were detached to support the right wing of the vanguard, commanded by Edmund Howard, and the centre of the vanguard had on its left, not Sir Marmaduke Constable's men, but the centre of the rearguard; in other words the troops under the immediate command of the Admiral and those under the immediate command of his father fought side by side.[1]

On the extreme left Stanley's men were still struggling across the marshy hollow when they heard the opening roar of the Scottish cannon. They continued their advance unperturbed, but among the Cheshire men on the right wing, who were nearer the enemy batteries, one might have seen white faces and trembling limbs[2] when the gunstones whistled overhead and buried themselves in the sodden ground in the rear. Again and again one heard the whistle and the thud, but never the cry of wounded men; the Scottish guns were placed so far up the hillside, and were handled so clumsily by the inexperienced gunners, that the shots flew high over the heads of the waiting English.[3] Soon the answering roar of the English guns was heard; it increased in volume, while the Scottish fire slackened, and then died away altogether. It was useless to call for retaliation from the Scottish artillery: the German experts who handled the English guns, which were lighter, more numerous, and more easily handled than the demi-curtals and culverins of their opponents, soon got their range and smothered their ineffectual fire.[4]

The King's own division had come under fire[5]; as shot after

---

[1] "Articles of Battle"; Hall, p. 562.   [2] "Articles of Battle".
[3] Lesley, pp. 94-5 Sc., 348 L.

[4] After the battle Surrey delivered to the town and castle of Berwick, in addition to the 17 guns captured from the Scots, 18 falcons—guns of $2\frac{1}{2}$-inch bore—and five serpentines. *L. and P. Henry VIII*, VOL. I, PT. II, No. 2651(ii). 11 of his gunners were Germans. *L. and P. Henry VIII*, VOL. I, PT. II, No. 2652(ii).

[5] Hall, pp. 561-2; "Trewe Encountre", pp. 147-8. In Hall, the account of the artillery duel, and of the havoc wrought by the English guns in the King's "battle", follows his account of the Admiral's appeal for help and the subsequent junction of the vanguard and rearguard. In the "Trewe Encountre", the

shot whanged through the air and plunged into the serried ranks, hitting and maiming the armour-clad warriors, James saw that if he kept his troops where they were, they would be demoralised and broken before they ever came to hand-strokes with the enemy. There was nothing for it but to give the order to advance; the trumpets rang out, and silently and in perfect order each phalanx of spearmen moved downhill to meet the approaching foe.[1] It was the last appearance on the battle field of the schiltrom of Bannockburn; though to those observers who had some experience of continental warfare it appeared not as something old but as something new, a copy of "the Almayns manner",[2] the favourite formation of the Swiss and German mercenaries.

The first hand-to-hand encounter took place on the English right. At the mere sight of the approaching line of levelled spears the men of Cheshire, already shaken by the sound of the cannonade, turned and fled, leaving Edmund Howard with only one or two attendants to fight his way to safety.[3] His standard-bearer was slain, he was thrice beaten to the ground himself, and he had to kill Sir David Hume with his own hands before he got to his brother's division.[4] Huntly and Hume, however, were not allowed to exploit this initial success; before they could wheel round and take the Admiral's division in flank, they were confronted by Dacre and his fifteen hundred horsemen, who drove them back to their original position.[5] The losses on either side

Admiral's appeal to Surrey is made *after* the English "gunnes did so break and constreyn the Scottisshe great army, that some part of thaim were enforced to come doune the said hilles towards our army".

[1] Hall, p. 561.

[2] "Articles of Battle"; Tuke to Pace (*La Rotta*, App., p. 4; *Cal. of State Papers, Venice*, VOL. II, No. 316; *Cal. of State Papers, Milan*, VOL. I, No. 660).

[3] "Trewe Encountre", p. 148.   [4] Hall, p. 562.

[5] "Articles of Battle"; Hall, p. 562; Tuke, *La Rotta*, App., p. 5; "Trewe Encountre". According to the "Trewe Encountre" it was the discovery that the Scots "did kepe thaim severall in iiij batelles" that made Surrey and the Admiral rearrange their men in four divisions. The position of Sir Marmaduke Constable's command, the left wing of the vanguard in the original order of battle, is unknown. Mr Mackenzie (*Secret of Flodden*, pp. 53-4) suggests that his command was merged with that of Stanley on the extreme left. But apart from the absence of any evidence for such a movement, it is difficult to see

were heavy, so heavy that neither the Scottish nor the English Warden dared to attack his opponent a second time, or to invite an attack from that opponent by attempting to move his forces to another part of the field.[1]

Almost immediately after the Scottish left wing and the English right wing clashed together, the division commanded by Crawford, Errol and Montrose closed with the Admiral's men, while the King's division, "so surely harnessed with complete harneys, jackes almayn, ryvettes, splentes, pavices and other habilimentes that shote of arrowes in regarde did thaim no harme", bore down with levelled spears on Surrey's command.[2] At first it seemed as if nothing could stop the advance of these gigantic warriors, but the English soldiers surged forward, and, with their brown bills, tried to hack and smash a way through the seemingly impregnable hedge of spears. Both Englishman and Scot fought with a cold and silent fury,[3] but it soon became apparent that at close quarters the fifteen-foot spear was a less effective weapon than the eight-foot halberd,[4] and that in prolonged hand-to-hand fighting the heavier armour of the Scots was a fatal encumbrance. The Scots fought on, dourly and silently, under the darkening sky, refusing to believe that they could be defeated. When their spears were shattered they drew their swords, but the terrible brown bills beat down their swords and crashed into their armour.[5] The King fought as bravely as his bravest follower; if we are to believe a contemporary Italian poet,[6] he slew five men with his spear before it was shattered in his hands. He had got within a spear's length of the English commander when he fell, pierced by an arrow and gashed by a brown bill.[7] "O what a noble and triumphaunt courage was thys

how it could have been made in the face of the enemy. The probability is that the left wing of the vanguard, like the remnants of the right wing, became merged in the Admiral's own division.

[1] Hall, p. 562; "Articles of Battle".

[2] Ruthal to Wolsey, *Fac. Nat. MSS*, PT. II, No. 4; Hall, p. 562; "Articles of Battle".   [3] "Trewe Encountre", p. 151.

[4] Ruthal to Wolsey, *Fac. Nat. MSS*, PT. II, No. 4.

[5] "Trewe Encountre", pp. 150, 151.

[6] *La Rotta*, p. 35.   [7] "Articles of Battle".

for a kyng to fyghte in a battayll as a meane souldier . . . but how soeuer it happened, God gaue the stroke, and he was no more regarded then a poore souldier, for all went one way."[1]

The King's banner of crimson and gold, the blue banners of St Andrew and St Matthew, had disappeared, thrown down and trampled underfoot by the combatants; the Howard banner with the white lion still floated above the mellay. A stupor seemed to seize on James's followers and deprive them of all power of concerted action[2]; the "serried phalanx tight" was broken up now into little knots of desperate men, some fighting on silently and hopelessly, others crying for a mercy that was not granted, and vainly promising great sums of money to their assailants. "For", says the author of the *Trewe Encounter*, "they wer soe vengeable and cruell in their feightyng that when Englisshmen had the better of thaim they wold not save thaim."[3]

No help could come from the division on the left, which had now ceased to exist, "after a great conflict vanquisshed, overcome, bettyn doune and put to flight"; its three leaders, Crawford, Errol and Montrose, lay dead on the field.[4] And Hume, who had lost several of his kinsmen as a result of Dacre's counter-attack, refused to attack a second time. "He dois weill that dois for himself," was his answer to Huntly's appeal; "lat the laif do thair pairt as we."[5] And so the English centre swept forward, and the remnants of the shattered phalanx "melted from the field like snow".

The division on the extreme right—the Highlanders and Islesmen commanded by Lennox and Argyll—was the last to be engaged. It was on the point of moving forward to attack Surrey's division, when Stanley, who had led his men up the slippery hillside unperceived by the Scots, launched a furious attack on its right flank.[6] The Highlanders broke, and were driven downhill, over the ground encumbered by the bodies of the King and his followers. Happily for the fugitives, at the sight of the armour and rich raiment the pursuers halted and began to

---

[1] Hall, p. 562.   [2] Polydore Vergil, *Historia Anglica*, VOL. II, p. 1622.
[3] "Trewe Encountre", p. 150.   [4] Hall, p. 562.
[5] Pitscottie, VOL. I, pp. 271-2.   [6] Hall, p. 562.

plunder the slain.[1] It was the same in other parts of the field; "King, bishops, lordes, knightes, nobles, and others were not so soon slain but forthwith despoiled out of thair harnais and array and lefte lying naked in the felde."[2]

Even while the issue of the battle was uncertain, men had been slipping to the rear in tens and twenties, making for the fords at Coldstream or for the "Dry Marches" farther south; now the whole Scottish army was in full flight. Though his own division was unbroken, Hume made no attempt to rally the fugitives or to save the guns.[3] Only when they were three miles from the battlefield, only when night hid their quarry from them, did the wearied English abandon the pursuit.[4] Some, who had pressed on too far, became entangled with the retreating Scots and were captured.[5] The English borderers were more prudent; they made straight for the Scottish camp, cut the throats of the camp-followers, and plundered at their leisure; then they vanished into the darkness, taking with them the draught oxen and some thousands of horses.[6]

When Surrey was informed by scouts that the enemy showed no signs of rallying he gathered his officers about him and knighted forty of them, including Edmund Howard.[7] Then, having posted a strong guard on his own artillery and the captured Scottish guns, he returned, probably by Etal Bridge, to the camp at Barmoor Wood.[8] But when the weary soldiers got back, they discovered that their tents had been plundered and their horses stolen.[9] They guessed who the culprits were—the English borderers—and swore that they would die rather than return to the Borders again.[10]

Surrey knew that his victory had been overwhelming and that

---

[1] Hall, p. 562. [2] Ruthal to Wolsey, *Fac. Nat. MSS*, PT. II, No. 4.
[3] Pitscottie, VOL. I, pp. 272-3. [4] "Articles of Battle". [5] Hall, p. 563.
[6] Ruthal to Wolsey (*Fac. Nat. MSS*, PT. II, No. 4; *L. and P. Henry VIII*, VOL. I, PT. II, No. 2283); "Articles of Battle"; "Trewe Encountre", p. 150.
[7] Hall, p. 564; "Trewe Encountre", p. 150. [8] Hall, p. 564.
[9] Hall, p. 564; Ruthal to Wolsey (*Fac. Nat. MSS*, PT. II, No. 4; *L. and P. Henry VIII*, VOL. I, PT. II, No. 2283).
[10] Ruthal to Wolsey (*Fac. Nat. MSS*, PT. II, No. 4; *L. and P. Henry VIII*, VOL. I, PT. II, No. 2283).

somewhere among the ghastly heaps of naked corpses lay the dead body of the King. Not till the following day, however, was it discovered.[1] Dacre, who knew the King well, identified the body.[2] It was conveyed to Berwick, where it was recognised by Sir John Forman, the King's Sergeant Porter, and Sir William Scott, a member of the Council.[3] But soon after the battle strange stories began to be whispered—that James had not fallen in battle; that he had been seen in Kelso[4] on the night of the battle; that he had been slain by the Humes[5]; that he had escaped and had gone on a pilgrimage to Jerusalem.[6] The corpse taken to Berwick, it was said, was really the body of someone who had been dressed in the King's coat-armour.[7] Buchanan alleges that he heard one Lawrence Telfer declare repeatedly that he had seen the King ride from the battlefield and cross the Tweed.[8] Even in 1571, Bishop Lesley tells us, there were people who believed that King James was still alive, journeying from shrine to shrine in distant lands.[9] The persistence of the legend is simply the measure of his people's need of him. Against these stories, born of defeat and humiliation, we can set the words of Dacre himself; the Scots "love me worst of any Inglisheman living, be reason that I fande the body of the King of Scotts, slayne in the felde."[10]

With the King perished—according to the English reckoning —at least ten thousand of his subjects.[11] The English put their losses at not more than 1,500 men, and few of these were of high rank.[12] The Scottish dead, on the other hand, included the young

---

[1] Hall, p. 564.

[2] Dacre to the Council (Pinkerton, VOL. II, p. 460; *L. and P. Henry VIII*, VOL. I, PT. II, No. 2913).

[3] Hall, p. 564.   [4] Lesley, pp. 95-6 Sc., 349 L.

[5] Buchanan, *Rerum Scoticarum historia*, BK. XIII, in *Opera omnia*, ed. Ruddiman, VOL. I, p. 254.   [6] Lesley, pp. 96 Sc., 349 L.

[7] Buchanan, *Rerum Scoticarum historia*, BK. XIII, in *Opera omnia*, ed. Ruddiman, VOL. I, p. 254.   [8] Ibid.   [9] Lesley, pp. 96 Sc., 349 L.

[10] Dacre to the Council (Pinkerton, VOL. II, p. 460; *L. and P. Henry VIII*, VOL. I, PT. II, No. 2913).

[11] "Articles of Battle"; "Trewe Encountre", p. 150.

[12] Hall, p. 563; Ruthal to Wolsey (*Fac. Nat. MSS*, PT. II, Nos. 4-5; *L. and P. Henry VIII*, VOL. I, PT. II, No. 2283).

Archbishop of St Andrews, two bishops, two abbots, eleven earls and fifteen lords.[1] And beside those whom he had lured along the road to disaster lay Jehan de la Motte, finished with plotting and scheming for ever. The Scots lost in addition the whole of their splendid park of artillery. One attempt, it is true, was made to recapture it. On the morning after the battle, while the Admiral, accompanied by a handful of men, was examining the guns, a body of 800 horsemen suddenly appeared on the crest of a neighbouring hill. It seemed as if they would overwhelm the Admiral's scanty force and ride off with the guns, but the situation was saved by the English master-gunner, William Brackenall, who fired a salvo that put the horsemen to flight.[2]

The guns were entrusted to Dacre, who took them to Berwick where they remained for many a year.[3] The bodies of the slain were thrust into great pits, one a little to the south-west of the hillock where the monument now stands; another, into which men and horses were thrust pell-mell, and covered with one foot of earth, in Branxton Churchyard.[4]

And so, in these charnel-pits, ended the great Crusade.

[1] "Trewe Encountre", pp. 149-50; Hall, p. 563; Ruthal to Wolsey (*Fac. Nat. MSS*, PT. II, No. 4; *L. and P. Henry VIII*, VOL. I, PT. II, No. 2283).

[2] Hall, p. 564.

[3] "Trewe Encountre", p. 149; Ruthal to Wolsey (*Fac. Nat. MSS*, PT. II, No. 4; *L. and P. Henry VIII*, VOL. I, PT. II, No. 2283).

[4] Letter of Rev. Robert Jones in *Archaeologia Aeliana*, III (2nd Series, 1859), p. 233; id., *Battle of Flodden Field*, p. 71.

XI

SALVAGE FROM THE WRECK

A wise Prince should be slow and loath to engage himself in a War, although he hath suffered some Wrong. He should consider that of all humane Actions and Hazards, there is no One of which the Precipitation is so dangerous, as that of beginning and undertaking a War. Neither, in humane Affairs, should there more Depths be sounded, nor hidden Passages searched and pryed into, than in this. He should remember, that besides the sad Necessity which is inseparable from the most innocent War . . . there is Nothing of which the Revolutions and Changes are more inconstant, and the Conclusions and Ends more uncertain. The Sea is not more treacherous, false, and deceiving, nor changeth more swiftly her Calms into Storms.

(Drummond of Hawthornden)[1]

EVEN before the news of the defeat arrived Edinburgh seemed to be a city of the dead. There was no stir of life in the streets; all the booths were closed; all the doors and windows of the houses fastened; here and there a white cloth, hung over the doorway or forestair of a house, showed that the pest had obtained a lodgment within. Then, on 10 September, the first rumours of the disaster arrived. The Burgh Council assembled at once, and issued a proclamation, which after four centuries still has power to move the reader by its simple and unpremeditated eloquence:

"We do yow to witt, Forsamekill as thair is ane greit rumour now laitlie rysin within this toun tuiching our Souerane Lord and his army, of the quhilk we understand thair is cumin na veritie as yit, thairfore we charge straitlie and commandis in our said Souerane Lord the Kingis name, and the presidentis for the provest and baillies within this burgh, that all maner of personis nychtbouris within the samyn haue reddye thair fensabill geir and wapponis for weir, and compeir thairwith to the said presi-

[1] *History of the five James's*, in *Works*, p. 78.

dentis at jowyng of the commoun bell, for the keiping and
defens of the toun aganis thame that wald invaid the samyn.

"And als chargis that all wemen, and specialie vagaboundis,
that thai pas to thair labouris and be nocht sene vpoun the gait
clamorand and cryand, vnder the pane of banesing of the personis
but fauouris, and that the vther wemen of gude pas to the kirk
and pray quhane tyme requiris for our Souerane Lord and his
armye and nychtbouris being thairat, and hald thame at thair
previe labouris of the gait within thair houssis as efferis."[1]

To Elphinstone the fulfilment of his prophecy brought no
comfort. "When William heard that our troops had met with a
disastrous defeat in their luckless encounter with the English,"
says his biographer, "he was overwhelmed with grief, and fell a
prey to that disease which clung to him for the remainder of his
life. After that he was never seen to laugh, nor did any jests delight
him, nor would he share in any mirth, however quiet it might
be."[2] The bishop's palace was not the only place where laughter
suddenly died, as even the dispassionate pages of the *Acta Dominorum Concilii* bear witness. Here, for example, is a petition presented to the Lords of Council by Isabel Dunbar eight months
after the battle. Her husband, Patrick McClellane of Galston,
had been slain "in our soverane lordis army and under his baner".
Their son and heir was aged four, and there were five other
children, the eldest less than seven years old. She therefore implored the Council to "ordane and mak me to have the profittes
of my barnis landis and gudis for the sustentacion of him and of
his five faderles brethir and sisteris".[3]

Of the actual return of the survivors all records have perished
except the grim little description of the fugitives seeking safety
and finding death, in treacherous fords of the Tweed,[4] and the
bitter account in Polydore Vergil of the demoralised army straggling home, pillaging right and left, cursed by all because
"bewildered and forgetful of their duty they had not attempted
either to avenge the death of the King or to help their comrades

[1] *Edinburgh Records*, VOL. I, pp. 143-4.   [2] Boece, *Vitae*, p. 105.
[3] *Acts of the Lords of Council in Public Affairs 1501-1554*, ed. Hannay, p. 5.
[4] *Cal. of State Papers, Venice*, VOL. II, No. 337.

in their extremity and so had branded their country with ever-lasting shame".[1] But at Tournai Mass was said and the *Te Deum* sung in a great tent of purple and gold, and the dead King had for his requiem the crash of the English guns.[2] As far away as Rome, where the rumour of a great English defeat had given the French and Scots a temporary popularity, bonfires were kindled when the news of Surrey's victory came to hand.[3]

To Ruthal the victory seemed to be a miracle, wrought by St Cuthbert because the Scots had damaged Norham, the pro-perty of his successor, the Bishop of Durham, and therefore under the Saint's protection. Everything was against the English, Ruthal wrote, they were much inferior in numbers, for three days they had been without beer or ale, they had to force their way uphill in the teeth of a great wind before they could encounter their stalwart opponents, who were clad in almost impenetrable armour. Yet they won, and so he was heartily glad that the Scots had assaulted his castle. Had they not offended the Saint at such an early stage in the campaign they might have done more mischief.[4]

The more sober author of the "Trewe Encountre" is almost as emphatic. The English artillery could not cover the advance of the English infantry; a "great wind and sudden rain" handicapped the English archers; the Scots fought manfully "determyned outher to wynne the ffelde or to dye".[5]

How is one to explain, in the words of Queen Katharine, a "mater soo marvelous that it semeth to bee of Godds doing aloone"?[6] How did it come about that an army not inferior in numbers to its opponents, more strongly posted, well provisioned and well equipped, should have sustained such an overwhelming defeat?

One explanation can be found in the instructions given in the

[1] Polydore Vergil, *Historia Anglica*, VOL. II, p. 1623.

[2] *L. and P. Henry VIII*, VOL. I, PT. II, No. 2391.

[3] *L. and P. Henry VIII*, VOL. I, PT. II, No. 2332; *Cal. of State Papers, Venice*, VOL. II, No. 325.

[4] Ruthal to Wolsey (*Fac. Nat. MSS*, PT. II, Nos. 4-5; *L. and P. Henry VIII*, VOL. I, PT. II, No. 2283). [5] "Trewe Encountre", p. 150.

[6] *Original Letters illustrative of English History*, ed. Ellis, VOL. I, pp. 89-91.

name of the infant James V to Sir Andrew Brownhill, when in January 1514 he went as ambassador to Denmark. "Our army was not handled with sufficient care", the young King is made to say, "and had already begun to break up: some had drifted home because they were unaccustomed to the exertions incident to military service, others because they were worn out by sickness and the evil weather. The King our father remained in the enemy's country with the peers of the realm and a body of nobles, expecting a battle at a prearranged time and place. But the English, intent on deceit, took care not to fight at the pre-arranged time or place on the day appointed, and delayed the battle till they appeared a little before sunset, in a marshy place protected on all sides. Our dearest father, made impatient by the very sight of the enemy, rushed too boldly on them, without putting his men into order, encountered them on ground that was unfavourable and positively dangerous, and fighting at the very head of his army, or in the foremost ranks, he threw away his own life and the lives of most of his nobles. The guns and baggage were lost, but the enemy's slain far outnumbered ours, but our nobles fell at the head of their men, or fighting side by side with them. It was different with the enemy: every one of their leaders remained with the supports or in the rear. Elated by this victory due to our lack of skill, not to the prowess of the enemy, the King of England . . ."[1] The rest is irrelevant.

This is an excuse for, rather than an impartial exposition of the causes of the defeat; it was designed to win the sympathy and active support of the King of Denmark; it cannot, therefore, be accepted at its face value. The English losses, for example, did not exceed those of the Scots. The writers plead the wastage by desertion, but do not venture to assert that on 9 September the Scottish army was smaller than the English. They accuse Surrey, with justice, of attacking James after the hour appointed; they fail to show that Surrey's surprise advance was responsible for the Scottish defeat. After all, the Scots were victorious in the race for Branxton Hill. Still, the document does indicate two of the most important factors in the defeat.

[1] *E.R.S.*, VOL. I, pp. 187-8.

One was bad leadership. On the Scottish side there was no evidence of a directing and co-ordinating brain, no sign of intelligent co-operation on the part of the subordinate commanders. At the very outset of the battle James failed to seize the opportunity that the Admiral presented to him of overwhelming the vanguard before the rearguard and the guns came up. When the fighting began James virtually resigned his command: he placed himself where he was most exposed to danger and least able to exercise any control over his troops, and the majority of his lieutenants followed his example. Consequently each division fought blindly, as an isolated unit: the left wing did not move while the centre was being cut to pieces; the right wing moved too late. We cannot but contrast this blundering and fumbling with the swift precision of the English commanders—Surrey's quick response to the Admiral's appeal; Dacre's spirited counter-attack after the English right wing had gone and half of his own men had bolted; Stanley's timely advance, which drove in the Scottish right and decided the battle.

The second was *imperitia*—the lack of military skill. The Scots were amateur soldiers, with no recent experience of war, with no military training beyond that provided at an occasional wapenschaw. Amateurs, it is true, made up the bulk of the English army, but it was stiffened by the five hundred green-and-white uniformed regulars of Surrey's retinue, and the thousand soldiers and sailors from the fleet who marched under the banner of the Admiral.

The results of this fatal *imperitia* were shown most clearly in the artillery duel which began the battle. James had the guns, but not the men: he had sent his highly skilled foreign gunners— Wolf, Heinrich Cut-lug and the rest—to the fleet, and now he had to watch novices like the clerkly Patrick Paniter mishandling the costly brazen pieces. On the other side were the expert German gunners, working guns that were more numerous and more manageable than James's demi-curtals and culverins.

Recent writers on the battle have tended to minimise the importance of the English superiority in artillery. Dr W. M. Mackenzie, for example, anxious to give all the credit of the victory to the English brown bill, says, "Whatever advantage there was in this boisterous exchange seems to have fallen to the English. Some of the Scottish gunners and many in the King's battle were slain."[1] Then, after noting the panic caused among the men of Tynemouth and Bamburghshire by the sound of the Scottish guns, he adds, "Otherwise the results for either side were out of all proportion to the vast labour exerted in moving about these cumbrous pieces and their equipment. . . . Thus a contemporary English account of Flodden can say bluntly that, in the decision, the guns 'were of little use'."[2] Against Dr Mackenzie's contention, however, and the quotation from Tuke which he cites in support of it, must be put the statement in the "Trewe Encountre"—"notwithstanding that othir our artillary for warre couth doe noe good nor advantage to our army because they were contynually goyng and advansyng up towarde the said hilles and mountaines, yit by the help of God, our gonnes did soe breke and constreyn the Scottisshe great army, that some parte of thaim wer enforsed to come doune the said hilles towards our army."[3] Hall is even more emphatic: "Then oute brast the ordinaunce on bothe sydes, with fyre flamme and hydeous noyse, and the Master gonner of the Englishe parte slew the Master gonner of Scotlande, and bet all hys men from theyr ordinaunce, so that the Scottishe ordynaunce dyd no harme too the Englishemen; but the Englishemens Artyllerie shotte into the myddes of the Kynges battayll, and slewe many persones; which seynge the kynge of Scottes and hys noble men, made the more haste too come too ioynynge."[4]

The Scottish failure in the preliminary artillery duel did much to determine the issue of the subsequent infantry contest: the King's division did not sweep with serried ranks against a shaken foe; it surged forward, *nullo . . . ordine servato*,[5] against troops

[1] Mackenzie, *Secret of Flodden*, p. 76.

[2] Mackenzie, *Secret of Flodden*, pp. 77-8; Tuke to Pace (*La Rotta*, App., p. 5; *Cal. of State Papers, Venice*, VOL. II, No. 316; *Cal. of State Papers, Milan*, VOL. I, No. 660).

[3] "Trewe Encountre", pp. 147-8.

[4] Hall, p. 561.

[5] *E.R.S.*, VOL. I, p. 187.

advancing in good order. But the large spears of the Scots were effective only when used by troops moving in close formation, with carefully ordered ranks; once the phalanx was broken, the eight-foot brown bill was a much more manageable and dangerous weapon than the cumbrous eighteen-foot spear. So it proved at Flodden. Tuke says that the whole credit for the victory was due to "those soldiers who are now called halberdiers"[1]; "the billes did beat and hew thaim downe," says the author of the "Trewe Encountre".[2] "Our bills qwite them veray welle", says Ruthal, "and did more goode that day thenne bowes for they shortely disapointed the Scotes of their long speres wherin was their greatest truste and whenne they came to hande stroke, though the Scotes faght sore and valiauntlye with their swerdes, yet they coude not resiste the billes that lighted so thicke and sore upon thaym."[3]

The explanation, then, of the miracle of Flodden seems to be that the English soldier was better armed than the Scottish soldier; that the English guns were more numerous, and were better served than the Scottish guns, and that the English commanders and their men knew their job better than their opponents.

No great achievement by the fleet came to redeem the disaster to the army; the naval expedition for which James had made such long and costly preparation, ended in complete and ignominious failure. Louis expected the fleet to arrive at Brest about the middle of August; and instructed the Grand Master of Brittany to have seven ships ready to sail northward with it as soon as it arrived, and join the squadron of Norman ships lying at the mouth of the Seine.[4] All through the last fortnight of August the *Petite Louise* lay off Villerville, waiting to pilot the Scottish fleet into Honfleur, where the *Lion*, Robert Barton's new French-built ship, lay at its moorings. The fleet did not appear

[1] Tuke to Pace (*La Rotta*, App., p. 5; *Cal. of State Papers, Venice*, VOL. II, No. 316; *Cal. of State Papers, Milan*, VOL. I, No. 660).

[2] "Trewe Encountre", p. 150.

[3] Ruthal to Wolsey (*Fac. Nat. MSS*, PT. II, No. 4; *L. and P. Henry VIII*, VOL. I, PT. II, No. 2283).

[4] Spont, *Letters and Papers relating to the War with France 1512-1513*, p. 174.

off the French coast till September; Arran, it appeared, had stopped to plunder the town of Carrickfergus.[1]

Early in November Arran and Fleming brought home the storm-battered Scottish fleet. Not a single shot had been exchanged with the enemy; though three of the finest ships were missing, they had not been sunk in battle, they had been lent by Arran to the French King. The *Michael*, which had been floated off after it ran aground, never returned to Scotland; in April 1514 she was sold to Louis for forty thousand francs.[2]

On the debit side we have to place disaster by land and failure by sea. There is little to put on the credit side beyond the privilege granted by Louis in September 1513 to Scotsmen resident in France.[3] Henceforth they would be on the same footing as Frenchmen resident in Scotland: they would be permitted to dispose of their goods by will without applying for letters of naturalisation. One Scotsman, however, gained a more substantial reward for his devotion to the cause of France. As early as June 1513 Louis had asked the reluctant chapter of Bourges to accept Forman as Archbishop. The chapter would have none of him even after Forman had been provided to the see by the Pope. On 7 August the King repeated his request, adding that it was Forman who had made the King of Scots openly declare himself on the side of France and make war on England. Still the canons refused to accept the foreigner; a third appeal from Louis, an appeal from "your brother and friend, for ever, if it please you. Andrew" had no better success. Not till the beginning of October did they give their consent, extorted from them, they were careful to say, by force and the fear inspired by the threats of the King. On 13 November, just about the time that John Barton was carried ashore to die in Kirkcudbright, the new Archbishop made his solemn entry into Bourges.[4]

More Scotland could not obtain from her ally. Arran, it is

---

[1] Pitscottie, VOL. I, p. 256.   [2] *E.R.S.*, VOL. I, p. 214.

[3] *L. and P. Henry VIII*, VOL. I, PT. II, No. 2322.

[4] Francisque Michel, *Les Ecossais en France, les Français en Ecosse*, VOL. I, pp. 320-4; Herkless and Hannay, *Archbishops of St Andrews*, VOL. II, Edinburgh 1909, pp. 73-5.

T

true, brought from France the request that the alliance should be confirmed, and on 26 November the Council gave its consent,[1] but Louis was already drawing nearer to his opponents. In October he had acknowledged the Lateran Council and made his peace with the Pope[2]; at the beginning of December he had authorised the opening of negotiations for an alliance with Ferdinand.[3] Six months later came a dramatic reconciliation with England. Louis was now a widower; Henry had at last become convinced that his former comrade-in-arms, Maximilian, no longer favoured the proposed marriage of his grandson Charles and Henry's younger sister, the Princess Mary. Disgusted by the duplicity of his allies, Henry turned to his enemy; in May 1514 ambassadors crossed from France to England to negotiate two treaties, one for an alliance between France and England, the other for the marriage of the elderly King and the youthful princess,[4] and on 7 August the two treaties were signed.[5] The Scots were to be included in the peace if they made application within three months; any raids into England, however, made with the connivance of the King and his Council, even unauthorised raids if made by more than three hundred men, would render their inclusion in the treaty null and void.

The Scots could not resist; Louis had kept the letter of his promise; Christian of Denmark had made it plain that only fair words were to be expected from him,[6] so on 24 August 1514 the Council informed Louis and his ambassadors in London that Scotland adhered to the treaty.[7]

When one contrasts the splendid promises of the French King with his shabby performance, when one reads Dacre's tale of the merciless forays in October and November 1513,[8] when one sees

---

[1] A.P.S., VOL. II, p. 281.   [2] L. and P. Henry VIII, VOL. I, PT. II, No. 2399.

[3] L. and P. Henry VIII, VOL. I, PT. II, No. 2486.

[4] L. and P. Henry VIII, VOL. I, PT. II, Nos. 2917-9.

[5] L. and P. Henry VIII, VOL. I, PT. II, No. 3129; Foedera, VOL. XIII, p. 413; Cal. of State Papers, Spain, VOL. II, Nos. 183-5.

[6] Becker, De rebus inter Ioannem et Christianum II . . . ac Ludovicum XII et Iacobum IV . . . actis, p. 92.

[7] L. and P. Henry VIII, VOL. I, PT. II, Nos. 3188-9.

[8] L. and P. Henry VIII, VOL. I, PT. II, Nos. 2386, 2390, 2406, 2443.

the smile struck from the lips of the good Bishop Elphinstone, or listens to the immortal lament that rose from the Forest of Ettrick, one is tempted to call for

> A blast of that dread horn
> On Fontarabian echoes borne.

What would have happened if James had defeated Surrey and survived the battle?

Probably in the long run victory at Flodden would have been even more disastrous to Scotland than defeat. What use could James have made of his victory? The summer was long past; the autumn nights were cold and the autumn rains were cruel. With an army thinned by disease and desertion before the battle, thinned in more drastic fashion by the battle itself, James would have found it difficult to advance far into England. And it is certain that his advance would not have been unopposed; Sir Thomas Lovell lay at Nottingham with 15,000 men, ready to go to the help of Surrey should the need arise; the Queen herself had taken the field at the head of a formidable army.[1] Nor would a Scottish victory have made any difference to the course of the war on the Continent—the French had been beaten at Guinegate, Thérouanne had surrendered, before 9 September—at the most it would have brought Henry home in mid-September instead of in mid-October.

In 1514 there would have been a different story to tell. Henry would not have forgotten the treachery of his ally and brother-in-law; his subjects, flushed with unaccustomed victory on the Continent, humiliated by an unaccustomed defeat at home, would not have rested till they could feel secure against invasion from the north. And the only way to humble the pride of King James and teach his subjects the folly of quarrelling with England was to invade Scotland. Henry would have led across the Tweed not a heterogeneous force like the one commanded by Surrey, but the disciplined troops who had overcome the chivalry of France at Guinegate; the guns which had thundered against

---

[1] Tuke to Pace (*La Rotta*, App., p. 6; *Cal. of State Papers, Venice*, VOL. II, No. 316; *Cal. of State Papers, Milan*, VOL. I, No. 660).

Tournai and Thérouanne would have been used to batter down the gates and towers of Edinburgh and Stirling. King Louis might vow and protest; as long as the English fleet had the command of the Channel he would be powerless to help his ally; he would see Scotland fare as the King of Navarre had fared a few months earlier. But Flodden was a Scottish defeat, and so, though the state of Scotland was wretched enough in 1514, Edinburgh remained unburned, and the Border abbeys unwrecked, for another thirty years.

Even so, one cannot help wishing that "Flodden had been Bannockbourne."

APPENDIX

A SCOTTS BALAD

London thow art of Townys A per se
Soverayn of Cytees, semelyest In sygth
Of hygth Renoun, Rycchesse and Royalte
Of lordys baronys, and many goodly knygth
Of most delectable, lusty ladyes brygth
Of ffamous prelattys, In habytys clerycall
Of marchauntys, fful of substaunce & mygth
London thow art, the fflowyr of Cytees all

Gladdyth aloon thow, lusty Troy Novant
Cyte that soom tyme, clepid was Newe Troye
In all the Erth, Imperyall as thow stant
Pryncess of Townys, of pleasure & of Joye
A Ryccher Restyth, undyr noo Crystyn Roye
For manly powar, wyth Crafftys Naturall
Fourmyth noon ffayrer, syth the fflood of Noye
London thow art, the fflowyr of Cytees all

Gemme of all Joye, Jasper of Jocundyte
Most mygthy Carbuncle, of vertu and valowr
Strong Troy In vygour, and In Strenuyte
Of Royall Cytees, Rose and Gerarfflowyr
Empress of Townys, exalt In honowyr
In Beawty beryng, the Throne Imperyall
Swete paradyse, precellyng In pleasure
London thow art, the fflowyr of Cytees all

Above all Ryvers, the Ryver hath Renoun
Whoos beryall stremys, playsant & preclare
Undyr thy lusty, wallys Rennyth doun
Where many a Swan, doth swym w^t wyngis ffayr
Where many a Barge, doth sayle & Rowe wyth are
Wher many a shypp, doth Rest wyth Topp Royall
O toun of townys, patron and noon compare
London thow art, the fflowyr of Cytees all

Upon thy lusty brygg, of pylers whyte
Been marchauntys, fful Royall to behold
Upon thy stretys, goth many a semely knygth
In velvet Gounys, and bere cheynys of Gold
By Julius Cezar, thy Towyr ffoundyd of old
Maybe the howse, of mars victoryall
Whoos artelery, wyth tung may nott be told
London thow art, the fflowyr of Cytees all

Strong be thy wallis, that abowth the standys
Wyse been the people, that wythyn the dwellys
Fresh Is thy Ryver, wyth his lusty strandys
Blythe be thy kyrkys, well sownyng be thy bellis
Rych be thy marchauntis, In substaunce that excellis
Fayer be theyr wyvys, Rygth lovesum white & small
Clere be thy vyrgyns, & lusty undyr kellys
London thow art, the fflowyr of Cytees all

Thy ffamous mayer, by pryncely governaunce
Wyth sword of Justice, the Rulyth prudently
Noo lord of parys, venyze or Floraunce
In dygnyte or honour, gooth to hym nyy
He ys exempler, loodster and Guy
Pryncypall patron, & Rose orygynall
Above all mayrys, as mastyr most worthy
London thow art, the fflowyr of Cytees all

Guildhall Library MS Great Chronicle of London, fols. 292^v-294.

BIBLIOGRAPHY

Aberdeen Register = *Extracts from the Council Register of the Burgh of Aberdeen 1378-1570*, edited by J. Stuart, VOL. I, Spalding Club, Aberdeen 1844.

Acta dominorum Concilii, Acts of the Lords of Council in Civil Causes, VOL. I (1478-1495) London 1839; VOL. II (1496-1501) edited by G. Neilson and H. Paton, Edinburgh 1918.

Acta Dominorum Concilii, MS, Edinburgh, General Register House, VOL. XXII.

Acts of the Lords Auditors of Causes and Complaints 1466-1494, London 1839.

Acts of the Lords of Council in Public Affairs 1501-1554, edited by R. K. Hannay, Edinburgh 1932.

A.P.S. = *Acts of the Parliament of Scotland*, VOLS. II-III edited by T. Thomson, London 1814; VOL. XII edited by A. Anderson, Edinburgh 1875.

"Articles of Battle" = "Account of the Battle of Flodden", in *Facsimiles of National Manuscripts*, photozincographed by Sir Henry James, PART II, Southampton 1865, No. 2; and "Gazette of the Battle of Flodden", in J. Pinkerton, *History of Scotland*, London 1797, Appendix, pp. 456-8.

Francis Bacon, Viscount St Albans, *The History of the Reign of King Henry VII*, in *Works*, edited by J. Spedding, R. L. Ellis and D. D. Heath, VOL. VI, London 1858.

Sir James Balfour of Kinnaird, *Annales of Scotland*, in *Historical Works*, edited by James Haig, London 1825.

The Bannatyne Manuscript, edited by W. Todd Ritchie, Scottish Text Society, Edinburgh 1928-34.

Cadwallader J. Bates, "Flodden Field", in *Archaeologia Aeliana*, XVI (1894), pp. 351-72.

J. W. Baxter, *William Dunbar, a biographical study*, Edinburgh 1952.

P. W. Becker, *De rebus inter Ioannem et Christianum II Daniae reges, ac Ludovicum XII et Iacobum IV Galliae Scotiaeque reges a. MDXI-MDXJV actis*, Copenhagen 1835.

Boece, *Vitae* = Hector Boethius, *Murthlacensium et Aberdonensium episcoporum vitae*, edited by J. Moir, Aberdeen 1894.

Boece, *Historia* = Hector Boethius, *Scotorum historiae prima gentis origine . . . libri XIX*, Paris, 1574.

The Book of Pluscarden, edited by F. J. H. Skene, Historians of Scotland, VOLS. VII and X, Edinburgh 1877-90.

W. Moir Bryce, *The Scottish Grey Friars*, Edinburgh 1909.

George Buchanan, *Rerum Scoticarum historia*, in *Opera omnia*, edited by T. Ruddiman, Edinburgh 1715.

Wilhelm Busch, *England under the Tudors*, translated by Alice M. Todd, London 1895.

Cal. Doc. Scot. = *Calendar of Documents relating to Scotland preserved in H.M. Public Record Office*, edited by Joseph Bain, VOL. IV, Edinburgh 1888.

Cal. of State Papers, Milan = *Calendar of State Papers and Manuscripts existing in the archives and collections of Milan*, VOL. I edited by A. B. Hinds, London 1912.

Cal. of State Papers, Spain = *Calendar of Letters, Despatches and State Papers relating to the negotiations between England and Spain*, VOLS. I-II edited by G. A. Bergenroth, London 1862-6.

Cal. of State Papers, Venice = *Calendar of State Papers and Manuscripts relating to English Affairs existing in the archives and collections of Venice and in other libraries of northern Italy*, edited by Rawdon Brown, VOLS. I-II, London 1864-7.

The Cambridge Modern History, edited by A. W. Ward, G. W. Prothero *et al.*, VOL. I, Cambridge 1902.

Annie I. Cameron, *The Apostolic Camera and Scottish Benefices 1418-1488*, Oxford 1934.

Charters and other Documents relating to the Burgh of Peebles, with extracts from the Records of the Burgh A.D. 1165-1710, edited by W. Chambers, Edinburgh 1872.

Charters, Writs and Public Documents of the Royal Burgh of Dundee 1292-1880, edited by W. Hay, Scottish Burgh Records Society, Dundee 1880.

Conway = Hon. Agnes Conway, *Henry VII's relations with Scotland and Ireland 1485-1498*, Cambridge 1932.

C.T.S. = *Compota Thesauriorum regum Scotorum, Accounts of the Lord High Treasurer of Scotland*, VOL. I edited by Thomas Dickson, VOLS. II-IV edited by James Balfour Paul, Edinburgh 1877-1902.

Gavin Douglas, *The Aeneid of Virgil translated into Scottish Verse*, edited by G. Dundas, Bannatyne Club, Edinburgh 1839.

— —, *The Palice of Honour*, edited by J. G. Kinnear, Bannatyne Club, Edinburgh 1827.

— —, *Poetical Works*, edited by J. Small, Edinburgh 1874.

John Dowden, *The Bishops of Scotland*, edited by J. Maitland Thomson, Glasgow 1912.

William Drummond of Hawthornden, *History of the Lives of the five James's Kings of Scotland*, in *Works*, Edinburgh 1711.

William Drummond, 1st Viscount Strathallan, *Genealogy of the most noble and ancient house of Drummond*, Edinburgh 1831.

Sir Archibald H. Dunbar, *Scottish Kings*, Edinburgh 1899.

William Dunbar, *Poems*, edited by D. Laing, Edinburgh 1834.

— —, *Poems*, edited by W. M. Mackenzie, Edinburgh 1932.

— —, *Poems*, edited by J. Small, Scottish Text Society, Edinburgh 1884-93.

Early Popular Poetry of Scotland and the Northern Border, edited by D. Laing, rearranged and revised by W. C. Hazlitt, London 1805.

Edinburgh Charters = *Charters and other Documents relating to the City of Edinburgh 1143-1540*, edited by J. D. Marwick, Edinburgh 1871.

Edinburgh Records = *Extracts from the Records of the Burgh of Edinburgh*, edited by J. D. Marwick, VOL. I, Scottish Burgh Records Society, Edinburgh 1869.

Hon. W. Fitzwilliam Elliot, *The Battle of Flodden and the Raids of 1513*, Edinburgh 1911.

The English and Scottish Popular Ballads, edited by Francis James Child, VOL. III, Boston 1888.

D. Erasmus, *Adages*, in *Opera omnia*, edited by G. Leclerc, VOL. II, Louvain 1703.

E.R.S. = *Epistolae Jacobi Quarti, Jacobi Quinti et Maria Regum Scotorum, eorumque tutorum et regni gubernatorum, ad Imperatores, Reges, Pontifices, Principes, civitates et alios ab anno 1505 ad annum 1545*, Edinburgh 1722-4.

Extracts from the Records of the Royal Burgh of Lanark, edited by R. Renwick, Scottish Burgh Records Society, Glasgow 1893.

Fac. Nat. MSS = *Facsimiles of National Manuscripts*, photozincographed by Sir H. James, PART II, Southampton 1865.

Fasti Aberdonenses, Selections from the Records of the University and King's College of Aberdeen 1494-1854, edited by C. Innes, Aberdeen 1854.

Ferrerius, *Continuatio* = *Scotorum historia . . . libri XIX Hectore Boethis Deidonano auctore continuatio per Ioannem Ferrerium*, Paris 1574.

Ferrerius, *Historia de Kynlos* = I. Ferrerius, *Historia abbatum de Kynlos, una cum vita Thomae Chrystalli abbatis*, edited by W. D. Wilson, Bannatyne Club, Edinburgh 1839.

Flodden Papers = *Flodden Papers, Diplomatic correspondence between the Courts of France and Scotland 1507-1517*, edited by Marguerite Wood, Scottish History Society, Ser. III, VOL. XX, Edinburgh 1933.

Foedera = T. Rymer, *Foedera, conventiones, literae, et cujuscunque acta publica inter reges Angliae et alios quovis imperatores, reges, pontifices, principes vel communitates*, VOLS. II, XI-XIII, London 1704-12.

Sir William Fraser, *The Douglas Book*, Edinburgh 1885.

U

Godscroft=David Hume of Godscroft, *The History of the Houses of Douglas and Angus*, Edinburgh 1644.

Great Chronicle of London, MS, London, Guildhall Library.

Donald Gregory, *History of the Western Highlands and Isles of Scotland*, 2nd edition, London and Glasgow 1881.

Hall=*Hall's Chronicle*, edited by Sir H. Ellis, London 1809.

R. K. Hannay, *The College of Justice*, Edinburgh 1933.

T. F. Henderson, *The Royal Stewarts*, Edinburgh 1914.

Robert Henryson, *Poems*, edited by G. Gregory Smith, Scottish Text Society, Edinburgh 1906-14.

John Herkless and R. K. Hannay, *The Archbishops of St Andrews*, VOLS. I-II, Edinburgh 1907-09.

— —, *The College of St Leonard*, Edinburgh 1905.

Thomas Hodgkin, "The Battle of Flodden", in *Archaeologia Aeliana*, XVI (1894), pp. 1-45.

John Hodgson, *History of Northumberland*, PART III, VOL.II, Newcastle upon Tyne 1828.

John Ireland, *The Meroure of Wyssdome*, edited by C. Macpherson, Scottish Text Society, Edinburgh 1926.

James IV, *Letters of James the Fourth*, edited by R. L. Mackie, Scottish History Society, Ser. III, VOL. XLV, Edinburgh 1953.

E. Jervoise, *The Ancient Bridges of the North of England*, London 1931.

Rev. Robert Jones, *The Battle of Flodden Field*, Edinburgh 1864.

C. L. Kingsford, *Chronicles of London*, Oxford 1905.

John Knox, *History of the Reformation in Scotland*, in *Works*, edited by D. Laing, VOL. I, Edinburgh 1846.

L. and P. Henry VIII=*Letters and Papers, Foreign and Domestic, of the Reign of Henry VIII*, VOL. I catalogued by J. S. Brewer, 2nd edition revised and enlarged by R. H. Brodie, London 1920; VOL. II edited by J. S. Brewer, London 1864.

L. and P. Richard and Henry VII=*Letters and Papers illustrative of the Reigns of Richard III and Henry VII*, edited by James Gairdner, London 1861-3.

The Lawes and Actes of Parliament maid be King James the First and his successours, Kingess of Scotland, compiled by Sir John Skene, Edinburgh 1597.

John Leland, *Collectanea*, London 1774.

John Lesley, *De origine, moribus et rebus gestis Scotorum libri decem*, 1675 edition.

— —, *The History of Scotland from the death of King James I in the year 1436 to the year 1561*, Bannatyne Club, Edinburgh 1830.

Sie David Lindsay of the Mount, *The Testament of the Papyngo*, in *Works*, edited by D. Hamer, Scottish Text Society, Edinburgh 1931-6.

Sir George Macdonald, "The Mint of Crossraguel Abbey", in *Proceedings of the Society of Antiquaries of Scotland*, LIV (1919-20).

W. M. Mackenzie, *The Scottish Burghs*, Edinburgh 1949.

—— , *The Secret of Flodden*, Edinburgh 1931.

J. D. Mackie, "The Auld Alliance and the Battle of Flodden", in *Transactions of the Franco-Scottish Society*, VIII (1919-35), pp. 37-56.

The Maitland Folio Manuscript, edited by W. A. Craigie, Scottish Text Society, Edinburgh 1919-27.

John Major, *History of Greater Britain*, translated and edited by A. Constable, Edinburgh 1892.

Martin Martin, Gent., *A Description of the Western Islands of Scotland*, edited by Donald J. Macleod, Stirling 1934.

Francisque Michel, *Les Ecossais en France, les Français en Ecosse*, London 1862.

Myln, *Vitae* = A. Myln, *Vitae Dunkeldensis ecclesiae episcoporum*, edited by T. Thomson, Bannatyne Club, Edinburgh 1823.

Original Letters illustrative of English History, edited by Sir H. Ellis, 1st series, London 1824.

Pinkerton = John Pinkerton, *History of Scotland from the accession of the House of Stuart to that of Mary*, London 1797.

Pitscottie = Robert Lindesay of Pitscottie, *The History and Cronicles of Scotland*, edited by Aeneas J. G. Mackay, Scottish Text Society, Edinburgh 1899-1911.

O. Raynald, *Annales ecclesiastici*, VOL. XIX, Cologne 1693.

Records Commission, *Forty-Sixth Annual Report of the Deputy Keeper of the Public Records*, London 1886.

Records of the Convention of the Royal Burghs of Scotland, VOL. I edited by J. D. Marwick, Edinburgh 1870.

Registrum episcopatus Moraviensis, edited by C. Innes, Bannatyne Club, Edinburgh 1837.

Rentale Dunkeldense, edited by R. K. Hannay, Scottish History Society, Ser. II, VOL. X, Edinburgh 1915.

G. Ridpath, *The Border History of England and Scotland*, new edition, Berwick upon Tweed 1848.

R.M.S. = *Registrun magni sigili regum Scotorum, The Register of the Great Seal of Scotland*, VOL. II (1424-1513) edited by James Balfour Paul, Edinburgh 1882.

William Roper, *The Lyfe of Sir Thomas Moore, knighte*, edited by E. V. Hitchcock, Early English Text Society, London 1935.

Rot. Scot. = *Rotuli Scotiae in turri Londinensi et in domo capitulari Westmonasteriensi asservati*, London 1814-19.

La Rotta = *La Rotta di Francciosi a Teroanna novamente facta, La Rotta de Scocesi*, Roxburghe Club, London 1825.

R. Scac. S. = *Rotuli Scaccarium regum Scotorum, The Exchequer Rolls of Scotland*, VOLS. IX-XII edited by G. Burnett, VOL. XIII edited by G. Burnett and Ae. J. G. Mackay, Edinburgh 1886-91.

R.S.S. = *Registrum secreti sigilli regum Scotorum, The Register of the Privy Seal of Scotland*, VOL. I edited by M. Livingstone, Edinburgh 1908.

Alfred Spont, *Letters and Papers relating to the War with France 1512-1513*, Navy Records Society VOL. X, London 1897.

Statutes of the Realm, VOL. II, London 1816.

John Stow, *Chronicles of England*, London 1580.

J. B. A. T. Teulet, *Inventaire chronologique des documents relatifs à l'histoire d'Ecosse, conservés aux archives du royaume à Paris*, Edinburgh 1839.

Theiner, *Vetera monumenta* = Augustin Theiner, *Vetera monumenta Hibernorum et Scotorum historiam illustrantia*, Rome 1864.

The Thre Prestis of Peblis, edited by T. D. Robb, Scottish Text Society, Edinburgh 1920.

"Trewe Encountre" = "A contemporary account of the battle of Flodden", in *Proceedings of the Society of Antiquaries of Scotland*, VII (1866-7), pp. 141-52.

Polydore Vergil, *Historia Anglica*, Douai 1603.

Robert White, "The Battle of Flodden", in *Archaeologia Aeliana*, III (2nd series, 1859), pp. 197-235.

INDEX

battle, 279; character, 45, 56, 113-4,
153-4, 200-1; and justice, 57, 58; and
taxation, 59, 198; ships, 63, 77, 202,
229-30, 235, 239-40; mistresses, 80-1,
92-3, 94, 100-1, 103-4, 104-5; and
alchemy, 103, 158-9; building, 114-
6; travels, 116-7, 124-8; interest in
learning, 118-9, 165, 166, 169-70;
sport, 119; daily life, 119-21, 133;
festivals, 121-4; feu farms, 131; and
burghs, 137-8, 139, 145; and Church,
157, 158-9, 160-1; and William
Dunbar, 176, 177.
James V, 220, 237, 273.
James, the, 230, 243 *n*.
Jean d'Albret, King of Navarre, 221,
225, 280.
Jedburgh, 200.
Jenny Pirwin, the, 209, 210.
John, King of Denmark, 113, 201, 208-
9, 213, 214-5, 218, 219, 220, 228.
Johnstone, Lord, 249-50.
Jones, Eleanor, 125-6.
Julius II, Pope, and Church in Scotland,
157, 158; and Venice, 202-3, 204;
and France, 203, 205, 206-7, 213, 214,
215, 217, 219, 220, 221, 226; and
James IV, 216, 227, 228-9, 230, 236;
death, 229, 231.
Jura, 194, 196.
Justice, administration of, 10, 11, 18,
31-2, 35-6, 38-9, 50-1, 57-8, 192-3,
198, 200-1.

Katharine of Aragon, Queen, 81, 94,
224-5, 237, 240, 241, 272, 279.
Katherine of York, Princess, 29.
Katherine, Lady, daughter of Countess
of Wiltshire, 67.
Katharine, the, 61, 176.
Kelso Abbey, 158.
Kennedy, Lord, John, 2nd, 28.
——, Sir David, 38 *n*.
——, James, Bishop of St Andrews, 8,
163.
——, Janet, 92-3, 94, 103, 125.
——, Walter, 61, 160, 175, 176, 182.
Kers, Alexander, 122.
Kilmarnock, 66.
Kilmary, 158.
King, Patrick, 27.
Kinloss Abbey, 155, 156, 162.
Kintyre, 75, 77, 190, 193.

Knapdale, 75, 77, 190, 193.
Knoydart, 197.

"L.A.", 103-4, 104-5.
Ladislaus, King of Hungary, 206.
Ladykirk, 154.
Laing, John, Bishop of Glasgow, 16 *n*.
Lamberton Kirk, 97, 106.
Lanark, 46, 136-7, 140, 147.
Lancaster Herald, 221.
Land tenure, 129-32.
Lateran Council, 213, 278.
La Tour, Anne de, 13.
Lauder, 80, 134.
—— episode, 13 *n*, 16, 19-20, 37.
Lawson, Patrick, 146.
——, Richard, 56 *n*, 88.
Le Casche, 132 *n*.
Leith, 12, 41, 63, 235, 240, 242.
Lennox, Earl of, John, 1st, 19, 53, 55,
56.
——, ——, Matthew, 2nd, 53, 260, 266.
Leo X, Pope, 229, 231-2, 233, 236, 243,
277, 278.
Leonard, 15, 16.
Levington, James, Bishop of Dunkeld,
22.
Lewis, 189, 190, 197.
Leyburn, Roger, Bishop of Carlisle,
126.
Liddell, Sir James, 23, 25.
Liddesdale, 18, 65, 66.
Lilbume, Christian, 145-6.
Lindores Abbey, 25, 41, 127.
Lindsay of the Byres, Lord, David,
44 *n*, 47 *n*, 48 *n*.
——, Alexander, 41.
——, Sir David, 244.
——, Patrick, 48 *n*.
Linlithgow, 40, 51, 54, 81, 104, 114-5,
116, 117, 120, 125, 126, 127, 135, 136,
237, 243.
Lion, the (first), 208, 209, 210.
——, (second), 276.
Lismore, diocese of, 52.
Literature, 170-87.
Lochaber, 190, 191, 193, 197.
Lochalsh, Alexander of, 76, 188-9.
——, Margaret of, 197.
Loch Finlagan, 74.
Loch Kilkerran Castle, 114, 189, 192.
Lochmaben, 18, 115, 126.
Lochwinnoch, 153.

SCOTLAND IN THE REIGN OF JAMES IV

THE FLODDEN CAMPAIGN